Cognitive Technologies

Editor-in-Chief

Daniel Sonntag, German Research Center for AI, DFKI, Saarbrücken, Saarland, Germany

Titles in this series now included in the Thomson Reuters Book Citation Index and Scopus!

The Cognitive Technologies (CT) series is committed to the timely publishing of high-quality manuscripts that promote the development of cognitive technologies and systems on the basis of artificial intelligence, image processing and understanding, natural language processing, machine learning and human-computer interaction.

It brings together the latest developments in all areas of this multidisciplinary topic, ranging from theories and algorithms to various important applications. The intended readership includes research students and researchers in computer science, computer engineering, cognitive science, electrical engineering, data science and related fields seeking a convenient way to track the latest findings on the foundations, methodologies and key applications of cognitive technologies.

The series provides a publishing and communication platform for all cognitive technologies topics, including but not limited to these most recent examples:

- Interactive machine learning, interactive deep learning, machine teaching
- Explainability (XAI), transparency, robustness of AI and trustworthy AI
- Knowledge representation, automated reasoning, multiagent systems
- Common sense modelling, context-based interpretation, hybrid cognitive technologies
- Human-centered design, socio-technical systems, human-robot interaction, cognitive robotics
- Learning with small datasets, never-ending learning, metacognition and introspection
- Intelligent decision support systems, prediction systems and warning systems
- Special transfer topics such as CT for computational sustainability, CT in business applications and CT in mobile robotic systems

The series includes monographs, introductory and advanced textbooks, state-of-the-art collections, and handbooks. In addition, it supports publishing in Open Access mode.

Georg Rehm
Editor

European Language Grid

A Language Technology Platform
for Multilingual Europe

 Springer

Editor
Georg Rehm ⓘ
Deutsches Forschungszentrum
für Künstliche Intelligenz GmbH (DFKI)
Berlin, Germany

The European Language Grid has received funding from the European Union's Horizon 2020 research and innovation programme under grant agreement no. 825627.

ISSN 1611-2482   ISSN 2197-6635   (electronic)
Cognitive Technologies
ISBN 978-3-031-17260-1   ISBN 978-3-031-17258-8   (eBook)
https://doi.org/10.1007/978-3-031-17258-8

This Springer imprint is published by the registered company Springer Nature Switzerland AG
The registered company address is: Gewerbestrasse 11, 6330 Cham, Switzerland

Foreword

I was proud to have the opportunity to present my report on *Language Equality in the Digital Age* to the European Parliament in 2018 and even prouder to see the overwhelming support it received. It was one of my final achievements as a Member of the European Parliament and I am delighted that it contributed to the groundbreaking work being done on the European Language Grid project. Despite it not being a legislative report, the level of cross-party support it received meant its recommendations could not be ignored.

When I first proposed a report on language equality in the digital age to the European Parliament's Culture and Education Committee it provoked a great deal of interest, as it did in the Industry Committee. This was due to the clear language inequality in Europe but also to the huge opportunities it presented for the digital industries. As both committees laid claim to the report, there was some debate before it was resolved that it would be a Culture Committee report with a written opinion from the Industry Committee. The latter's participation strengthened the report and its impact. It widened the scope to emphasise the importance of the role of private companies alongside public bodies and of facilitating cross border trade in the Digital Single Market.

It was clear from the early days that the European Commission was keen to support the report and take the proposals forward. As a spokesperson for the Commissioner stated in a conference I organised in parliament in September 2018, "You are never so wealthy as when you can speak in your own language". The European Language Equality project is currently developing a roadmap to achieve language equality by 2030, which will be presented to the European Institutions later this year.

Minority languages in particular have most to lose but also most to gain from the digital age, given the right support. Cultural and linguistic diversity depends largely on the technological resources available to all languages.

It was a report by the EU Panel for the Future of Science and Technology, STOA, that sparked the idea of a parliamentary report. STOA highlighted the social and economic consequences of language barriers and the widening of the technological gap. As someone who had long campaigned for equal status for the Welsh language, I was inspired by the potential that a major EU project could offer.

Even though the dominance of a few well-resourced languages in the digital world was obvious, the impact of this on other languages had not been adequately explored. When the discussion began, the interest grew. The increase in technology presented new threats and new opportunities. This was an issue which literally affected everyone, and most notably children growing up in this digital world. The role of education is crucial in teaching and understanding language technologies but also in raising awareness of career opportunities in this industry across Europe.

The European Union itself, of course, could could play a major role. The institutional framework for the provision of language technology could be improved considerably. I believed that this was such a crucial issue that it deserved the specific allocation of the portfolio to a European Commissioner. This did not materialise in the appointment of a new Commission following the European elections in 2019, but I believe the proposal should be maintained and could be adopted in future.

The strong support given to my report by the European Parliament was an indication of support for the exciting language equality work that is taking place now. The report proposed a dedicated funding programme for research, development and innovation in language technologies with the aim of closing the gap between European languages.

This suggestion was a direct result of seeing the existing research being done in many countries. Identifying the problem went hand in hand with discovering that there were many individuals and organisations already addressing it and working to overcome it. They had the information and expertise but needed far more support and a higher profile. It was clear that the EU could become a trailblazer in research on digital language technology, given the political will.

As a politician, the rights of minority languages like my own, Welsh, were at the heart of my work for justice and equality. For me, language was not merely a means of communication but central to our culture and identity. The EU claims equality in diversity but when it came to language equality it fell far short. So in my role as a Member of the European Parliament I saw an opportunity to help correct this. I could play my role in parliament but to ensure the report was effective in achieving its aim it needed the input of the experts, the practitioners and the pioneers in this field of work to ensure that it was accurate and informed.

I never fail to be inspired by their work and their dedication and I repeat my thanks to all those who contributed to the success of the *Language Equality in the Digital Age* report and to the remarkable European Language Grid project which established the primary platform for "language technologies *for* Europe built *in* Europe".

Rhondda Valley, April 2022   *Jill Evans*

Preface

The origins of this book date back to 2012. Back then, under the umbrella of the EU Network of Excellence META-NET, we prepared the recommendations and priority research themes specified in the first Strategic Research Agenda (SRA) for the European Language Technology (LT) field in a complex, community-driven process.[1] While the European LT community is quite extensive, with hundreds of commercial and academic organisations working on a large and heterogeneous set of technologies, it is also extremely fragmented with many community members operating only in narrow niches and limited regions, on very specific topics and quite often only taking into account one or two regionally confined languages. Through the META-NET SRA process, we have been able to identify the community's need for a joint technology platform that brings the European LT community together, that fosters collaboration and synergies, that acts as a marketplace and deployment platform, that functions like the "yellow pages" of the European LT community and through which essentially all European resources, corpora, datasets and grammars as well as tools, services and source code can be discovered and actually used, straight from the platform itself. Back in 2013, in the published META-NET SRA, we called this concept the *European Service Platform for Language Technologies*. The SRA document only contained a rather coarse-grained description of this ambitious technology vision, which has been demanded, for a number of different reasons, by an overwhelming majority of the members of the LT community.

Later on, in the three Strategic Research and Innovation Agendas prepared under the umbrella of the EU project CRACKER (Cracking the Language Barrier; 2015-2017), we refined the notion of the European LT Service Platform and we extended the possible use cases and a large number of LT-driven applications, primarily focusing the multilingual digital single market. Further boosted by the scientific breakthroughs produced in the area of Artificial Intelligence, Machine Learning and Deep Learning, early on applied to LT applications such as Machine Translation, not only the topic of Language Technology but also the vision of a joint European Language Technology Platform became more and more relevant. The topic was mentioned in

---

[1] http://www.meta-net.eu/sra

a prominent way in the STOA study *Language equality in the digital age*[2], commissioned by the European Parliament and also in a European Parliament resolution[3] with the same title, adopted by the European Parliament in a landslide vote in 2018 (cf. Jill Evans' foreword).

Roughly at the same time, in late 2017, we started preparing a project proposal for the Horizon 2020 ICT call, topic ICT-29 a), *European Language Grid*, which fortunately reflected the vast interest within the community in such a platform. After various unsuccessful attempts at coming up with a good title for the proposal, we decided to use the title of the actual call because it fit perfectly. Having passed the evaluation with a positive result, the project started in January 2019. We had an enthusiastic kick-off meeting, exciting hackathons and developed the first prototype of the platform in a fast and agile way. It was first presented to the public at META-FORUM 2019, which took place in Brussels in October that year.

Only a few weeks later, the global SARS-CoV-2 pandemic hit. The whole world was affected and so was our project plan. We were unable to have face-to-face project meetings or additional hackathons, we were unable to organise any on-site workshops with our 32 ELG National Competence Centres as part of the "ELG European Roadshow". All meetings, including our annual META-FORUM conferences in 2020 and 2021, had to go virtual, which was new to us at first and quickly became the new normal. Recently, in early June 2022, we had our last META-FORUM conference under the umbrella of the ELG EU project. META-FORUM 2022 went back, at least partially, to the *old* normal with approx. 100 participants in the conference centre in Brussels and hundreds more participating remotely.

It was nothing but a pleasure to act as Coordinator of the European Language Grid project and to work together with such a strong and dedicated team. Our original plan in this Innovation Action was already quite ambitious yet we managed to exceed our joint expectations in terms of the technology platform and its features, in terms of the services and resources developed, collected and ingested into the platform, in terms of the acceptance and feedback by the community and also in terms of the various collaborations we conducted with other projects. Many of the features envisioned for the *European Service Platform for Language Technologies* in 2013 are in fact now finally available in the *European Language Grid*, which is, by a large margin, the biggest all-purpose Language Technology platform on the planet covering the whole breadth and technology spectrum of the field.

All of the activities and results produced by the nine partners of the ELG consortium during the project's runtime are described in this book in detail. I would like to thank all consortium partners and team members for their extremely hard and dedicated work towards our common goal of developing and establishing the ELG platform, community and marketplace. In addition, I would like to thank the 15 selected pilot projects for their innovative proposals and the more than 200 organisations who applied for funding through one of our pilot projects. Thanks are also due to the projects ELG collaborated with, especially, in 2021/2022, the European

---

[2] https://www.europarl.europa.eu/stoa/en/document/EPRS_STU(2017)598621

[3] https://www.europarl.europa.eu/doceo/document/TA-8-2018-0332_EN.html

Language Equality project, the results of which will also be documented in the form of a book in the same series, but also others such as Bergamot, COMPRISE, ELITR, EMBEDDIA, Gourmet, Prêt-à-LLOD, AI4EU, HumanE AI Net, VISION, TAILOR, WeVerify, NTEU, Microservices at your Service, MAPA, QURATOR, PANQURA, SPEAKER and many others.

This book is the definitive documentation of the EU project European Language Grid.[4] I would like to thank all colleagues from the ELG consortium and also from the ELG pilot projects wholeheartedly for the chapters they contributed, without which this book would not have been possible.

While this book can only cover the results achieved during the project's runtime (January 2019 until June 2022), the ELG initiative will continue. In the second half of 2022 we will establish a legal entity that will take over maintenance and operation of the platform. We hope that ELG will serve its many purposes and, among others, address the stark community fragmentation and contribute to digital language equality in Europe, functioning indeed as one joint umbrella platform for the whole European LT community. Furthermore, while none of these can be considered a direct follow-up just yet, in a few projects (including OpenGPT-X, NFDI4DataScience and AI as well as the EU projects DataBri-X and SciLake) we will have the opportunity to continue our work with and on the ELG platform.

Berlin, July 2022

Georg Rehm

Acknowledgements The European Language Grid EU project has received funding from the European Union's Horizon 2020 research and innovation programme under grant agreement no. 825627.

---

[4] https://european-language-grid.readthedocs.io provides more details with regard to technical aspects of the ELG platform. The online documentation is actively maintained and kept up to date.

Contents

Part II ELG Inventory of Technologies and Resources

List of Contributors

European Language Grid EU Project (Parts I, II and III)

Victoria Arranz
ELDA, France, arranz@elda.org

Gerhard Backfried
HENSOLDT Analytics GmbH, Austria, gerhard.backfried@hensoldt.net

Cristian Berrìo Aroca
Expert AI, Spain, cberrio@expert.ai

Kalina Bontcheva
University of Sheffield, UK, k.bontcheva@sheffield.ac.uk

Rémi Calizzano
Deutsches Forschungszentrum für Künstliche Intelligenz GmbH (DFKI), Germany,
remi.calizzano@dfki.de

Khalid Choukri
ELDA, France, choukri@elda.org

Miltos Deligiannis
Institute for Language and Speech Processing, R. C. "Athena", Greece,
mdel@athenarc.gr

Dimitris Galanis
Institute for Language and Speech Processing, R. C. "Athena", Greece,
galanisd@athenarc.gr

Andres Garcia Silva
Expert AI, Spain, agarcia@expert.ai

Ulrich Germann
University of Edinburgh, UK, ulrich.germann@ed.ac.uk

Maria Giagkou
Institute for Language and Speech Processing, R. C. "Athena", Greece,
mgiagkou@athenarc.gr

Katerina Gkirtzou
Institute for Language and Speech Processing, R. C. "Athena", Greece,
katerina.gkirtzou@athenarc.gr

Dimitris Gkoumas
Institute for Language and Speech Processing, R. C. "Athena", Greece,
dgkoumas@athenarc.gr

Jose Manuel Gómez-Pérez
Expert AI, Spain, jmgomez@expert.ai

Annika Grützner-Zahn
Deutsches Forschungszentrum für Künstliche Intelligenz GmbH (DFKI), Germany,
annika.gruetzner-zahn@dfki.de

Jan Hajič
Charles University, Czech Republic, hajic@ufal.mff.cuni.cz

Jana Hamrlová
Charles University, Czech Republic, hamrlova@ufal.mff.cuni.cz

Stefanie Hegele
Deutsches Forschungszentrum für Künstliche Intelligenz GmbH (DFKI), Germany,
stefanie.hegele@dfki.de

Miroslav Jánošík
HENSOLDT Analytics GmbH, Austria, miroslav.janosik@hensoldt-analytics.com

Lukáš Kačena
Charles University, Czech Republic, kacena@ufal.mff.cuni.cz

Florian Kintzel
Deutsches Forschungszentrum für Künstliche Intelligenz GmbH (DFKI), Germany,
florian.kintzel@dfki.de

Athanasia Kolovou
Institute for Language and Speech Processing, R. C. "Athena", Greece,
akolovou@athenarc.gr

Ondřej Košarko
Charles University, Czech Republic, kosarko@ufal.mff.cuni.cz

Jens-Peter Kückens
Deutsches Forschungszentrum für Künstliche Intelligenz GmbH (DFKI), Germany,
jens_peter.kueckens@dfki.de

Penny Labropoulou
Institute for Language and Speech Processing, R. C. "Athena", Greece,
penny@athenarc.gr

Andis Lagzdiņš
Tilde, Latvia, andis.lagzdins@tilde.lv

Valérie Mapelli
ELDA, France, mapelli@elda.org

Katrin Marheinecke
Deutsches Forschungszentrum für Künstliche Intelligenz GmbH (DFKI), Germany,
katrin.marheinecke@dfki.de

Stelios Piperidis
Institute for Language and Speech Processing, R. C. "Athena", Greece,
spip@athenarc.gr

Katja Prinz
HENSOLDT Analytics GmbH, Austria, katja.prinz@hensoldt.net

Georg Rehm
Deutsches Forschungszentrum für Künstliche Intelligenz GmbH (DFKI), Germany,
georg.rehm@dfki.de

Mickaël Rigault
ELDA, France, mickael@elda.org

Ian Roberts
University of Sheffield, UK, i.roberts@sheffield.ac.uk

Milan Straka
Charles University, Czech Republic, straka@ufal.mff.cuni.cz

Andrejs Vasiļjevs
Tilde, Latvia, andrejs@tilde.lv

Leon Voukoutis
Institute for Language and Speech Processing, R. C. "Athena", Greece,
leon.voukoutis@athenarc.gr

European Language Grid FSTP Pilot Projects (Part IV)

Begoña Altuna
Fondazione Bruno Kessler, Italy, HiTZ Centre, University of the Basque Country,
Spain, begona.altuna@ehu.eus

Sebastian Andersson
Lingsoft, Finland, sebastian.andersson@lingsoft.fi

Arkaitz Anza
Skura Mobile, Spain, arkaitz@skuramobile.com

Mikko Aulamo
University of Helsinki, Finland, mikko.aulamo@helsinki.fi

Valerio Basile
University of Turin, Italy, valerio.basile@unito.it

Andrea Bolioli
CELI, Italy, andrea.bolioli@h-farm.com

Alessio Bosca
CELI, Italy, alessio.bosca@h-farm.com

Cristina Bosco
University of Turin, Italy, cristina.bosco@unito.it

Mark Breuker
EDIA b. v., The Netherlands, mark@edia.nl

Cesare Campagnano
Sapienza University of Rome, Italy, campagnano@di.uniroma1.it

Li-Hsin Chang
University of Turku, Finland, lhchan@utu.fi

Simone Conia
Sapienza University of Rome, Italy, conia@di.uniroma1.it

Ander Corral
Elhuyar Fundazioa, Spain, a.corral@elhuyar.eus

Michael Fell
University of Turin, Italy, michael.fell@unito.it

Filip Ginter
University of Turku, Finland, figint@utu.fi

Dagmar Gromann
University of Vienna, Austria, dagmar.gromann@univie.ac.at

Sam Hardwick
University of Helsinki, Finland, sam.hardwick@helsinki.fi

Barbara Heinisch
University of Vienna, Austria, barbara.heinisch@univie.ac.at

Gregor Jarisch
Labs.ai, Austria, gregor@labs.ai

Pavel Jedlička
University of West Bohemia, Czech Republic, jedlicka@ntis.zcu.cz

Beñat Jimenez
Talaios Koop., Spain, jimakker@talaios.coop

Jenna Kanerva
University of Turku, Finland, jmnybl@utu.fi

Jemina Kilpeläinen
University of Turku, Finland, jemina.j.kilpelainen@utu.fi

Svetla Koeva
Institute for Bulgarian Language, Bulgarian Academy of Sciences, Bulgaria,
svetla@dcl.bas.bg

Zdeněk Krňoul
University of West Bohemia, Czech Republic, zdkrnoul@ntis.zcu.cz

Hanna-Mari Kupari
University of Turku, Finland, hmknie@utu.fi

Christian Lang
University of Vienna, Austria, christian.lang@univie.ac.at

Alberto Lavelli
Fondazione Bruno Kessler, Italy, lavelli@fbk.eu

Igor Leturia
Elhuyar Fundazioa, Spain, i.leturia@elhuyar.eus

Helmut Ludwar
Sign Time GmbH, Austria, helmut.ludwar@signtime.media

Bernardo Magnini
Fondazione Bruno Kessler, Italy, magnini@fbk.eu

Jaione Martinez
Skura Mobile, Spain, jaione@skuramobile.com

Anne-Lyse Minard
Université d'Orléans, France, anne-lyse.minard@univ-orleans.fr

Luděk Müller
University of West Bohemia, Czech Republic, muller@kky.zcu.cz

Roberto Navigli
Sapienza University of Rome, Italy, navigli@diag.uniroma1.it

Tommi Nieminen
University of Helsinki, Finland, tommi.nieminen@helsinki.fi

Riccardo Orlando
Sapienza University of Rome, Italy, orlando@diag.uniroma1.it

Viviana Patti
University of Turin, Italy, viviana.patti@unito.it

Aurora Piirto
University of Turku, Finland, aurora.e.piirto@utu.fi

Silvia Portela
Skura Mobile, Spain, silvia@skuramobile.com

Jenna Saarni
University of Turku, Finland, jensaay@utu.fi

Xabier Sarasola
Elhuyar Fundazioa, Spain, x.sarasola@elhuyar.eus

Julia Schuster
Sign Time GmbH, Austria, julia.schuster@signtime.media

Maija Sevón
University of Turku, Finland, maija.suonpaa@gmail.com

Valtteri Skantsi
University of Turku, Finland, valtteri.skantsi@oulu.fi

Manuela Speranza
Fondazione Bruno Kessler, Italy, manspera@fbk.eu

Michael Stormbom
Lingsoft, Finland, michael.stormbom@lingsoft.fi

Otto Tarkka
University of Turku, Finland, ohitar@utu.fi

Steffen Thoma
FZI Research Center for Information Technology, Germany, thoma@fzi.de

Jörg Tiedemann
University of Helsinki, Finland, jorg.tiedemann@helsinki.fi

Rossella Varvara
University of Turin, Italy, rossella.varvara@unito.it

Alena Vasilevich
Coreon GmbH, Germany, alena@coreon.com

Lennart Wachowiak
University of Vienna, Austria, lennart.wachowiak@univie.ac.at

Franz Weber
Labs.ai, Austria, franz@labs.ai

Michael Wetzel
Coreon GmbH, Germany, michael@coreon.com

Patrick Wiener
FZI Research Center for Information Technology, Germany, wiener@fzi.de

Roberto Zanoli
Fondazione Bruno Kessler, Italy, zanoli@fbk.eu

Miloš Železný
University of West Bohemia, Czech Republic, zelezny@ntis.zcu.cz

Acronyms

AI	Artificial Intelligence
AMR	Abstract Meaning Representation
API	Application Programming Interface
ASL	American Sign Language
ASR	Automatic Speech Recognition
ATE	Automated Term Extraction
BMC	Business Model Canvas
CAS	Common Analysis System
CAT	Computer-assisted Translation
CC	Creative Commons
CD	Continuous Deployment
CEF	Connecting Europe Facility
CEFR	Common European Framework of Reference
CI	Continuous Integration
CLAIRE	Confederation of Laboratories for AI Research in Europa
CLARIN	Common Language Resources and Technology Infrastructure
CLI	Command-Line Interface
CMDI	Component Metadata Infrastructure
CMS	Content Management System
COAR	Controlled Vocabularies for Repositories
COMPRISE	Cost-effective, Multilingual, Privacy-driven, Voice-enabled Services
CPU	Central Processing Unit
CRACKER	Cracking the Language Barrier
CSE	Czech Sign Language
CSS	Cascading Style Sheets
CURLICAT	Curated Multilingual Language Resources for CEF AT
DC	Data Controller
DC	Dublin Core
DCAT	Data Catalog Vocabulary
DMP	Data Management Plan

DOI	Digital Object Identifier
DSDE	Development of Slovene in a Digital Environment
EEA	European Economic Area
EEIG	European Economic Interest Grouping
EFNIL	European Federation of National Institutions for Language
ELE	European Language Equality
ELG	European Language Grid
ELG R1	European Language Grid Release 1
ELG R2	European Language Grid Release 2
ELG R3	European Language Grid Release 3
ELITR	European Live Translator
ELRA	European Language Resource Association
ELRC	European Language Resource Coordination
ELT	European Language Technology
EMBEDDIA	Cross-lingual Embeddings for Less-Represented Languages in European News Media
EOSC	European Open Science Cloud
EUCPT	EU Council Presidency Translator
FAIR	Findable, Accessible, Interoperable, Reusable
FSTP	Financial Support to Third Parties
GATE	General Architecture for Text Engineering
GDPR	General Data Protection Regulation
GPU	Graphics Processing Unit
GUI	Graphical User Interface
HF	Hugging Face
HLT	Human Language Technology
HMM	Hidden Markov Models
HPA	Horizontal Pod Autoscaler
HTML	Hypertext Markup Language
HTTP	Hypertext Transfer Protocol
IAA	Inter-Annotator Agreement
ICT	Information and Communication Technology
IE	Information Extraction
IRI	Internationalised Resource Identifier
JSON	JavaScript Object Notation
JVM	Java Virtual Machine
KG	Knowledge Graph
KPI	Key Performance Indicator
KWS	Keyword-Spotting
LCR	Lexical or Conceptual Resource
LLOD	Linguistic Linked Open Data
LOD	Linked Open Data
LR	Language Resource
LRT	Language Resources and Language Technologies
LSDISCO	Lingsoft Solutions as Distributable Containers

LT	Language Technology
MAPA	Multilingual Anonymisation for Public Administrations
MARCELL	Multilingual Resources for CEF.AT in the Legal Domain
META	Multilingual Europe Technology Alliance
META-NET	Network of Excellence forging the Multilingual Europe Technology Alliance
MIME	Multipurpose Internet Mail Extensions
MT	Machine Translation
MVP	Minimum Viable Product
NAP	National Anchor Point
NCC	National Competence Centre
NCP	National Contact Point
NER	Named Entity Recognition
NLP	Natural Language Processing
NLU	Natural Language Understanding
NMT	Neural Machine Translation
NTEU	Neural Translation for the European Union
OA	Open Access
OAI-PMH	Open Archives Initiative Protocol for Metadata Harvesting
OCR	Optical Character Recognition
OLAC	Open Language Archives Community
OWL	Web Ontology Language
PB	Pilot Board
PID	Persistent Identifier
POS	Part of Speech
PRINCIPLE	Providing Resources in Irish, Norwegian, Croatian and Icelandic for Purposes of Language Engineering
PROVENANCE	Providing Verification Assistance for New Content
QURATOR	QURATOR – Curation Technologies
RDF	Resource Description Framework
REST	Representational State Transfer
SDK	Software Development Kit
SEO	Search Engine Optimisation
SKOS	Simple Knowledge Organisation System
SL	Sign Language
SME	Small and Medium Size Enterprises
SOA	Service-Oriented Architecture
SPDX	Software Package Data Exchange
SQL	Structured Query Language
SR	Subword Regularisation
SRL	Semantic Role Labeling
TBX	Termbase Exchange
TC	Text Classification
TCS	Terminological Concept System
TMX	Translation Memory Exchange

TTS	Text To Speech Synthesis
UI	User Interface
UML	Unified Modeling Language
URI	Uniform Resource Identifier
URL	Uniform Resource Locator
USP	Unique Selling Proposition
WFST	Weighted Finite State Transducer
WMT	Workshop/Conference on Machine Translation
WSD	Word Sense Disambiguation
XGAPP	XML GATE Application
XMI	XML Metadata Interchange
XML	Extensible Markup Language
XSD	XML Schema Definition
YAML	YAML Ain't Markup Language

Chapter 1
European Language Grid: Introduction

Georg Rehm

Abstract Europe is a multilingual society with 24 European Union Member State languages and dozens of additional languages including regional and minority languages as well as languages spoken by immigrants, trade partners and tourists. While languages are an essential part of our cultural heritage, language barriers continue to be unbreachable in many situations. The only option to enable and to benefit from multilingualism is through Language Technologies (LTs) including Natural Language Processing (NLP), Natural Language Understanding (NLU) and Speech Technologies. The commercial European LT landscape is dominated by hundreds of SMEs that develop many different kinds of LTs. While the industrial and also the academic European LT community is world-class, it is also massively fragmented. This chapter is an introduction to the present volume, which describes the European Language Grid (ELG) cloud platform, initiative and EU project. The ELG system is targeted to evolve into the primary platform and marketplace for LT in Europe by providing one umbrella platform for the entire European LT community, including research and industry, enabling all stakeholders to showcase, share and distribute their services, tools, products, datasets and other resources. At the time of writing, the ELG platform provides access to more than 13,000 commercial and non-commercial language resources and technologies covering all official EU languages and many national, co-official, regional and minority languages.

1 Overview and Context

Europe is a multilingual society with 24 EU Member State languages and dozens of additional languages including regional and minority languages as well as languages spoken by immigrants, trade partners and tourists. While languages are an important part of our cultural heritage, language barriers continue to be unbreachable in many situations. The only option to enable and to benefit from multilingualism is through Language Technologies (LTs) including Natural Language Processing (NLP), Nat-

Georg Rehm
Deutsches Forschungszentrum für Künstliche Intelligenz GmbH, Germany, georg.rehm@dfki.de

G. Rehm (ed.), *European Language Grid*, Cognitive Technologies,
https://doi.org/10.1007/978-3-031-17258-8_1

ural Language Understanding (NLU), and Speech Technologies. The commercial European LT landscape is dominated by hundreds of SMEs and a few larger enterprises (Rehm et al. 2020b). While the European LT community is world class, it is also very fragmented, significantly holding back its impact (Vasiljevs et al. 2019).

This book is the definitive documentation[1] of the EU project *European Language Grid*, which has developed the ELG cloud platform (Figure 1), available online at:

https://www.european-language-grid.eu

The European Language Grid is targeted to evolve into the primary platform for Language Technology in Europe. We provide one umbrella platform for all LTs and LRs developed by the whole European LT landscape, including research and industry, addressing a major gap, i. e., the lack of a common LT platform, that has been repeatedly raised by the whole community for many years (Rehm and Uszkoreit 2013; Rehm et al. 2016; STOA 2018; Rehm and Hegele 2018; European Parliament 2018). The ELG platform is also meant to be a virtual home and marketplace for all products, services and organisations active in this space in Europe, significantly boosting the EU Digital Single Market by helping to make it multilingual. ELG is an initiative *from* the European LT community *for* the European LT community. It provides one platform that can be used by all stakeholders to showcase, share and distribute their products, services, tools, datasets, corpora and other relevant resources. At the time of writing, the ELG platform enables access to more than 13,000 commercial and non-commercial language resources and technologies for all official EU languages and many national, co-official, regional and minority languages.

The European LT community had been demanding a dedicated LT platform for years – the ELG cloud platform fills this gap. The ambition of the ELG project and initiative is to unite a strong and extensive network of European experts and concentate on *commercial* as well as *non-commercial LTs*, both *functional* (analysis, processing and generation for written and spoken language) and *non-functional* (datasets, corpora, lexicons, models etc.). A related goal is to establish the ELG as a marketplace for the fragmented European LT landscape (Vasiljevs et al. 2019; Rehm et al. 2020b) to connect demand and supply, strengthening Europe's position in this field. The ELG platform enables the whole European LT community to upload their services and datasets, to deploy them, connect with, and make use of those resources made available by others (taking into account IPR and licences, as soon as the ELG legal entity is in place, including payment and billing options, especially with regard to commercial services and resources).

ELG is also meant to support *digital language equality* in Europe (STOA 2018; European Parliament 2018), i. e., bringing about a situation in which *all* languages are supported through technologies equally well. Currently, there is still an extreme imbalance, characterised by a stark predominance of LRTs for English, while almost all other languages are only marginally supported (Gaspari et al. 2022; Grützner-Zahn and Rehm 2022). In fact, many of these languages are in danger of digital

---

[1] The ELG cloud platform is actively being used, i. e., new services, tools and resources are made available on or through ELG on a daily basis. The data, numbers and statistics presented in this book regarding the use of ELG reflect the respective time of writing.

Fig. 1 The European Language Grid cloud platform

language extinction (Rehm and Uszkoreit 2012; Kornai 2013). With an initial consortium of 52 partners, ELG's sister project ELE (European Language Equality; Jan. 2021 – June 2022) and its immediate follow-up project ELE 2 (July 2022 – June 2023) are developing a strategic agenda and roadmap for digital language equality in Europe by 2030 to address this issue by means of a coordinated, pan-European research, development and innovation programme (Rehm and Way 2023).[2]

---

[2] https://european-language-equality.eu

2 The European Language Grid EU Project

The original proposal for the Innovation Action "European Language Grid" (ELG) was prepared by a consortium of nine partners (Table 1) and submitted on 17 April 2018, responding to the European Commission Horizon 2020 call topic ICT-29-2018 ("A multilingual Next Generation Internet", sub-topic "European Language Grid").[3] The ELG EU project[4] started in January 2019 and finished in June 2022.[5]

1 Deutsches Forschungszentrum für Künstliche Intelligenz GmbH DFKI (Coordinator)		Germany
2 Athena Research and Innovation Center in Information, Commu-nication and Knowledge Technologies, Institute for Language and Speech Processing	ILSP	Greece
3 University of Sheffield	USFD	UK
4 Charles University	CUNI	Czech Republic
5 Evaluations and Language Resources Distribution Agency	ELDA	France
6 Tilde SIA	TILDE	Latvia
7 HENSOLDT Analytics GmbH	HENS	Austria
8 Expert System Iberia SL	EXPSYS	Spain
9 University of Edinburgh	UEDIN	UK

Table 1 Consortium of the ELG EU project

The project was structured into three broader *areas*. The *ELG Platform* area (WP 1, WP 2, WP 3) took care of developing the technology platform, which was built with robust, scalable, reliable and widely used open source technologies, enabling it to scale with the growing demand and supply. As an important part of the platform, the ELG catalogue contains metadata records of all resources (including services, datasets etc.), service and application types, languages as well as records of LT companies, research organisations, projects, etc. This is where the first area overlapped with the second, i. e., *ELG Content* (WP 4, WP 5), referring to the actual content of the European Language Grid in terms of processing or generation services, tools, datasets, corpora, models, language resources etc. We distinguished between *functional* content (running services that can be uploaded into and deployed from the ELG cloud platform and integrated into other systems) and *non-functional* content (datasets, corpora, lexicons, etc.). Functional LT services are created by container-ising and ingesting them into ELG. One of our key goals was to make this process as easy and efficient as possible for commercial and non-commercial LT providers. These are two of the main classes of users of the third area, i. e., *ELG Community* (WP 6, WP 7), which includes all stakeholders of the ELG. Apart from commercial or academic developers of LT, these stakeholders also include companies, NGOs or

---

[3] https://ec.europa.eu/info/funding-tenders/opportunities/portal/screen/opportunities/topic-details/ict-29-2018

[4] https://cordis.europa.eu/project/id/825627

[5] The original runtime of 36 months was extended by six months due to the COVID-19 pandemic.

public administrations interested in purchasing or integrating Language Technologies into their own systems and applications. The ELG project collaborated – and still collaborates – with various other EU-supported research and innovation projects as well as with international networks and associations. Furthermore, ELG established a network of 32 National Competence Centres (NCCs) in as many European countries, who acted as national bridges to the project, generating interest in participating in the ELG initiative amongst relevant stakeholders from their own regions. In 2020, ELG published two open calls through which a total of 15 pilot projects were financially supported. These pilot projects extended ELG's catalogue with relevant services or datasets and realised innovative applications based on the ELG platform and available services and resources, demonstrating the usefulness of the platform. Table 2 shows all work packages of the ELG EU project.

Area	Work Package	Lead
ELG Platform	WP 1 Base Infrastructure	DFKI
	WP 2 Language Grid	ILSP
	WP 3 Interactive Interface and Information System	TILDE
ELG Content	WP 4 Services, Tools, Components	USFD
	WP 5 Language Resources, Data Sets and Models	ELDA
ELG Community	WP 6 Piloting the ELG	CUNI
	WP 7 Communication and Competence Centres	DFKI
	WP 8 Project Management and Coordination	DFKI

Table 2 Work packages of the ELG EU project

The ELG project resulted in more than 40 deliverables, the public ones of which are available online.[6] In addition to what had been originally specified in the project plan in early 2018, the project also worked on a number of activities that were not foreseen to be executed in the project proposal or grant agreement. For example, ELG organised the First International Workshop on Language Technology Platforms (IWLTP 2020).[7] Driven by the success of this workshop (Rehm et al. 2020a), a special issue of the *Language Resources and Evaluation* journal focusing on LT Platforms is currently in preparation, scheduled to be published in 2023. Motivated by the very positive feedback we have received from many different stakeholders since the beginning of the project, we decided, in 2020, to compile the present book as the definitive documentation of the project.

---

[6] https://www.european-language-grid.eu/deliverables

[7] https://www.european-language-grid.eu/iwltp-2020

3 Beyond the ELG EU Project

Throughout the years it has been repeatedly argued that Europe should not outsource its multilingual communication and digital language infrastructure to other continents and markets since the European demands are complex, challenging and above all unique. Instead, Europe should support and make use of its own LT community. One of the obstacles to overcome along the way has been the development of a shared technology and community platform for all European stakeholders. Now that the ELG cloud platform is finally in place, it is able to foster Language Technologies *for Europe* built *in Europe*, tailored to our languages and cultures and to our societal and economical demands, benefitting European citizens, society, innovation and industry. ELG plays the role of a shared, scalable cloud platform for the whole European LT community and it also functions as a joint marketplace and broker for a broad variety of services, products and datasets.

The ELG EU project was successfully completed in June 2022, and Release 3 of the ELG platform is ready to be used. At the time of writing, ELG provides access to more than 13,000 commercial and non-commercial language resources and technologies for all official EU languages and many national, co-official, regional and minority languages. In addition, the ELG project has contributed to validating and extending the platform with 15 pilot projects, building a pan-European community of users and providers, establishing communication and outreach channels and organising a number of large-scale conferences and smaller workshops.

Since the start of the project, we have been collaborating with the European AI on demand platform, especially with the AI4EU project, to ensure compatibility of our approaches in terms of describing resources semantically. Furthering these collaborative efforts will facilitate cross-platform search and discovery enabling ELG resources and other assets to be visible, discoverable and usable by the wider AI community. Considering the EU's plan to deploy the emerging European AI on demand platform, ELG is ready to act as the central language-related AI hub and marketplace providing access to and direct use of several thousands of LT services and datasets.

The ELG legal entity will take over further development and maintenance of ELG in the second half of 2022. At the same time, the ELG platform plays a role in several new funded projects. ELE (Jan. 2021 – June 2022) and ELE 2 (July 2022 – June 2023) have already been mentioned – ELG's sister projects are developing a strategic agenda and roadmap for achieving full digital language equality in Europe by 2030.[8] The ELG platform was and is heavily used in ELE – of special importance is the ELE dashboard, which provides a number of visualisations of the ELG catalogue, enabling various comparisons of the technology support of Europe's languages.[9] The project OpenGPT-X (Jan. 2022 – Dec. 2024), funded by the German Federal Ministry for Economic Affairs and Climate Action, develops large language models that will enable new data-driven business solutions, specifically address-

---

[8] https://european-language-equality.eu
[9] https://live.european-language-grid.eu/catalogue/dashboard

ing European needs.[10] In this project, many different language resources provided by ELG are used for research and development purposes. In addition, ELG will be further extended so that it complies to the specifications of the emerging Gaia-X[11] infrastructure and ecosystem, eventually integrating ELG into Gaia-X, making available many of the OpenGPT-X results (and *all* ELG resources) through Gaia-X. The project NFDI4DataScience and Artificial Intelligence (Oct. 2021 – Sept. 2026) is part of the initiative *Nationale Forschungsdateninfrastruktur* (German Research Data Infrastructure).[12] In this project, the ELG platform will be integrated into the emerging NFDI[13] infrastructure. A similar goal will be addressed by the upcoming EU project SciLake (Jan. 2023 – Dec. 2025), in which we will establish technical bridges between the ELG platform and the European Open Science Cloud (EOSC).[14] Finally, the upcoming EU project DataBri-X (Oct. 2022 – Sept. 2025) will interlink ELG and the emerging DataBri-X platform.

4 Summary of this Book

This book is structured into four different parts. Parts I, II and III describe the main results of the ELG project, while Part IV focuses on the ELG open calls and the 15 pilot projects. Below we include short summaries of the four parts.

4.1 Part I: ELG Cloud Platform

Part I provides an in-depth description of the *European Language Grid Cloud Platform*. First, Chapter 2 (p. 13 ff.) introduces the architecture and setup of the ELG cloud platform, including fundamental concepts such as the user and provider roles, the semantic metadata scheme and the different types of technologies currently supported by the platform. Afterwards, Chapter 3 (p. 37 ff.) concentrates on using ELG as a *consumer*. For this purpose, the web-based user interface, the public-facing APIs and the ELG Python SDK can be used. The complementary Chapter 4 (p. 67 ff.) examines using ELG as a *provider* of Language Technologies and Language Resources including the corresponding dashboard, service integration and various helper tools. Chapter 5 (p. 95 ff.) goes even deeper and provides a description of the ELG cloud infrastructure, e. g., the Kubernetes cluster, the storage solution etc. Finally, Chapter 6 (p. 107 ff.) examines the relation between ELG and other projects and infrastructures in terms of various technical collaborations (e. g., metadata harvesting).

---

[10] https://opengpt-x.de

[11] https://gaia-x.eu

[12] https://www.nfdi4datascience.de

[13] https://www.nfdi.de

[14] http://eosc.eu, https://eosc-portal.eu

4.2 Part II: ELG Inventory of Technologies and Resources

Part II focuses on the actual content of the ELG platform, i. e., it examines the *ELG Inventory of Technologies and Resources*. First, Chapter 7 (p. 131 ff.) describes the hundreds of functional Language Technology tools and services available in the ELG platform, covering machine translation, automatic speech recognition, text-to-speech synthesis as well as text analysis tools, among others. These tools and services have been and are being provided by companies as well as academic organisations. Chapter 8 (p. 151 ff.) then takes a look at the diverse set of Language Resources covering datasets, corpora, language models and other types of resources for all European languages. Many of these are hosted in ELG, available for direct download, while for others metadata records are collected from external repositories, enabling discovery through ELG as a one-stop-shop platform for the European LT community. Chapter 9 (p. 171 ff.) concludes Part II and describes the organisations, i. e., companies and research institutions, as well as projects currently represented in ELG. Our vision is for ELG to become the primary platform for Language Technology in Europe and, thus, for all organisations that develop LT to actively maintain their ELG pages, provide language tools and services as well as language resources, linking them to their own ELG pages.

4.3 Part III: ELG Community and Initiative

Part III provides an in-depth look at four different dimensions of the *ELG Community and Initiative*. First, Chapter 10 (p. 189 ff.) describes the main group of stakeholders that the EU project ELG collaborated with including various LT providers, different EU and national research projects as well as several wider initiatives. This chapter also describes the different ELG communication channels including social media. Chapter 11 (p. 205 ff.) focuses on the 32 National Competence Centres (NCCs) that the ELG project set up. The NCCs function as an international network of national networks, they support the overall mission of the ELG project. On a more abstract level, Chapter 12 (p. 219 ff.) provides a glimpse at various aspects and processes that revolve around open innovation and the marketplace concept as one of the main visions we have for the European Language Grid. Finally, Chapter 13 (p. 233 ff.) describes the ELG legal entity – including setup, challenges, products etc. – as the main instrument to sustain the ELG initiative beyond the EU project.

4.4 Part IV: ELG Open Calls and Pilot Projects

Part IV is dedicated to the *ELG Open Calls and Pilot Projects*. A considerable amount of the overall budget of the EU project European Language Grid was set aside to support a number of pilot projects that either make use of the technologies and resources provided by ELG or that extend the ELG inventory and portfolio by contributing additional technologies or resources. First, Chapter 14 (p. 257 ff.) describes the setup of the ELG open calls including designed and implemented procedures, boards, evaluation criteria etc. The following 15 chapters – Chapter 15 (p. 271 ff.) to Chapter 29 (p. 355 ff.) – report on the 15 pilot projects, selected from more than 200 project proposals in an expert-driven evaluation procedure.

References

European Parliament (2018). *Language Equality in the Digital Age. European Parliament resolution of 11 September 2018 on Language Equality in the Digital Age (2018/2028(INI)*. URL: http://www.europarl.europa.eu/doceo/document/TA-8-2018-0332_EN.pdf.

Gaspari, Federico, Owen Gallagher, Georg Rehm, Maria Giagkou, Stelios Piperidis, Jane Dunne, and Andy Way (2022). "Introducing the Digital Language Equality Metric: Technological Factors". In: *Proceedings of the Workshop Towards Digital Language Equality (TDLE 2022; co-located with LREC 2022)*. Ed. by Itziar Aldabe, Begoña Altuna, Aritz Farwell, and German Rigau. Marseille, France, pp. 1–12. URL: http://www.lrec-conf.org/proceedings/lrec2022/workshops/TDLE/pdf/2022.tdle-1.1.pdf.

Grützner-Zahn, Annika and Georg Rehm (2022). "Introducing the Digital Language Equality Metric: Contextual Factors". In: *Proceedings of the Workshop Towards Digital Language Equality (TDLE 2022; co-located with LREC 2022)*. Ed. by Itziar Aldabe, Begoña Altuna, Aritz Farwell, and German Rigau. Marseille, France, pp. 13–26. URL: http://www.lrec-conf.org/proceedings/lrec2022/workshops/TDLE/pdf/2022.tdle-1.2.pdf.

Kornai, Andras (2013). "Digital Language Death". In: *PLoS ONE* 8.10. DOI: 10.1371/journal.pone.0077056. URL: https://doi.org/10.1371/journal.pone.0077056.

Rehm, Georg, Kalina Bontcheva, Khalid Choukri, Jan Hajic, Stelios Piperidis, and Andrejs Vasiljevs, eds. (2020a). *Proc. of the 1st Int. Workshop on Language Technology Platforms (IWLTP 2020, co-located with LREC 2020)*. Marseille, France. URL: https://www.aclweb.org/anthology/volumes/2020.iwltp-1/.

Rehm, Georg and Stefanie Hegele (2018). "Language Technology for Multilingual Europe: An Analysis of a Large-Scale Survey regarding Challenges, Demands, Gaps and Needs". In: *Proceedings of the 11th Language Resources and Evaluation Conference (LREC 2018)*. Ed. by Nicoletta Calzolari, Khalid Choukri, Christopher Cieri, Thierry Declerck, Sara Goggi, Koiti Hasida, Hitoshi Isahara, Bente Maegaard, Joseph Mariani, Hélène Mazo, Asuncion Moreno, Jan Odijk, Stelios Piperidis, and Takenobu Tokunaga. Miyazaki, Japan: ELRA, pp. 3282–3289. URL: https://aclanthology.org/L18-1519.pdf.

Rehm, Georg, Katrin Marheinecke, Stefanie Hegele, Stelios Piperidis, Kalina Bontcheva, Jan Hajic, Khalid Choukri, Andrejs Vasiļjevs, Gerhard Backfried, Christoph Prinz, José Manuel Gómez Pérez, Luc Meertens, Paul Lukowicz, Josef van Genabith, Andrea Lösch, Philipp Slusallek, Morten Irgens, Patrick Gatellier, Joachim Köhler, Laure Le Bars, Dimitra Anastasiou, Albina Auksoriūtė, Núria Bel, António Branco, Gerhard Budin, Walter Daelemans, Koenraad De Smedt, Radovan Garabík, Maria Gavriilidou, Dagmar Gromann, Svetla Koeva, Simon Krek, Cvetana Krstev, Krister Lindén, Bernardo Magnini, Jan Odijk, Maciej Ogrodniczuk, Eiríkur Rögnvaldsson, Mike Rosner, Bolette Pedersen, Inguna Skadina, Marko Tadić, Dan Tufiş, Tamás Váradi, Kadri Vider, Andy Way, and François Yvon (2020b). "The European Language Technology Landscape in 2020: Language-Centric and Human-Centric AI for Cross-Cultural Communication in Multilingual Europe". In: *Proceedings of the 12th Language Resources and Evaluation Conference (LREC 2020)*. Ed. by Nicoletta Calzolari, Frédéric Béchet, Philippe Blache, Christopher Cieri, Khalid Choukri, Thierry Declerck, Hitoshi Isahara, Bente Maegaard, Joseph Mariani,

Asuncion Moreno, Jan Odijk, and Stelios Piperidis. Marseille, France: ELRA, pp. 3315–3325. URL: https://www.aclweb.org/anthology/2020.lrec-1.407/.

Rehm, Georg and Hans Uszkoreit, eds. (2012). *META-NET White Paper Series: Europe's Languages in the Digital Age*. 32 volumes on 31 European languages. Heidelberg etc.: Springer.

Rehm, Georg and Hans Uszkoreit, eds. (2013). *The META-NET Strategic Research Agenda for Multilingual Europe 2020*. Heidelberg, New York, Dordrecht, London: Springer. URL: http://www.meta-net.eu/vision/reports/meta-net-sra-version_1.0.pdf.

Rehm, Georg, Hans Uszkoreit, Sophia Ananiadou, Núria Bel, Audronė Bielevičienė, Lars Borin, António Branco, Gerhard Budin, Nicoletta Calzolari, Walter Daelemans, Radovan Garabík, Marko Grobelnik, Carmen García-Mateo, Josef van Genabith, Jan Hajič, Inma Hernáez, John Judge, Svetla Koeva, Simon Krek, Cvetana Krstev, Krister Lindén, Bernardo Magnini, Joseph Mariani, John McNaught, Maite Melero, Monica Monachini, Asunción Moreno, Jan Odijk, Maciej Ogrodniczuk, Piotr Pęzik, Stelios Piperidis, Adam Przepiórkowski, Eiríkur Rögnvaldsson, Mike Rosner, Bolette Sandford Pedersen, Inguna Skadiņa, Koenraad De Smedt, Marko Tadić, Paul Thompson, Dan Tufiş, Tamás Váradi, Andrejs Vasiļjevs, Kadri Vider, and Jolanta Zabarskaite (2016). "The Strategic Impact of META-NET on the Regional, National and International Level". In: *Language Resources and Evaluation* 50.2, pp. 351–374. DOI: 10.1007/s10579-015-9333-4. URL: http://link.springer.com/article/10.1007/s10579-015-9333-4.

Rehm, Georg and Andy Way, eds. (2023). *European Language Equality: A Strategic Agenda for Digital Language Equality*. Cognitive Technologies. Forthcoming. Springer.

STOA (2018). *Language equality in the digital age – Towards a Human Language Project*. STOA study (PE 598.621), IP/G/STOA/FWC/2013-001/Lot4/C2. URL: https://data.europa.eu/doi/10.2861/136527.

Vasiļjevs, Andrejs, Khalid Choukri, Luc Meertens, and Stefania Aguzzi (2019). *Final study report on CEF Automated Translation value proposition in the context of the European LT market/ecosystem*. DOI: 10.2759/142151. URL: https://op.europa.eu/de/publication-detail/-/publication/8494e56d-ef0b-11e9-a32c-01aa75ed71a1/language-en.

Part I
ELG Cloud Platform

Chapter 2
The European Language Grid Platform: Basic Concepts

Stelios Piperidis, Penny Labropoulou, Dimitris Galanis, Miltos Deligiannis, and Georg Rehm

Abstract In the fragmented Language Technology (LT) landscape of multilingual Europe, ELG has set out to bring together language resources and technologies (LRTs) and boost the LT sector and its activities. The primary goal is to build a scalable and comprehensive cloud platform for providers, developers, integrators and consumers of language resources and technologies. We describe the basic concepts of the ELG platform in terms of its architecture, the functionalities and services offered to its types of users and the policies it implements. We present the ELG repository, its catalogue features, the LT services execution environment as well as the metadata model underlying the platform operations and the resources life cycle, from creation to publication. We also discuss the compliance of ELG with the FAIR principles and the relation to other platforms and infrastructure initiatives which have inspired certain aspects and with which ELG has been establishing strong links.

1 Introduction

The overarching objective of the European Language Grid (ELG, Rehm et al. 2021) is to tackle the observed fragmentation in the European Language Technology (LT) landscape by bringing together Language Resources and Technologies (LRTs), commercial and non-commercial, and through multiple multi-level services support and boost the LT sector and LT activities in Europe. The primary technological goal is to build a scalable cloud-based platform through which developers and providers of language resources and technologies can not only deposit and upload their resources and technologies into ELG, but also deploy them through the platform and make use of the services, technologies and resources made available by others. ELG is a marketplace through which consumers and integrators of LRTs can discover, try out

Stelios Piperidis · Penny Labropoulou · Dimitris Galanis · Miltos Deligiannis
Institute for Language and Speech Processing, R. C. "Athena", Greece, spip@athenarc.gr,
penny@athenarc.gr, galanisd@athenarc.gr, mdel@athenarc.gr

Georg Rehm
Deutsches Forschungszentrum für Künstliche Intelligenz GmbH, Germany, georg.rehm@dfki.de

13

G. Rehm (ed.), *European Language Grid*, Cognitive Technologies,
https://doi.org/10.1007/978-3-031-17258-8_2

and integrate the resources and technologies they require for their own research and application development.

The primary services of the platform are dedicated to the deposition, discovery, distribution and deployment of Language Resources and Technologies. ELG already offers access to thousands of commercial and non-commercial LTs and ancillary LRs for all European languages and more. These include processing and generation services, tools, applications for written and spoken language, as well as datasets, corpora, lexical resources, language models and computational grammars.

ELG also supports the promotion and collaboration of LT stakeholders through an extensive catalogue of organisations (companies, SMEs, academic and research organisations and groups, etc.) active in the LT community. Organisations can describe, promote and distribute their services and resources all in one place. Complemented with an expanding catalogue of European and national projects that have funded the production of LRTs and related activities, the catalogue of the ELG platform offers an overview of the European LT landscape. ELG, therefore, also acts as an observatory of LT, consolidating existing and legacy tools, services, LRs, and information about them, as well as newly emerging ones. This, in turn, enables the identification of gaps and imbalances between the LRTs offered for all European languages, a valuable instrument for the support of digital language equality in Europe.

ELG is conceived as a platform for the whole LT community. Primarily for Europe, ELG is a platform built *by* the European LT community *for* the European LT community, including industry, innovation and research. For the population of the catalogue of its platform, ELG builds bridges to existing initiatives and reaches agreements for harvesting and importing information (i. e., metadata) and resources from other infrastructures, platforms and repositories under mutually agreed conditions, business policies, acknowledgement and attribution of the source, and collaborates in joint initiatives and crowdsourcing campaigns.

This chapter introduces the basic concepts of the ELG platform, while the subsequent chapters go into more detail with regard to functionalities offered to consumers (Chapter 3) and providers (Chapter 4), the cloud infrastructure (Chapter 5) and the synergies with other initiatives (Chapter 6). We first give an overview of the platform features (Section 2) and its users (Section 3). Section 4 presents the architecture of ELG. Sections 5 and 6 present the models and policies that influence the design and operations of the ELG platform, i. e., the metadata model, and the publication life cycle of catalogue entries. Section 7 positions the ELG platform with regard to the FAIR principles (Wilkinson et al. 2016).

2 Overview of the ELG Platform

The ELG platform combines the features of a catalogue (Section 2.1), a repository (Section 2.2), and an execution environment for running services (Section 2.3).

2.1 Catalogue

All LRTs are accessed through their metadata records in the catalogue (Figure 1). Providers can describe and share their LRTs; they can upload them to be hosted in ELG, or they can only describe them and provide access to them through other locations, such as institutional or national repositories, or private repositories of commercial organisations. They can also create dedicated pages for their organisations, describe their offerings and services and interlink all their LRTs through their own pages.

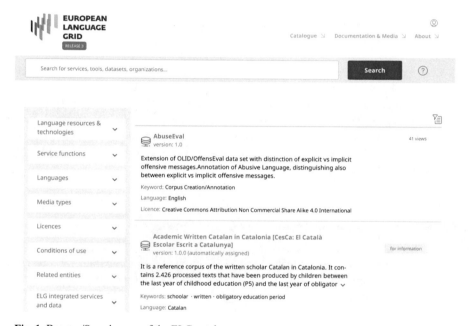

Fig. 1 Browse/Search page of the ELG catalogue

Additionally, the ELG catalogue includes metadata records imported automatically from other sources, through standard harvesting protocols and dedicated converters, thus resulting in an extensive and continuously growing inventory of LRTs as well as of organisations and projects in the LT domain.

LRT consumers, i. e., users, and other interested parties can search for and discover LRTs using free text search and faceted views of the catalogue. Users can select and view the detailed descriptions of LRTs to see if they fit the users' needs. Users can access the resources, either directly if hosted in ELG, or be re-directed to the URL from where the resources are accessible. Users can also search for organisations, browse them, and view their activities on their profile pages. If these organisations have also described the LRTs they developed, users can navigate to the respective pages for more details. Last, users can also discover the LT-related

projects in which organisations participated and that have helped fund the organisations' LRT development. Finally, users can export and download the metadata
descriptions or share the pages on social media.

2.2 Repository of Language Resources and Technologies

LRT providers can upload their resources to be hosted in the ELG cloud infrastructure, and to be made available to consumers for direct download. Providers must
specify the licensing conditions under which the resources can be used. Depending
on the terms, ELG will allow immediate download (for open access resources) or
impose further measures (authentication and authorisation). Commercial LRTs, distributed for download at a fee, will be available for purchase using a user-friendly
billing service.

ELG as a repository is committed to making data, services and their metadata
FAIR, i. e., findable, accessible, interoperable and reusable (Wilkinson et al. 2016).
The assignment of persistent identifiers in the form of Digital Object Identifiers
(DOIs)[1] for the data and services hosted in ELG is among the main steps towards this
objective; the FAIR principles, detailed in Section 7, form an integral part of the ELG
policies aiming to support the requirements posed by research results reproducibility
objectives and practices.

2.3 Running Language Technology Cloud Services

To benefit from the advanced features of ELG, providers can integrate LT tools as
ready-to-deploy services, following our specifications (Chapter 4). In this case, consumers can test the tools and services using the trial UIs or APIs offered by ELG,
and, ultimately, integrate them in their workflows and systems. For commercial services, billing services will be available to allow pay-for-use services with seamless
access and use in the minimum possible number of steps.

ELG provides a set of standard APIs which cover all principal service types (see
Chapter 3, Section 3, p. 50 ff., for more details): *information extraction and annotation services* for *text and speech*, *text-to-text* services (most notably machine translation services, but also summarisers, anonymisers, etc.), *classification services for
text or image*, such as language identifiers, fake news detectors, sentiment analysers,
etc., *speech recognition* services, *text-to-speech synthesis* services, and *image OCR*
(optical character recognition) services.

The technical specifications give service providers a set of easy-to-implement
integration options from which they can select the one that best fits their needs. All
that is required is that they upload an image of their tool or service using one of these
options in a container registry and provide access to ELG.

---

[1] https://www.doi.org

ELG maintains a dedicated container registry for LT services.[2] As the images of LT services are partly pulled from registries external to the ELG project, this registry serves as a point to collect LT service images when they are ingested into the ELG and to apply versioning. This approach enables us to ensure that older versions of images remain available even if their original site no longer provides them.

To provide easy access and interaction with the ELG platform also for programmers, a Python SDK has been developed on top of the various ELG programmatic interfaces providing simple methods to easily interact with the platform and consume resources in Python (see Chapter 3, Section 4, p. 55 ff., for more details).

3 User Types and User Model

Specified by its mission, ELG targets various types of users, broadly classified into:

Providers of LRTs, both commercial and academic, albeit with different requirements (the former seek to promote and sell their products and activities, while the latter wish to make their resources available for research or look for cooperation to further develop them in new projects or commercialize them),

Consumers of LRTs, including companies developing LT tools, services and applications, integrators, researchers using LRT for their studies, etc.,

LT laypersons interested in finding out more about LT and its uses,

Funding authorities and stakeholders that wish to get an overview of the LT field and landscape, trends and prospects with regard to languages, domains etc.

All users can browse the catalogue and access, view and inspect the detailed descriptions of the assets listed in the catalogue, and download resources available with open access licences. For further interactions with the ELG platform, registration is required and can be performed with a simple and user-friendly self-service procedure. The types of permitted actions and access level are determined by the user role: *registered consumers* can run integrated services and download resources that are available for free download to authenticated users; *providers* can, in addition, describe all types of assets, upload content files, and integrate services according to the ELG technical requirements; two specific user roles (*validator* and *administrator*) are reserved for ELG team members responsible for the management of the catalogue, metadata records and data files, in accordance with the ELG policies (Section 6) including the overall platform maintenance and administrative operations.

---

[2] registry.european-language-grid.eu

4 Architecture

The ELG platform uses state-of-the art technologies and is designed to evolve over time to address new requirements or technological advancements. The choices made in the architectural design and implementation allow for scaling with the growing demand and supply for compute resources and lay the foundation for interoperable data and service spaces.

All subsystems are built with robust, scalable, reliable, widely used open source technologies, as described below. Docker containers[3] are used for all services and applications which comprise the ELG platform, while Kubernetes[4] is used for container orchestration. Conceptually, ELG takes the form of a three-layered platform, with each layer grouping together the main subsystems responsible for the platform's functionalities: *base infrastructure, platform back end, platform front end* (Figure 2).

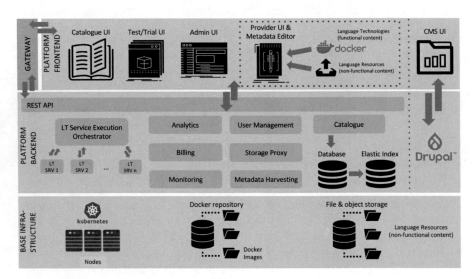

Fig. 2 ELG platform architecture

The *base infrastructure* is the layer on which all ELG software components are deployed and run. It includes the supporting tools that facilitate development and management of the ELG platform software. It is composed, first and foremost, of the compute nodes running the platform, alongside their respective volume storage and networking facilities; these are organised in two different clusters, one for development and one for production purposes. It also comprises public and private

---

[3] A Docker image of an application contains its actual code and all required dependencies required to run it; e. g., the operating system, frameworks, settings, configuration files, libraries, etc. Containers are instantiations of images and can be thought of as lightweight virtual machines.

[4] Kubernetes is a framework that enables and simplifies the deployment, scaling and management of containers, see https://kubernetes.io.

container registries, which host all images for the ELG platform components and for the LT services integrated in the platform. In addition, it includes an S3-compatible file and object storage, through which data resources uploaded by providers as well as backups of core platform components are persisted. This layer also includes a set of Git[5] repositories for the source code of the platform software apps and for the individual LT services implementations of specific providers. Chapter 5 (p. 95 ff.) provides more information on the base infrastructure.

The *platform back end* consists of all the components that enable the operation of the ELG platform, i.e., the catalogue core components, the component for processing LT services and platform support as well as management components. The catalogue component, implemented using Django[6], interfaces with a PostgreSQL[7] database for storing the metadata records and an index, which uses ElasticSearch[8]. The LT service execution server offers a common REST API for calling LT services integrated in the platform, and handles failures, time-outs, etc. Finally, separate modules are used for the user management and authentication module (based on Keycloak[9], an identity and access management solution), the analytics, monitoring, metadata harvesting and the proxy for interacting with the S3-compatible storage.

The *platform front end* layer consists of the static pages maintained in a Content Management System (CMS). These provide information on the ELG project and initiative, and the platform UIs for the different types of users, i.e., consumers, providers, validators, and administrators. These include the catalogue pages (browse, search, view), and the dashboard pages customised for the different user types, UIs for registering (describing and uploading) LRTs and other assets and supporting the publication life cycle, implemented using React[10], and the trial UIs for services integrated in ELG. The catalogue UI consumes REST services exposed by the ELG platform back end (e.g., catalogue application, LT Service execution server).

Chapters 3 (p. 37 ff.) and 4 (p. 67 ff.) provide more information on the back end and front end layers of the European Language Grid platform.

5 Catalogue Contents and Metadata Model

All types of LT assets as well as all LT-related meta-information are brought together, aligned and interlinked. This set of information[11] is formally structured and harmonised in ELG using the ELG-SHARE metadata model[12] catering for the full

---

[5] https://git-scm.com

[6] https://www.djangoproject.com

[7] https://www.postgresql.org

[8] https://www.elastic.co

[9] https://www.keycloak.org

[10] https://reactjs.org

[11] https://european-language-grid.readthedocs.io/en/stable/all/A2_Metadata/Metadata.html

[12] https://gitlab.com/european-language-grid/platform/ELG-SHARE-schema

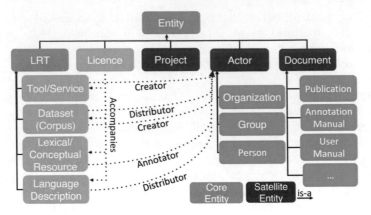

Fig. 3 ELG entities

language data and services life cycle and their related entities (Labropoulou et al. 2020). The ELG model covers the following types of entities (Figure 3).

- *Language resources and technologies (LRTs)*, further classified into:
    - *Corpora*, i. e., datasets of mono/bi/multilingual text documents, audio/video recordings, multimedia datasets, parallel corpora, translation memories, etc.
    - *Lexical/conceptual resources*, including lexica, ontologies, gazetteers, term lists, computational dictionaries, etc.
    - *Language descriptions*, which mainly refer to computational grammars, statistical and machine learning models
    - *Tools/services*, i. e., pieces of software offered as locally executable code or web services, hosted and running in the ELG cloud platform or remotely

- Related/satellite entities, such as actors, be it *persons* or *organizations* that have created or that curate resources, *projects* that have funded them or in which they have been used, as well as *licences* and accompanying *documents* (e. g., publications related to the resource, user manuals, technical documents, etc.)

The ELG model lies at the heart of the platform and supports its key operations. In particular, it aims to 1. support the discoverability of all catalogue contents; 2. enable accessibility by human users and, where possible or required, machines (e. g., including links to URLs that offer direct access to a resource or service); 3. address (at the metadata level) interoperability requirements of resources belonging to the same types and media, but coming from different sources with different descriptions, as well as between resources of different types and media (e. g., between datasets and services to be used for their processing); and, 4. finally, satisfy documentation needs at different levels of granularity, ranging from the strict enforcement of technical metadata required for the deployment of ELG-compatible services to rather loose descriptions of resources imported from general purpose catalogues.

The metadata model builds upon previous work from the META-SHARE metadata model (Gavrilidou et al. 2012), which caters for the description of language resources and language-processing technologies, and its application profiles, i. e., ELRC-SHARE (Piperidis et al. 2018a), OMTD-SHARE (Labropoulou et al. 2018), CLARIN-SHARE (Piperidis et al. 2018b), which extend, restrict and adapt the basic model to specific domains and areas (e. g., public domain resources, text and data mining domain, etc.), and the MS-OWL ontology[13] (McCrae et al. 2015; Khan et al. 2022), which is the RDF/OWL representation of the model.

The model builds along three key concepts, each of which is associated with a distinctive set of metadata elements:

- *resource type*, with the four subtypes described above;
- *media type*, which specifies the form or physical medium of the resource. The notion of medium is preferred over the written, spoken or multimodal distinction, as it has clearer semantics and allows us to view LRs as a set of modules, each of which can be described through a distinctive set of features. Thus, the following media type values are foreseen: *text, audio, image, video* and *numerical text* (referring to numerical data, such as biometrical, geospatial data, etc.). To cater for multimedia and multimodal language resources (e. g., a corpus of videos and subtitles, or a corpus of audio recordings and transcripts, a sign language corpus with videos and texts, etc.), language resources are represented as *consisting* of at least one media part;
- *distribution*, which, following the DCAT[14] model (Albertoni et al. 2020; Maali and Erickson 2014), refers to any physical form of the resource that can be distributed and deployed by end-users.

These elements give rise to a modular structure, in which metadata elements are attached to the appropriate level ("class"). The "LanguageResource" class includes properties common to all resource and media types, such as those used for identification purposes (title, description, etc.), recording provenance (creation, publication dates, creators, providers, etc.), contact points, etc. More technical features and classification elements differ across resource and media types and are, thus, attached to combinations thereof; for example, a corpus may take elements specific to annotation processes, while the description of a computational lexicon encodes, e. g., whether it includes lemmas, examples, grammatical information, translation equivalents, etc. Technical features, such as format, size, information on licensing and mode of access are properties of the distribution. They can also differ across resource type. For example, corpora can be distributed as PDF files or as simple text files, lexical resources in tabular form or queried through an interface, while tools may be available as source code, executable files or web services. Each of these forms can be licensed under different terms: source code may be available at a price for integration in other applications, while an API may be offered for research purposes without any fee. Figure 4 illustrates a subset of the elements for a tool/service.

---

[13] http://w3id.org/meta-share/meta-share

[14] https://www.w3.org/TR/vocab-dcat-3/

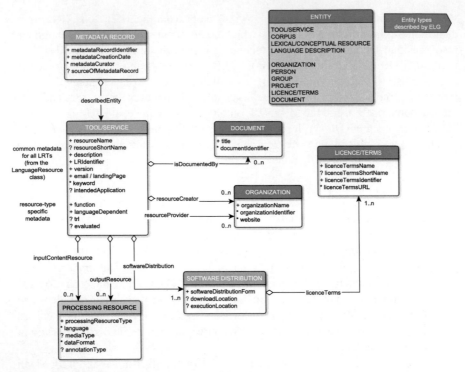

Fig. 4 Excerpt of the minimal schema for tools/services

The schema allows for the description of the full life cycle of language resources (see, e. g., Rehm 2016), from conception and creation to integration in applications and usage. All this information leads to a complex and demanding schema; to ensure flexibility and uptake by resource providers, the elements are classified into three levels of optionality:

- *mandatory:* elements that are necessary
- *recommended:* elements that can help the current or future use of the resource, or useful information that providers have not yet standardised
- *optional:* all remaining information

The minimal schema comprises all mandatory elements which must be filled for a metadata record to be considered ELG-compliant and eligible to be registered in the platform. Recently, a "relaxed" version of the ELG schema was introduced as a way of handling metadata records with "lighter" information imported from other catalogues in ELG, but this version of the schema is allowed only under specific circumstances. Chapter 6 discusses this in more detail. Below, we summarise the metadata categories considered mandatory for the description of resources (Figures 6 to 10 in the Appendix provide an overview for each resource type).

- Administrative information: these features are important for the identification of an LRT (resource name, version, description which includes information on the contents, provenance information, any other information deemed useful and helpful for consumers, etc.), contact information (landing page with additional information or a contact email).
- Classification information: one or more free text keywords that support the findability of the resource.
- Usage information: separate distributions for each distributable form of the resource, with the following elements: the distribution form (i. e., whether it can be downloaded, accessed through an interface, deployed as a web service, etc.), the licensing terms under which it can be used (licence name and URL); if the resource is not uploaded in ELG, an access or download link.
- Legal/ethical information for data resources: whether personal or sensitive data is included and, if applicable, information on anonymisation.
- Technical information: depending on the resource type

  - for tools/services: the function (i. e., the task it performs, e. g., named entity recognition, machine translation, speech recognition, etc.), the technical specifications of its input (at least the resource type it processes, e. g., corpus, text, etc.), whether it is language independent and, if not, the input languages; depending on the function, further information may be required (e. g., the languages of the output resource for machine translation services);
  - for all data resources[15]: features on the language following the BCP 47[16] guidelines, multilinguality type, resource subtype with different values (e. g., terminological glossary, ontology, etc. for lexical/conceptual resources, raw or annotated for corpora); size and format information must also be added separately for each distribution and media part;
  - in addition, specifically for models: the intended application (e. g., machine translation, named entity recognition, etc.), the model function (e. g., zero-shot classification), and model type (e. g., embeddings, Bayesian model, n-gram model, etc.);
  - specifically for grammars and lexical/conceptual resources: the encoding level of their contents (i. e., whether they contain morphological, syntactic, semantic, etc. information).

For organisations and projects, all that is required is the name (official title). However, we also recommend a free text description with the activities of the organisation or the project summary respectively, and the URL of its website. The LT area(s) in which the organisation/project activities are related to and one or more keywords increase its visibility and findability. For big organisations with multiple divisions (e. g., academic institutions with schools, faculties, departments, or multinational

---

[15] A resource can consist of one or more media parts, which must be described separately, for example, for a corpus of video recordings and their subtitles in various languages, the language value must be indicated separately for each part.

[16] https://www.rfc-editor.org/info/bcp47

companies with branches), both the parent organisation and division(s) can be registered and a link between them added.

For standardisation purposes, the ELG schema favours controlled vocabularies over free-text fields, especially when these are associated with internationally acknowledged standards, best practices or widespread vocabularies, e. g., ISO 3166 for region codes (ISO 2020), RFC 5646 for languages[17] (Phillips and Davis 2009), etc. The implementation in the form of an XML Schema Definition (XSD) imports elements from two ontologies, i. e., the MS-OWL ontology, which includes most elements and controlled vocabularies, and the OMTD-SHARE ontology[18] (Labropoulou et al. 2018) reserved for the controlled vocabularies of LT categories (also referred to as "LT taxonomy"), data formats, annotation types and methods.

6 Publication Life Cycle

ELG considers the quality of metadata records to be of primary importance as it contributes to the discovery and usage of resources. We defined a set of policies that take into account the source and the process through which a record has been entered in the ELG catalogue.

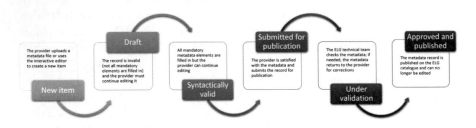

Fig. 5 ELG publication life cycle

The ELG publication life cycle consists of a set of states through which an entry progresses, from its creation in the ELG platform until it is published (Figure 5). A *new item* is created each time a provider adds a new metadata record. The record can remain at the *draft* status as long as the provider wishes, in which case no validation checks are made – apart from validation of the data types of the metadata elements (e. g., that a URL is properly formulated). At the *syntactically valid* status, a metadata record must comply with the minimal version of the ELG schema (i. e., all mandatory elements must be filled in). The provider can still continue to edit it until they are satisfied with the description and can then submit it for publication; once submitted, the provider is notified by email. While the record is *submitted for publication* the

---

[17] https://datatracker.ietf.org/doc/html/rfc5646

[18] http://w3id.org/meta-share/omtd-share/

entry is validated at the metadata, technical and legal level. The validation, which is described in more detail in Chapter 3, aims to check the consistency of the description and, where required, its technical compliance with the ELG specifications; it does not include any qualitative evaluation of the resource itself. The validation is currently performed by the ELG team. When validators identify a problem, they contact the provider and recommend changes and additions to the metadata; in such cases, the status is changed to *syntactically valid* again and the provider is notified to make the appropriate amendments. When the validators have approved an item, it is automatically visible via the ELG catalogue. Published metadata records cannot be edited any more, i. e., they are immutable.

Metadata records added by individuals go through the whole publication life cycle. Human validation aims at ensuring a minimum level of quality included in the records, which can be achieved through interactions with the provider. This procedure cannot be adopted for metadata records automatically imported from other catalogues. For these, the responsibility for the quality and extent of information lies with the source catalogue. The same policy, that of accepting records as is, has been adopted for records added through bulk initiatives, such as the collaborative survey of LRTs undertaken in the context of the European Language Equality project[19] and described in Chapter 6.

7 ELG and the FAIR Principles

The publication of the FAIR principles (Wilkinson et al. 2016) marked a landmark for infrastructures that support the sharing and re-use of data resources. The FAIR principles are guidelines set to enhance re-usability of data by improving their findability, accessibility, interoperability and re-usability. They are intended both for humans and machines, and put an emphasis on machine actionability, i. e., the capacity of computational systems to find, access, interoperate, and reuse data with no or minimal human intervention.[20] ELG has implemented mechanisms and policies to ensure that resources (data and software) included in ELG as well as the metadata that describe them are FAIR, i. e., adhere to the FAIR principles.[21]

Findability principles

- *F1 – (Meta)data are assigned a globally unique and persistent identifier*
  Resources hosted in ELG and ELG-compatible services are assigned a DOI (Digital Object Identifier)[22] provided by DataCite[23]. Metadata for resources will also have their own unique identifier created on the basis of the resource

---

[19] https://european-language-equality.eu

[20] https://www.go-fair.org/fair-principles/

[21] https://force11.org/info/the-fair-data-principles/

[22] https://www.doi.org

[23] https://datacite.org

DOI. For metadata records that do not have an accompanying file and hence cannot be assigned a DOI, we use their URL as an identifier.

- *F2 – Data are described with rich metadata*
  The ELG metadata schema is rich in information. Providers are encouraged to add not only the mandatory but also recommended information. The validation process for resources and services aims at improving metadata quality.
- *F3 – Metadata clearly and explicitly include the identifier of the data they describe*
  The element "identifier" (with the "identifier scheme" attribute) is included in the metadata record.
- *F4 – (Meta)data are registered or indexed in a searchable resource*
  All metadata records are indexed and searchable in the ELG catalogue and also accessible to search engines. In addition, we expose the metadata records of LRTs to Google's dedicated search engine for research datasets.[24]

Accessibility principles

- *A1 – (Meta)data are retrievable by their identifier using a standardised communications protocol*
  All metadata in ELG are accessible via the ELG catalogue. Resources hosted in ELG and ELG-compatible are accessible via their DOI and directly retrievable via a URL. The HTTPS protocol is used.
- *A1.1 The protocol is open, free, and universally implementable*
  HTTPS is used for providing access to metadata and resources.
- *A1.2 The protocol allows for an authentication and authorisation procedure, where necessary*
  HTTPS is used for providing access to metadata and resources. ELG uses an authentication and authorisation system.
- *A2 – Metadata are accessible, even when the data are no longer available*
  When a resource or a metadata record is deleted, a tombstone page with all the required elements following DataCite recommendations is put in place.

Interoperability principles

- *I1 – (Meta)data use a formal, accessible, shared, and broadly applicable language for knowledge representation*
  All metadata records are exported in XML format, a subset is available in JSON-LD format; work is ongoing for the export into RDF using the MS-OWL ontology.
- *I2 – (Meta)data use vocabularies that follow FAIR principles*
  The metadata elements and values are taken from two RDF/OWL ontologies, MS-OWL and OMTD-SHARE[25].

---

[24] https://datasetsearch.research.google.com

[25] http://w3id.org/meta-share/omtd-share

- *I3 – (Meta)data include qualified references to other (meta)data*
  Qualified relations are used for linking between versions of the resources and, in cases of imported records, for linking with their source metadata records.

Re-usability principles

- *R1 – (Meta)data are richly described with a plurality of accurate and relevant attributes*
  Alongside the "description" element where providers are advised to add as much information as possible for the benefit of human users, the ELG schema includes elements that can be used to identify potential uses of a resource and properties that make clear where they can be of use, e. g., "intended application", "service function", "domain", etc.
- *R1.1 – (Meta)data are released with a clear and accessible data usage license*
  All resources must have a licence; the licence value and a link to the licence text are included in the metadata. Metadata are also permissively licensed with a Creative Commons licence.
- *R1.2 – (Meta)data are associated with detailed provenance*
  The source for the metadata record is explicitly added in the metadata record ("metadata creator" or "source repository"). Properties about the creation of a resource are included in the metadata.
- *R1.3 – (Meta)data meet domain-relevant community standards*
  With regard to the metadata, the ELG schema is based on META-SHARE, a well-established metadata vocabulary in the LT community. For the tools and services added in the ELG catalogue, the technical specifications follow current best practices (e. g., preparing a Docker image). For data, a set of recommendations, taking into account established file formats, standards, and de facto best practices, is under construction.

8 Related Platforms and Infrastructures

ELG builds upon previous work of the ELG consortium partners and the wider European LT community (Rehm et al. 2020b), especially META-NET[26] and ELRC[27].

The ELG platform shares common features and goals with other platforms, repositories, projects or other initiatives: 1. a collection of LT/NLP tools or datasets, 2. a platform, which harvests metadata records from distributed sources, 3. a platform for the sharing of tools or datasets, 4. a platform for the deployment of services, 5. a repository for storing data files. Comparisons can be made along various dimensions. We include here an overview at the level of the main functionalities provided, while the respective background and technical details are presented in Chapters 3 and 4. An alternative and minimally outdated comparison is provided in Rehm et al. (2020a).

---

[26] http://www.meta-net.eu

[27] https://www.elrc-share.eu

META-SHARE[28] is a network of repositories (Piperidis 2012; Piperidis et al. 2014). Each repository, or node, hosts various types of resources (datasets, services, etc.) described with the META-SHARE metadata schema (Gavrilidou et al. 2012). Each node is deployed at a different organisation. The nodes periodically harvest metadata records from each other. Architecture and conceptual design of the ELG platform have been inspired by the META-SHARE setup but designed and implemented from scratch. ELG adopts a different approach as it operates as a centralised platform where individuals can directly register, download and run resources and services. Harvesting is also performed but from external catalogues (e. g., ELRC-SHARE[29], LINDAT/CLARIAH-CZ[30], etc.), as described in Chapter 6. From an engineering point of view, ELG is a radically improved version of META-SHARE, e. g., 1. ELG offers REST APIs while META-SHARE does not, 2. the ELG front end and back end are implemented as different layers that can be developed in parallel, 3. the metadata schema has been updated and extended to cover new resource types and description requirements.

The OpenMinTeD platform[31] was designed as an open, service-oriented e-Infrastructure for Text and Data Mining of scientific content (Labropoulou et al. 2018). It includes a catalogue for datasets, NLP and text mining services, worfklows, lexica etc., described with a rich metadata schema, OMTD-SHARE. REST APIs for searching, metadata and resource upload/download are provided, as in the case of ELG. OpenMinTeD was a centralised repository, and harvesting was employed as a one-off procedure for importing metadata records from a few content providers. It supported the creation of workflows from tools contained in the catalogue, and their execution on datasets provided through the same platform; the functionality was based on the Galaxy[32] worfklow management system (Afgan et al. 2018).

ELRC-SHARE[33] (Piperidis et al. 2018a) is an infrastructure developed by the European Language Resource Coordination action[34] with the objective to host, document, manage and distribute LRs pertinent to MT, with a particular focus on the needs of the eTranslation[35] service of the European Commission. It is a centralised repository with a catalogue of datasets, which are added and documented by individuals. Metadata records of tools and services are listed as for information only.

The European AI-on-demand platform, as initiated by the EU project AI4EU seeks to bring together the European AI community while promoting European values.[36] The platform is a facilitator of knowledge transfer from research to multiple

---

[28] http://www.meta-share.org

[29] https://www.elrc-share.eu

[30] https://lindat.mff.cuni.cz

[31] https://github.com/openminted – the OpenMinTeD platform is not available online any more.

[32] https://galaxyproject.org/learn/advanced-workflow/

[33] https://www.elrc-share.eu

[34] https://lr-coordination.eu

[35] https://cor.europa.eu/en/engage/Pages/e-translation.aspx

[36] https://www.ai4europe.eu

business and industry domains. The AI catalogue[37] is designed for hosting datasets and services in the area of AI; for instance, it includes NLP resources, computer vision services, etc. The capabilities of the metadata schema used are rather limited compared to the ELG schema. It also provides catalogues for organisations involved in AI[38], collaborating projects[39] and educational resources[40], but the catalogues are all separate, without any linking between the entities as offered in the ELG catalogue.

CLARIN[41] (Hinrichs and Krauwer 2014; Eskevich et al. 2020) is a European Research Infrastructure providing access to digital language resources and tools to researchers in the humanities and social sciences. CLARIN does not host a single repository; instead, it is organised in the form of a network of centres that operate their own repositories and catalogues. The individual centres are free in their choice of repository software and metadata schema (Broeder et al. 2008). The CLARIN Virtual Language Observatory[42] is the central catalogue which harvests metadata from all centres as well as other catalogues of interest to scholars in the target disciplines and displays them in a uniform way, although only a subset of the metadata elements are common. Processing services are catalogued centrally in the Language Switchboard[43], while some CLARIN centres make available processing services connected to their catalogues or offered separately (e. g., LINDAT/CLARIAH-CZ[44], PORTULAN-CLARIN[45], CLARIN:EL[46], etc.). Unlike ELG, there is no central compute infrastructure for deploying and running processing services.

The Language Application Grid (LAPPS Grid)[47] (Ide et al. 2014, 2016) is an open, interoperable web service platform for NLP research and development. It provides facilities for selecting and combining NLP tools and services to create workflows, composite services, and applications, and to evaluate, reproduce, and share them. It is based largely on the Galaxy[48] worfklow management system and does not actually include a catalogue. Some limited metadata have to be provided in order to create the files that are required for adding tools used in Galaxy wokflows, e. g., the name of the tool, a description, input parameters etc. For datasets no metadata are required since they are not permanently stored in Galaxy.

Hugging Face[49] is an AI/NLP company, offering repository and deployment functionalities for machine learning (Wolf et al. 2020). It hosts a large set of models and

---

[37] https://www.ai4europe.eu/research/ai-catalog

[38] https://www.ai4europe.eu/ai-community/organizations

[39] https://www.ai4europe.eu/ai-community/projects

[40] https://www.ai4europe.eu/education/education-catalog

[41] https://www.clarin.eu

[42] https://vlo.clarin.eu

[43] https://switchboard.clarin.eu

[44] https://lindat.mff.cuni.cz

[45] https://portulanclarin.net

[46] https://inventory.clarin.gr

[47] https://www.lappsgrid.org

[48] https://galaxyproject.org/learn/advanced-workflow/

[49] https://HuggingFace.co

datasets that can be used for model training. It offers a catalogue with a limited REST API, e. g., the API does not allow filtering search results, etc. Similar to this, there are other catalogues and repositories, such as Kaggle[50] and Papers With Code[51], which target the machine learning community. These are also community-driven, i. e., resources are registered by individuals and have their own metadata schemas.

Finally, we should mention the long lasting initiative of ELRA and the LREC community in establishing the LREC Map (Calzolari et al. 2010), as well as the growing popularity of initiatives that include general (e. g., European Open Science Cloud[52]) or federated catalogues (e. g., Gaia-X[53]) and also general repositories (e. g., Zenodo[54]), which bring together a large range of resources from and for various disciplines. See Chapter 6 for more details.

9 Conclusions

ELG has been designed as the primary platform for the European LT community, adopting a holistic view of technology development, deployment and use, bringing together language data, resources and processing services as well as the commercial and non-commercial LT actors and initiatives. ELG has established and implemented a standardised resource life cycle catering for all stages, from creation to publication and version evolution. The primary services offered are dedicated to the deposition, discovery, distribution and deployment of language resources and technologies through appropriate interfaces for technical and non-technical providers, developers, consumers and integrators. Such interfaces include web GUIs, REST APIs and a Python Software Development Kit (SDK). Its operations are supported by a metadata model underlying the description, search, discovery and distribution of resources and services, conforming to the FAIR principles. On this basis, ELG has started building bridges to existing initiatives for harvesting and importing information and resources from other infrastructures, platforms and repositories under mutually agreed conditions, business policies, acknowledgement and attribution of the source, and collaborates in joint initiatives and crowdsourcing campaigns.

References

Afgan, Enis, Dannon Baker, Bérénice Batut, Marius van den Beek, Dave Bouvier, Martin Čech, John Chilton, Dave Clements, Nate Coraor, Björn A Grüning, Aysam Guerler, Jennifer Hillman-Jackson, Saskia Hiltemann, Vahid Jalili, Helena Rasche, Nicola Soranzo, Jeremy Goecks, James

---

[50] https://www.kaggle.com

[51] https://paperswithcode.com

[52] https://eosc-portal.eu

[53] https://www.gaia-x.eu

[54] https://zenodo.org

Taylor, Anton Nekrutenko, and Daniel Blankenberg (2018). "The Galaxy platform for accessible, reproducible and collaborative biomedical analyses: 2018 update". In: *Nucleic Acids Research* 46.W1, W537–W544. DOI: 10.1093/nar/gky379. URL: https://academic.oup.com/nar/article/46/W1/W537/5001157.

Albertoni, Riccardo, David Browning, Simon Cox, Alejandra Gonzalez-Beltran, Andrea Perego, and Peter Winstanley, eds. (2020). *Data Catalog Vocabulary (DCAT) – Version 2*. W3C Recommendation. URL: https://www.w3.org/TR/vocab-dcat-2/.

Broeder, Daan, Thierry Declerck, Erhard Hinrichs, Stelios Piperidis, Laurent Romary, Nicoletta Calzolari, and Peter Wittenburg (2008). "Foundation of a Component-based Flexible Registry for Language Resources and Technology". In: *Proceedings of the Sixth International Conference on Language Resources and Evaluation (LREC 2008)*. Marrakech, Morocco: ELRA. URL: http://www.lrec-conf.org/proceedings/lrec2008/pdf/364_paper.pdf.

Calzolari, Nicoletta, Claudia Soria, Riccardo Del Gratta, Sara Goggi, Valeria Quochi, Irene Russo, Khalid Choukri, Joseph Mariani, and Stelios Piperidis (2010). "The LREC Map of Language Resources and Technologies". In: *Proceedings of the Seventh International Conference on Language Resources and Evaluation (LREC 2010)*. Valletta, Malta: ELRA. URL: http://www.lrec-conf.org/proceedings/lrec2010/pdf/370_Paper.pdf.

Eskevich, Maria, Franciska de Jong, Alexander König, Darja Fišer, Dieter Van Uytvanck, Tero Aalto, Lars Borin, Olga Gerassimenko, Jan Hajic, Henk van den Heuvel, Neeme Kahusk, Krista Liin, Martin Matthiesen, Stelios Piperidis, and Kadri Vider (2020). "CLARIN: Distributed Language Resources and Technology in a European Infrastructure". In: *Proc. of the 1st Int. Workshop on Language Technology Platforms (IWLTP 2020, co-located with LREC 2020)*. Ed. by Georg Rehm, Kalina Bontcheva, Khalid Choukri, Jan Hajic, Stelios Piperidis, and Andrejs Vasiljevs. Marseille, France: ELRA, pp. 28–34. URL: https://aclanthology.org/2020.iwltp-1.5.

Gavrilidou, Maria, Penny Labropoulou, Elina Desipri, Stelios Piperidis, Haris Papageorgiou, Monica Monachini, Francesca Frontini, Thierry Declerck, Gil Francopoulo, Victoria Arranz, and Valerie Mapelli (2012). "The META-SHARE Metadata Schema for the Description of Language Resources". In: *Proceedings of the Eighth International Conference on Language Resources and Evaluation (LREC 2012)*. Istanbul, Turkey: ELRA, pp. 1090–1097. URL: http://www.lrec-conf.org/proceedings/lrec2012/pdf/998_Paper.pdf.

Hinrichs, Erhard and Steven Krauwer (2014). "The CLARIN Research Infrastructure: Resources and Tools for eHumanities Scholars". In: *Proceedings of the Ninth International Conference on Language Resources and Evaluation (LREC 2014)*. Reykjavik, Iceland: ELRA, pp. 1525–1531. URL: http://www.lrec-conf.org/proceedings/lrec2014/pdf/415_Paper.pdf.

Ide, Nancy, James Pustejovsky, Christopher Cieri, Eric Nyberg, Denise DiPersio, Chunqi Shi, Keith Suderman, Marc Verhagen, Di Wang, and Jonathan Wright (2016). "The Language Application Grid". In: *Worldwide Language Service Infrastructure*. Ed. by Yohei Murakami and Donghui Lin. Cham: Springer, pp. 51–70. DOI: 10.1007/978-3-319-31468-6_4.

Ide, Nancy, James Pustejovsky, Christopher Cieri, Eric Nyberg, Di Wang, Keith Suderman, Marc Verhagen, and Jonathan Wright (2014). "The Language Application Grid". In: *Proc. of the Ninth International Conference on Language Resources and Evaluation (LREC 2014)*. Reykjavik, Iceland: ELRA. URL: http://www.lrec-conf.org/proceedings/lrec2014/pdf/926_Paper.pdf.

ISO (2020). *ISO 3166 – Country Codes*. International Organization for Standardization. URL: https://www.iso.org/iso-3166-country-codes.html.

Khan, Anas Fahad, Christian Chiarcos, Thierry Declerck, Daniela Gifu, Elena González-Blanco García, Jorge Gracia, Maxim Ionov, Penny Labropoulou, Francesco Mambrini, and John P. McCrae (2022). "When Linguistics Meets Web Technologies. Recent advances in Modelling Linguistic Linked Open Data". In: *Semantic Web Journal*. Accepted for publication.

Labropoulou, Penny, Dimitris Galanis, Antonis Lempesis, Mark Greenwood, Petr Knoth, Richard Eckart de Castilho, Stavros Sachtouris, Byron Georgantopoulos, Stefania Martziou, Lucas Anastasiou, Katerina Gkirtzou, Natalia Manola, and Stelios Piperidis (2018). "OpenMinTeD: A Platform Facilitating Text Mining of Scholarly Content". In: *Proceedings of WOSP 2018 (co-located with LREC 2018)*. Miyazaki, Japan: ELRA, pp. 7–12. URL: http://lrec-conf.org/workshops/lrec2018/W24/pdf/13_W24.pdf.

Labropoulou, Penny, Katerina Gkirtzou, Maria Gavriilidou, Miltos Deligiannis, Dimitris Galanis, Stelios Piperidis, Georg Rehm, Maria Berger, Valérie Mapelli, Michael Rigault, Victoria Arranz, Khalid Choukri, Gerhard Backfried, José Manuel Gómez Pérez, and Andres Garcia-Silva (2020). "Making Metadata Fit for Next Generation Language Technology Platforms: The Metadata Schema of the European Language Grid". In: *Proceedings of the 12th Language Resources and Evaluation Conference (LREC 2020)*. Ed. by Nicoletta Calzolari, Frédéric Béchet, Philippe Blache, Christopher Cieri, Khalid Choukri, Thierry Declerck, Hitoshi Isahara, Bente Maegaard, Joseph Mariani, Asuncion Moreno, Jan Odijk, and Stelios Piperidis. Marseille, France: ELRA, pp. 3421–3430. URL: https://www.aclweb.org/anthology/2020.lrec-1.420/.

Maali, Fadi and John Erickson, eds. (2014). *Data Catalog Vocabulary (DCAT) – Version 1*. W3C Recommendation. URL: https://www.w3.org/TR/2020/SPSD-vocab-dcat-20200204/.

McCrae, John Philip, Penny Labropoulou, Jorge Gracia, Marta Villegas, Víctor Rodríguez-Doncel, and Philipp Cimiano (2015). "One Ontology to Bind Them All: The META-SHARE OWL Ontology for the Interoperability of Linguistic Datasets on the Web". In: *The Semantic Web: ESWC 2015 Satellite Events*. Ed. by Fabien Gandon, Christophe Guéret, Serena Villata, John Breslin, Catherine Faron-Zucker, and Antoine Zimmermann. Lecture Notes in Computer Science. Springer International Publishing, pp. 271–282. URL: https://link.springer.com/chapter/10.1007/978-3-319-25639-9_42.

Phillips, Addison and Mark Davis (2009). *Tags for Identifying Languages*. Tech. rep. RFC 5646. Internet Engineering Task Force. URL: https://datatracker.ietf.org/doc/rfc5646.

Piperidis, Stelios (2012). "The META-SHARE Language Resources Sharing Infrastructure: Principles, Challenges, Solutions". In: *Proceedings of the Eight International Conference on Language Resources and Evaluation (LREC'12)*. Ed. by Nicoletta Calzolari, Khalid Choukri, Thierry Declerck, Mehmet Uğur Doğan, Bente Maegaard, Joseph Mariani, Asuncion Moreno, Jan Odijk, and Stelios Piperidis. Istanbul, Turkey: ELRA.

Piperidis, Stelios, Penny Labropoulou, Miltos Deligiannis, and Maria Giagkou (2018a). "Managing Public Sector Data for Multilingual Applications Development". In: *Proceedings of the Eleventh International Conference on Language Resources and Evaluation (LREC 2018)*. Ed. by Nicoletta Calzolari, Khalid Choukri, Christopher Cieri, Thierry Declerck, Sara Goggi, Koiti Hasida, Hitoshi Isahara, Bente Maegaard, Joseph Mariani, Hélène Mazo, Asuncion Moreno, Jan Odijk, Stelios Piperidis, and Takenobu Tokunaga. Miyazaki, Japan: ELRA. URL: http://www.lrec-conf.org/proceedings/lrec2018/pdf/648.pdf.

Piperidis, Stelios, Penny Labropoulou, and Maria Gavriilidou (2018b). "clarin:el An infrastructure for the documentation, sharing and processing of language data (in Greek)". In: *Proceedings of the 12th International Conference on Greek Linguistics (ICGL12)*. Vol. 2. Berlin, Germany: Edition Romiosini/CeMoG, Freie Universität Berlin, pp. 851–869. URL: http://www.cemog.fu-berlin.de/en/icgl12/offprints/piperidis-lampropoulou-gavriilidou/icgl12_Piperidis-et-al.pdf.

Piperidis, Stelios, Harris Papageorgiou, Christian Spurk, Georg Rehm, Khalid Choukri, Olivier Hamon, Nicoletta Calzolari, Riccardo del Gratta, Bernardo Magnini, and Christian Girardi (2014). "META-SHARE: One year after". In: *Proceedings of the 9th Language Resources and Evaluation Conference (LREC 2014)*. Ed. by Nicoletta Calzolari, Khalid Choukri, Thierry Declerck, Hrafn Loftsson, Bente Maegaard, Joseph Mariani, Asuncion Moreno, Jan Odijk, and Stelios Piperidis. Reykjavik, Iceland: ELRA, pp. 1532–1538. URL: http://www.lrec-conf.org/proceedings/lrec2014/pdf/786_Paper.pdf.

Rehm, Georg (2016). "The Language Resource Life Cycle: Towards a Generic Model for Creating, Maintaining, Using and Distributing Language Resources". In: *Proceedings of the 10th Language Resources and Evaluation Conference (LREC 2016)*. Ed. by Nicoletta Calzolari, Khalid Choukri, Thierry Declerck, Marko Grobelnik, Bente Maegaard, Joseph Mariani, Asuncion Moreno, Jan Odijk, and Stelios Piperidis. Portorož, Slovenia: ELRA, pp. 2450–2454. URL: https://aclanthology.org/L16-1388.pdf.

Rehm, Georg, Maria Berger, Ela Elsholz, Stefanie Hegele, Florian Kintzel, Katrin Marheinecke, Stelios Piperidis, Miltos Deligiannis, Dimitris Galanis, Katerina Gkirtzou, Penny Labropoulou, Kalina Bontcheva, David Jones, Ian Roberts, Jan Hajic, Jana Hamrlová, Lukáš Kačena, Khalid Choukri, Victoria Arranz, Andrejs Vasiļjevs, Orians Anvari, Andis Lagzdiņš, Jūlija Meļņika,

Gerhard Backfried, Erinç Dikici, Miroslav Janosik, Katja Prinz, Christoph Prinz, Severin Stampler, Dorothea Thomas-Aniola, José Manuel Gómez Pérez, Andres Garcia Silva, Christian Berrío, Ulrich Germann, Steve Renals, and Ondrej Klejch (2020a). "European Language Grid: An Overview". In: *Proceedings of the 12th Language Resources and Evaluation Conference (LREC 2020)*. Ed. by Nicoletta Calzolari, Frédéric Béchet, Philippe Blache, Christopher Cieri, Khalid Choukri, Thierry Declerck, Hitoshi Isahara, Bente Maegaard, Joseph Mariani, Asuncion Moreno, Jan Odijk, and Stelios Piperidis. Marseille, France: ELRA, pp. 3359–3373. URL: https://www.aclweb.org/anthology/2020.lrec-1.413/.

Rehm, Georg, Katrin Marheinecke, Stefanie Hegele, Stelios Piperidis, Kalina Bontcheva, Jan Hajic, Khalid Choukri, Andrejs Vasiļjevs, Gerhard Backfried, Christoph Prinz, José Manuel Gómez Pérez, Luc Meertens, Paul Lukowicz, Josef van Genabith, Andrea Lösch, Philipp Slusallek, Morten Irgens, Patrick Gatellier, Joachim Köhler, Laure Le Bars, Dimitra Anastasiou, Albina Auksoriūtė, Núria Bel, António Branco, Gerhard Budin, Walter Daelemans, Koenraad De Smedt, Radovan Garabík, Maria Gavriilidou, Dagmar Gromann, Svetla Koeva, Simon Krek, Cvetana Krstev, Krister Lindén, Bernardo Magnini, Jan Odijk, Maciej Ogrodniczuk, Eiríkur Rögnvaldsson, Mike Rosner, Bolette Pedersen, Inguna Skadina, Marko Tadić, Dan Tufiş, Tamás Váradi, Kadri Vider, Andy Way, and François Yvon (2020b). "The European Language Technology Landscape in 2020: Language-Centric and Human-Centric AI for Cross-Cultural Communication in Multilingual Europe". In: *Proceedings of the 12th Language Resources and Evaluation Conference (LREC 2020)*. Ed. by Nicoletta Calzolari, Frédéric Béchet, Philippe Blache, Christopher Cieri, Khalid Choukri, Thierry Declerck, Hitoshi Isahara, Bente Maegaard, Joseph Mariani, Asuncion Moreno, Jan Odijk, and Stelios Piperidis. Marseille, France: ELRA, pp. 3315–3325. URL: https://www.aclweb.org/anthology/2020.lrec-1.407/.

Rehm, Georg, Stelios Piperidis, Kalina Bontcheva, Jan Hajic, Victoria Arranz, Andrejs Vasiļjevs, Gerhard Backfried, José Manuel Gómez Pérez, Ulrich Germann, Rémi Calizzano, Nils Feldhus, Stefanie Hegele, Florian Kintzel, Katrin Marheinecke, Julian Moreno-Schneider, Dimitris Galanis, Penny Labropoulou, Miltos Deligiannis, Katerina Gkirtzou, Athanasia Kolovou, Dimitris Gkoumas, Leon Voukoutis, Ian Roberts, Jana Hamrlová, Dusan Varis, Lukáš Kačena, Khalid Choukri, Valérie Mapelli, Mickaël Rigault, Jūlija Meļņika, Miro Janosik, Katja Prinz, Andres Garcia-Silva, Cristian Berrio, Ondrej Klejch, and Steve Renals (2021). "European Language Grid: A Joint Platform for the European Language Technology Community". In: *Proceedings of the 16th Conference of the European Chapter of the Association for Computational Linguistics: System Demonstrations (EACL 2021)*. Kyiv, Ukraine: ACL, pp. 221–230. URL: https://www.aclweb.org/anthology/2021.eacl-demos.26.pdf.

Wilkinson, Mark D., Michel Dumontier, IJsbrand Jan Aalbersberg, Gabrielle Appleton, Myles Axton, Arie Baak, Niklas Blomberg, Jan-Willem Boiten, Luiz Bonino da Silva Santos, Philip E. Bourne, Jildau Bouwman, Anthony J. Brookes, Tim Clark, Mercè Crosas, Ingrid Dillo, Olivier Dumon, Scott Edmunds, Chris T. Evelo, Richard Finkers, Alejandra Gonzalez-Beltran, Alasdair J.G. Gray, Paul Groth, Carole Goble, Jeffrey S. Grethe, Jaap Heringa, Peter A.C 't Hoen, Rob Hooft, Tobias Kuhn, Ruben Kok, Joost Kok, Scott J. Lusher, Maryann E. Martone, Albert Mons, Abel L. Packer, Bengt Persson, Philippe Rocca-Serra, Marco Roos, Rene van Schaik, Susanna-Assunta Sansone, Erik Schultes, Thierry Sengstag, Ted Slater, George Strawn, Morris A. Swertz, Mark Thompson, Johan van der Lei, Erik van Mulligen, Jan Velterop, Andra Waagmeester, Peter Wittenburg, Katherine Wolstencroft, Jun Zhao, and Barend Mons (2016). "The FAIR Guiding Principles for Scientific Data Management and Stewardship". In: *Scientific Data* 3. DOI: 10.1038/sdata.2016.18. URL: http://www.nature.com/articles/sdata201618.

Wolf, Thomas, Lysandre Debut, Victor Sanh, Julien Chaumond, Clement Delangue, Anthony Moi, Pierric Cistac, Tim Rault, Rémi Louf, Morgan Funtowicz, Joe Davison, Sam Shleifer, Patrick von Platen, Clara Ma, Yacine Jernite, Julien Plu, Canwen Xu, Teven Le Scao, Sylvain Gugger, Mariama Drame, Quentin Lhoest, and Alexander M. Rush (2020). "Transformers: State-of-the-art Natural Language Processing". In: *Proceedings of the 2020 Conference on Empirical Methods in Natural Language Processing: System Demonstrations*. ACL, pp. 38–45. DOI: 10.18653/v1/2020.emnlp-demos.6. URL: https://aclanthology.org/2020.emnlp-demos.6.

Appendix

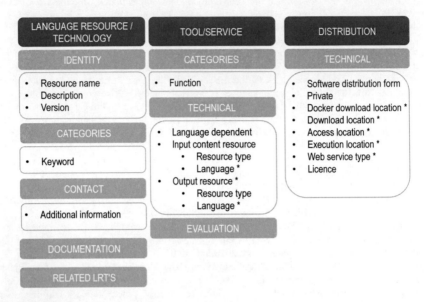

Fig. 6 ELG minimal schema version for a tool/service

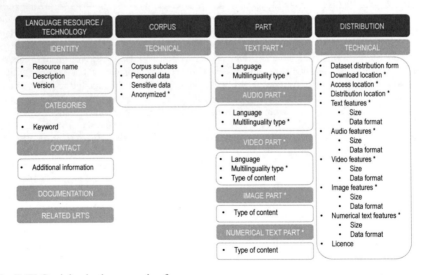

Fig. 7 ELG minimal schema version for a corpus

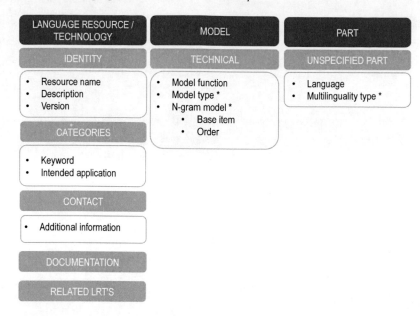

Fig. 8 ELG minimal schema version for a model

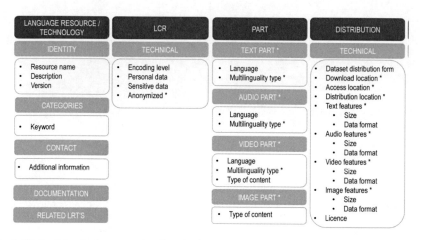

Fig. 9 ELG minimal schema version for a lexical/conceptual resource

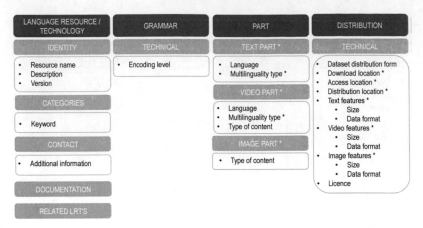

Fig. 10 ELG minimal schema version for a grammar

Chapter 3
Using the European Language Grid as a Consumer

Ian Roberts, Penny Labropoulou, Dimitris Galanis, Rémi Calizzano, Athanasia Kolovou, Dimitris Gkoumas, Andis Lagzdiņš, and Stelios Piperidis

Abstract This chapter describes the European Language Grid cloud platform from the point of view of a *consumer* who wishes to access language resources or make use of language technology tools and services. Three aspects are discussed: 1. the web-based user interface (UI) for casual and non-technical users, 2. the underlying REST APIs that drive the UI but can also be called directly by third parties to integrate ELG functionality in their own tools, and 3. the Python Software Development Kit (SDK) that we have developed to simplify access to these APIs from Python code. The chapter concludes with a preview of the upcoming payment module that will enable the sale of commercial LT services and resources through ELG, and a discussion of how ELG compares and relates to other similar platforms and initiatives.

1 Introduction

The European Language Grid (ELG) platform (Rehm et al. 2021) provides access to Language Technology (LT) tools and services, both basic Natural Language Processing (NLP) tools and end-to-end applications, as well as data resources, such as structured and unstructured datasets and corpora, Machine Learning models, lexica, ontologies, terminologies, etc. Chapters 7 (p. 131 ff.) and 8 (p. 151 ff.) present the current state of LT services as well as datasets and language resources included in the ELG platform respectively.

Ian Roberts
University of Sheffield, UK, i.roberts@sheffield.ac.uk

Penny Labropoulou · Dimitris Galanis · Athanasia Kolovou · Dimitris Gkoumas · Stelios Piperidis
Institute for Language and Speech Processing, R. C. "Athena", Greece, penny@athenarc.gr, galanisd@athenarc.gr, akolovou@athenarc.gr, dgkoumas@athenarc.gr, spip@athenarc.gr

Rémi Calizzano
Deutsches Forschungszentrum für Künstliche Intelligenz GmbH, Germany,
remi.calizzano@dfki.de

Andis Lagzdiņš
Tilde, Latvia, andis.lagzdins@tilde.lv

© The Author(s) 2023
G. Rehm (ed.), *European Language Grid*, Cognitive Technologies,
https://doi.org/10.1007/978-3-031-17258-8_3

ELG enables consumers of Language Technology to browse through the ELG catalogue and have an overview of its contents, search for specific resources and select as well as view the features of a resource through its formal description (metadata record). Users can download resources hosted in the ELG cloud infrastructure in accordance with their licensing conditions, or, in the case of external resources, be re-directed to the location where they can be downloaded from or accessed. They can also try out services in order to assess whether they comply with their needs; for this to happen, the services must comply with the ELG technical interoperability specifications, which are outlined in Chapter 4. Furthermore, ELG includes a catalogue of commercial companies and academic and research organisations that are active in the LT domain and of EU and national projects that have funded the development and maintenance of LRTs (see Chapter 9); LRTs, actors and projects are interlinked offering a comprehensive image of the LT landscape in Europe.

Different types of users have different requirements and different levels of technical expertise, and the ELG platform provides a variety of access methods to address these; all the principal functionality of the ELG is offered through both web-based user interfaces (UIs, see Section 2) for interactive use and Application Programming Interfaces (APIs, see Section 3) for programmatic access. In addition, the ELG team supports the advanced needs of LT integrators with dedicated tools and helpers; most notably a Software Development Kit (SDK) for Python (see Section 4), which is currently the most widely used programming language in the LT community.

Supporting consumers to easily discover resources is of utmost importance, especially when a catalogue contains many entries, as in the case of ELG (over 13,000 metadata records for LRTs and 1,800 related entities at the time of writing and constantly increasing). Best practices and recommendations (Wu et al. 2019; Wilkinson et al. 2016) have been taken into account in the design and implementation of the ELG catalogue pages and interaction mechanisms with the consumers.

At present all functionality of the ELG platform is offered free of charge. All users can view the catalogue and metadata descriptions as well as download open access resources. In order to download resources with restrictive licences and try out ELG-compatible services, users must register in the platform, as described in Section 5. It should be noted that while the ELG platform does not currently charge fees for access to any resources or services, restrictions may apply with regard to the intended use(s) of the resource (e. g., available only for non-commercial use), request for explicit consent to licensing conditions, etc. Resources available with commercial licences are described in the ELG catalogue but for now re-directed to the providers for further information. A prototype billing module, described in Section 6, has been implemented and will be fully launched following the setup of the ELG legal entity (see Chapter 13). Finally, in Section 7 we compare the ELG platform to other similar services and initiatives, from the point of view of the service or resource consumer. A similar comparison from the point of view of the provider can be found in Chapter 4.

2 Web-based Interface

The ELG platform targets a diverse set of user types with different needs and levels of technical expertise. The primary access route for non-technical users is via the web user interface (UI), which prioritises user-friendliness and ease of use alongside raw performance considerations. The catalogue UI includes two main pages: the *catalogue page*, which offers access to the catalogue contents, and the *view pages* for each metadata record or resource (LT, LR, organisation, project).

2.1 Viewing the Catalogue

After ELG's homepage, the dedicated catalogue page (Figure 1) is the primary entry point through which users have access to the ELG platform contents and functions. Users can browse through the entire catalogue to find entries that might interest them. They can also look for specific entries, using the free text search bar, filtering the catalogue with one or more facets, or combining these two modes.

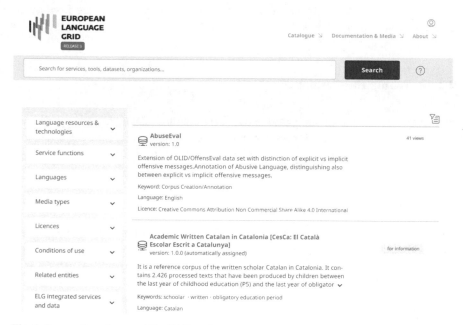

Fig. 1 Browse/Search page of the ELG catalogue

The main section of the catalogue page shows all published entries sorted by name in alphabetical order. Users can also sort the entries according to the update date of the metadata record, so that they can view the most recently added entries first. The catalogue shows only the most recent version of each entry if multiple versions are registered. The snippet informs the users of additional older entries, which can be viewed and accessed through the view page of the newest version (see Section 2.3). This allows users to always keep up to date with the most recent version of a service, but also access older versions when needed, for instance, when reproducing previously published experiments.

Each entry is shown with an informative snippet, designed to serve as a preview of the full metadata record and to help users decide whether they want to explore the entry further. Following well-established practices in catalogues, each entry is represented by its name, an excerpt of its description, a set of metadata tags, and popularity indicators. The set of metadata tags has been carefully selected to accommodate consumer requirements, as identified in a user survey conducted during the ELG design and specification phase (Melnika et al. 2019) and subsequently enriched based on user feedback. All types of entries include their free-text keywords. Entries representing LRTs additionally include the resource type (represented with an icon), language(s), and licence(s). The popularity indicators, displayed at the right hand side of the snippet, consist of counts of visits of the view page of all versions of an entry, counts of downloads (for ELG-hosted resources only) and number of calls (for ELG-compatible services only; again for all versions of the entry). Finally, dedicated badges are shown for resources hosted in ELG and ELG-compatible services, as well as for a subset of the metadata records that have been imported from other catalogues with minimal metadata (see Chapter 6).

2.2 Searching the Catalogue

Search of the catalogue is supported in two different modes, which can be combined in order to refine search queries and support users in easily finding entries of interest: free text search (Section 2.2.1) and faceted search (Section 2.2.2).

2.2.1 Free Text Search

Users enter a word or phrase in the search box at the top of the catalogue page (see Figure 1) and click the "Search" button to submit the query. By default, the search functionality matches whole words using the OR operator. Advanced queries, utilising the Lucene query syntax[1], are supported, allowing users to search for partial or exact matches, words or phrases, etc. Only certain metadata elements have been indexed to make them searchable; these include a resource's name(s), short name(s), keywords and a subset of technical elements appropriate for each entry type and deemed important as a search criterion. For example, for all LRTs, additional in-

---

[1] https://www.lucenetutorial.com/lucene-query-syntax.html

dexed elements are the "resource type", "language" and "licence"; for LT tools/services, "service function" is also added to the search elements.

In addition, to improve recall of search results, for those metadata elements that take values from controlled vocabularies, i. e., "service function","intended LT application", and "language", the query is expanded with the use of synonyms. Synonyms for the first two elements are derived from a taxonomy of LT activities[2], which provides the values. For alternative names of languages, besides the official ones included in the ISO 639-3 standard for language codes[3] (International Organization for Standardization 2007), we exploit open access vocabularies published as linked data, i. e., the Glottolog list of languoids (families, languages, dialects)[4], the lexvo ontology of languages[5], and the WALS list of languages[6]; all these vocabularies are offered through Glottolog.

2.2.2 Faceted Search

Users can filter the catalogue or previous search results by selecting values from the list of facets (Figure 2) on the left side of the catalogue page (Figure 1). For facets with a long list of values, such as languages and licences, the facet values are broken down into subsections or a search bar is included to refine the list.

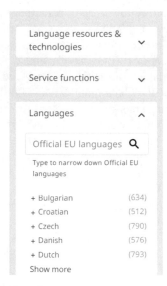

Fig. 2 Faceted search in the ELG catalogue

---

[2] Part of the OMTD-SHARE ontology, see http://w3id.org/meta-share/omtd-share.

[3] https://iso639-3.sil.org/code_tables/639/data

[4] https://glottolog.org

[5] http://lexvo.org/ontology

[6] https://wals.info/languoid

The facets were selected in the initial phase of the ELG development based on user preferences collected through a survey conducted for the technical platform specifications (Melnika et al. 2019). Important criteria for users searching for are language coverage (62%), licence and access conditions (59%) and availability of open source code (56%). Later on, more facets have been added to reflect updates in the metadata schema and improve search capabilities (Wu et al. 2019).

There are two facets, based on the *resource type* and *entity type* elements, that create dedicated subsets of the catalogue contents. The values are taken from the respective elements of the ELG metadata schema, but are tuned to current LT approaches. Thus, with regard to LRTs, users can view specific catalogues of tools and services, corpora, lexical/conceptual resources, models, grammars and other language descriptions. In the ELG schema the last three are subclasses of the *language description* type, but we opted to treat them as separate resource types primarily to improve the visibility of models; these are what define the state of the art for many NLP tasks and are likely to be particularly popular, so need to be easily discoverable. The two catalogues of organisations and projects are a valuable asset for boosting and activating interactions within and across the LT community (including match-making in the ELG marketplace) and eventually also for monitoring funding outcomes.

LRTs can be further filtered using the facet *ELG integrated services and data* to restrict the catalogue view to the ELG-compatible services and resources hosted in ELG, for users who wish to take advantage of the "try out" functionality offered by ELG for services or of the direct download of resources uploaded in ELG.

The facet *languages* shows the language coverage of the LRTs in the ELG catalogue, i. e., the languages of the contents of data resources and the ones that tools/services cater for. Given the scope of ELG, the official EU languages are presented in a separate group shown at the top of the facet. The encoding of language values in the catalogue follows the BCP 47 recommendations (Phillips and Davis 2009), i. e., it allows for users adding a tag consisting of subtags for language, region, script and language variants, but for simplicity of the UI the facet browser includes only the values of the *language* subtag. Moreover, it includes only one of the known names of a language; e. g., for "Catalan; Valencian", only the first name is shown. For languages and language varieties without an ISO 639 code, we show the name associated with the respective Glottocode[7] if it has one.

The facets *intended LT application* and *service function* are used for classifying LRTs and related entities with concepts specific to the LT community; consumers can search for services that perform specific functions (e. g., dependency parsers, Machine Translation tools), but also for corpora or models that have been created or can be used for a a specific application (e. g., bilingual or multilingual corpora to be used for building machine translation models), as well as for organisations and projects active in an LT area; the values of these two elements are both taken from the taxonomy of LT areas[8], and free text values that have been added by users.

---

[7] https://glottolog.org/meta/glossary

[8] http://w3id.org/meta-share/omtd-share/

Licensing and access conditions are among the search criteria most requested by users: *licences* gives the detailed list of licences used for LRTs in the catalogue.[9] The more coarse-grained facet *Conditions of use* groups licences by the general types of conditions they impose (e. g., "no commercial use", "share-alike"), intended for users with little knowledge of legal terms. Users are still advised to carefully read the licence specified on the view page of each LRT for all terms and conditions.

The *media types* facet was introduced at a later stage when the number of multimodal resources included in the catalogue increased. As for languages, this refers to the media type of the contents of resources or the media type of the input/output of tools, and can be used to quickly search not only for text-related applications and resources, but also for audio, video and image ones.

The ELG catalogue includes both entries added by individuals and entries aggregated from other catalogues.[10] Thus, the facet *source* refers to the source of the metadata record. It includes the name of the catalogue from which the record has been imported or the value "ELG/ELE" for records originating in ELG or added by the collaborating project European Language Equality (ELE)[11] through processes described in Chapter 6.

2.3 Viewing Metadata Records and Resources

By clicking the title of an entry on the catalogue page, users can view its full description. Figures 3 and 4 show the view page of a tool/service and a corpus respectively. Specific view pages have been implemented for all LRT types published in ELG. Their design takes into account user preferences and requirements, design and accessibility considerations and the ELG metadata schema. They allow users to access detailed information about an item, test it, if it is a service integrated in the platform, and, finally, obtain and use it for their purposes.

Even though the types of information shown on the view pages differ for each category, we apply a consistent visual look and feel for all of them. The information on the view page of each item comes from the respective metadata record. Taking into consideration the specificities and richness of the metadata schema, but also user-friendliness, the information is layered along specific sections of the page. Thus, view pages share a common layout that consists of a header, a right-hand sidebar, a main content area and a bottom content region; the positioning of the elements on the page and the formatting of the text is carefully thought through to draw users' attention to the most important information.

The header shows the name and version of the resource, its resource type and optionally important flags (e. g., to indicate that a certain service is deployed in ELG).

---

[9] Chapter 6 discusses why this element was made mandatory.

[10] See Chapters 4 and 6 for more information on the respective modes of population.

[11] https://european-language-equality.eu

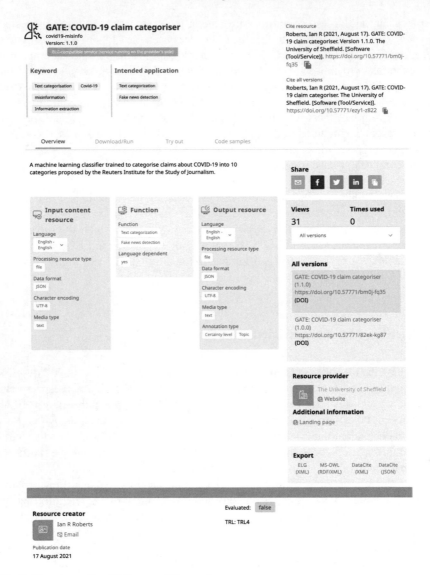

Fig. 3 View page of an ELG-compatible service

At the top of the right-hand sidebar, the button "Claim" may appear for some of the metadata records; these are records with minimal metadata that have been imported through automatic harvesting and bulk collection procedures (see Chapter 6). The claiming process enables interested users, i. e., the rightful owners of these LRTs, to ask to curate and enrich them. The same area provides for all records information on how they can be cited, according to data and software citation principles (Smith

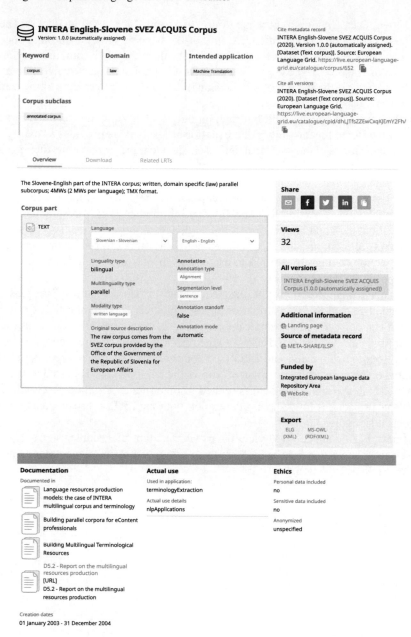

Fig. 4 View page of a corpus

et al. 2016; Data Citation Synthesis Group 2014) and DataCite guidelines[12]. They also have the option to share the URL link of the page by email or through social media and export the metadata record as an XML file in the ELG-compliant schema. Statistics of resource usage are shown both for the particular resource version and for all versions (if there are multiple versions). Links to other versions of the same resource are also displayed here.

In the content area, tabs split information into smaller views and enable users to navigate to offered functionalities of the platform. The first tab provides an overview of the main features of the entry that help users decide if the resource fits their needs. In terms of layout it is similar across resource types, but the information types (metadata elements) differ. Compare, for instance, Figures 3 and 4 that show the overview tab for a service and a corpus. The top shows a free text description for all record types, followed by a section for classification information (keywords, domain, service function, etc.) and an area for technical metadata, e. g., the media type(s) and language(s) of a corpus, the input and output data formats for a service, etc. The bottom section contains hyperlinks to useful documents, creation details, etc. and is again specific to resource types.

Depending on the resource type, the "Download" or "Download/Run" tab presents information related to the distribution of the resource, such as the licence under which it can be accessed, a technical description of its content files (e. g., size and format for data resources), and access to the resource itself – a direct download link if the resource is uploaded into ELG (see Section 3.2), otherwise a redirect to the resource on its provider's site. Figure 5 shows the tab for a corpus hosted in ELG.

A third tab appears if the item is related to other items, e. g., a project with the LRTs this project has funded, an organisation with the LRTs it has created and the projects it is involved in.

Finally, ELG-compatible services have two more tabs that enable users to try out the service (see Section 2.5) and inform them how to use it via the command line or Python SDK (see Section 4).

2.4 Consumer's Grid

Individuals can browse the catalogue, view detailed metadata cards and download open access resources without any registration. To access restricted resources and run ELG-compatible services, they must be registered with an ELG account and also logged in. For registered users, ELG offers a dashboard ("grid") for managing and performing actions on catalogue items depending on their rights (see Chapter 2 for more information on user roles and rights). As for view pages, the grid follows a similar layout which is customised for each user type.

The consumer's grid (Figure 6) allows registered users to monitor their usage of daily quotas, view details on downloads of LRTs they performed and of the services

---

[12] https://datacite.org/cite-your-data.html

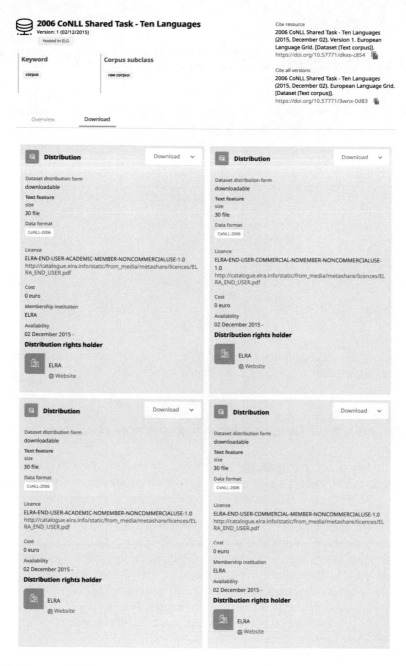

Fig. 5 Download tab for a corpus

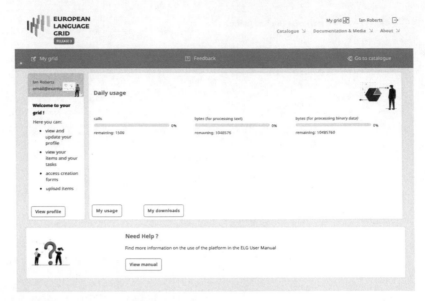

Fig. 6 Consumer's grid (see Figure 4 in Chapter 4, p. 73, for the Provider's grid)

they have deployed. Additional elements of the "My grid" section that are relevant only to *provider* users are discussed in Chapter 4.

2.5 Try out UIs for Language Technology Services

One of the key benefits of having an LT service fully integrated in ELG is that users have access to a "try out" UI from which they can test the service directly using their web browser. ELG provides standard trial UIs[13] covering all principal service types:

- *Information Extraction (IE) & text analysis* services take text input and produce standoff *annotations* over that text.
  In addition to this generic text analysis UI there is also a specific one for dependency parsers that renders CoNLL-U style annotations as a tree structure.[14]
- *Text-to-text* services (most notably Machine Translation, but also summarisation, anonymisation, etc.) take text and return new text that is derived from the input.
- *Text classification* services take text input and classify it somehow (e. g., language identification, "fake news" detection, etc.)
- *Speech recognition* services accept audio and return a text transcription.

---

[13] Service providers whose tools do not fit one of the above UIs are free to provide their own.

[14] https://universaldependencies.org/format.html

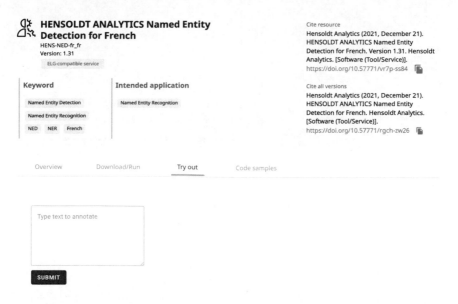

Fig. 7 An example "try out" UI for a named entity service

- *Audio annotation* services take audio and return standoff annotations over particular time segments of the audio stream.
- *Text-to-speech* services take text and return audio.
- *Image OCR* (optical character recognition) services take image data and return text extracted from the image.

The trial UIs for services are available to any user who has logged in to the ELG portal. The UI appears in the "Try out" tab when viewing a service in the catalogue; Figure 7 shows an example for a simple service that only requires plain text. However, some services can be much more complex, requiring additional parameters or providing snippets of sample data that users can test the service with – if a service declares these kinds of items in its metadata record, then the try out UI will automatically adapt, as shown in Figure 8. This service – also see Chapter 18 – declares two optional parameters and offers a selection of samples in different languages.

The UIs have been designed to render all of the main service response types in a user-friendly way, for example, annotations over text are shown as colour highlights (Figure 9), translated text is displayed alongside the original, audio can be played directly in the browser, etc.

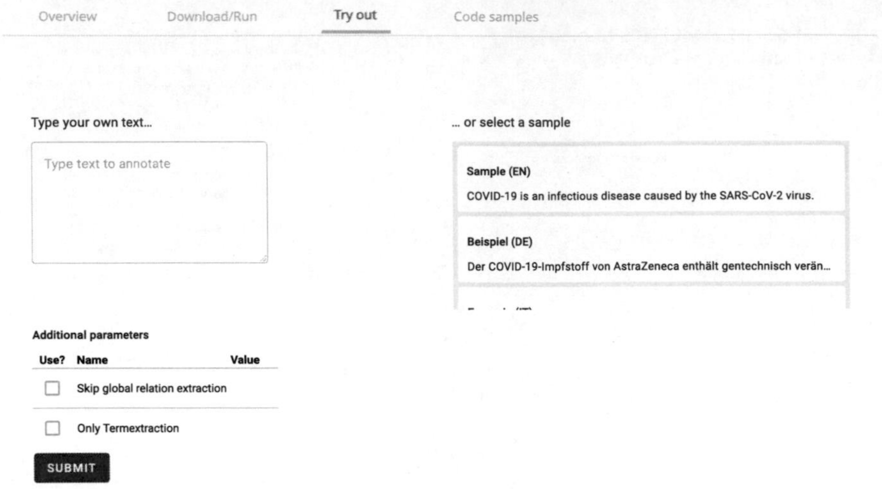

Fig. 8 A more complex "try out" UI for the Text2TCS service

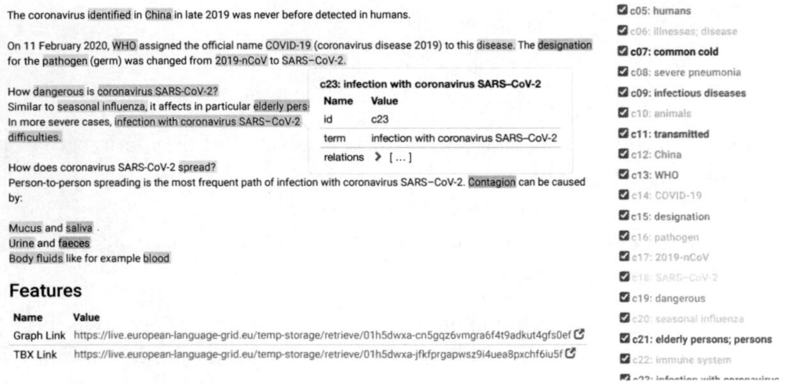

Fig. 9 Example result for the Text2TCS service showing rendered text annotations

3 Public REST APIs

The web user interfaces described above are built on top of a set of REST APIs, and the same APIs can also be called directly by third parties, allowing ELG functionality to be accessed programmatically and embedded into other tools. The current public APIs break down into three principal groups: 1. accessing/using the catalogue (Section 3.1), 2. accessing and downloading ELG-hosted data resources (Section 3.2), 3. calling ELG-hosted LT services (Section 3.3).

All APIs are HTTPS-based and use JSON as the primary data representation format. Where authentication is required, this is performed using OAuth2 access tokens issued by the ELG user management layer (see Section 5).

3.1 Accessing and Using the Catalogue

The ELG catalogue is a Python web application based on the Django REST Framework.[15] It offers a number of services as REST APIs, including the following ones which are useful for consumers: 1. searching the catalogue, 2. authorising the download of a resource or access of any resource or page, 3. retrieving the metadata description of a resource.

3.2 Downloading a Resource

ELG allows providers to upload and store the actual contents of their LRTs within the platform (data files for corpora, source code for software, etc.), and the catalogue offers an API to allow consumers to download this data subject to licensing terms.

LRT data is stored in a storage service compatible with the API of Amazon S3. Access by consumers is mediated by a Storage Proxy.[16] The proxy defers to a data management module within the catalogue application (see Section 6) to determine, based on authentication information provided by the user who attempts the download, whether that user has the permission to download the requested resource. Factors considered in making a decision include whether the resource is open access to all requesters (authenticated or not), if it requires authentication, or if the user must explicitly accept the terms of the licence prior to download.

3.3 Language Technology Service Public API

One of the great strengths of ELG is its use of a single harmonised set of APIs for all ELG-compatible LT services regardless of provider. This differs from other API aggregator platforms such as RapidAPI[17], where each service provider defines their own API and the caller must adapt their code for each different service.

For each LT service the platform provides two endpoints at which the service can be called, which implement synchronous and asynchronous modes of operation. These endpoints are implemented in the LT Service Execution Server. The endpoint URLs can be found in the `service_info` section of the metadata record JSON structure returned by the catalogue API.

The synchronous mode simply consists of a single API call in which the caller will POST the data to be processed and receive the results via the response to the same request. The asynchronous mode accepts the same type of request but instead of blocking the caller until the results are ready it returns a polling URL, which the

---

[15] https://www.django-rest-framework.org

[16] https://gitlab.com/european-language-grid/platform/s3proxy

[17] https://rapidapi.com

caller must repeatedly poll for status updates. This requires more HTTP requests but for long-running services (or those that take some time to scale up from idle) the asynchronous mode is more resilient to connection failures or intermediary proxy timeouts between the client and the ELG platform.

Any query parameters appended to the URL will be passed through to the service and may affect its behaviour – each service declares the parameters that it supports in its metadata. All available versions of a given service are exposed at the same endpoint, the `?version=...` parameter is used to select between them, with the latest version used by default if no parameter is given.

The `POST` data must have an appropriate `Content-Type` header for the service in question; services that take text (such as text analysis or MT services) expect "text/plain"[18], services that take audio (such as speech recognition) expect "audio/x-wav" or "audio/mpeg", and services that take images expect the "image/png", "image/jpeg", etc. A few services expect their input to be "structured text" that has been pre-segmented by the caller, for these the request must be presented in an ELG-defined JSON format. The response will be in JSON, in one of a variety of formats depending on the data type:

- *Standoff annotations* are represented in a style inspired by the format used by Twitter, each *type* of annotation mapping to a JSON array of objects referencing the start and end locations of the annotation (characters for text, fractional seconds for audio), and an optional set of *features*.
- *Classifications* of the whole input have their own format giving an ordered list of classes, each with an optional score.
- *New texts* such as translations of text or transcriptions of audio are returned in a structured format referred to as a "texts" response (note texts is plural). This is described in more detail below.
- *Audio* responses such as text-to-speech are still represented in JSON. Short snippets of audio can be returned inline in base 64 encoding, longer audio will typically be stored at a short-lived temporary URL for the caller to download via a separate HTTPS request.

The full specification of these response types can be found in the ELG documentation.[19] The "texts" response type is the most complex one as it is able to encode a nested tree structure of texts, where each node in the tree can be either a leaf node containing a single string of content, or a branch node containing another level of texts. The vast majority of services currently using this response format produce one of the three basic forms shown in Listing 1: a single text, a flat list of segments or alternatives, or a two-level list where each segment has a set of alternatives.

The property `role` is used to distinguish the cases. Not all services populate this property but it is encouraged; conventionally a role of "sentence", "paragraph" or "segment" denotes segments of text that are all part of the same transcript or translation, and "alternative" denotes different translations or transcriptions of the same

---

[18] UTF-8 encoding is the default but can be overridden by adding the `charset=...` parameter.

[19] https://european-language-grid.readthedocs.io/en/stable/all/A3_API/LTPublicAPI.html

```
 1   // A single text
 2   {
 3     "response":{
 4       "type":"texts",
 5       "texts":[
 6         {"content":"This is some text"}
 7       ]
 8     }
 9   }
10
11   // A flat list of segments or alternatives
12   {
13     "response":{
14       "type":"texts",
15       "texts":[
16         {"content":"First sentence", "role":"sentence"},
17         {"content":"Second sentence", "role":"sentence"},
18       ]
19     }
20   }
21
22   // A two level list of segments that each have a number of alternatives
23   {
24     "response":{
25       "type":"texts",
26       "texts":[
27         {
28           "role":"sentence",
29           "texts":[
30             {"content":"Translation one", "role":"alternative"},
31             {"content":"First translation", "role":"alternative"}
32           ]
33         },
34         ...
35       ]
36     }
37   }
```

Listing 1 The three most common types of "texts" response

input segment. In the case of alternatives, each entry may also have a "score" representing the relative quality of the different options.

For errors (and also for warning messages), ELG, being a multilingual platform, uses a format designed to be amenable to internationalisation (i18n). Each message is represented as a JSON object with three properties "code", "text" and "params" (see Listing 2). The property "code" is the primary identifier for the error; there is a list of standard message codes provided in the ELG documentation but providers are free to create their own codes if the standard messages do not adequately cover their needs. The property "text" is a string for the message text in English, and it may include numbered placeholders {0}, {1}, etc. If the message has placeholders,

```
1  {
2    "code":"elg.request.type.unsupported",
3    "text":"Request type {0} not supported by this service",
4    "params":["audio"]
5  }
```

Listing 2 An example "status message" object from the ELG API, designed to be easily translated into many languages.

```
1  POST https://live.european-language-grid.eu/i18n/resolve?lang=fr
2  Content-Type: application/json
3
4  [
5    {
6      "code":"elg.request.type.unsupported",
7      "text":"Request type {0} not supported by this service",
8      "params":["audio"]
9    }
10 ]
11
12 // response
13 Content-Type: application/json
14
15 ["La demande du type audio n'est pas supportée par ce service"]
```

Listing 3 Resolving a status message to a translated string

the corresponding values are given in the "params" array (as a zero-based index, so 0 refers to the first item, 1 to the second, etc.). The error message may also include an optional "detail" object providing more technical details about the error.

The standard ELG message codes have translations into a number of different languages (twelve at the time of writing, with more in the pipeline), and ELG provides a special API endpoint that accepts an array of errors and an ISO 639 language code, and returns an array of message strings in the requested language (if available) with all placeholders filled in. If the requested message code is not available in that language the endpoint falls back to English, and if the message code is not known at all then the "text" fallback from the original error is used instead.

Listing 3 shows an example of calling the "resolver" API; the ?lang=... parameter specifies the desired language. If it is not provided then the resolver will respect any Accept-Language HTTP header on the request.[20] If no language is requested by the parameter or the header then messages will be returned in English by default.

Some long running services will return more meaningful progress updates as they work through their various stages of processing, and these updates will be passed back to the caller if they use the asynchronous API mode – requests to the polling

---

[20] For browser-based clients this will typically result in the messages being returned in the user's preferred browsing language.

URL for a given job will return the latest progress update if the process is not yet complete. These updates are represented as i18n message objects in the same way as the errors and warnings described above, and they can be resolved to strings using the same resolver API endpoint.

4 Python SDK for Users

ELG provides many APIs to access the catalogue and search for specific resources, to download corpora hosted in ELG, to call services or many other uses (see Section 3). This provides ELG users with a lot of flexibility in the way they want to interact with the platform, however, the basic APIs are rather low level. For example, the search endpoint is paginated and returns only 20 results per call, which means that multiple API calls are needed to obtain more than 20 results. Similarly, calling a service via the public LT service API in the asynchronous mode requires multiple API calls to be made at the correct times and in the correct sequence to perform what is, from the user's perspective, a single action.

In order to simplify interactions with the platform, we developed a Python SDK that operates on top of the various ELG APIs and provides simple methods to easily interact with ELG and consume the resources in Python. We chose Python as the language for this first ELG SDK as it is probably the most widely-used programming language within the LT community.

The SDK is included in the ELG Pypi package which can be installed using the `pip` command familiar to any Python programmer. The basic SDK for consumer use is installed using `pip install elg`. The SDK provides access to most ELG functions through Python. It provides access to the catalogue with methods that allow users to search the catalogue and look for corpora, services, and organisations. The SDK enables users to call ELG-compatible services, and even to combine them using a simple pipeline mechanism.

4.1 Browsing the Catalogue

The SDK enables access to the ELG catalogue. It uses the same filters as the UI, i. e., we can filter for the type of resource or LT service, languages and licence; free text search can also be used. Listing 4 shows how to search for an English to French machine translation service. The SDK handles issues such as pagination automatically and returns the result as a list of entities, where each entity is a Python object that encapsulates the information about the respective ELG resource.

```
 1  from elg import Catalog
 2
 3  catalog = Catalog()
 4
 5  # Search and get the result as a list of Python objects
 6  results = catalog.search(
 7      resource = "Tool/Service", # "Corpus", "Lexical/Conceptual
 8                                 # resource" or "Language
 9                                 # description"
10      function = "Machine Translation", # only for "Tool/Service"
11      languages = ["en", "fr"],  # string or list if multiple
12                                 # languages
13  )
```

Listing 4 Example code to use the ELG catalogue

4.2 Downloading a Resource

The Python SDK has a Corpus class that corresponds to a corpus or data set. It can be initialised using the identifier of the resource. If the resource is stored in ELG, it can be downloaded using the download method of the Corpus class. Listing 5 shows the most simple usage and parameters are available to choose the distribution or specify the download location for example.

```
 1  from elg import Corpus
 2
 3  corpus = Corpus.from_id(913) # initialise the Corpus using its ID
 4  corpus.download()            # download corpus method
```

Listing 5 Example code to download an ELG corpus

4.3 Obtaining an Access Token

Some functions are restricted to authorised users of ELG (see Section 5). For the restricted APIs, an access token must be retrieved to identify the user behind the API call. It is possible to obtain a short-lived valid access token through the UI but this is not convenient for programmatic use.

To address this limitation, the Python SDK includes the Authentication class that interacts directly with the ELG OpenID Connect authentication service to obtain tokens, i. e., the access token to authenticate the API call and the refresh token which is used to refresh the access token when it expires.

```
1  from elg import Authentication
2
3  auth = Authentication.init()
4  # here the user is asked to authenticate in the browser
5
6  auth = Authentication.init(scope="offline_access")
7  # here we are requesting an ``offline'' token that remains valid until
8  # revoked, as opposed to the usual token that requires re-authentication
9  # after 6 hours
10
11 auth.to_json("tokens.json") # export the tokens to a json file
12
13 auth = Authentication.from_json("tokens.json")
14 # creation of an Authentication object from the tokens in the json file
```

Listing 6 Example of code to obtain, store, and retrieve authentication tokens

Listing 6 shows an example usage of the Authentication class. During the process, the user has to authenticate using their browser and paste the resulting authorisation code back to the Python program. Once the Authentication object is initialised, it is possible to save the tokens in a json file and reuse them. Obtained tokens are by default valid for only six hours. It is possible to get tokens that are valid indefinitely by setting the scope parameter to offline_access.

4.4 Calling Language Technology Services

The Service class of the Python SDK corresponds to an ELG LT service, and can be initialised using the identifier of the service. As users need to be authenticated to use ELG services, a login step is necessary. Alternatively, it is possible to provide an Authentication object or a json file containing the tokens during the initialisation of the service, which allows the login step to be skipped. Various ways of authenticating during the service initialisation of a service are shown in Listing 7.

A service that is initialised in Python can be called easily (see Listing 8). The Python SDK handles the creation of the input message, any necessary refreshing of the access token, the communication with the REST API, etc.

When calling a service, the input request can be provided in various formats: a plain text, a path to a text or an audio file, or a Request object.[21] The result is a Python object that corresponds to one of the response messages (see Section 3.3).

---

[21] https://european-language-grid.readthedocs.io/en/stable/all/A1_PythonSDK/notebooks/Service.html#Usage

```
  from elg import Service

  lt = Service.from_id(474) # login step necessary (unless tokens
      are cached) and the tokens will expire after 6 hours
  lt = Service.from_id(474, scope="offline_access") # login step
      necessary (unless tokens are cached) and the tokens will
      never expire
  lt = Service.from_id(474, auth_object=auth) # 'auth' is an
      Authentication object. No login step and the expiration of
      the tokens depends on the `auth` object
  lt = Service.from_id(474, auth_file="tokens.json") # file
      containing existing tokens. No login step and the expiration
      of the tokens depends on the scope used to create them
```

Listing 7 Different ways of providing authentication during Service initialisation

```
  from elg import Service

  lt = Service.from_id(474) # initialise LT service using its ID
  result = lt("Nikola Tesla did not live in Berlin.") # run service
  print(result)
```

Listing 8 Example code for calling an ELG service

5 User Authentication

While general exploration and search in the ELG catalogue is open to all, various other operations in ELG are restricted to certain users. For example, access to the LT service public API (via the Python SDK, curl or the "try out" UIs) requires the caller to be logged in so that the platform can enforce API call quotas to limit how much data can be processed by each user per day, following the ELG licensing strategy (see Section 6). Similarly, the submission of new resources and metadata records is limited to users who are registered as *providers*; administrative tasks are restricted to the technical ELG team.

Registering a regular user account is a simple self-service procedure. The registration form is available through the sign up/sign in icon in the top right corner of the catalogue page. All registered users are assigned the *consumer* role by default. To get *provider* status, users can submit a request through their profile page. All other roles are assigned internally by the ELG administrators.

ELG uses Keycloak[22], a user management, authentication and authorisation server based on the OAuth2 and OpenID Connect[23] standards. Keycloak supports both interactive authentication of users through the web UI, and programmatic access to the REST APIs using JSON Web Tokens. Users sign in to Keycloak, then they (or

---

[22] https://www.keycloak.org
[23] https://openid.net/connect/

the client tool they are using, such as the ELG Python SDK) can acquire an access token, which is a cryptographically signed "permit" that encodes their identity and permissions. API endpoints can verify the validity of the token by checking its signature, and then make access decisions based on the "claims" encoded in the token without needing to check every request directly with the authentication server.

The adoption of OpenID Connect opens up the possibility for third party applications to allow their own users to authenticate using ELG accounts, in the same way as many existing websites and applications support "sign in with Google" or "sign in with Facebook". The OpenID Connect specification allows this without compromising the protection of users' personal information. When a given user attempts to "log in with ELG" to a particular third party application for the first time, Keycloak requires the user to grant *explicit consent* before any of their data is shared with the provider, and that consent can be revoked at any time. At the time of writing the first proof of this concept is under development with one of the ELG pilot projects.

6 Licensing and Billing

ELG includes mechanisms that support the consumption of services and resources that are available without any restrictions in terms of commercial aspects. It supports the download of resources under the condition that they are offered free of charge with open access licences or with restrictive licences that require only user authentication and, optionally, accepting the licensing terms. Technical safeguards have been implemented to ensure that access to LRTs is granted in accordance with the above terms, for example, access to LRTs distributed with restricted licences is made available only to those users that fulfil the criteria specified in the licences. With regard to LT services, only the "try out" functionality is available and only for registered users. Each user has two independent daily quotas for the quantity of data processed, one for plain text and the other for binary (audio or image) data, to reflect the fact that binary formats generally require much more data than plain text.

In addition, we also designed and implemented the prototype of a billing module that will enable ELG to offer resources and services distributed with commercial licences. The module is based on the commercial platform Chargebee, which was selected because it fulfilled our requirements: it ensures security and includes various services, such as handling subscriptions, payments, pricing, taxes, emails, ensuring customer satisfaction and conformance to all EU and national laws, and offers several functionalities, such as checkout pages, self-service after the payment, cancellation, creating and managing subscription plans, subscription changes, etc. The integration of the external billing module is based on the interaction between the two platforms, ELG and Chargebee. Information about the pricing of a resource or service is formally encoded in the metadata record in ELG; administrative and execution costs may also be added and calculated on the ELG side. In the Chargebee catalogue we maintain a set of all monetised products and plans, and their prices.

The relationship between the ELG catalogue products and the Chargebee catalogue is not necessarily one-to-one; Chargebee can contain paid plans that allow the use of multiple products from the ELG catalogue, or the download of multiple resources. The relation between the two catalogues depends on the ELG business strategy. All transactions, subscription changes, logs, billing information, subscription data and similar information are stored on the Chargebee side, i. e., a database that is external to ELG. Any information needed from Chargebee can be synchronised through a webhook mechanism. For the ELG platform, this information includes the identity of the user who has performed an action through a subscription plan and/or a purchase, the action performed, the billing plan to which the user subscribed, etc. Chargebee sends this information via HTTPS POST to the ELG back end so that it can register changes in the ELG platform. The ELG back end monitors the user's quota usage and, taking into account the user's subscription plans from the Chargebee platform, decides whether to allow or block a request for running a service. A similar procedure is used for the download of a purchased resource.

7 Consumer-Related Functionalities in ELG and other Platforms

In this section we present platforms and catalogue-based systems that share features with ELG, with a special focus on functionalities for consumers.

7.1 Catalogue and Repository Functionalities

With regard to the presentation and organisation of the contents of such a digital catalogue of artefacts, the users of ELG can see all types of entities on the same page or go through quick links from the top menu to the subset that interests them. Offering such resource type-specific filtering functionalities is an approach adopted by many catalogues, for example, Hugging Face[24] has separate pages for models and datasets, Papers with Code[25] for datasets and benchmarks, some CLARIN centres distinguish between data resources and services (e. g., CLARIN-PL[26], etc.), the European AI on demand platform[27] maintains separate catalogues for AI assets, organisations, projects and educational resources. This approach is particularly useful for expert users with clear search objectives. In addition, distinguishing between separate resource types allows for the selection of different metadata elements and subgroupings of entries along the parameters most suitable to each type (e. g., grouping together services based on the tasks they perform or the degree of complexity

---

[24] https://huggingface.co

[25] https://paperswithcode.com

[26] https://clarin-pl.eu

[27] https://www.ai4europe.eu

of use, and datasets based on modality or language). On the other hand, the one-size-fits-all page has the benefit of allowing users to have an overview of resources and activities using the same set of filters. ELG combines the two approaches by providing quick links in the top menu and filters for the targeted pages.

With regard to search functionalities, free text search is the most popular one. In some cases, an autocomplete function (e. g., Hugging Face) is used while advanced queries are less used. Faceted search is also common, but in most cases with limited facets (e. g., European AI on Demand platform, Hugging Face, etc.). Search with programmatic modes through REST APIs is offered by many platforms on a limited set of metadata elements in the same way that ELG does.

With regard to the functionalities offered for hosted data resources, direct download of open access resources is common. A download link that can be used from outside the platform (e. g., through a command line mode, or as a URL link) is provided in most cases. The deployment of integrated services on hosted resources is a feature offered in only a few platforms (e. g., OpenMinTeD, clarin:el[28]). Machine Learning platforms, like Hugging Face, can feed hosted datasets into applications, but this is not among the objectives of the ELG platform.

7.2 Language Technology Service Execution

ELG's LT service execution functionality has been designed and implemented from scratch. Below, we compare this functionality with similar related infrastructures or frameworks and highlight the similarities and differences in various aspects, e. g., interchange format, trial/visualisation UIs and support of workflows.

The DKPro[29] family of tools and resources (Gurevych et al. 2007) consists of a growing number of projects addressing different NLP tasks and aspects, such as pre-processing, machine learning, and lexical resources. It offers a collection of tools wrapped as UIMA components (Unstructured Information Management Architecture)[30], i. e., the components implement the interfaces and specifications of the UIMA framework. A UIMA reader component should extend the `ResourceCollectionReaderBase` class and also implement the `getNext(CAS aJCas)` method. A processor must extend `JCasAnnotator_ImplBase` and, furthermore, implement `process(JCas aJCas)` and a writer extends `JCasFileWriter_ImplBase` and implements `process(JCas aJCas)`. A UIMA reader loads data from a text file and creates a Common Analysis System (CAS) object. A processor gets a CAS object, runs the wrapped NLP tool and adds the results to the CAS object. A writer gets a CAS object and serialises its content to a file in a specific format. UIMA is Java-based but it can be used to wrap non-Java tools as well. UIMA allows to programmatically define pipelines (workflows), i. e., chain a reader, various processors, a

---

[28] https://inventory.clarin.gr

[29] https://dkpro.github.io

[30] https://uima.apache.org

writer and run the pipeline locally; it does not run remote services as in the case of ELG. The DKPro components are interoperable because they all follow the DKPro typesystem[31], which defines which annotations can be added to a CAS object, which features an annotation can contain, how these are serialised etc. The typesystem is actually an ontology for annotations, how they are organised etc. The ELG JSON format does not follow a typesystem. Another difference with ELG is that a CAS object is serialised (by default) in XML Metadata Interchange (XMI) format[32], a standard for exchanging metadata information via XML; other formats are also supported. If the results of a DKPro pipeline are exported in an appropriate format (e. g., XMI) they can be loaded, visualised and even edited with the annotation tool IN-CEpTION[33] (Klie et al. 2018), which is not possible in the ELG trial UIs.

GATE[34] (Cunningham et al. 2013) is an open source toolkit capable of solving numerous text processing problem. The GATE framework is written in Java and similar to DKPro/UIMA. As with UIMA there are additional modules to support integration with non-Java tools. It allows creating, either via a UI builder or progra-matically, a pipeline of NLP tools for specific tasks. The completed pipeline can be saved in the XML "recipe" format XGAPP, which can, in turn, be loaded into the developer UI to process small numbers of documents and visualise the resulting an-notations, run using a batch processing tool for larger scale processing, or packaged as a service on either the ELG or GATE's own GATE Cloud platform (see Chap-ter 7, Section 4.2, 140 ff.). Each GATE processing component gets as input a GATE Document which is enriched with annotations. Again, as in DKPro, GATE readers and writers load the data and write the processing results. A GATE Document is by default serialised to GATE XML, however, other formats are also supported. The annotations that are added in GATE Document do not follow a specific typesystem but follow some generic rules – each document has one or more sets of annotations, each set can contain annotations of many types, each annotation can have zero or more features, and while there is no *enforced* typesystem, all standard GATE com-ponents share a set of informal conventions for the types and features they use. This logic is very similar to the one adopted in ELG's JSON-based format. Contrary to ELG, the DKPro/UIMA and GATE tools are not dockerized (by default) and run as command line tools locally. Furthermore, the ELG services always process raw text while DKPro and UIMA components can also handle other formats such as PDF, and documents that have already been partially annotated.

GATE Cloud[35] (Tablan et al. 2013) is a platform very similar in spirit to ELG, but specifically built around the requirements of GATE-based text analysis tools. It was developed by the same team at the University of Sheffield that was responsible for the initial design of the ELG LT service execution layer and thus shares many of the same API design decisions. GATE Cloud offers a REST API accepting documents

---

[31] http://dkpro.github.io/dkpro-core/releases/1.8.0/docs/typesystem-reference.html

[32] https://www.omg.org/spec/XMI/2.5.1/About-XMI/

[33] https://inception-project.github.io

[34] https://gate.ac.uk

[35] https://cloud.gate.ac.uk

via HTTP post and returning annotations in the native JSON or XML formats of the GATE framework. GATE Cloud services process only text (not audio or other media types), but can accept formats such as XML, PDF (with machine-readable text) or Word documents as well as plain text. As well as the single document API, GATE Cloud also supports batch processing of larger amounts of data using on-demand processing capacity from Amazon Web Services. GATE Cloud services are defined as XGAPP "recipes" in the native GATE format, which are wrapped as Docker containers for the REST API or executed as-is by the batch processing engine. GATE Cloud has recently added support for other types of APIs such as image OCR (a service which has itself been integrated into the ELG platform).

The LAPPS Grid platform, as DKPro, is based on a typesystem, the LAPPS Web Service Exchange Vocabulary (Ide et al. 2016), "an ontology of terms for a core of linguistic objects and features exchanged among NLP tools that consume and produce linguistically annotated data. It is intended to be used for module description and input/output interchange to support service discovery, composition, and reuse in the natural language processing domain." In LAPPS Grid, as in ELG, tools are wrapped as web services, packaged as Docker images and exchange JSON messages. However, LAPPS Grid also offers workflows by using Galaxy, a workflow management system. Galaxy includes a visual editor for creating and parameterising workflows and an engine for executing these workflows. LAPPS Grid does *not* have a catalogue and each service is described with a limited set of metadata elements that are required for adding it to the Galaxy tool inventory. ELG was not designed to offer workflows, i. e., it does not include a workflow editor or a workflow execution engine. In addition, all services get as input raw text and they were not designed for playing the role of components in a workflow. However, some pipelines can be created by using external tools, e. g., the Python SDK and some code/adapters (Rehm et al. 2020; Moreno-Schneider et al. 2022). For example, using the ELG Python SDK, a Machine Translation service can be called, the result can extracted from the output JSON message and fed to an ELG NER service.

The OpenMinTeD execution service (Labropoulou et al. 2018) is also built on top of Galaxy. A large number of tools from the DKPro and GATE collections were ingested to OpenMinTeD. Several tools from other providers were also added. All tools were dockerized and are executed inside the container as command line tools, i. e., not as web services. An OpenMinTeD workflow is executed by running a series of Docker images (one after the other) in a cluster managed by Mesos[36], a framework similar to Kubernetes[37]. The workflow itself is created using the Galaxy editor. In OpenMinTeD no specific interchange format was enforced, the recommendation was to use the DKPro typesystem and XMI serialization. However, the GATE tools were using GATE XML format and several others were using their own custom format (e. g., based on JSON). In order to create a "mixed" workflow the creator had to combine the respective components with corresponding format adapters. If the results of

---

[36] https://mesos.apache.org

[37] https://kubernetes.io

the workflow were in XMI format, they could be visualised using WebAnno[38], a predecessor of INCEpTION.

The European AI on Demand platform[39] covers the whole European AI landscape rather than being restricted to LT or NLP. For example, computer vision is also included. The services are gRPC-based (not REST-based as in ELG) and are packaged as Docker images. The messages that they consume and produce are based on the ProtoBuf serialisation format[40] and no specific typesystem is used. The platform does not offer an execution environment. However, the worfklows that are created with the AI4EU Experiments editor[41], an editor similar to the one offered by Galaxy, are exported to a format that allows their execution in a Kubernetes cluster.

Hugging Face offers a large collection of Transformer-based models for computer vision, language processing, audio processing etc. Transformers are a specific type of neural networks (Vaswani et al. 2017) that have revolutionised machine learning since they achieve state of the art results in many tasks. Hugging Face allows training of Transformer-based models via the AutoNLP API[42], which is not free of charge. While we have performed initial experiments, ELG does not offer integrated model training. In Hugging Face, training as well model deployment is based on Amazon SageMaker, which is built on top of Docker. Hugging Face users can call a model via the trial UIs/widgets that are embedded in the respective page (as in ELG). For doing the same in a programmatic way, Hugging Face offers an inference REST API along with a Python client API[43]. Similar inference functionalities are offered through the ELG REST APIs and the Python SDK. Upon request, Hugging Face also offers an inference solution delivered as a container with the Transformer model for on-premise usage.[44] It can be used via a HTTP API (as in ELG). Finally, Hugging Face has developed a Python-based library (called "transformer") that allows to download a model and either fine-tune it in a specific task or use it for inference. Such functionality is not offered by the ELG Python SDK.

8 Conclusions

The ELG platform has fully achieved all objectives it had set for serving consumers. It allows consumers to browse through the whole ELG catalogue, already populated with more than 13,000 metadata records, apply faceted filtering and exploration, search for specific resources and services, download them (if hosted in ELG) and try out more than 800 functional services, both basic processing NLP services and

---

[38] https://webanno.github.io/webanno/

[39] https://www.ai4europe.eu

[40] https://developers.google.com/protocol-buffers

[41] https://aiexp.ai4europe.eu

[42] https://huggingface.co/autotrain

[43] https://api-inference.HuggingFace.co/docs/python/html/quicktour.html

[44] https://HuggingFace.co/infinity

end-to-end applications. Users can also access the directory of LT-developing companies and academic organisations, find organisations active in a specific LT area,
and initiate collaborations with them. The links between LRTs, organisations and
projects allows users to navigate between them and have an overview of the overall European LT landscape. Consumers can access all these functionalities through
user-friendly web user interfaces, or in programmatic ways, using the public REST
APIs and Python SDK.

References

Cunningham, Hamish, Valentin Tablan, Angus Roberts, and Kalina Bontcheva (2013). "Getting
    More Out of Biomedical Documents with GATE's Full Lifecycle Open Source Text Analytics".
    In: *PLOS Computational Biology* 9.2, pp. 1–16. DOI: 10.1371/journal.pcbi.1002854.
Data Citation Synthesis Group (2014). *Joint Declaration of Data Citation Principles – FORCE11*.
    Ed. by M. Martone. DOI: 10.25490/a97f-egyk. URL: https://doi.org/10.25490/a97f-egyk.
Gurevych, Iryna, Max Mühlhäuser, Christof Müller, Jürgen Steimle, Markus Weimer, and Torsten
    Zesch (2007). "Darmstadt Knowledge Processing Repository based on UIMA". In: *Proc. of
    the First Workshop on Unstructured Information Management Architecture (co-located with
    GLDV 2007)*. Tübingen, Germany, p. 89.
Ide, Nancy, Keith Suderman, Marc Verhagen, and James Pustejovsky (2016). "The Language Ap-
    plication Grid Web Service Exchange Vocabulary". In: *Worldwide Language Service Infrastruc-
    ture*. Lecture Notes in Computer Science. Springer, pp. 18–32.
International Organization for Standardization (2007). *Codes for the representation of names of
    languages – Part 3: Alpha-3 code for comprehensive coverage of languages*. URL: https://ww
    w.iso.org/cms/render/live/en/sites/isoorg/contents/data/standard/03/95/39534.html.
Klie, Jan-Christoph, Michael Bugert, Beto Boullosa, Richard Eckart de Castilho, and Iryna Gure-
    vych (2018). "The INCEpTION Platform: Machine-Assisted and Knowledge-Oriented Inter-
    active Annotation". In: *Proceedings of the 27th International Conference on Computational
    Linguistics (COLING 2018): System Demonstrations*. Santa Fe, USA: ACL, pp. 5–9. URL: htt
    p://tubiblio.ulb.tu-darmstadt.de/106270/.
Labropoulou, Penny, Dimitris Galanis, Antonis Lempesis, Mark Greenwood, Petr Knoth, Richard
    Eckart de Castilho, Stavros Sachtouris, Byron Georgantopoulos, Stefania Martziou, Lucas Anas-
    tasiou, Katerina Gkirtzou, Natalia Manola, and Stelios Piperidis (2018). "OpenMinTeD: A
    Platform Facilitating Text Mining of Scholarly Content". In: *Proceedings of WOSP 2018 (co-
    located with LREC 2018)*. Miyazaki, Japan: ELRA, pp. 7–12. URL: http://lrec-conf.org/works
    hops/lrec2018/W24/pdf/13_W24.pdf.
Melnika, Julija, Andis Lagzdiņš, Uldis Siliņš, Raivis Skadins, and Andrejs Vasiļjevs (2019). *De-
    liverable D3.1 Requirements and Design Guidelines*. Project deliverable; EU project European
    Language Grid (ELG); Grant Agreement no. 825627 ELG. URL: https://www.european-langu
    age-grid.eu/wp-content/uploads/2021/02/ELG-Deliverable-D3.1-final.pdf.
Moreno-Schneider, Julián, Rémi Calizzano, Florian Kintzel, Georg Rehm, Dimitris Galanis, and
    Ian Roberts (2022). "Towards Practical Semantic Interoperability in NLP Platforms". In: *Pro-
    ceedings of the 18th Joint ACL-ISO Workshop on Interoperable Semantic Annotation (ISA 2022;
    co-located with LREC 2022)*. Ed. by Harry Bunt. Marseille, France, pp. 118–126. URL: http:
    //www.lrec-conf.org/proceedings/lrec2022/workshops/ISA-18/pdf/2022.isa18-1.16.pdf.
Phillips, Addison and Mark Davis (2009). *Tags for Identifying Languages*. Tech. rep. RFC 5646.
    Internet Engineering Task Force. URL: https://datatracker.ietf.org/doc/rfc5646.
Rehm, Georg, Dimitrios Galanis, Penny Labropoulou, Stelios Piperidis, Martin Welß, Ricardo
    Usbeck, Joachim Köhler, Miltos Deligiannis, Katerina Gkirtzou, Johannes Fischer, Christian
    Chiarcos, Nils Feldhus, Julián Moreno-Schneider, Florian Kintzel, Elena Montiel, Víctor Ro-

dríguez Doncel, John P. McCrae, David Laqua, Irina Patricia Theile, Christian Dittmar, Kalina Bontcheva, Ian Roberts, Andrejs Vasiljevs, and Andis Lagzdiņš (2020). "Towards an Interoperable Ecosystem of AI and LT Platforms: A Roadmap for the Implementation of Different Levels of Interoperability". In: *Proc. of the 1st Int. Workshop on Language Technology Platforms (IWLTP 2020, co-located with LREC 2020)*. Ed. by Georg Rehm, Kalina Bontcheva, Khalid Choukri, Jan Hajic, Stelios Piperidis, and Andrejs Vasiljevs. Marseille, France, pp. 96–107. URL: https://www.aclweb.org/anthology/2020.iwltp-1.15.pdf.

Rehm, Georg, Stelios Piperidis, Kalina Bontcheva, Jan Hajic, Victoria Arranz, Andrejs Vasiljevs, Gerhard Backfried, José Manuel Gómez Pérez, Ulrich Germann, Rémi Calizzano, Nils Feldhus, Stefanie Hegele, Florian Kintzel, Katrin Marheinecke, Julian Moreno-Schneider, Dimitris Galanis, Penny Labropoulou, Miltos Deligiannis, Katerina Gkirtzou, Athanasia Kolovou, Dimitris Gkoumas, Leon Voukoutis, Ian Roberts, Jana Hamrlová, Dusan Varis, Lukáš Kačena, Khalid Choukri, Valérie Mapelli, Mickaël Rigault, Jūlija Meļņika, Miro Janosik, Katja Prinz, Andres Garcia-Silva, Cristian Berrio, Ondrej Klejch, and Steve Renals (2021). "European Language Grid: A Joint Platform for the European Language Technology Community". In: *Proceedings of the 16th Conference of the European Chapter of the Association for Computational Linguistics: System Demonstrations (EACL 2021)*. Kyiv, Ukraine: ACL, pp. 221–230. URL: https://www.aclweb.org/anthology/2021.eacl-demos.26.pdf.

Smith, Arfon M., Daniel S. Katz, and Kyle E. Niemeyer (2016). "Software citation principles". In: *PeerJ Computer Science* 2. URL: https://peerj.com/articles/cs-86.

Tablan, Valentin, Ian Roberts, Hamish Cunningham, and Kalina Bontcheva (2013). "GATECloud-.net: A Platform for large-scale, Open-Source Text Processing on the Cloud". In: *Philosophical Transactions of the Royal Society A: Math., Phys. and Eng. Sciences* 371.20120071.

Vaswani, Ashish, Noam Shazeer, Niki Parmar, Jakob Uszkoreit, Llion Jones, Aidan N Gomez, Łukasz Kaiser, and Illia Polosukhin (2017). "Attention is all you need". In: *Proceedings of the 31st International Conference on Neural Information Processing Systems*, pp. 6000–6010.

Wilkinson, Mark D., Michel Dumontier, IJsbrand Jan Aalbersberg, Gabrielle Appleton, Myles Axton, Arie Baak, Niklas Blomberg, Jan-Willem Boiten, Luiz Bonino da Silva Santos, Philip E. Bourne, Jildau Bouwman, Anthony J. Brookes, Tim Clark, Mercè Crosas, Ingrid Dillo, Olivier Dumon, Scott Edmunds, Chris T. Evelo, Richard Finkers, Alejandra Gonzalez-Beltran, Alasdair J.G. Gray, Paul Groth, Carole Goble, Jeffrey S. Grethe, Jaap Heringa, Peter A.C 't Hoen, Rob Hooft, Tobias Kuhn, Ruben Kok, Joost Kok, Scott J. Lusher, Maryann E. Martone, Albert Mons, Abel L. Packer, Bengt Persson, Philippe Rocca-Serra, Marco Roos, Rene van Schaik, Susanna-Assunta Sansone, Erik Schultes, Thierry Sengstag, Ted Slater, George Strawn, Morris A. Swertz, Mark Thompson, Johan van der Lei, Erik van Mulligen, Jan Velterop, Andra Waagmeester, Peter Wittenburg, Katherine Wolstencroft, Jun Zhao, and Barend Mons (2016). "The FAIR Guiding Principles for Scientific Data Management and Stewardship". In: *Scientific Data* 3. DOI: 10.1038/sdata.2016.18. URL: http://www.nature.com/articles/sdata201618.

Wu, Mingfang, Fotis Psomopoulos, Siri Jodha Khalsa, and Anita de Waard (2019). "Data Discovery Paradigms: User Requirements and Recommendations for Data Repositories". In: *Data Science Journal* 18.1. URL: http://datascience.codata.org/articles/10.5334/dsj-2019-003/.

Chapter 4
Contributing to the European Language Grid as a Provider

Dimitris Galanis, Penny Labropoulou, Ian Roberts, Miltos Deligiannis, Leon Voukoutis, Katerina Gkirtzou, Rémi Calizzano, Athanasia Kolovou, Dimitris Gkoumas, and Stelios Piperidis

Abstract The ELG platform enables producers of language resources and language technology tools and services to upload, describe, share, and distribute their services and products as well as to describe their companies, academic organisations and projects. This chapter presents the functionalities offered through web-based user interfaces for describing LT resources or related entities with metadata and for managing their publication. It gives a detailed description of the options that providers of LT tools can exploit to integrate them into ELG as ready-to-deploy services and the tools that ELG offers in their support during the preparation, upload and integration phases. The tools and packaging recommendations for resources to be uploaded in ELG are also presented. The chapter concludes with a discussion of functionalities offered to providers by ELG and other related platforms.

1 Introduction

The European Language Grid platform (Rehm et al. 2021) offers various functionalities for providers of Language Resources and Technologies (LRTs) through which they can share their assets with the Language Technology (LT) community and interested clients, customers or users of these technologies. The minimum requirement is that they make them accessible (by uploading them to ELG or through another website) and describe them with a metadata record that complies with the ELG specifications (see Chapter 2), where they specify the access location and licensing con-

Dimitris Galanis · Penny Labropoulou · Miltos Deligiannis · Leon Voukoutis · Katerina Gkirtzou · Athanasia Kolovou · Dimitris Gkoumas · Stelios Piperidis
Institute for Language and Speech Processing, R. C. "Athena", Greece,
galanisd@athenarc.gr, penny@athenarc.gr, mdel@athenarc.gr, leon.voukoutis@athenarc.gr, katerina.gkirtzou@athenarc.gr, akolovou@athenarc.gr, dgkoumas@athenarc.gr, spip@athenarc.gr

Ian Roberts
University of Sheffield, UK, i.roberts@sheffield.ac.uk

Rémi Calizzano
Deutsches Forschungszentrum für Künstliche Intelligenz GmbH, Germany,
remi.calizzano@dfki.de

© The Author(s) 2023
G. Rehm (ed.), *European Language Grid*, Cognitive Technologies,
https://doi.org/10.1007/978-3-031-17258-8_4

ditions under which they can be used. To take advantage of the advanced features of ELG, providers can also integrate LT tools as ready-to-deploy services, following the ELG specifications, or upload the resource itself, in which case it will be stored and preserved according to the Data Management Plan (see Chapter 8) and made readily available to LRT consumers. Furthermore, descriptions of organisations that are active in the LT area can be added in order to promote their activities and products. Descriptions of projects that have been funded in the broader LT area can also be included in the ELG catalogue. LRTs, organisations that have provided or created them and projects that have contributed to their funding are linked together.

Detailed documentation is provided and a suite of helper tools have been developed aiming to make the contribution and integration of all entities briefly sketched above as simple as possible, taking into account the technical expertise and preferences of users. In ELG, the provision and management of catalogue entries is supported through web user interfaces (UIs) and REST application programming interfaces (APIs). Section 2 describes the steps a provider must take to contribute entries to the catalogue, and the tools provided by ELG to support this process. The ELG catalogue intends to be a reliable source for resources that can be accessed and (re-)used by commercial and non-commercial, research and public organisations as well as individuals. For this purpose, management and curation policies and processes for the metadata, data and services included in ELG have been set up, albeit with variations depending on the source and type of contribution. Only authorised and authenticated individuals can add LRTs in ELG; the registration and assignment of the "provider" user role is a simple process for all interested users (see Chapter 3). In addition, all entries go through a formal publication life cycle (see Chapter 2). Before being published in the catalogue, added metadata records are validated by the ELG core team (Section 3). Section 4 looks into the requirements for the different types of resources and entities in ELG, either integrated in ELG or available remotely and added to ELG as metadata records only. Further technical specifications are set for LT services that are intended to be deployed through the ELG cloud infrastructure, and for data resources hosted in ELG. Before being published in ELG, these resources go through a process that aims to ensure their technical validity and, for services, to set up the required environment for their deployment. Section 5 presents similar platforms and infrastructures and discusses the approach and tools they offer for providers of LRTs, in analogy to the comparison made for the platform functionalities from the point of view of consumers in Chapter 3.

2 Adding Resources to the ELG Platform

LRT providers come from a variety of backgrounds, some within Language Technology fields such as NLP or Computational Linguistics, and others from neighbouring fields such as Digital Humanities. Different providers have different levels of technical knowledge and familiarity with formal metadata descriptions, so ELG attempts to offer an integrated environment suitable for both expert and non-expert users. The functions exposed for registering and managing catalogue entries and their accompanying data files are designed to be user-friendly while still offering advanced features to users with the relevant skills.

All metadata records must comply with the ELG metadata schema (Labropoulou et al. 2020). The schema offers a rich set of metadata elements for each type of LRT or entity (organisation, project) to be added. Individual elements are either *mandatory*, *recommended* or *optional*, depending on the record type. Providers can add entries with only the mandatory elements, although they are also encouraged to add the recommended ones. See Chapter 2 for more details.

2.1 Creating Metadata Records

Providers can add records in one of two ways: either by creating and uploading XML files compliant to the ELG schema (Section 2.1.1), or by using the interactive editor offered by ELG (Section 2.1.2). In practice many users will adopt a combination of the two approaches, for example, a provider who wishes to submit many similar records (such as MT services based on the same underlying engine but with models for different language pairs) may create their first record using the editor, export it as XML, and use this file as a template to generate the remaining records.

2.1.1 Creation and Upload of Metadata Files

This first option is probably more appealing to expert and technical users, especially those that wish to register multiple related records or produce frequently updated versions of LRTs registered in ELG. To facilitate the process of adding records, prefilled metadata templates and examples (with the mandatory and recommended elements) are available in the ELG GitLab repository[1]. As mentioned above, any existing metadata record can be exported from ELG as XML to be used as a template.

A REST endpoint for metadata validation of single files or zipped archives of XML files is publicly available and offered for providers that want to validate their metadata files and ensure they comply with the ELG schema before uploading them to the platform.[2] The XSD validator checks that all mandatory elements are filled in and that filled-in values are consistent with the data type declared for the elements – for example, if elements take values from controlled vocabularies or should follow a specific pattern – and returns the results in JSON form.

Users can upload their metadata records through the provider's grid (see Section 2.3) as single files or in batch mode. The import step includes additional validation rules, which check the syntactic and, to a certain extent, semantic integrity of the record. For example, checks are performed for metadata elements that depend

---

[1] https://gitlab.com/european-language-grid/platform/ELG-SHARE-schema

[2] https://live.european-language-grid.eu/catalogue/#/validate-xml

on the presence or value of other elements (e. g., the element "multilinguality type" which is mandatory for bilingual and multilingual resources), or for duplicate values (e. g., the same "language" value used twice). Validation errors are reported to the user for correction. If the file is valid, it is imported to the platform and the provider can perform further edits with the editor or submit it for publication in accordance with the publication life cycle (see Chapter 2).

2.1.2 Metadata Editor

The editor can be accessed through the provider's grid (see Section 2.3). It supports users in creating new metadata records, as well as editing and updating existing ones. The editor includes the mandatory and recommended fields of the ELG schema. Chapter 2 provides a summary of all mandatory metadata elements.

The editor has been designed with non-expert users in mind, and intends to hide the richness of the ELG schema. For this reason, we offer a full-fledged UI with metadata elements grouped into semantically coherent sets and layered along horizontal and vertical tabs, following the ELG conceptual structure. Different editor forms with the same look and feel have been implemented for each resource or entity type. Figure 1 shows the editor for tools/services; the horizontal tabs correspond to the main classes of the schema – in this case, LRT, tool/service and distribution – and the vertical tabs to categories of elements within that main section. The figure shows the LRT horizontal tab, whose options include "identity" (identification metadata such as the resource name, long description, and name of the creator responsible for the record), "categories" (classification elements such as keywords and subject domain), and "documentation" (links to publications, user manuals, or other documents describing the resource).

Fig. 1 ELG metadata editor

The editor guides the user to fill in at least all of the mandatory elements with appropriate values. Help tips and examples are available for metadata elements, and different editing controls are used for elements depending on their data type. For instance, the elements of controlled vocabularies are shown using dropdown lists. For vocabularies with many values (e. g., languages, service functions, etc.), we use a combination of dropdown lists with suggested values as the user types in the text.

The combination of dropdown lists and dynamically suggesting values is also applied to improve normalisation. For example, some elements such as keywords allow free text entry, however as the user types, a popup suggests matching values that have previously been used for the same element in other records, "nudging" the user to choose identical values instead of slight variations. The same lookup mechanism, of suggesting values from those already imported in the catalogue, is used for reducing the chance for duplicates of related entities such as agents, projects, documents, licences, and other resources.[3] For such entities, the ELG schema requires a set of minimal information, a name/title, and, optionally, an identifier and metadata elements that could uniquely distinguish it from similar entities (e. g., email for persons, website for organisations, a URL with the text for licences, etc.). Thus, when adding related entities through the editor, users type in a name/title, and are shown matching entries (if any) to select from; if not, they are prompted to fill in the required elements mentioned above. The same set of metadata elements is also used at the import of metadata records to uniquely identify the related entities.

Through the editor, providers have the option of saving incomplete metadata records ("draft"), for which only the data type of the metadata elements is validated (e. g., that they have entered a valid URL). When they decide to properly save the metadata record, we validate the entry using the yup library[4], implementing at least the same rules used at the import of metadata files. In case of errors, messages describe the error and location where it occurred (see Figure 2); clicking on the error, users are forwarded to its location.

2.2 Uploading and Managing Data Files

Data files, i. e., the physical files that contain the contents of a resource, must be uploaded as a ZIP file. Section 4.2.2 presents recommendations for the packaging of data resources, especially for those that can be split into subsets.

Providers can upload data files as a first step when they upload an XML file[5], or during the editing process with the editor. The editor includes a tab entitled "Data" (Figure 3) through which users can manage the files (upload, replace and delete).

---

[3] This is a well-known issue across catalogues; the adoption of unique persistent identifiers is recommended to resolve it, but not all entities are assigned such a unique identifier or it may not be known to the provider that submits the metadata record.

[4] https://github.com/jquense/yup

[5] At the time of writing, the upload of data files during the batch import of XML metadata records is not supported.

Fig. 2 ELG metadata editor with error messages

A resource may be available in a range of distributable forms ("distributions"), for example, in different file formats (e. g., as PDF, XML or TXT files). ELG supports the upload of multiple data files for the same resource. For this reason, when users upload more than one package of data files, they are prompted to associate each package with the respective distribution (i. e., the one that includes the metadata that describe the size and format of the particular set of files). This action is performed by selecting the specific package on the "distribution" tab.

2.3 Managing Catalogue Entries

The ELG platform presents users that have the "provider" role set with a "grid" (dashboard), through which they can access and manage the catalogue items they have created, as well as create new items (Figure 4). Since every provider is by definition

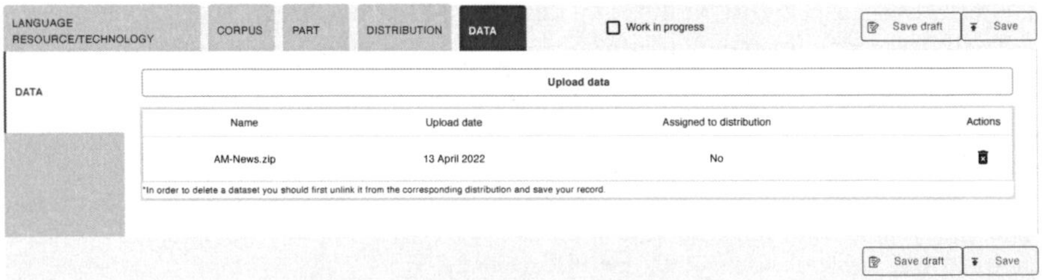

Fig. 3 ELG metadata editor – "data" tab for uploading data files

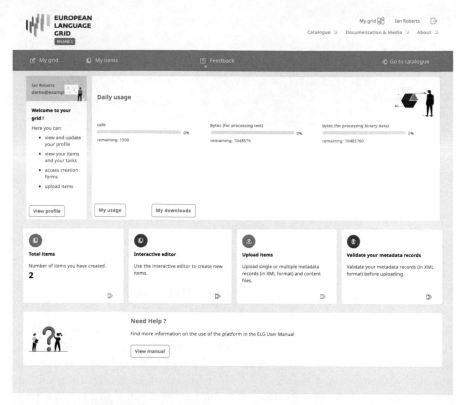

Fig. 4 Provider's grid (see Figure 6 in Chapter 3, p. 48, for the Consumer's grid)

also a consumer, the provider's dashboard is an extension of the consumer's dashboard shown in Chapter 3, adding a counter of the number of records this user has created and links to the editor, XML upload, and XML validator tools.

Users can manage the metadata records they have created through a dedicated page ("My items", Figure 5), and, in accordance with their user rights and the publication status of the record, perform the following actions: edit a metadata record, submit it for publication, create a new version of a published record, copy a metadata record (in order to use it as a model and create a similar record), delete a metadata record that has not yet been published, and request the unpublication of one of their records.[6] The "My items" page is a focused version of the catalogue, this time filtering records according to each user's role. This page also implements browse and search functionalities like the main catalogue page.

---

[6] Records cannot be completely deleted after publication except in exceptional circumstances, and then only by request to the ELG administrators.

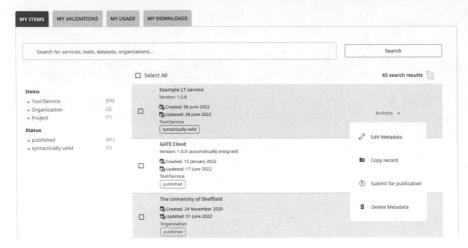

Fig. 5 "My items" page

3 Validating and Publishing Metadata Records

Metadata records added by individuals[7] enter a validation process, as specified in the ELG publication life cycle (see Chapter 2), before they are published in the catalogue: we perform technical/metadata and legal validation for ELG-compatible services and resources with uploaded data files, and validation at the metadata level only for all other metadata records. ELG-compatible services also go through a set of actions required for the registration of the service in the ELG platform (see Section 4.1.8).

Validators have access to the metadata records that have been assigned to them through the "validator's grid", and more specifically the "My validations" page (Figure 6). The validation form includes fields in which the validator can add internal comments (visible only to the other validators), and in the case of rejected records, a field for noting the reasons and suggested changes that are communicated to the provider for corrections. Providers can go through the changes and resubmit the record, which initiates a new round of validation, until final approval. When the metadata record has been approved by the responsible validator or validators, it is automatically made visible in the public catalogue.

4 Entity-Type Specific Requirements

There are several technical requirements that need to be met for LT services (Section 4.1) or resources (Section 4.2) to be deployed through or hosted in ELG successfully. We also present the requirements for metadata-only resources (Section 4.3).

---

[7] For harvesting and batch import functionalities from other catalogues, see Chapter 6.

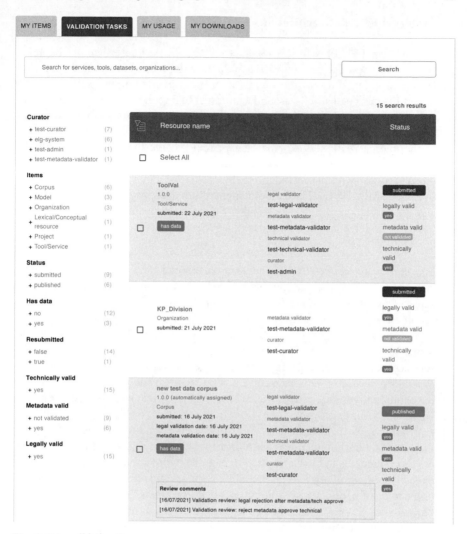

Fig. 6 "My validations" page

4.1 ELG-compatible Services

A service is ELG-compatible if it is packaged in a Docker image and follows the ELG LT internal API, i. e., the service consumes and produces messages in the ELG-specified format, as defined in Section 4.1.1 below. When a provider adds a tool or service to ELG either using XML metadata upload or through the metadata editor, they are asked if the service will actually be integrated in ELG, so that conformance to our specifications can be monitored.

4.1.1 Internal LT API Specification

The ELG internal LT API is closely related to the public API described in Chapter 3. The public API is a simplified derivative of the internal API. While both the internal and public APIs make use of the same JSON messages for input and output, the internal API is designed strictly around a single HTTP request-response transaction for each processing task, rather than the multi-step asynchronous mode supported by the public API.

For the internal API, services that accept text receive their requests as JSON, while services that process binary audio or image data receive a MIME "multipart/-form-data" request with the metadata in JSON and the binary data as the relevant audio or image MIME type. The endpoint must return the appropriate JSON response message depending on its function (standoff "annotations", classifications, audio, or new "texts" – which could be a single text, a series of sentences, a list of alternative translations, etc.). Examples include:

- *Information extraction (IE) services for text* accept a "text" request and return an "annotations" response; i. e., annotations whose position is described in terms of zero-based character offsets. Such services include tokenisers, sentence splitters, sentiment analysers, named entity recognisers, dependency parsers, etc.
- *Text classification services* accept a "text" request and return a "classification" response with the classes that have been assigned to the whole input text by the service. Examples are language identifiers, text-level sentiment classifiers etc.
- *Machine translation services* receive a "text" request and generate a new text or list of alternatives returned in a "texts" message. Services such as summarisation would use a similar format.
- *Information extraction services from speech* take "audio" requests and return the same standoff annotations as IE-from-text, but in this case the annotations are time segments in the audio stream, e. g., keyword spotting for audio files.
- *Speech recognition services* take "audio" requests and return a text transcription or a choice of n-best transcriptions, encoded as a "texts" message.
- *Text-to-speech services* take "text" messages and return "audio" messages, which can either include the returned audio inline as base64-encoded data, or as a URL reference to audio which has been uploaded to the temporary storage helper service (see Section 4.1.2).
- *Optical character recognition services* take "image" requests and return the extracted text as a "texts" response.
- *Image classification services* take "image" requests and return "classification" responses.

The formats of the input and output messages are generic and can be easily reused for integrating new types or classes of services. For example, Speech-to-Text services, such as a speech summariser that would consume an "audio" request and return a "texts" response in the same way as a pure speech recogniser, can easily be added. Other examples can be found in Chapter 7.

Detailed, up-to-date guidance on the process of integrating an LT service and selecting the most appropriate integration option can be found in the ELG documentation[8]; more information is provided in Section 4.1.3.

As described in Chapter 3, error, warning and progress report messages are represented as structured objects with a message *code*, representing a message that can be localised into many languages. The ELG team provides a set of standard message codes for common messages, and maintains their translations, but service providers who use their own custom messages are welcome to contribute their own localisations for integration into the public message resolver by contacting the ELG team.

Services that take a long time to process data have the option of returning a series of "progress" messages prior to generating the final response using the standard HTTP "server-sent events" format.[9]

4.1.2 Helper Services

ELG provides certain helper services that can be called at fixed URLs by LT service containers if they run within the platform. Notably, ELG provides a temporary storage helper which LT services can use in order to return data that does not naturally map on to the standard JSON-based response formats. This helper allows an LT service to store arbitrary blobs of binary data on a short-term basis (for any time from ten seconds up to 24 hours), and receive a randomly generated URL that can be included in the response JSON, and which the caller can retrieve up until its expiry time. Typical uses for this service include text-to-speech services that need to return larger chunks of audio data, or services that visualise structures such as parse trees in a binary image format. This is discussed further in the context of the Text2TCS service in Chapter 7, Section 5.1, p. 144 ff.

4.1.3 Integration Requirements and Options

The requirements for integrating an LT tool or service into ELG are as follows.

Expose an ELG-compatible endpoint: The provider needs to make sure that the LT tool or service to be integrated into ELG exposes an HTTP endpoint, i. e., either such an endpoint already exists or it needs to be implemented. The corresponding endpoint application must consume HTTP requests that follow the ELG JSON format, call the included or underlying LT tool and produce responses again in the ELG JSON format as specified in the the ELG LT internal API (Section 4.1.1). Developers working in Python or Java, Groovy, Kotlin, or other JVM-based languages, can make use of helper libraries provided by the ELG team to handle much of the boilerplate code for creating the HTTP listener, parsing and

---

[8] https://european-language-grid.readthedocs.io/en/stable/all/3_Contributing/Service.html
[9] https://html.spec.whatwg.org/multipage/server-sent-events.html#server-sent-events

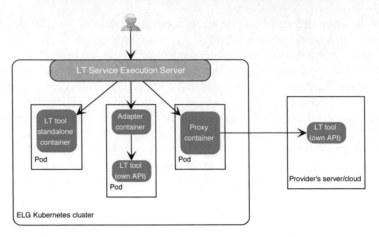

Fig. 7 Integration options

producing the JSON messages, etc., so that the provider can concentrate on their own business logic (see Sections 4.1.6 and 4.1.5 for more details).

Provide the application in the form of a Docker image: The whole application must be packaged as a container image using Docker or similar tools, and uploaded to a Docker registry, such as GitLab[10], DockerHub[11] or Azure Container Registry[12]. More than one image might be needed for one service, depending on how the service is made available. From the three options described in Fig. 7, providers can pick the one that best fits their needs.

- *LT tool packaged in one standalone image:* One image is created that contains the application that exposes the ELG-compatible endpoint and the actual LT tool. This is the most common approach when wrapping tools that are callable as libraries from custom code, such as Python machine learning models.
- *LT tool running remotely outside the ELG infrastructure:* In this case, one *proxy* image is created that exposes one (or more) ELG-compatible endpoints; the proxy container communicates with the actual LT service that runs outside the ELG infrastructure.
- *LT tool requiring an adapter:* This is a compromise between the standalone and remote approaches. A tool that is available as a Docker image but whose API is not natively ELG-compatible can be run alongside a separate ELG-compatible *adapter* image as a single pod in the ELG infrastructure. The adapter receives ELG API requests, communicates with the tool's native API in the pod, and translates the responses back to ELG format.

---

[10] https://gitlab.com

[11] https://hub.docker.com

[12] https://azure.microsoft.com/en-us/services/container-registry/

```
 1  # Base image.
 2  FROM openjdk:8-jdk-alpine
 3
 4  # SET TARGET DIRECTORY
 5  ENV TARGETDIR /elg/
 6  # This is required for wait.sh
 7  RUN apk update && apk add bash
 8
 9  # Install tini and create unprivileged user
10  RUN apk add --no-cache tini && \
11          addgroup --gid 1001 "elg" && \
12          adduser --disabled-password --gecos "ELG User,,," \
13          --home /elg --ingroup elg --no-create-home --uid 1001 elg
14
15  # Create target directory
16  RUN install -d -o elg -g elg $TARGETDIR
17  # Copy everything to target directory
18  COPY --chown=elg:elg dockerCmd ${TARGETDIR}dockerCmd
19  # Copy/Rename server app jar.
20  ADD --chown=elg:elg  /elg-ilsp-lt-services-rest-simple-0.0.1-
        SNAPSHOT-exec.jar ${TARGETDIR}dockerCmd/app.jar
21
22  # Set working directory
23  USER elg:elg
24  WORKDIR ${TARGETDIR}dockerCmd
25
26  # Make sure script can be executed
27  RUN chmod +rx ./wait.sh
28
29  # The command that is run when the container starts
30  ENTRYPOINT ["sh", "runInContainer.sh"]
```

Listing 1 Example of a dockerfile for an integrated ELG LT service

4.1.4 Creation of Docker Images

The Docker image of an application contains the code of the tool and all dependencies required to run it, e. g., the operating system, frameworks, settings, configuration files and libraries etc. Containers are instantiations of images and can be thought of as lightweight virtual machines.

The process of packaging a service as a Docker image involves creating a dockerfile that describes the build process, running that build, and pushing, i. e., copying the resulting image to a Docker registry that is accessible to the ELG infrastructure. An example dockerfile is shown in Listing 1. The most important parts are:

- Line 2 states that an image containing a lightweight Linux-based operating system that includes Java programming language will be used as the base.
- Line 20 adds the Java-based application (.jar file) that exposes an ELG-compliant LT service to the image (see Section 4.1.5 for more details).

```
1  # Login to Gitlab container registry
2  $ docker login registry.gitlab.com
3
4  # Build the image and tag it with the name registry.gitlab.com/
     ilsp-nlpli-elg/elg-ilsp-lt-services and a version number
5  $ docker build -t registry.gitlab.com/ilsp-nlpli-elg/elg-ilsp-lt-
     services:1.0.0 .
6
7  # Push the image to the container registry
8  $ docker push registry.gitlab.com/ilsp-nlpli-elg/elg-ilsp-lt-
     services:1.0.0
```

Listing 2 Example sequence of commands to build and push a Docker image to a registry

- Line 30 specifies the script (.sh) that is run when a container is created from this image; this script starts the Java application.

A simple and robust way to build and store the image of a service in a registry is to put the service code into a source code repository such as GitHub[13] or GitLab, and then to use the repository's continuous integration (CI) mechanism. There are various examples of services built like this, i. e., using GitLab CI, in the ELG GitLab space.[14] Gitlab CI is triggered immediately after a commit on the repository or on demand and runs the build process specified in .gitlab-ci.yml.

An image can also be built and stored by running a set of commands locally. This option is helpful because CI services are often restricted, e. g., Gitlab has monthly quotas. In this case, users must first download the source code to a local folder (including the dockerfile), and then run a sequence of commands similar to Listing 2.

Some languages and build systems provide alternatives for building Docker images that do not require developers to write their own dockerfile, or to use Docker at all. For example, Java services based on the Micronaut[15] helper described below can use the Micronaut built-in dockerPush or dockerPushNative gradle tasks to build and push an image in one step using an automatically generated dockerfile, or Google Jib[16], which is designed specifically around the needs of Java applications and produces intelligently layered images that make more efficient use of space in the container registry. Additional files such as models can also be included.

To be deployed in ELG, a Docker image must meet the following requirements:

- It must be built for the amd64 architecture (also known as x86_64); multi-architecture images may be appreciated by users who want to run the service on their own hardware, but ELG itself runs on amd64.
- It must be compatible with the Broadwell micro-architecture, which supports SSE4.2, AVX and AVX2 but *not* AVX512 instructions.

---

[13] https://github.com

[14] https://gitlab.com/european-language-grid

[15] https://micronaut.io

[16] https://github.com/GoogleContainerTools/jib

- The container must run in *at most* 6GB of RAM, but the smaller its foot-print the better. By default, containers are limited to 512MB RAM; if the container requires more memory, this must be specified in the metadata record (using `additionalHWRequirements`). Services requiring more than 6GB are approved only in exceptional cases.
- It must be tagged with an explicit version number such as `:1.0.0`, not the implicit `:latest` tag which typically changes over time.
- The network socket on which the container listens for HTTP requests must bind to all the container's IP addresses (typically by using `0.0.0.0`). Some HTTP libraries only listen on the local loopback `127.0.0.1` by default, which will not be sufficient in ELG.
- Ideally the container should run without needing outgoing network connections to locations outside the hosting cluster. In particular, any model files must be cached within the image at build time, not downloaded at runtime from a repository such as Hugging Face. If outgoing network access is *required*, the target IP address ranges must be specified.

It is recommended for the service to only start listening once it is fully initialised and ready to start handling requests. If this is not possible (e. g., if the code requires some asynchronous initialisation process and the library used opens its sockets before that process is complete), then a separate "readiness" endpoint should also be provided at a separate URL path from the main service endpoint (typically `/elg-ready`) that returns the response code 503 ("service unavailable") if the service is not yet initialised, and 200 or 204 once it is ready to handle requests.

Sections 4.1.5 and 4.1.6 present Java- and Python-based libraries for easily creating an application that offers an ELG-compatible service. Some of these include utilities for creating the Docker image in which the service will be packaged.

4.1.5 Helper Libraries for Java

For LT service developers working in Java or other Java Virtual Machine (JVM) languages such as Groovy[17] or Kotlin[18], ELG provides helper libraries for two popular frameworks, Spring Boot[19] and Micronaut[20]. The programming style is similar in both cases, though Micronaut is better optimised towards creating smaller, lighter images with faster startup times, so if the service implementation does not already have a dependency on Spring, Micronaut is the recommended option. Both libraries depend on a common bindings library[21] of Java model classes that represent the various JSON message structures in a more Java-native way.

---

[17] https://groovy-lang.org

[18] https://kotlinlang.org

[19] https://spring.io/projects/spring-boot

[20] https://micronaut.io

[21] https://javadoc.io/doc/eu.european-language-grid/elg-java-bindings

An ELG-compatible LT service can be built in three steps[22] using Micronaut:

1. Create a blank Micronaut application using the Micronaut Launch tool.[23]
2. Add the ELG helper as a dependency, which is published to the central repository
   – for Gradle this means

```
implementation("eu.european-language-grid:lt-service-
    micronaut:1.0.0")
```

3. Create a controller that extends `LTService` (for services that process text-based requests) or `BinaryLTService` (for services that process requests with binary content) and implement the relevant handle or handleSync method.

The process[24] is similar for Spring Boot:

1. Create a blank Spring Boot application using the "Spring Initializr"[25] – additional dependencies are not needed, unless the specific code requires them.
2. Add the ELG helper as a dependency, which is published to the central repository
   – for Gradle this means

```
implementation("eu.european-language-grid:elg-spring-boot-
    starter:1.0.0")
```

3. Create one or more beans annotated `@ElgHandler`, with one or more public methods annotated `@ElgMessageHandler`. Each method should take an ELG request type such as `TextRequest` as a parameter (and for binary requests a second parameter of type `Flux<DataBuffer>` for the actual data) and return an ELG response type such as `AnnotationsResponse` or a reactive streams Publisher producing that type.

In both cases, Micronaut and Spring Boot, developers must add their code in the appropriate places to call the actual LT tool and build a response based on the tool's results, using the model classes, e. g., an `AnnotationsResponse` object in the case that the results are standoff annotations. Once the objects are created, the frameworks and libraries are able to automatically serialise them into ELG-compliant JSON response messages. Similarly, the frameworks automatically translate the received input JSON messages to objects that can be easily handled by the developer, e. g., in the Spring Boot case a "text" JSON request is deserialised to a `TextRequest` object.

4.1.6 Helper Tools for Python

Similar to Java, the ELG team provides helper tools to create an ELG-compatible service from a Python-based LT service. The helper tools are included in the ELG Pypi package presented in Chapter 3. The package provides two Python classes that

---

[22] https://gitlab.com/european-language-grid/platform/lt-service-micronaut

[23] https://micronaut.io/launch

[24] https://gitlab.com/european-language-grid/platform/elg-spring-boot-starter

[25] https://start.spring.io

```
1  from elg import FlaskService
2  from elg.model import TextRequest, AnnotationsResponse
3  import langdetect
4
5  class ELGService(FlaskService):
6      def process_text(self, request: TextRequest):
7          langs = langdetect.detect_langs(request.content)
8          ld = {}
9          for l in langs:
10             ld[l.lang] = l.prob
11         return AnnotationsResponse(features=ld)
12
13 service = ELGService("LangDetection")
14 app = service.app
```

Listing 3 Example ELG service created using the FlaskService class of the ELG Python package

can be extended to create a simple HTTP server that exposes an ELG-compatible endpoint of the LT tool. The ELG Python package also comes with a command-line interface (CLI) that helps with the creation of the Docker image.

For the ELG-compatible endpoint, the developer creates a Python class extending either FlaskService or QuartService as a base class, and must implement one of the four following handler methods: process_text, process_structured_text, process_audio or process_image, depending on the required input type for the LT service. This method will contain the code of the LT tool, it takes as input an ELG request object of the relevant type and should return a valid ELG response object. As a simple example, Listing 3 shows an LT tool that detects the language of the input text. The ELGService class inherits from the FlaskService class, which already contains all the code needed to create the server. This allows the developer to focus on the LT tool by only having to define the handler method. The FlaskService and QuartService classes work the same way; the first is based on Flask[26], which is more suited to CPU-bound synchronous code, the second uses the asyncio-based Quart framework[27], which is better for I/O bound code – QuartService is the only supported option if the handler method uses async/await[28]. Both base classes support the progress reporting mechanism and correctly handle exceptions raised by the tool, mapping them to ELG-compliant failure responses.

After having defined the HTTP server compatible with the ELG LT internal API using the FlaskService or QuartService class, the next step is to create the Docker image. The ELG CLI that comes with the Python package contains the elg docker create command to help during this step. The command automatically generates the dockerfile based on the arguments. Listing 4 shows an example for the language detection service presented in Listing 3. All the available options of the

---

[26] https://flask.palletsprojects.com/en/2.0.x/

[27] https://pgjones.gitlab.io/quart/

[28] https://www.european-language-grid.eu/2021/10/04/choose-the-right-tool-to-create-your-elg-service-in-python/

```
elg docker create -n ELGService -p elg_service.py -r langdetect
```
Listing 4 CLI command to generate the dockerfile automatically

command are accessible with `elg docker create --help`. Once the dockerfile is generated, the creation and the publication of the Docker image follows the same process as described in Section 4.1.4.

The ELG documentation includes a complete tutorial on how to create an ELG-compatible service using the Python package.[29] With these helper tools, we seek to facilitate as much as possible the creation of an ELG-compatible service from an LT tool implemented in Python. Using the Python helper ensures that the resulting service follows best practice in terms of error handling, request parsing, etc. and the construction of the dockerfile. This makes the services deployed in the ELG infrastructure efficient and secure.

4.1.7 Metadata Requirements

In addition to the metadata requirements for tools and services (see Chapter 2), the metadata records of ELG-compatible services must also include a set of technical metadata that are necessary for their deployment in the platform:

- `dockerDownloadLocation`: location of the image with the LT service;
- `serviceAdapterDownloadLocation`: location of the adapter image (if any);
- `executionLocation`: REST endpoint at which the LT tool is exposed within the Docker image (`http://localhost:{port}{/path}`);
- `additionalHWRequirements`: can be used to specify hardware requirements for this tool beyond the default limits of 512MB RAM and one CPU core;
- We also recommend providing *sample data* on which the service produces sensible results. Sample data help speed up the validation process, and can be used through the trial UIs and the "Code samples" tab by consumers who want to test the service. Providers can upload a file with samples, add a URL where the samples are located, or simply add the data in a dedicated free text element.

Figure 8 shows the mandatory elements replicating the editor (with sections horizontally and tabs vertically); elements marked with an asterisk are mandatory, given certain conditions, or required depending on the presence of another value or element.

---

[29] https://european-language-grid.readthedocs.io/en/stable/all/A1_PythonSDK/TutoServiceIntegration.html

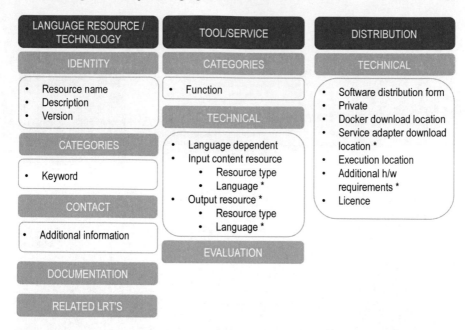

Fig. 8 Mandatory metadata for an ELG-compatible service

4.1.8 Technical Validation and Registration of ELG-Compatible Services

When LT providers have completed the packaging of their service, they can add it to ELG by supplying a metadata record via either the XML upload or editor mechanisms described in Section 2.1, specifying that it is an "ELG-compatible service" when prompted. Submitting the record initiates the validation process, which is performed internally by the ELG team.

The validation starts with the service registration process: The metadata or technical validator inspects the metadata record (accessed through the validator's grid) and deploys the service in the ELG Kubernetes cluster by creating the respective entries in the Helm charts that control the cluster. After that, the validator registers the service using a registration form (Figure 9), which specifies:

- Kubernetes-specific endpoint to be used by the LT execution server when calling the service, derived from the executionLocation metadata element value.
- ID of the trial UI to be used for rendering the processing results.
- Type of service (e. g., Speech Recognition, Text-to-Speech, Text Classification, etc.), which determines the appearance of the "Code samples" tab.
- Accessor ID that is used to form the public API endpoint URLs at which the service can be called. If the service was created as a new version of an existing service then it will share the same accessor ID as the service it replaces, but other than this, two distinct services must have different accessor IDs.

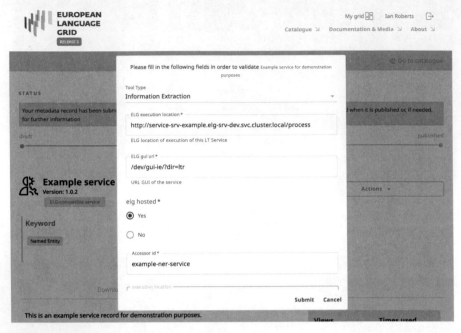

Fig. 9 Registration form for ELG-compatible LT services

When the registration is completed, the service is visible only to the validator and the provider. The technical validator and the provider check that the service behaves as expected using test input, and that the results it returns can be rendered adequately by the assigned trial UI – this is where good sample data is particularly useful. When required, the validator may communicate with the provider to recommend changes in the technical implementation of the service or metadata. When the service is finally running as it should the technical validator approves it; it will be published once it also receives approval from the legal validator (see Chapter 2 for more information on the ELG publication life cycle).

4.1.9 Custom Try Out Interface

The ELG-provided trial UIs[30] have been designed to support common service types in a generic way, but there may be specific services for which the standard UIs either do not work or do not represent the results in a particularly intuitive way. If this is the case, it is possible to supply an alternative trial UI that better suits the service to be

---

[30] https://gitlab.com/european-language-grid/usfd/gui-ie

```
1   // set up message listener
2   window.addEventListener('message', (e) => {
3     if(e.origin ===
4        'https://live.european-language-grid.eu') {
5       const serviceInfo = JSON.parse(e.data);
6       // configure UI here - store ServiceUrl and Authorization, fetch
7       // parameter metadata from ApiRecordUrl, etc.
8     }
9   });
10
11  // request configuration from the parent frame
12  setTimeout(() => {
13    // the content of the message is unimportant, any message will trigger
14    // the configuration reply.
15    window.parent.postMessage("GUI:Ready for config",
16            "https://live.european-language-grid.eu");
17  }, 500);
```

Listing 5 Typical JavaScript setup code for a trial UI

added. The standard UIs are open source under the Apache Licence[31], and providers
are free to use this code as a basis for their own UI.

A trial UI is a single-page HTML/JavaScript application which is loaded into an
<iframe> by the catalogue page when the user views an ELG-compatible service.
Trial UIs run entirely in the browser and must not send user data to anywhere other
than the ELG service endpoint and the i18n message resolver service. The JavaScript
inter-frame messaging mechanism is used to supply the UI with the data it needs to
configure itself for use with this particular service – when the UI <iframe> loads
it must register a message listener that expects to receive message data that can be
parsed as JSON, then dispatch a message to the parent frame to trigger the configuration message in return.[32] An example of this mechanism is shown in Listing 5.

The message event data sent by the parent frame will be JSON containing the
following properties:

ServiceUrl   The public LT service API URL at which the service can be called.
The URL may include query string parameters if the service has more than one
deployed version.

ApiRecordUrl   The catalogue API URL from which the metadata record for this
service may be retrieved with a GET request. This provides access to service parameter declarations, sample data, etc.

Authorization   An HTTP Authorization header value that will authenticate
calls to the ServiceUrl and ApiRecordUrl as the user who is logged in.

---

[31] https://www.apache.org/licenses/LICENSE-2.0
[32] To avoid the parent frame sending the configuration data before the UI frame is ready to receive
it.

Language   (optional) ISO code for the preferred language of the user. If present, this should be used as the `lang` parameter when resolving status messages to strings using the i18n resolver (see Section 4.1.1)

The custom UI can be hosted at any HTTPS URL – the `ServiceUrl` and `ApiRecordUrl` return the appropriate CORS headers to support cross-origin requests. Trial UIs run as Docker images in the ELG Kubernetes cluster. UIs can be created either by the ELG team or by a provider that needs a custom visualisation interface for the tools they contribute. Custom UIs can be integrated into ELG together with the ELG technical team.

4.2 ELG-hosted Resources

Together with metadata descriptions, providers are encouraged to upload the corresponding data files of their language resources so that they are readily available for download through ELG. To register their resources, they can select their preferred option from the ones presented in Section 2.1 and upload the accompanying files following the instructions in Section 2.2.

4.2.1 Requirements for ELG-hosted Resources

ELG requires data files to be uploaded as compressed ZIP files. There are no other specific metadata requirements apart from those defined for records of the resource type to which they belong (i. e., corpora, models, etc.). Chapter 2, Section 5, (p. 19 ff.) describes the metadata schema in more detail.

4.2.2 Packaging Data and Splitting Metadata Records: Recommendations

Datasets are composed of files that can be organised according to different criteria. For example, a multilingual corpus of texts from various domains can be described as a whole (one metadata record) or split into subsets (with corresponding metadata records) using the language or domain criteria. Depending on their intended use, different ways of packaging datasets and making them available can be suggested.[33]

We prepared a set of recommendations for the packaging of data files to enable users, especially those accessing ELG through programmatic APIs, to automatically identify, download and use corpora as is, without having to download them and manually search among them the subsets that interest them.[34]

---

[33] https://www.w3.org/TR/vocab-dcat-3 provides a similar argumentation for data distributions.

[34] These recommendations can be applied in different contexts, depending on whether the resource will be uploaded in ELG: when providers upload their corpora into ELG, they can use them to package the files and register the resource as one or multiple metadata records; if they decide to

The following cases are foreseen:

Multilingual resources   are recommended to be split into bilingual pairs, so that users can easily find and use them, for example, in the case of bilingual corpora, to train bilingual models.

Resources from shared tasks   are usually already split into training, development, gold, and test datasets, with a direct link to each of these. This is an established practice, and adopted in ELG as is. We recommend to register them as separate metadata records.

In both cases, a parent metadata record, to which the metadata records of all subsets can point is recommended using the "isPartOf" relation.

4.3 Metadata Records for External LRTs, Organisations and Projects

When external LRTs, organisations or projects are added to ELG, the only requirement for such metadata records is that they conform to the minimal version of the ELG metadata schema, i. e., they include the mandatory metadata elements described in Chapter 2, Section 5 (p. 19 ff.). Providers can use one of the options described in Section 2.1 (p. 69 ff.). For these records, the validation process aims to ensure that the metadata description is consistent and informative for users.

5 Provider-Related Functionalities in ELG and other Platforms

In this final section of the chapter we discuss some aspects of the functionalities offered to LT providers in ELG in relation to those available in other similar platforms. This discussion cannot be exhaustive. It rather attempts to give an overview of their design and implementation, highlight the main options utilised by the platforms, and offer explanations of the adopted approaches.

5.1 Metadata Requirements

Although the use of certain metadata schemas (e. g., DC[35], DCAT[36], schema.org[37], etc.) is growing, these schemas are usually restricted to the documentation of gen-

---

grant access to external corpora through hyperlinks, they can follow them for splitting the resource into one or multiple records and marking the availability through a direct link (element "download-Location").

[35] https://www.dublincore.org/specifications/dublin-core/dcmi-terms/

[36] https://www.w3.org/TR/vocab-dcat-3/

[37] https://schema.org

eral properties and do not satisfy domain- or community-specific requirements, especially with regard to discovery. Thus, most platforms use their own metadata schemas or ask for a minimum set of elements which are community-, domain-, or resource type specific (see Chapter 6 for a discussion of metadata schemas). Technical metadata are typically mandatory when resources are deployed in a platform. ELG has a detailed schema with a minimum set of required metadata to allow for flexibility and strictness when this is mandated for operational reasons (i. e., resources deployed in ELG, added by individuals, harvested from other sources).

CLARIN has initiated the Component MetaData Infrastructure[38], which provides a framework to describe and reuse different "metadata profiles" for resource types and communities. Specific metadata profiles, e. g., those of web services, are "recommended" with an aim to ensure interoperability and operational requirements. However, these profiles may promote different mandatory elements, depending on the use of the profile by each CLARIN Centre. Hugging Face[39] uses a dataset and model card, in which part of the required information is specified via YAML[40] tags.

5.2 Provider User Interface and Metadata User Interface

User-friendly editors that can cover *multiple* metadata schemas are difficult to implement, especially when the schemas have a complex structure. Nevertheless, most platforms include such an option. ELG, like META-SHARE[41] (Piperidis 2012; Piperidis et al. 2014), OpenMinTeD[42] (Labropoulou et al. 2018) and the European AI-on-demand platform[43], offer provider-specific UIs and a metadata editor supporting their respective schemas for describing resources. Hugging Face offers a rather simple UI with limited functionality. LAPPS Grid[44] (Ide et al. 2016) does not provide such UIs, a provider must communicate with the technical team in order to add services to the Galaxy[45] toolbox. Various CLARIN teams have created editors that support CMDI metadata (e. g., COMEDI[46], ARBIL[47], etc.). For more technical users, platforms offer APIs through which they can upload metadata records with JSON being the most widely used format for the records.

---

[38] https://www.clarin.eu/content/component-metadata

[39] https://huggingface.co

[40] https://huggingface.co/docs/datasets/v1.12.0/dataset_card.html

[41] http://www.meta-share.org

[42] https://openminted.github.io

[43] https://www.ai4europe.eu

[44] https://www.lappsgrid.org

[45] http://galaxy.lappsgrid.org

[46] https://clarino.uib.no/comedi/page

[47] https://portal.clarin.nl/node/14320

5.3 Try Out User Interface

Hugging Face offers embedded trial UIs to access their public "inference API". These are similar in spirit to the ELG "try out" UI mechanism, with a publicly documented API being called by a generic user interface. In addition, Hugging Face provides "Spaces"[48] which enable users to create and deploy their own UIs for demonstrating a model. The approach followed by Hugging Face Spaces is different from ELG; it is based on developers coding their own back-end server code and front-end UI as a single unit using the Streamlit[49] or Gradio[50] Python libraries. The developer adds this source code to a Git repository and Hugging Face then deploys the code to their infrastructure directly from the source code rather than from a developer-supplied Docker image. The UI is tightly coupled to the server-side code and the "API" is an implementation detail that varies from "space" to "space". ELG does not offer this kind of option by default, but the documented APIs mean that third parties could create a similar service on top of the LT services offered by ELG.

5.4 Helper Tools for Packaging Resources

As described in the previous sections, ELG offers command line utilities and SDKs for creating and submitting metadata for resources, preparing ELG-compatible services, etc. OpenMinTeD offered only a metadata validation service, without a corresponding command line tool. The European AI-on-demand platform, however, provides such utilities through Acumos[51] an open source framework, that makes it easy to build, share, and deploy AI applications.

5.5 Packaging Data Resources

ELG has adopted a lightweight policy for the packaging of uploaded datasets, given that direct deployment is currently not foreseen. In the CLARIN infrastructure, each centre has its own processes and recommended formats for uploaded resources, taking into account preservation or deployment purposes (e. g., submitting the resources to processing). Hugging Face maintains a detailed set of instructions for the upload of datasets and models, which is crucial for ensuring that they can be deployed.

---

[48] https://huggingface.co/spaces

[49] https://streamlit.io

[50] https://gradio.app

[51] https://www.acumos.org

6 Conclusions

ELG enables producers of language resources and language technology tools and services to upload, describe, share, and distribute their services and products as well as to describe their companies, academic organisations and projects. ELG offers to providers web-based user interfaces for describing LT resources or related entities with metadata records and provides them with functionalities for managing the life cycle of their assets; a billing component for commercial services and resources has been implemented (see Chapter 3, Section 6, p. 59 f.) and will be activated as soon as the ELG legal entity is in place (see Chapter 13). Providers of LT tools can exploit such functionalities to integrate LT tools in the ELG platform as ready-to-deploy services. LT data and tool providers are requested to follow the specifications and recommendations for packaging tools and resources to be uploaded in ELG. In the wider language technology ecosystem, provider-related functionalities are offered by other platforms, too, respecting their own target groups, objectives and policies. ELG has built bridges to some of these platforms, see Chapter 6 for more details.

References

Ide, Nancy, James Pustejovsky, Christopher Cieri, Eric Nyberg, Denise DiPersio, Chunqi Shi, Keith Suderman, Marc Verhagen, Di Wang, and Jonathan Wright (2016). "The Language Application Grid". In: *Worldwide Language Service Infrastructure*. Ed. by Yohei Murakami and Donghui Lin. Cham: Springer, pp. 51–70. DOI: 10.1007/978-3-319-31468-6_4.
Labropoulou, Penny, Dimitris Galanis, Antonis Lempesis, Mark Greenwood, Petr Knoth, Richard Eckart de Castilho, Stavros Sachtouris, Byron Georgantopoulos, Stefania Martziou, Lucas Anastasiou, Katerina Gkirtzou, Natalia Manola, and Stelios Piperidis (2018). "OpenMinTeD: A Platform Facilitating Text Mining of Scholarly Content". In: *Proceedings of WOSP 2018 (co-located with LREC 2018)*. Miyazaki, Japan: ELRA, pp. 7–12. URL: http://lrec-conf.org/works hops/lrec2018/W24/pdf/13_W24.pdf.
Labropoulou, Penny, Katerina Gkirtzou, Maria Gavriilidou, Miltos Deligiannis, Dimitris Galanis, Stelios Piperidis, Georg Rehm, Maria Berger, Valérie Mapelli, Michael Rigault, Victoria Arranz, Khalid Choukri, Gerhard Backfried, José Manuel Gómez Pérez, and Andres Garcia-Silva (2020). "Making Metadata Fit for Next Generation Language Technology Platforms: The Metadata Schema of the European Language Grid". In: *Proceedings of the 12th Language Resources and Evaluation Conference (LREC 2020)*. Ed. by Nicoletta Calzolari, Frédéric Béchet, Philippe Blache, Christopher Cieri, Khalid Choukri, Thierry Declerck, Hitoshi Isahara, Bente Maegaard, Joseph Mariani, Asuncion Moreno, Jan Odijk, and Stelios Piperidis. Marseille, France: ELRA, pp. 3421–3430. URL: https://www.aclweb.org/anthology/2020.lrec-1.420/.
Piperidis, Stelios (2012). "The META-SHARE Language Resources Sharing Infrastructure: Principles, Challenges, Solutions". In: *Proceedings of the Eight International Conference on Language Resources and Evaluation (LREC'12)*. Ed. by Nicoletta Calzolari, Khalid Choukri, Thierry Declerck, Mehmet Uğur Doğan, Bente Maegaard, Joseph Mariani, Asuncion Moreno, Jan Odijk, and Stelios Piperidis. Istanbul, Turkey: ELRA.
Piperidis, Stelios, Harris Papageorgiou, Christian Spurk, Georg Rehm, Khalid Choukri, Olivier Hamon, Nicoletta Calzolari, Riccardo del Gratta, Bernardo Magnini, and Christian Girardi (2014). "META-SHARE: One year after". In: *Proceedings of the 9th Language Resources and Evaluation Conference (LREC 2014)*. Ed. by Nicoletta Calzolari, Khalid Choukri, Thierry Declerck,

Hrafn Loftsson, Bente Maegaard, Joseph Mariani, Asuncion Moreno, Jan Odijk, and Stelios Piperidis. Reykjavik, Iceland: ELRA, pp. 1532–1538. URL: http://www.lrec-conf.org/proceed ings/lrec2014/pdf/786_Paper.pdf.

Rehm, Georg, Stelios Piperidis, Kalina Bontcheva, Jan Hajic, Victoria Arranz, Andrejs Vasiļjevs, Gerhard Backfried, José Manuel Gómez Pérez, Ulrich Germann, Rémi Calizzano, Nils Feldhus, Stefanie Hegele, Florian Kintzel, Katrin Marheinecke, Julian Moreno-Schneider, Dimitris Gala-nis, Penny Labropoulou, Miltos Deligiannis, Katerina Gkirtzou, Athanasia Kolovou, Dimitris Gkoumas, Leon Voukoutis, Ian Roberts, Jana Hamrlová, Dusan Varis, Lukáš Kačena, Khalid Choukri, Valérie Mapelli, Mickaël Rigault, Jūlija Meļņika, Miro Janosik, Katja Prinz, Andres Garcia-Silva, Cristian Berrio, Ondrej Klejch, and Steve Renals (2021). "European Language Grid: A Joint Platform for the European Language Technology Community". In: *Proceedings of the 16th Conference of the European Chapter of the Association for Computational Linguistics: System Demonstrations (EACL 2021)*. Kyiv, Ukraine: ACL, pp. 221–230. URL: https://w ww.aclweb.org/anthology/2021.eacl-demos.26.pdf.

Chapter 5
Cloud Infrastructure of the European Language Grid

Florian Kintzel, Rémi Calizzano, and Georg Rehm

Abstract The European Language Grid (ELG) is a cloud-based platform, utilising a variety of software packages as well as infrastructure components and virtual hardware. The additional software components developed by the ELG project are usually provided as open source to facilitate re-use by third parties. This chapter provides an overview of the infrastructural setup used by the ELG cloud platform. The selected architecture also has implications for providers as well as users of the platform, e. g., in terms of the scaling behaviour of individual Language Technology (LT) services.

1 Introduction

One of the key technical goals of the ELG cloud platform is the ability to integrate functional Language Technology (LT) services from a variety of sources, i. e., to build a large platform and a corresponding community of providers and users of these services. The LT tools and services to be continuously integrated into the ELG platform are, thus, heterogeneous and vary in their technical setup, which is why a set of common approaches needs to be established to make the integration of the tools and services possible. One of the most basic joint technical approaches is the requirement for all functional services to be containerised so that they can run on the ELG cloud infrastructure. Providers can optionally benefit from utilising additional support functionality, e. g., source code repositories, container registries and deployment pipelines offered by the ELG platform.

Conceptually, the ELG platform consists of three layers, the user interface (UI) layer, the back end layer and the base infrastructure (see Figure 1). While the UI and back end are described in more detail in Chapters 2, 3 and 4, the present chapter focuses on the base infrastructure setup along with supporting functionality. Among others, this chapter is helpful for providers of functional LT tools and services or users interested in running parts of the ELG platform on their own hardware.

Florian Kintzel · Rémi Calizzano · Georg Rehm
Deutsches Forschungszentrum für Künstliche Intelligenz GmbH, Germany,
florian.kintzel@dfki.de, remi.calizzano@dfki.de, georg.rehm@dfki.de

G. Rehm (ed.), *European Language Grid*, Cognitive Technologies,
https://doi.org/10.1007/978-3-031-17258-8_5

The rest of this chapter is structured as follows. First, Section 2 gives an overview of the building blocks of the ELG infrastructure. Section 3 provides information about the deployment side of the ELG platform, while Section 4 describes how the platform's scaling profile lends itself to usage in different real-world scenarios. Finally, Section 5 concludes the chapter with an overview of future work on the ELG platform infrastructure.

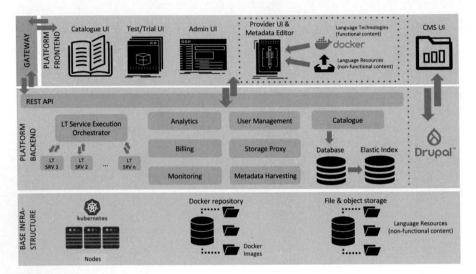

Fig. 1 ELG platform architecture

2 Cloud Infrastructure

The base infrastructure consists, first and foremost, of the compute nodes on which the European Language Grid runs, alongside their respective volume storage and networking facilities. On these, the Kubernetes[1] core components are installed (Section 2.1) including S3-compatible object storage (Section 2.2). We use a *managed* approach to Kubernetes, i. e., the installation, update and operation of the Kubernetes system itself is taken care of by a cloud provider. Together, this forms the hardware basis of the European Language Grid.

Conceptually, the base infrastructure also consists of a larger set of Git[2] repositories and container registries which are described in Sections 2.3 and 2.4.

---

[1] https://kubernetes.io

[2] https://git-scm.com

2.1 Kubernetes and Cloud Native

Kubernetes is an open source system for automating deployment, scaling, and management of containerised applications. It has seen widespread usage in recent years as *the* container orchestration tool of choice. Adoption of Kubernetes in a *managed* setup was still in a relatively early stage at the time the ELG project was exploring different cloud providers in early 2019. While various products by the typical hyperscalers already existed, European providers had only very recently started offering comparable solutions.

Our selection of Kubernetes as the framework of choice for ELG was primarily based on the following criteria:

- Kubernetes provides self-healing capabilities that can detect common failure situations and restart affected containers automatically.
- Through the use of a managed approach to Kubernetes, failures of the core Kubernetes system itself are the responsibility of the cloud provider.
  These first two criteria together allowed the ELG project to have a relatively small footprint in terms of operational complexity as failures are either self-healed or taken care of by the cloud provider, at least in theory. While exceptions *do* exist, this still has reduced the operational effort considerably.
- Kubernetes facilitates the usage of OCI-compatible containers.[3] As ELG aims to integrate different technologies used for the implementation of LT services and tools, OCI-compatible containers form a common approach for integration.
- Kubernetes provides off-the-shelf functionality for scaling up resources based on dynamic load. As ELG integrates hundreds of different LT tools and services, this functionality was deemed essential.
- Kubernetes namespaces[4] are useful to separate the different platform components from one another.
- Continuous adoption of Kubernetes within the industry assures continued support and development of this technology.

An ecosystem of compatible technologies has been established around Kubernetes with the Cloud Native Computing Foundation (CNCF).[5] CNCF promotes the use of a large set of base technologies for solving, e. g., authentication, monitoring, deployment and other common challenges. Most supporting technologies used in ELG (Section 3.2) are part of CNCF. Alongside this, a set of architecture patterns has emerged that aim to support properties such as Gannon et al. (2017):

- Cloud-native applications often operate at the global level.
- Cloud-native applications must scale well with thousands of concurrent users.
- Built on the assumption that infrastructure is fluid and failure is constant.
- Designed so that upgrade and test occur without disrupting production.
- Security must be part of the underlying application architecture.

---

[3] https://opencontainers.org – Open Container Initiative

[4] https://kubernetes.io/docs/concepts/overview/working-with-objects/namespaces

[5] https://www.cncf.io

2.2 Storage

The various components of the European Language Grid platform utilise persistent storage differently, as follows:

- Static Language Resources, i. e., corpora, models etc. available for direct download on the European Language Grid platform are persisted on S3-compatible object storage and can be fetched from there.
- The major infrastructural part of the ELG platform – the hundreds of LT tools services – do not utilise persistent storage at all, as they are designed stateless. All application code is shipped within an OCI-compatible container. This includes additional resources needed to run the service, e. g., language models and additional configuration files.
- The core ELG platform components (catalogue, authentication, CMS etc.) utilise network block storage attached to their running containers for persistence. This block storage is in turn backed up to the object storage on a regular basis.

Therefore, static resources *can* potentially be available for direct download and be included in the respective service container image as well. We decided for this approach to simplify deployment and management of images and resources, e. g., for a local installation of a set of LT services, it is only necessary to pull and run the respective images, i. e., no additional language resources need to be handled. Though this potentially results in duplication of resource files (within an image and as an additional separate file for download) it was deemed a necessary trade-off to keep the deployment model easier.

2.3 Software Repositories

ELG is comprised of various independent software packages for, e. g., platform components and individual LT services. The main ELG GitLab project repository[6] is set up as a GitLab group, consisting of various sub-groups and repositories. The different repositories in this group can be categorised as follows.

- The ELG Infrastructure Repository consists of a set of configuration files, mostly in the form of Helm[7] charts (see Section 3.1). These define which packages, i. e., containers, the ELG system consists of, as well as numerous additional configuration parameters such as the number of replicas and package-specific configurations. It can be used to set up multiple clusters. We maintain different branches within the repository, usually at least one for the development and one for the production cluster. The branches are not only used to distinguish between specific configurations for each cluster, but present different versions

---

[6] https://gitlab.com/european-language-grid

[7] https://helm.sh

of the ELG system as it matures during development. This is used to facilitate a staged roll-out to the production cluster. The actual source code for these components is not part of this repository. It only includes references to the container registries with the specific components. When installing the ELG cluster, these images are then downloaded ("pulled") from these registries.

- The ELG Cluster Admin repository holds cluster-specific configurations for each ELG instance that are applied separately from the settings of the ELG Infrastructure Repository. These mostly consist of the list of active administrative users for accessing the ELG infrastructure (those needing access to the infrastructure the ELG is running on, not users of the ELG platform), their roles and access rights as well as the configuration for build-bot, our continuous integration utility of choice. Included are also various utilities to manage the cluster. This repository is not needed for local deployment of the ELG, as such a deployment is usually only meant for a single user, typically a developer, and does not participate in continuous deployment.
- The main ELG GitLab platform project repository.[8] This repository hosts the individual components that make up the the core ELG platform and ELG website. These are mainly the platform (catalogue back end and front end components and the website content management system, along with a larger set of internal supporting and utility components.
- Individual sub-groups with repositories for individual LT services, grouped by provider. These consist solely of the LT services provided by members or associates of the ELG project consortium.

Implementation code for LT services not provided by ELG project consortium members is not usually held in the ELG GitLab group but rather managed via provider-specific repositories.

2.4 Container Registries

The images for instantiating containers in the ELG cluster are stored in various container registries. The Kubernetes installation powering ELG pulls the images from these registries on demand. These can be categorised as follows.

- The ELG GitLab project registry[9] is the registry that corresponds to the main ELG GitLab group, it hosts all images for all ELG core platform components (e. g., UI, back end, utilities) and for several ELG LT services developed by ELG project consortium partners. This registry allows public access to facilitate download and re-use of ELG components.
- Public registries for various externally implemented third-party components such as database system, identity and access management.

---

[8] https://gitlab.com/european-language-grid/platform
[9] registry.gitlab.com/european-language-grid

- Private registries of partners who do not publish their LT services under an open source license (proprietary LT services) or need to use their own registries for technical reasons.
- Various other public registries for open source LT services.
- The dedicated ELG registry.[10] As LT service images are partly pulled from registries external to the ELG project, this registry was set up to serve as a point to collect LT service images when they are ingested into ELG in order to perform versioning. Using this approach, ELG can ensure the availability of older versions of certain tools even if their original site is no longer serving them.

3 Installation

ELG utilises a GitOps approach (see, e. g., Beetz and Harrer 2021) to deployment, i. e., the configuration necessary to set up the compute cluster is managed by version control. The base artefact for deployment is the Helm chart.[11] Helm charts are used to manage the installation and update the ELG platform. Each chart bundles a set of components along with their configuration. All custom charts are defined in the ELG platform repository GitLab group (Section 3.1). Alongside the custom charts, a larger set of third-party charts is utilised to set up the respective components (Section 3.2).

We apply the charts to the cluster using a Continuous Integration (CI) approach, i. e., automatic deployment happens whenever changes to the configuration are detected by the CI (Figure 2).

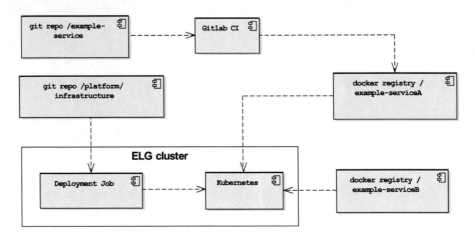

Fig. 2 ELG continuous integration

---

[10] registry.european-language-grid.eu

[11] https://helm.sh

If a new version of the infrastructure setup is detected, the CI checks out the respective changes and applies them to the cluster state. Any new container versions are then pulled from their distributed container registries. The Kubernetes cluster is updated with the latest configuration and takes care of gracefully shutting down and instantiating new containers.

Continuous integration regarding the ELG infrastructure only deals with updating the ELG cluster with the latest set of images (as specified by their version number) and configuration. It does not deal with building the respective images themselves.

3.1 ELG Charts

These charts were specifically developed for ELG and control its setup and installation. The packages are meant to be installed together, though it is possible to install only a subset for specific use cases (e. g., custom local installations). The architecture of the ELG is described in Chapter 2 as well as, e. g., Rehm et al. (2021), which is why we focus only on the software packages themselves.

- The ELG core package consists of definitions for various supporting functionalities of ELG. These are the Ingress[12] definitions for routing incoming traffic into the ELG cluster, the configuration for the rest server component as well as the configuration for the temporary storage component (used for large file operations). Various smaller configurations can also be found here, e. g., priority classes for pod scheduling, support for maintenance operations and others.
- The ELG back end chart consists of the definitions for the main back end components, the Django[13] and React[14] powered applications that form the ELG catalogue and the ELG back end and administrative applications. Included in this chart are also a set of utility functions that deal with housekeeping.
- The ELG LT services chart bundles the whole set of individual LT services installed in ELG. It is actually a collection of charts that follow a common structure, each sub-chart consisting of the definitions for the LT services of a specific LT services provider as well as a common chart for open source LT services by providers who only offer a small set of services. A definition for each individual LT service consists at the minimum of the reference to its image location, but can consist of numerous additional configurations, e. g., specific hardware requirements, helper images, parameters for scaling the service up and down and various other parameters.

---

[12] https://kubernetes.io/docs/concepts/services-networking/ingress

[13] https://www.djangoproject.com

[14] https://reactjs.org

3.2 Third-Party Charts

Apart from the core components, we use a set of third-party components, which provide their functionality to the ELG cluster. In the following, we briefly describe the main third-party components.

- Cert-manager[15] is a tool to manage issuing and updating of TLS certificates. It is used to install and refresh TLS certificates to allow for the encryption of all HTTPS traffic that reaches the cluster via one of the configured ingress-rules.
- The Horizontal Pod Autoscaler (HPA)[16] is a standard Kubernetes component used to scale pods based on their load and runtime behaviour. For scalability and load monitoring, Kubernetes collects certain metrics, e. g., CPU and memory load, from each pod. Therefore, it is necessary to have at least one instance of each type of pod to be up and running at all times. Otherwise, no metrics can be collected. This setup is useful to scale ELG core components, e. g., the portal website and back end. It cannot be utilised as is to scale the hundreds of LT services offered by the platform, as these need to be scaled down to zero replicas if they are not needed to not exceed the cluster capacity. Therefore, we introduced KNative (see below), which is feeding the standard autoscaler with a new metric "concurrency", based on the number of active requests to that LT service. Scaling those services still makes use of cluster-autoscaler functionality, but with the new metric also being available if no active replica of an LT service is instantiated.
- KNative[17] and Kourier[18] give ELG the possibility to scale down LT services based on the current number of parallel requests to them (concurrency). The concurrency metric is available even if there is no active replica of an LT service. KNative buffers HTTP requests to one of the ELG APIs until the specific LT service's container has started and keeps track of the concurrency metric to terminate the replica if it is no longer needed. We cannot overstate the importance of this functionality for ELG as the platform consists of hundreds of individual LT service components, not all of which need to run all the time, i. e., it would not be efficient to have all these services consume resources while in idle state. Starting up a container takes a certain amount of time though, while the service initialises. Using a service after it has not been used in a while therefore requires a certain spin-up time. KNative does not natively provide facilities to reduce the spin-up time further, but additional methods might be helpful in the ELG context, e. g., predictive auto scaling (Nanayakkara 2021). If frequent traffic is expected for a particular service, it can easily be configured to have one or more instances running at any given time, depending on hardware availability.

---

[15] https://cert-manager.io/docs

[16] https://kubernetes.io/de/docs/tasks/run-application/horizontal-pod-autoscale

[17] https://knative.dev/docs

[18] https://github.com/3scale-archive/kourier

- Ingress-Ningx[19] is installed to act as ingress-controller, i. e., handling HTTP traffic received and forwarding them to their respective endpoint within the cluster.
- Keycloak[20] is an open source solution for authentication and authorisation. It interfaces with front end, back end and LT services to provide single-sign on.
- Elasticsearch[21] is used to index the catalogue database for fast faceted search.
- Prometheus[22], Grafana, Loki and AlertManager form the ELG monitoring solution. They collect and analyse logs and metrics from all running components in the cluster (including the hardware) and provide visualisations in the form of dashboards and diagrams (Figure 3).

Fig. 3 Monitoring ELG using Prometheus and Grafana

- The ELG back end database uses PostgreSQL[23], a well-supported open source database engine. It holds all relevant data concerning the ELG catalogue, e. g., projects, organisations, LT resources, LT service as well as user information.
- MariaDB[24] is used for persistence of the Drupal CMS that powers the ELG portal. We plan to move this over to PostgreSQL for ease of maintenance.
- Not an off-the-shelf component, but rather specifically adapted for ELG, the s3proxy[25] facilitates the upload of LT resources (models, corpora, but also project and organisation logos etc.) to ELG. It acts as a proxy to the S3-compatible object storage that takes care of validating upload authorisation with the ELG back end and streams data to the object storage.

---

[19] https://nginx.org

[20] https://github.com/keycloak/keycloak

[21] https://github.com/elastic/elasticsearch

[22] https://prometheus.io

[23] https://www.postgresql.org

[24] https://mariadb.org

[25] https://gitlab.com/european-language-grid/platform/s3proxy

4 Scalability of LT Tools and Services

ELG is optimised for stateless LT tools and services. Its database systems are exclusively used by the platform back end for the metadata catalogue, user data etc. LT services do not have persistence enabled for them, with the exception of temporary files used for large file uploads. In the following, we describe our approach for scaling up individual LT services and describe its impact for service usability.

4.1 Implementation

With the goal of hosting thousands of individual LT tools and services with very different hardware needs, it is neither feasible nor practical to have all of them instantiated at the same time as this would require hundreds of Gigabytes of RAM even in idle mode, i. e., even if none of them are actually used. Therefore, ELG leverages the capabilities of KNative[26] which make is possible to automatically scale down services not currently in use to zero replicas. In this state, an LT service does not consume any hardware resources.

Scaling up an LT service happens automatically to an initial number of replicas once a request has been received for that individual service. Requests are buffered while new containers are starting up. This setup is especially suitable for services seeing little or irregular traffic. Further scale-up happens when a configurable threshold of concurrent requests for a given service is exceeded.

LT services deployed on ELG need to be aware that their life-cycle is exclusively controlled by Kubernetes and they need to expect to be started, stopped and horizontally scaled regularly, e. g., when the scheduler detects low resource situations on one of the nodes, if a container fails to respond, if high traffic is received to an LT service and other situations. LT services, therefore, highly benefit from quick start-up times and this is one of the reasons, why we opted for LT services to include necessary resources like models into their OCI images directly.

4.2 Use Cases

Given its scalability (Section 4.1), a number of use cases can be solved with ELG.

- Demonstration of service functionality: providers of LT tools and services can freely deploy their services to the platform and can expect to be discoverable via the platform's catalogue. For the try out functionality of services, a certain spin-up time from idle mode will not impact its usefulness. More performant installations of a given service could, e. g., be offered by the providers themselves.

---

[26] https://knative.dev/docs

- Batch processing of multiple documents: as the containers of an individual LT service will stay instantiated for some time after usage before scale-down happens, ELG is a good fit for batch processing as the initial scale-up time will not be a major contributing factor to processing time.
- For services intended to power applications where quick response times are required (e. g., mobile apps), however, the time it takes to spin up a container is likely too long (some seconds, depending on a service's implementation). This is why services on ELG can be configured to stay instantiated all the time and still benefit from dynamic scaling in high load situations. To be feasible, dedicated hardware is necessary, which service providers will be able to reserve on the ELG platform for a fee in the future so their services will show the responsiveness and performance they require.
- Remote processing is a second alternative for LT service providers who want to offer their services to the public. In this setup, the ELG platform uses a proxy to forward user requests to an external installation of a service, managed by the service providers themselves. This offers a flexible approach for providers to tune the hardware setup according to their own requirements.
- Management of non-functional LT resources, where only bandwidth limits scalability instead of compute capacity.

5 Conclusions

The ELG platform is growing continuously and the capacity, availability, operational readiness and tooling support of the base infrastructure need to evolve accordingly. We foresee a need to evolve in the following areas in particular.

- Hardware capacity and cost distribution: through the use of cloud technology, ELG has the technical capability to grow horizontally as required by the encountered load. In practice, though, the available hardware is restricted by budget considerations. Batches of utilised compute resources would need to be individually matched to the user requesting them or the provider offering them, to allow the ELG to calculate operational costs on a per request basis. With this and the emerging payment functionality, individual resource usage can be reimbursed.
- Hardware acceleration: ELG currently runs on CPUs exclusively. Already now, a larger number of LT services in ELG would benefit from GPU support. Apart from higher costs, GPU support will pose a number of technical challenges, among them a need to map LT services to specific compute nodes (with or without GPU support).
- Integration and deployment support: the initial integration of a functional LT service will need further automation and tooling support to be able to cope with increased demand and an increased number of running services.
- Workflow support: ELG would benefit from a possibility for easy workflow composition, spanning multiple LT services. Initial efforts have been started towards this goal (Moreno-Schneider et al. 2020).

- Gaia-X: in the Gaia-X[27] project OpenGPT-X[28] the ELG platform is currently being integrated into the wider Gaia-X ecosystem, i. e., ELG is further extended so that it complies to the technical Gaia-X specifications. This will enable all ELG LT services and resources to be discoverable and usable within Gaia-X.

This list only includes a selection of likely areas of improvement. Many additional use cases and requirements for ELG can be imagined – the platform infrastructure will need to grow and evolve as required.

References

Beetz, Florian and Simon Harrer (2021). "GitOps: The Evolution of DevOps?" In: *IEEE Software* 39.4, pp. 70–75. DOI: 10.1109/MS.2021.3119106.

Gannon, Dennis, Roger Barga, and Neel Sundaresan (2017). "Cloud-Native Applications". In: *IEEE Cloud Computing* 4.5, pp. 16–21. DOI: 10.1109/MCC.2017.4250939.

Moreno-Schneider, Julián, Peter Bourgonje, Florian Kintzel, and Georg Rehm (2020). "A Workflow Manager for Complex NLP and Content Curation Pipelines". In: *Proc. of the 1st Int. Workshop on Language Technology Platforms (IWLTP 2020, co-located with LREC 2020)*. Ed. by Georg Rehm, Kalina Bontcheva, Khalid Choukri, Jan Hajic, Stelios Piperidis, and Andrejs Vasiljevs. Marseille, France, pp. 73–80. URL: https://www.aclweb.org/anthology/2020.iwltp-1.12.pdf.

Nanayakkara, Pallage Kamindu (2021). "Serverless Performance Improvement for Knative using Predictive Auto Scaling". PhD thesis. Sri Lanka: Informatics Institute of Technology. URL: http://dlib.iit.ac.lk/xmlui/handle/123456789/702.

Rehm, Georg, Stelios Piperidis, Kalina Bontcheva, Jan Hajic, Victoria Arranz, Andrejs Vasiļjevs, Gerhard Backfried, José Manuel Gómez Pérez, Ulrich Germann, Rémi Calizzano, Nils Feldhus, Stefanie Hegele, Florian Kintzel, Katrin Marheinecke, Julian Moreno-Schneider, Dimitris Galanis, Penny Labropoulou, Miltos Deligiannis, Katerina Gkirtzou, Athanasia Kolovou, Dimitris Gkoumas, Leon Voukoutis, Ian Roberts, Jana Hamrlová, Dusan Varis, Lukáš Kačena, Khalid Choukri, Valérie Mapelli, Mickaël Rigault, Jūlija Meļņika, Miro Janosik, Katja Prinz, Andres Garcia-Silva, Cristian Berrio, Ondrej Klejch, and Steve Renals (2021). "European Language Grid: A Joint Platform for the European Language Technology Community". In: *Proceedings of the 16th Conference of the European Chapter of the Association for Computational Linguistics: System Demonstrations (EACL 2021)*. Kyiv, Ukraine: ACL, pp. 221–230. URL: https://www.aclweb.org/anthology/2021.eacl-demos.26.pdf.

---

27 https://www.gaia-x.eu, https://www.data-infrastructure.eu

28 https://www.opengpt-x.de

Chapter 6
Interoperable Metadata Bridges to the wider Language Technology Ecosystem

Penny Labropoulou, Stelios Piperidis, Miltos Deligiannis, Leon Voukoutis, Maria Giagkou, Ondřej Košarko, Jan Hajič, and Georg Rehm

Abstract One of the objectives of the European Language Grid is to help overcome the fragmentation of the European Language Technology community by bringing together language resources and technologies, information about them, Language Technology consumers, providers and the wider public. This chapter describes the mechanisms ELG has put in place to build interoperable bridges to related initiatives, infrastructures, platforms and repositories in the wider Language Technology landscape. We focus on the different approaches implemented for the exchange of metadata records about, in a generic sense, resources and exemplify them with the help of four use cases through which the ELG catalogue has been further populated. The chapter presents the protocols used for the population processes as well as the adaptations of the ELG metadata schema and platform policies that proved necessary to be able to ingest these new records. Last, we discuss the challenges emerging in large-scale metadata aggregation processes and propose a number of alternative options to address them.

1 Introduction

One of the objectives of the European Language Grid is to help overcome the fragmentation of the European Language Technology community by bringing together language resources and technologies, information about them, Language Technology consumers, providers and the wider public.

Additionally, ELG is meant to support digital language equality in Europe (STOA 2018; European Parliament 2018), i. e., to create a situation in which *all* European

Penny Labropoulou · Stelios Piperidis · Miltos Deligiannis · Leon Voukoutis · Maria Giagkou
Institute for Language and Speech Processing, R. C. "Athena", Greece, penny@athenarc.gr, spip@athenarc.gr, mdel@athenarc.gr, leon.voukoutis@athenarc.gr, mgiagkou@athenarc.gr

Ondřej Košarko · Jan Hajič
Charles University, Czech Republic, kosarko@ufal.mff.cuni.cz, hajic@ufal.mff.cuni.cz

Georg Rehm
Deutsches Forschungszentrum für Künstliche Intelligenz GmbH, Germany, georg.rehm@dfki.de

© The Author(s) 2023
G. Rehm (ed.), *European Language Grid*, Cognitive Technologies,
https://doi.org/10.1007/978-3-031-17258-8_6

languages are supported through technologies equally well. Technological support for human languages has been characterised by a stark predominance of LTs for English, while almost all other languages are only marginally supported and, thus, in danger of digital extinction (Kornai 2013; Rehm et al. 2014, 2020b; ELRC 2019; Calzolari et al. 2011; Soria et al. 2012). More than ten years after the initial findings (Rehm and Uszkoreit 2012), Europe's languages are still affected by this stark imbalance in 2022, as attested in the most recent series of Language Reports (Giagkou et al. 2022) prepared by the European Language Equality[1] project, which develops a strategic research, innovation and implementation agenda as well as a roadmap for achieving full digital language equality in Europe by 2030. In collaboration with ELG, one of the first steps towards Digital Language Equality has been the creation of an inventory of language resources and technologies available for Europe's languages and its regular monitoring.

In tandem with its operation as an integrated LT platform, through a battery of selection, conversion and ingestion processes described in this chapter, ELG aims to act as a one-stop shop and single entry point to homogenised descriptions of language resources and technologies. Section 2 positions the ELG approach towards this goal in the broader context of the exchange of metadata between catalogues and repositories. Section 3 presents four use cases through which the ELG catalogue has been populated with metadata records from other sources, highlighting the features that have influenced the different solutions we adopted. Section 4 presents the adaptations made in the ELG metadata schema and platform policies to take into account the outputs of these import procedures. Finally, in Section 5 we discuss, based on the experience gained in this process, the challenges that need to be addressed in the aggregation of metadata from multiple sources in order to share and promote the use and re-use of resources, data and software among community members.

2 Approach

There are a wide range of digital catalogues, repositories and, in general, infrastructures[2] that support the publication and dissemination of digital artefacts and resources, which can be classified along various dimensions. Institutional catalogues hosting all types of resources (publications, datasets, tools, etc.) produced by practitioners affiliated with an institution, catalogues that focus on resources produced by specific communities (e. g., OLAC[3] for resources related to language and linguistics, CLARIN[4] and ELRA[5] for language resources, Europeana[6] for cultural works,

---

[1] https://european-language-equality.eu

[2] For the sake of brevity, we will use the cover term "catalogue" for all institutions of this kind.

[3] http://www.language-archives.org

[4] https://www.clarin.eu

[5] http://elra.info

[6] https://www.europeana.eu

ELIXIR[7] for bioinformatics, LLOD cloud[8] for linguistic linked data, etc.), catalogues that collect specific content types (e. g., Hugging Face[9] for Machine Learning models and datasets, ELRC-SHARE[10] for Machine Translation-related resources or portals for open government data).[11]

At the same time, we witness a strong movement towards the sharing of resources from multiple sources and various disciplines through a common point of access, so that they are easily discoverable, accessible and re-usable by all interested stakeholders, fostering interdisciplinary research and cross-community collaborations as well as Open Science (e. g., European Commission 2022). Google has implemented its Dataset Search[12], a service dedicated to facilitating the discovery of datasets stored across the World Wide Web based on keyword search (Benjelloun et al. 2020). The European Open Science Cloud (EOSC)[13], initiated by the European Commission, is conceived as a federated and open multi-disciplinary environment for hosting and processing research data and all other digital objects produced along the research life cycle, e. g., methods, software and publications (Abramatic et al. 2021). Some European countries have launched corresponding national initiatives, including the National Research Data Infrastructure in Germany (NFDI).[14] Gaia-X[15] seeks to establish a federated ecosystem in which data is made available, collated, shared and processed in trustworthy environments, associated with the concept of data spaces, a type of data relationship between trusted partners, each of whom apply the same high policies, standards and technical components to the description, storage and sharing of their data and other resources.

All these initiatives offer catalogues, or inventories, employing, in many cases, different metadata schemas for the description of resources. The differences between the schemas can be attributed to the varying requirements defined by the relevant object of description (e. g., dataset vs. software or publication or geospatial data), the need to cover a wide range of users (for general catalogues) in contrast to the specialised practices common among scholars of a discipline, as well as to the different purposes that catalogues may serve (e. g., preservation, dissemination, or processing). Sharing metadata across catalogues presupposes interoperability, in particular, *semantic* interoperability. Initiatives for the adoption of common standards in metadata vocabularies, documentation of the vocabularies themselves, and the creation and publication of mappers between them are among the primary instruments to achieve such interoperability (Chan and Zeng 2006; Zeng and Chan 2006; Haslhofer and Klas 2010; Alemu et al. 2012; Broeder et al. 2019).

---

[7] https://elixir-europe.org

[8] https://linguistic-lod.org/llod-cloud

[9] https://huggingface.co

[10] https://www.elrc-share.eu

[11] https://www.re3data.org/browse/ provides a registry of research data repositories.

[12] https://datasetsearch.research.google.com

[13] https://eosc-portal.eu

[14] https://www.nfdi.de

[15] https://www.gaia-x.eu

Equally important is the establishment of protocols and mechanisms for the sharing of metadata, and subsequently of the resources themselves. The OAI-PMH protocol[16] is one of the most popular mechanisms used for repository interoperability at the metadata level. The ResourceSync[17] specification is a framework for the synchronisation of both metadata and resources. Finally, APIs are frequently offered nowadays as a solution for downloading dumps of metadata records.

ELG has established technical bridges with other infrastructures and initiatives in order to enrich its catalogue with information about data resources and tools from other catalogues and repositories. The catalogues of interest to ELG are usually discipline-specific, targeting the LT/NLP and neighbouring areas, such as Machine Learning, Artificial Intelligence as well as social sciences and humanities. Potentially interesting resources for LT development purposes are also hosted in general repositories and catalogues, the identification and filtering of which poses challenges which are briefly discussed in Section 3.

3 Establishing Interoperable Connections: Four Use Cases

Depending on the source repositories' respective contents, metadata schemas and vocabularies, and the available export functionalities of their catalogues, we have adopted different approaches towards establishing interoperable connections, a selection of which is presented in the following use cases. For each use case, we describe the source repository's technical and metadata features, explain how these impact the import of metadata records into ELG and present the methodology and tools used in the integration process.

3.1 Use Case 1: OAI-PMH (CLARIN Nodes and ELRC-SHARE)

The CLARIN (Common Language Resources and Technology Infrastructure) Research Infrastructure (Hinrichs and Krauwer 2014; Eskevich et al. 2020) supports the sharing, use and sustainability of digital language resources and tools for research in the social sciences and humanities. It is established in the form of a networked federation of centres (Wittenburg et al. 2010), consisting of language data repositories, service centres and knowledge centres, with single sign-on access for all members of the academic community in all participating countries.

As part of the technical interoperability specifications, CLARIN data repositories are required to expose their metadata records to the Virtual Language Observatory[18] using OAI-PMH. With regard to metadata interoperability, CLARIN has designed

---

[16] https://www.openarchives.org/pmh/

[17] http://www.openarchives.org/rs/1.1/resourcesync

[18] https://vlo.clarin.eu

and implemented the Component MetaData Infrastructure (CMDI)[19], a framework for the description and reuse of metadata "components" (semantic groups of elements) which can be combined to build "profiles", i. e., metadata templates for specific resource types by specific communities or groups (Broeder et al. 2008, 2012). Both are stored and shared through a dedicated registry, with metadata records being shared in the form of XML files compatible with one of these profiles.

The ELG platform implements an OAI-PMH client for harvesting metadata from external repositories which expose their metadata via OAI-PMH. The process of harvesting requires the registration of a third-party provider as an "OAI-PMH Provider" in the ELG catalogue. As soon as communication is established, the third-party provider shares their OAI-PMH endpoint, which ELG will call at regular intervals (currently once a week) in order to harvest the metadata the external repository exposes. Thus, for linking with the CLARIN infrastructure, the OAI-PMH harvesting protocol is the ideal candidate.

The metadata schema is a crucial parameter to be taken into account in the harvesting process. The ELG harvester accepts metadata records compliant with the minimal version of the ELG metadata schema (see Section 5 in Chapter 2). LINDAT/CLARIAH-CZ[20], the Czech CLARIN national node, does indeed expose its metadata records described using the META-SHARE minimal schema through its OAI-PMH endpoint (Gavrilidou et al. 2012). The fact that the ELG schema (Labropoulou et al. 2020) builds upon META-SHARE proved valuable in the conversion process of the original LINDAT/CLARIAH-CZ metadata into the ELG schema (see Chapter 8, Section 4, p. 157 ff., for more technical details).

CLARIN-DSpace, the repository software[21] (forked from DSpace[22]) developed mainly by the LINDAT/CLARIAH-CZ team, is used by several CLARIN centres for their repositories (Straňák et al. 2019). After pulling the latest changes, these repositories are ready-to-import into ELG using the same harvesting mechanism and procedure. At the time of writing, the mechanism described above is also used for harvesting CLARIN-PL[23] and CLARIN-SI[24].

The same harvesting approach was followed for the harvesting of metadata records from the ELRC-SHARE repository, which is used for the storage of and access to language resources collected through the European Language Resource Coordination[25] initiative (Lösch et al. 2018) and for feeding the CEF Automated Translation (CEF.AT) platform.[26] ELRC-SHARE (Piperidis et al. 2018) uses a metadata schema based on the META-SHARE schema tuned to text resources for Machine

---

[19] https://www.clarin.eu/content/component-metadata

[20] https://lindat.mff.cuni.cz

[21] https://github.com/ufal/clarin-dspace

[22] https://duraspace.org/dspace/

[23] https://clarin-pl.eu/dspace/

[24] https://www.clarin.si/repository/xmlui/?locale-attribute=en

[25] https://lr-coordination.eu

[26] https://ec.europa.eu/cefdigital/wiki/display/CEFDIGITAL/eTranslation

Translation purposes. Again, the mapping of the metadata records from the original schema to ELG was undertaken by the two teams.

3.2 Use Case 2: Custom API and Proprietary Schema (Hugging Face)

A different procedure is used for catalogues that expose metadata records through custom APIs and proprietary metadata schemas. This procedure is used only for catalogues that are of high interest to the ELG objectives. The Hugging Face catalogue (Wolf et al. 2020) is such a case. It is a large collection of machine learning models and datasets that can be used for training models, with a focus on the Transformer architecture. Since 2021 ELG and Hugging Face have been collaborating with the goal of importing metadata records from the Hugging Face catalogue into ELG.

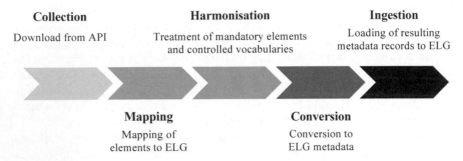

Collection

Download from API

Harmonisation

Treatment of mandatory elements
and controlled vocabularies

Ingestion

Loading of resulting
metadata records to ELG

Mapping

Mapping of
elements to ELG

Conversion

Conversion to
ELG metadata

Fig. 1 Workflow for the import of metadata records from Hugging Face to ELG

One of the goals of Hugging Face is to enable its users to upload datasets and models following a set of specifications so that they can be deployed for testing and building other models or integrating models in their applications. Although they encourage users to add descriptions for the resources, this is not enforced. Furthermore, the suggested metadata elements do not follow a standard schema. Users are asked to upload a "card" for datasets[27] or models[28], with a combination of free text fields and a set of tags (e. g., language, licence) with values from recommended controlled vocabularies, which are, however, not strictly validated.

Hugging Face exposes two APIs with JSON files for datasets and models respectively. These JSON files include a subset of the metadata elements displayed in their catalogue, however, not all records have values for all of the elements. Since importing into ELG presupposes that the metadata records comply with the ELG metadata schema, which means that at least the mandatory elements of the minimal version (see Section 5 in Chapter 2) are filled in, the conversion and import of records from Hugging Face into ELG has so far been limited to datasets with at least the de-

---

[27] https://huggingface.co/docs/datasets/dataset_card.html

[28] https://huggingface.co/docs/hub/model-repos

scription, language and licence elements filled in as these are deemed the minimum threshold for findability and usability purposes in the context of ELG.

A conversion process has been set up based on the mapping of the elements and, in the case of controlled vocabularies, their values. Further enrichment of the resulting records has been performed for specific elements. The most prominent case was that of the licencing information, since ELG requires, besides its name, a URL with the text of the licence. Hugging Face includes a list of licence identifiers taken from the SPDX list[29] (which are also used in ELG), but it allows users as well to add a licence name without further information. Thus, in addition to the mappings of the licence identifiers from Hugging Face into the ones used in ELG, we looked for the licence URL of unmapped values; if no URL was found, the resource was not imported into ELG. Finally, where required, default values have been used for mandatory elements whose values could not be inferred from the original metadata records (e. g., all datasets have been assigned the text value for media type). Figure 1 shows the workflow that was followed in this process.

3.3 Use Case 3: General Catalogues and Standard Schemas (Zenodo)

Catalogues with heterogeneous resources from multiple sources and disciplines present various challenges. We use Zenodo[30] to discuss these challenges.

Zenodo[31] is a repository for storing and sharing EC-funded research results to support Open Science established and run by CERN, which was created in response to the European Commission's (EC) assignment to the OpenAIRE project.[32]. Since its launch, Zenodo has grown steadily and is currently used for the publication of all types of resources beyond EC-funded ones by research communities and individuals. The constant update of the Zenodo catalogue and its uptake by researchers for the upload of datasets, and, more recently, software, makes it particularly interesting for ELG purposes. The size and increasing number, however, of catalogue contents makes the selection of resources very challenging. During the first phase of the ELG project, we used a manual process for the identification of resources, which is described in Chapter 8. This process, though, does not allow for regular updates and has been abandoned in favour of an automatic process.

---

[29] https://spdx.org/licenses/

[30] https://zenodo.org

[31] https://about.zenodo.org

[32] https://www.openaire.eu

Zenodo exposes its metadata records through two channels: a REST API[33], which outputs records as JSON files, and an OAI-PMH API[34] in a set of standard metadata formats, i. e., DC[35], DataCite[36], MARC21[37] and DCAT[38].

With regard to the ELG import mechanism, our preferred solution is OAI-PMH, a standard protocol for interoperability and exchange of metadata records, which includes a mechanism for regular harvesting. However, the Zenodo OAI-PMH endpoint does not allow the selection based on resource types, which would allow us to focus on "datasets" and "software". The only option is to download the whole set of metadata records in order to subsequently filter them. Furthermore, harvesting from the OAI-PMH endpoint is rate limited, hence not appropriate for large numbers of metadata records. We have, therefore, resorted to a combined solution:

- We downloaded a full dump of 2,060,674 metadata records included in Zenodo up until 31 August 2021. This dump, which is available from Zenodo, contains all records in JSON format, was filtered according to resource-type.
- For records added to Zenodo after this date, we are incrementally harvesting from the OAI-PMH endpoint. Through this channel, a set of additional 147,621 records has been harvested in a three-month period.

The next step is that of identifying the candidate resources for ELG. From the 2,208,295 metadata records available up until 31 December 2021, those of resource type "dataset" and "software" amount to 592,509 entries. This number is rather high, and since the majority of these records are of little or no interest to ELG users[39], we are experimenting with automated filtering methods to identify the records of interest.

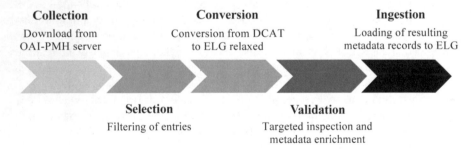

Collection	**Conversion**	**Ingestion**
Download from OAI-PMH server	Conversion from DCAT to ELG relaxed	Loading of resulting metadata records to ELG

Selection	**Validation**
Filtering of entries	Targeted inspection and metadata enrichment

Fig. 2 Workflow for the import of metadata records from Zenodo to ELG

---

[33] https://developers.zenodo.org/#rest-api

[34] https://developers.zenodo.org/#oai-pmh

[35] https://www.dublincore.org/specifications/dublin-core/dcmi-terms/

[36] https://schema.datacite.org/meta/kernel-4.4/

[37] https://www.loc.gov/marc/bibliographic/

[38] https://www.w3.org/TR/vocab-dcat-3/

[39] As a comparison, the ELG catalogue has approx. 13,000 metadata records at the time of writing.

The conversion of the metadata records is based on the DCAT metadata schema (Albertoni et al. 2022), which is in widespread use. We expect that mapping DCAT to ELG will enable the re-use of these converters as a base for import from other repositories. Moreover, DCAT is the schema with the richest information among the ones exposed from Zenodo, and the only one that includes a direct link to the downloadable files ("downloadURL" element), an important feature for ELG consumers.

Mapping from DCAT is, however, not straightforward. DCAT is an RDF vocabulary, and restrictions and extensions are implemented in the form of profiles and applications. The OAI-PMH endpoint makes the metadata records available in XML format; the XSD schema used by Zenodo is not publicly available[40]. A closer inspection of the XML files has revealed discrepancies in the representation of some elements. For instance, "subject" (defined in DCAT as a SKOS[41] Concept) appears in Zenodo XML files either as a SKOS Concept or as an element with the IRI of the subject value in the form of an attribute. We have analysed the Zenodo XML files, to the extent possible, and based our mapping on this analysis. We also had to apply some modifications in the ELG schema so that we could take into account the DCAT features (Section 4.1). Finally, a converter for the elements in the JSON files offered through the REST API for the first batch of files has also been implemented.

As a result of this endeavour, the procedure for regular updates from Zenodo is foreseen as a workflow integrating the following steps: harvesting from the Zenodo endpoint, offline filtering and conversion of the metadata records, possibly with some manual targeted inspection, and import into ELG (Figure 2).

3.4 Use Case 4: Collaborative Community Initiatives (ELE, ELG)

We also populated the ELG catalogue using bulk lists of metadata records, potentially containing limited information, that serve as seeds for further enrichment. We present here two such cases, one set of resources collected collaboratively in ELE and a second set collected by the ELG consortium.

The European Language Equality (ELE) project (Rehm and Way 2023)[42], which collaborates with ELG to promote digital language equality in Europe, launched a project-internal initiative in 2021 to collect as many LRTs as possible available for the languages under investigation by the project.[43] Operationally, a web form was set up, which included a subset of the mandatory metadata elements of the ELG schema. Given the size and breadth of this activity (dozens of respondents throughout Europe for approx. 80 official, regional, minority languages), we considered requiring every informant to fill in even the minimal version of the metadata schema for every single resource identified too demanding and not pariculary realistic, perhaps

---

[40] The XSD schema included in the OAI-PMH API for DCAT is in fact that of DataCite v4.1.

[41] https://www.w3.org/2004/02/skos/

[42] https://european-language-equality.eu

[43] https://european-language-equality.eu/languages/

even negatively impacting the collection process itself, potentially resulting in fewer resources being reported by the informants if the process of registering a resource took too much time. The modifications required to accommodate this collaborative scenario resulted in a "relaxed" version of the schema (see Section 4.1).

The results of this collection process were exported in a tabular format. Before the conversion and final import of the approx. 6,500 records into ELG, a long and demanding process of curation was undertaken using semi-automatic methods. The final output was imported into ELG through various scripts (Figure 3).

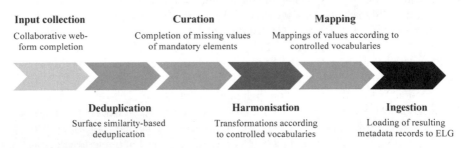

Input collection
Collaborative web-form completion

Curation
Completion of missing values of mandatory elements

Mapping
Mappings of values according to controlled vocabularies

Deduplication
Surface similarity-based deduplication

Harmonisation
Transformations according to controlled vocabularies

Ingestion
Loading of resulting metadata records to ELG

Fig. 3 Workflow for the import of ELE results to ELG

The curation process included normalising, correcting, and enriching values of elements that were absent or not used consistently. Despite the effort to control the input through prompting for the selection of values from recommended vocabularies and filling in mandatory values, web forms do not allow strict enforcement strategies, especially for cases of long lists of values or multiple values. For example, although a set of "language" values was offered for selection in the form, the informants could also add other values, which resulted in values with alternative, unofficial or simply unusual names. Therefore, language information had to be normalised and mapped to the ISO 639 language codes, as required by ELG. Although the tabular format presents some advantages, given its simplicity and users' familiarity, it still poses a number of challenges for validation purposes, especially for elements with patterns, or with multiple values. For instance, the "email" element was filled in with free text values, URL links, etc., since no validation pattern was used for the element. For elements with multiple values, such as languages, functions, etc., different delimiters were used in between values and had to be normalised. Moreover, nested information cannot be represented in a flat form; for example, the values of language and region (where the language is spoken) were split in two complementary columns so that controlled vocabularies could be used, but there can be no guarantee that both columns are consistently filled in. For these cases, we had to check and ensure that the same number of values was consistently used across the two complementary columns and, moreover, that the values were matched correctly.

In a similar collaborative population setting, the catalogue was populated with European organisations that develop or use LTs or LRs, which were collected by the ELG team and the National Competence Centres (NCCs; see Chapter 11 for more details), thus enabling ELG to quickly become the "yellow pages" of organisations active in the broader LT community. As described in more detail in Chapter 9, lists of organisations from various sources have been merged, together with information on list items – mainly contact data and key terms describing their LT-related activities. The resulting enriched list, divided into sub-lists by country, was checked again by the respective NCCs, and, after checking the consistency, more than 1,700 records were converted into the ELG-compatible XML format and imported into ELG. At the time of writing, a similar procedure is being followed for LT-related R&D projects and their funding agencies.

3.5 Summary of Use Cases

Table 1 summarises the technical and the metadata conditions in each of the use cases presented in this section and the ways these are catered for in ELG. Depending on the export functionalities offered by the source, the ELG platform can establish a connection at regular intervals and benefit from continuous updates. Table 1 also shows the ELG metadata schema version that can be used, depending on the source metadata schema, as well as the quantity and information richness of metadata records.

Repository	Export Functionality	Metadata Schema	ELG Schema Version	Update Frequency
CLARIN nodes	OAI-PMH	META-SHARE	minimal	regular
ELRC-SHARE	OAI-PMH	ELRC-SHARE	minimal	regular
Hugging Face	REST API	Proprietary (JSON)	relaxed	one-off
Zenodo	REST API	Proprietary (JSON)	relaxed	one-off
Zenodo	OAI-PMH	DCAT (XML)	relaxed	regular
ELE survey	–	Subset of ELG schema	relaxed	one-off
ELG collection	–	Subset of ELG schema	relaxed	one-off

Table 1 Overview of use cases

4 Implementing Metadata Interoperability

Primarily motivated by our various interoperability use cases, some of which are described in Section 3, we modified the ELG platform import procedures and policies, especially with regard to the metadata schema and the publication life cycle (described in Chapter 2), so that they are able to handle the different interoperability scenarios. These adaptations are not restricted to the requirements of the use cases but lay the foundational principles for accommodating a broader range of metadata import scenarios.

4.1 ELG Metadata Schema – Relaxed Version

The "relaxed" version of the ELG metadata schema aims to accommodate mismatches between the ELG schema and schemas used for metadata records that are automatically imported into the ELG catalogue, especially those from catalogues with limited information or catalogues populated with metadata records of interest to a broader range of communities (e. g., Zenodo, EOSC, etc.) and, thus, using more general schemas, e. g., DCAT (Albertoni et al. 2022) or DataCite[44] (DataCite Metadata Working Group 2021). This version of the schema features additional alternative elements for mandatory metadata elements that may be missing from the source records or that have different data types.

The first case refers to two elements that are deemed important for ELG purposes: "media type" and "licence".

- The element "media type part" is crucial for ELG, as it is used for attaching important metadata properties, such as language, format, size, etc. Even in cases where these are included in source records, they may come with *different* classification vocabularies and semantics and, therefore, cannot be imported into ELG. For these cases, the additional alternative value "unspecified media part" can be used.
- The element "licence" is crucial for re-usability purposes; for a licence, both a name and a URL hyperlink to the respective legal document are required. However, in many cases, such as legacy resources, or records in catalogues allowing free text as the value of "licence", the name and URL cannot be determined automatically. This is why we introduced the "access rights" element that takes a free text value as an alternative to "licence", specifying the rights of access and use at a higher level of abstraction.

The second case groups together elements which take a value from controlled vocabularies in ELG, while in other schemas they have a free text value (e. g., "service function", "size unit", etc.) and combined elements that cannot be distinguished from the source metadata record (e. g., when size is encoded as free text combining amount and size unit together). To address the first case, we modified the data type of the element so that it takes a value from a recommended vocabulary or free text entered by the user; to address the second case, we introduced a new element that takes free text as a value (e. g., "sizeText" can be used as an alternative to the combination of "amount" and "size unit").

4.2 Publication Policies for Imported Metadata Records

ELG rates the quality of the metadata records highly. High quality metadata contributes to the discovery and usage of the resources themselves. A standardised pub-

---

[44] https://schema.datacite.org

lication life cycle has been established in ELG for metadata records (see Chapter 2, Section 6, 24 ff.). However, the same level of quality cannot be enforced across all metadata records. This is also taken into account in the publication policies. Thus, while metadata records registered by individuals go through a validation process, for records automatically imported from other catalogues the same manual validation processes cannot be set up in a feasible way, i. e., the quality and extent, in terms of information, of external metadata records remains under the responsibility of the respective source catalogue. Depending on the harvesting process and source catalogue, a three-level classification of metadata records is used:

- *Metadata records harvested automatically from collaborating catalogues (CLARIN nodes, ELRC-SHARE)*, which have similar metadata requirements as ELG. These records are added by individuals, the resource is stored in the repository. This is why these metadata records are considered trustworthy, and the records are published in the ELG catalogue as is, i. e., without any human validation.
- *Metadata records automatically imported from catalogues with "lighter" metadata requirements (Hugging Face, Zenodo)* have originally been added to the source catalogue by individuals together with the physical resource. The metadata record and resource is considered trustworthy but it may lack information which is important for ELG purposes, and thus marked as "for information" to indicate to ELG users that important information may be missing.
- *Metadata records that resulted from bulk collection initiatives (ELE collection, ELG collection)* are often incomplete, i. e., only a subset of the required information was collected and converted to the ELG schema. These records adhere to the relaxed ELG schema, the physical resource may be stored anywhere online. These records do not undergo the validation process, they are marked and can be claimed for further enrichment by their rightful owners (see Chapter 9, Section 3.3, p. 179). When a user claims a metadata record, the technical ELG team is notified and can approve or reject the claim, taking into account the professional email account of the user; if the claim is approved, the metadata record is unpublished and assigned to the user for further editing. Once the user finishes the editing, the record is submitted for publication and goes through the normal publication procedure. Users are notified about the claim procedure of these metadata records via e-mail.

5 Interoperability across Repositories

The interoperability across multiple repositories and platforms is of utmost importance in a broader, federated environment of data and services, as envisaged in initiatives like EOSC (European Open Science Cloud, see, e. g., Corcho et al. 2021), NFDI, Gaia-X or the European Commission's Data Spaces and in accordance with the FAIR principles (Wilkinson et al. 2016), see Section 2. In the following, we discuss some of the open issues that need to be addressed in order to achieve this based on the endeavours presented in this chapter.

5.1 Technical Interoperability across Repositories

The first prerequisite for the sharing of metadata records and the construction of a common master inventory based on the contents of all participating repositories is that of exchange services. The OAI-PMH protocol, despite its limitation to the exchange of metadata, constitutes the most widespread and hence usually preferred option. REST services are becoming more popular, but they are not yet standardised and thus require customised solutions. Rehm et al. (2020a) explore technical and semantic interoperability in more detail.

5.2 Semantic Interoperability across Repositories

The use of shared vocabularies for the documentation of resources is the next necessary step towards interoperability. The standardisation and documentation of metadata schemas is a requirement that many initiatives have articulated (Hugo et al. 2020; Behnke et al. 2021). While certain metadata vocabularies, such as DC[45], DCAT, schema.org[46] and DataCite, have become de facto standards, these are general schemas that can be used to express core metadata elements required for the description of any type of digital resource. This, however, competes with the much more fine-grained documentation needs of specific communities and more detailed requirements set to achieve machine actionability. For example, "resource type" is an element that poses problems for all catalogues: in contrast to the general vocabularies (e. g., COAR resource type vocabulary[47], a limited set of values from DC[48], Zenodo[49]), communities prefer finer distinctions (cf. the values of "resource type" in the CLARIN VLO[50]). This creates a burden when moving from general to specialised catalogues (e. g., from Zenodo to ELG).

Bridges and mappers between vocabularies are developed, especially between the popular schemas.[51] Yet this is not a scalable approach, as for each new vocabulary a new mapper has to be built. Instead, a "shared semantic space" is needed as a joint, ontologically grounded and machine-readable vocabulary, into which all concepts and terminologies can be mapped (Rehm et al. 2020a). This space can be envisaged as a reference model able to represent all crucial information typically contained in the respective metadata schema. However, a single RDF/OWL ontology covering general and domain or community-specific semantic categories is an almost impossible task to achieve (Labropoulou et al. 2018). An alternative could be a Linked

---

[45] https://www.dublincore.org/specifications/dublin-core/dcmi-terms/

[46] https://schema.org

[47] https://vocabularies.coar-repositories.org/resource_types/

[48] https://www.dublincore.org/specifications/dublin-core/resource-typelist/

[49] https://developers.zenodo.org/#representation

[50] https://vlo.clarin.eu

[51] For the mapping of metadata schemas in the wider LT ecosystem, see McCrae et al. (2015b,a).

Data approach[52], in which different communities maintain their independent formal models and vocabularies and subsequently refer to reference vocabularies or concepts developed in a distributed fashion by the broader community. As an example of such an approach, a collaboration was initiated between ELG and the AI4EU project on the mapping of the ontologies used in the two platforms. This work is continued under the umbrella of the AI Ontology Working Group which includes members from the European AI on Demand Platform and collaborating projects.[53]

Even in this scenario, though, an important issue to be addressed is that of the appropriate semantic relations. Equivalence relations are not always one-to-one and also need to take into account the type of elements. Additionally, there are an abundance of similar vocabularies recommended by different communities or serving different documentation needs. For example, in terms of "language", a value taken from ISO 639[54] may suffice for general catalogues. But for the metadata of resources in language-related catalogues, such as ELG, a more detailed value space is required, that takes into account dialects and other varieties, and these are not included in ISO 639 (Gillis-Webber and Tittel 2019). In ELG we use the BCP 47 recommendation (Phillips and Davis 2009) alongside values taken from the Glottolog[55] vocabulary (Hammarström et al. 2021) so that we can exploit the finer distinctions made in it for language varieties. The fact that Glottolog includes a mapping to ISO 639-3 values, when these exist, facilitates this endeavour and the exchange of metadata records with catalogues that prefer using ISO 639.

5.3 Minimal Metadata Requirements

The different purposes served by the catalogues have an impact on the exchange of metadata records, too. For example, Zenodo is used for the publication of research outcomes by many different organisations and individuals. The fact that there is a very small set of mandatory elements as well as the fact that providers do not have a strong incentive to make their resources findable lowers the quality of the metadata descriptions. In a similar way, individuals that add their resources to the Hugging Face catalogue are mostly interested in testing their dataset and do not pay attention to its description. Many metadata elements that are important for ELG purposes, such as "language", are simply not included in the formal descriptions of these records. Often, even free text descriptions are of very low quality and cannot be used for discovery purposes. There is, therefore, a strong need for training resource owners on the importance of metadata together with the continuous curation by experts (Gordon and Habermann 2019). The "claim" procedure adopted in ELG is a step along these lines. Semi-automatic methods for enriching metadata records by extracting

---

[52] https://www.w3.org/DesignIssues/LinkedData.html

[53] https://www.ai4europe.eu/ai-community/working-groups-d/ontology

[54] https://www.iso.org/iso-639-language-codes.html

[55] https://glottolog.org

information from the datasets themselves, as well as other sources, will also play an important role in ensuring that minimal documentation requirements are met.

5.4 Duplicate Resources

Looking at the resources themselves, the exchange of metadata records across catalogues comes with the risk of creating duplicates and near-duplicates. The same resource may appear with slightly different names in catalogues and similar descriptions, while the same name is often used for subsets of the resource. The use of persistent identifiers (PIDs) has been proposed to address this, but it cannot be guaranteed that persistent identifiers are indeed unique. Explicit relations between similar resources (subsets, raw or annotated versions, versions and updates, etc.) must be formally recorded in the metadata so that they can be used for deduplication purposes. Establishing relations between the metadata records of the same resource in different catalogues should also be recorded.

6 Conclusions

In this chapter we have focused on the sharing of metadata between catalogues. This is only the basis for what is going to be the next level of sharing data and software which is the ultimate goal. This involves not only a shared semantic space to anchor and cross-link metadata vocabularies but also technical compatibility and cooperation. ELG has closely collaborated with other platforms to explore platform interoperability at various levels (Rehm et al. 2020a). Experiments were conducted with AI4EU[56], SPEAKER[57] and QURATOR[58] for the creation of cross-platform workflows, where data and services were accessed from one platform and either transferred to another platform or used for building a pipeline or workflow of different processing services in another platform. Our initial experiments, explored further by Moreno-Schneider et al. (2022), demonstrate that interoperability can be partially achieved, with a certain degree of manual and automatic interventions.

Finally, we should also mention an alternative that can be used for sharing resources and their documentations across platforms and communities. This consists of supporting cross-platform search through making search and discovery APIs used by a platform available to third parties so that they can integrate them in their own search space (Rehm et al. 2020a). This way, a single query would return matches from multiple platforms whose publicly available search APIs are integrated in the platform queried by the user. In this case, search results would show only a minimal

---

[56] https://www.ai4europe.eu

[57] https://www.speaker.fraunhofer.de

[58] https://qurator.ai

set of metadata redirecting the user to the platform that offers the respective resource. Again, a shared common space is required but only for a limited set of metadata – a similar situation to the general catalogues presented above, but only for a small subset. However, this option presents a scalability problem as soon as the number of collaborating platforms and respective search APIs grows.

Decentralised infrastructures such as Gaia-X, in which individual trusted platforms follow a common standard (i. e., the Gaia-X federation services) and become a networked system freely sharing and exchanging data and services across multiple actors, offer a viable solution addressing this challenge. OpenGPT-X[59] is a German national project in which large language models are currently being developed, especially for German but also for English and other European languages. In this project, which has started in January 2022, we will have the chance to implement the emerging Gaia-X specifications in the ELG platform so that it joins this emerging ecosystem.

References

Abramatic, Jean-François, Jan Hrušák, and Sarah Jones, eds. (2021). *European Open Science Cloud (EOSC) Executive Board: Final Progress Report*. Publications Office. DOI: 10.2777/46019.

Albertoni, Riccardo, David Browning, Simon Cox, Alejandra Gonzalez-Beltran, Andrea Perego, and Peter Winstanley, eds. (2022). *Data Catalog Vocabulary (DCAT) – Version 3*. W3C Working Draft. URL: https://www.w3.org/TR/vocab-dcat-3/.

Alemu, Getaneh, Brett Stevens, and Penny Ross (2012). "Towards a conceptual framework for user-driven semantic metadata interoperability in digital libraries: a social constructivist approach". In: *New Library World* 113.1/2, p. 15.

Behnke, Claudia, Kees Burger, Yann le Franc, Wim Hugo, Pekka Järveläinen, Jessica Parland-von Essen, and Gerard Coen (2021). "D2.6 First reference implementation of the data repositories features". In: DOI: 10.5281/zenodo.5362027. URL: https://zenodo.org/record/5362027/export /hx.

Benjelloun, Omar, Shiyu Chen, and Natasha Noy (2020). "Google Dataset Search by the Numbers". In: *The Semantic Web (ISWC 2020) – 19th International Semantic Web Conference*. Ed. by Jeff Z. Pan, Valentina A. M. Tamma, Claudia d'Amato, Krzysztof Janowicz, Bo Fu, Axel Polleres, Oshani Seneviratne, and Lalana Kagal. Vol. 12507. Lecture Notes in Computer Science. Athens, Greece: Springer, pp. 667–682. DOI: 10.1007/978-3-030-62466-8_41. URL: https://doi.org/1 0.1007/978-3-030-62466-8_41.

Broeder, Daan, Thierry Declerck, Erhard Hinrichs, Stelios Piperidis, Laurent Romary, Nicoletta Calzolari, and Peter Wittenburg (2008). "Foundation of a Component-based Flexible Registry for Language Resources and Technology". In: *Proceedings of the Sixth International Conference on Language Resources and Evaluation (LREC 2008)*. Marrakech, Morocco: ELRA. URL: http://www.lrec-conf.org/proceedings/lrec2008/pdf/364_paper.pdf.

Broeder, Daan, Thorsten Trippel, Emiliano Degl'Innocenti, Roberta Giacomi, Maurizio Sanesi, Mari Kleemola, Katja Moilanen, Henri Ala-Lahti, Caspar Jordan, Iris Alfredsson, Hervé L'Hours, and Matej Ďurčo (2019). "SSHOC D3.1 Report on SSHOC (meta)data interoperability problems". In: DOI: 10.5281/ZENODO.3569868. URL: https://zenodo.org/record/3569868.

Broeder, Daan, Dieter van Uytvanck, Maria Gavrilidou, Thorsten Trippel, and Menzo Windhouwer (2012). "Standardizing a Component Metadata Infrastructure". In: *Proceedings of the Eighth In-*

---

[59] https://opengpt-x.de

ternational Conference on Language Resources and Evaluation (LREC 2012). Istanbul, Turkey: ELRA, pp. 1387–1390. URL: http://www.lrec-conf.org/proceedings/lrec2012/pdf/581_Paper .pdf.

Calzolari, Nicoletta, Valeria Quochi, and Claudia Soria, eds. (2011). *The Strategic Language Resource Agenda*. URL: https://www.academia.edu/1651334/The_Strategic_Language_Resourc e_Agenda.

Chan, Lois Mai and Marcia Lei Zeng (2006). "Metadata Interoperability and Standardization – A Study of Methodology Part I: Achieving Interoperability at the Schema Level". In: *D-Lib Magazine* 12.6. DOI: 10.1045/june2006-chan. URL: http://www.dlib.org/dlib/june06/chan/06 chan.html.

Corcho, Oscar, Magnus Eriksson, Krzysztof Kurowski, Milan Ojsteršek, Christine Choirat, Mark van de Sanden, Frederik Coppens, and European Commission, Directorate-General for Research and Innovation (2021). *EOSC Interoperability Framework: Report from the EOSC Executive Board Working Groups FAIR and Architecture*. Publications Office. DOI: 10.2777/620649. URL: https://data.europa.eu/doi/10.2777/620649.

DataCite Metadata Working Group (2021). "DataCite Metadata Schema Documentation for the Publication and Citation of Research Data and Other Research Outputs v4.4". In: DOI: 10.144 54/3W3Z-SA82. URL: https://schema.datacite.org/meta/kernel-4.4/.

ELRC (2019). *ELRC White Paper: Sustainable Language Data Sharing to Support Language Equality in Multilingual Europe*. Second online edition. URL: https://lr-coordination.eu/sit es/default/files/Documents/ELRCWhitePaper.pdf.

Eskevich, Maria, Franciska de Jong, Alexander König, Darja Fišer, Dieter Van Uytvanck, Tero Aalto, Lars Borin, Olga Gerassimenko, Jan Hajic, Henk van den Heuvel, Neeme Kahusk, Krista Liin, Martin Matthiesen, Stelios Piperidis, and Kadri Vider (2020). "CLARIN: Distributed Language Resources and Technology in a European Infrastructure". In: *Proc. of the 1st Int. Workshop on Language Technology Platforms (IWLTP 2020, co-located with LREC 2020)*. Ed. by Georg Rehm, Kalina Bontcheva, Khalid Choukri, Jan Hajic, Stelios Piperidis, and Andrejs Vasiljevs. Marseille, France: ELRA, pp. 28–34. URL: https://aclanthology.org/2020.iwltp-1.5.

European Commission (2022). *European Research Area policy agenda: overview of actions for the period 2022–2024*. Publications Office. DOI: 10.2777/52110. URL: https://data.europa.eu/doi /10.2777/52110.

European Parliament (2018). *Language Equality in the Digital Age. European Parliament resolution of 11 September 2018 on Language Equality in the Digital Age (2018/2028(INI)*. URL: http://www.europarl.europa.eu/doceo/document/TA-8-2018-0332_EN.pdf.

Gavrilidou, Maria, Penny Labropoulou, Elina Desipri, Stelios Piperidis, Haris Papageorgiou, Monica Monachini, Francesca Frontini, Thierry Declerck, Gil Francopoulo, Victoria Arranz, and Valerie Mapelli (2012). "The META-SHARE Metadata Schema for the Description of Language Resources". In: *Proceedings of the Eighth International Conference on Language Resources and Evaluation (LREC 2012)*. Istanbul, Turkey: ELRA, pp. 1090–1097. URL: http://www.lrec -conf.org/proceedings/lrec2012/pdf/998_Paper.pdf.

Giagkou, Maria, Stelios Piperidis, Georg Rehm, and Jane Dunne, eds. (2022). *Language Technology Support of Europe's Languages in 2020/2021*. Various project deliverables (language reports); EU project European Language Equality (ELE); Grant Agreement no. LC-01641480 – 101018166 ELE. European Language Equality Project. URL: https://european-language-equal ity.eu/deliverables/.

Gillis-Webber, Frances and Sabine Tittel (2019). "The Shortcomings of Language Tags for Linked Data When Modeling Lesser-Known Languages". In: *2nd Conference on Language, Data and Knowledge (LDK 2019)*. Ed. by Maria Eskevich, Gerard de Melo, Christian Fäth, John P. McCrae, Paul Buitelaar, Christian Chiarcos, Bettina Klimek, and Milan Dojchinovski. Vol. 70. OpenAccess Series in Informatics (OASIcs). Dagstuhl, Germany: Schloss Dagstuhl–Leibniz-Zentrum fuer Informatik, 4:1–4:15. DOI: 10.4230/OASIcs.LDK.2019.4. URL: http://drops.da gstuhl.de/opus/volltexte/2019/10368.

Gordon, Sean and Ted Habermann (2019). *Visualizing The Evolution of Metadata*. Version Number: v0.0.1. DOI: 10.5281/zenodo.2538983. URL: https://doi.org/10.5281/zenodo.2538983.

Hammarström, Harald, Robert Forkel, Martin Haspelmath, and Sebastian Bank (2021). *Glottolog database 4.5*. Version Number: v4.5, Type: dataset. Leipzig, Germany: Max Planck Institute for Evolutionary Anthropology. DOI: 10.5281/ZENODO.5772642. URL: https://zenodo.org/recor d/5772642.

Haslhofer, Bernhard and Wolfgang Klas (2010). "A survey of techniques for achieving metadata interoperability". In: *ACM Computing Surveys* 42.2, pp. 1–37. DOI: 10.1145/1667062.1667064. URL: https://dl.acm.org/doi/10.1145/1667062.1667064.

Hinrichs, Erhard and Steven Krauwer (2014). "The CLARIN Research Infrastructure: Resources and Tools for eHumanities Scholars". In: *Proceedings of the Ninth International Conference on Language Resources and Evaluation (LREC 2014)*. Reykjavik, Iceland: ELRA, pp. 1525–1531. URL: http://www.lrec-conf.org/proceedings/lrec2014/pdf/415_Paper.pdf.

Hugo, Wim, Yann Le Franc, Gerard Coen, Jessica Parland-von Essen, and Luiz Bonino (2020). "D2.5 FAIR Semantics Recommendations Second Iteration". In: DOI: 10.5281/zenodo.536201 0. URL: https://zenodo.org/record/5362010.

Kornai, Andras (2013). "Digital Language Death". In: *PLoS ONE* 8.10. DOI: 10.1371/journal.pon e.0077056. URL: https://doi.org/10.1371/journal.pone.0077056.

Labropoulou, Penny, Dimitris Galanis, Antonis Lempesis, Mark Greenwood, Petr Knoth, Richard Eckart de Castilho, Stavros Sachtouris, Byron Georgantopoulos, Stefania Martziou, Lucas Anastasiou, Katerina Gkirtzou, Natalia Manola, and Stelios Piperidis (2018). "OpenMinTeD: A Platform Facilitating Text Mining of Scholarly Content". In: *Proceedings of WOSP 2018 (co-located with LREC 2018)*. Miyazaki, Japan: ELRA, pp. 7–12. URL: http://lrec-conf.org/works hops/lrec2018/W24/pdf/13_W24.pdf.

Labropoulou, Penny, Katerina Gkirtzou, Maria Gavriilidou, Miltos Deligiannis, Dimitris Galanis, Stelios Piperidis, Georg Rehm, Maria Berger, Valérie Mapelli, Michael Rigault, Victoria Arranz, Khalid Choukri, Gerhard Backfried, José Manuel Gómez Pérez, and Andres Garcia-Silva (2020). "Making Metadata Fit for Next Generation Language Technology Platforms: The Metadata Schema of the European Language Grid". In: *Proceedings of the 12th Language Resources and Evaluation Conference (LREC 2020)*. Ed. by Nicoletta Calzolari, Frédéric Béchet, Philippe Blache, Christopher Cieri, Khalid Choukri, Thierry Declerck, Hitoshi Isahara, Bente Maegaard, Joseph Mariani, Asuncion Moreno, Jan Odijk, and Stelios Piperidis. Marseille, France: ELRA, pp. 3421–3430. URL: https://www.aclweb.org/anthology/2020.lrec-1.420/.

Lösch, Andrea, Valérie Mapelli, Stelios Piperidis, Andrejs Vasiļjevs, Lilli Smal, Thierry Declerck, Eileen Schnur, Khalid Choukri, and Josef van Genabith (2018). "European Language Resource Coordination: Collecting Language Resources for Public Sector Multilingual Information Management". In: *Proc. of the Eleventh International Conference on Language Resources and Evaluation (LREC 2018)*. Miyazaki, Japan: ELRA. URL: https://aclanthology.org/L18-1213.

McCrae, John Philip, Philipp Cimiano, Victor Rodriguez-Doncel, Daniel Vila Suero, Jorge Gracia, Luca Matteis, Roberto Navigli, Andrejs Abele, Gabriela Vulcu, and Paul Buitelaar (2015a). "Reconciling Heterogeneous Descriptions of Language Resources". In: *Proceedings of the 4th Workshop on Linked Data in Linguistics: Resources and Applications*. Beijing, China: ACL, pp. 39–48. DOI: 10.18653/v1/W15-4205. URL: http://aclweb.org/anthology/W15-4205.

McCrae, John Philip, Penny Labropoulou, Jorge Gracia, Marta Villegas, Víctor Rodríguez-Doncel, and Philipp Cimiano (2015b). "One Ontology to Bind Them All: The META-SHARE OWL Ontology for the Interoperability of Linguistic Datasets on the Web". In: *The Semantic Web: ESWC 2015 Satellite Events*. Ed. by Fabien Gandon, Christophe Guéret, Serena Villata, John Breslin, Catherine Faron-Zucker, and Antoine Zimmermann. Lecture Notes in Computer Science. Springer International Publishing, pp. 271–282. URL: https://link.springer.com/chapter /10.1007/978-3-319-25639-9_42.

Moreno-Schneider, Julián, Rémi Calizzano, Florian Kintzel, Georg Rehm, Dimitris Galanis, and Ian Roberts (2022). "Towards Practical Semantic Interoperability in NLP Platforms". In: *Proceedings of the 18th Joint ACL-ISO Workshop on Interoperable Semantic Annotation (ISA 2022; co-located with LREC 2022)*. Ed. by Harry Bunt. Marseille, France, pp. 118–126. URL: http: //www.lrec-conf.org/proceedings/lrec2022/workshops/ISA-18/pdf/2022.isa18-1.16.pdf.

Phillips, Addison and Mark Davis (2009). *Tags for Identifying Languages*. Tech. rep. RFC 5646. Internet Engineering Task Force. URL: https://datatracker.ietf.org/doc/rfc5646.

Piperidis, Stelios, Penny Labropoulou, Miltos Deligiannis, and Maria Giagkou (2018). "Managing Public Sector Data for Multilingual Applications Development". In: *Proceedings of the Eleventh International Conference on Language Resources and Evaluation (LREC 2018)*. Ed. by Nicoletta Calzolari, Khalid Choukri, Christopher Cieri, Thierry Declerck, Sara Goggi, Koiti Hasida, Hitoshi Isahara, Bente Maegaard, Joseph Mariani, Hélène Mazo, Asuncion Moreno, Jan Odijk, Stelios Piperidis, and Takenobu Tokunaga. Miyazaki, Japan: ELRA. URL: http://www.lrec-conf.org/proceedings/lrec2018/pdf/648.pdf.

Rehm, Georg, Dimitrios Galanis, Penny Labropoulou, Stelios Piperidis, Martin Welß, Ricardo Usbeck, Joachim Köhler, Miltos Deligiannis, Katerina Gkirtzou, Johannes Fischer, Christian Chiarcos, Nils Feldhus, Julián Moreno-Schneider, Florian Kintzel, Elena Montiel, Víctor Rodríguez Doncel, John P. McCrae, David Laqua, Irina Patricia Theile, Christian Dittmar, Kalina Bontcheva, Ian Roberts, Andrejs Vasiljevs, and Andis Lagzdiņš (2020a). "Towards an Interoperable Ecosystem of AI and LT Platforms: A Roadmap for the Implementation of Different Levels of Interoperability". In: *Proc. of the 1st Int. Workshop on Language Technology Platforms (IWLTP 2020, co-located with LREC 2020)*. Ed. by Georg Rehm, Kalina Bontcheva, Khalid Choukri, Jan Hajic, Stelios Piperidis, and Andrejs Vasiljevs. Marseille, France, pp. 96–107. URL: https://www.aclweb.org/anthology/2020.iwltp-1.15.pdf.

Rehm, Georg, Katrin Marheinecke, Stefanie Hegele, Stelios Piperidis, Kalina Bontcheva, Jan Hajic, Khalid Choukri, Andrejs Vasiļjevs, Gerhard Backfried, Christoph Prinz, José Manuel Gómez Pérez, Luc Meertens, Paul Lukowicz, Josef van Genabith, Andrea Lösch, Philipp Slusallek, Morten Irgens, Patrick Gatellier, Joachim Köhler, Laure Le Bars, Dimitra Anastasiou, Albina Auksoriūtė, Núria Bel, António Branco, Gerhard Budin, Walter Daelemans, Koenraad De Smedt, Radovan Garabík, Maria Gavriilidou, Dagmar Gromann, Svetla Koeva, Simon Krek, Cvetana Krstev, Krister Lindén, Bernardo Magnini, Jan Odijk, Maciej Ogrodniczuk, Eiríkur Rögnvaldsson, Mike Rosner, Bolette Pedersen, Inguna Skadina, Marko Tadić, Dan Tufiş, Tamás Váradi, Kadri Vider, Andy Way, and François Yvon (2020b). "The European Language Technology Landscape in 2020: Language-Centric and Human-Centric AI for Cross-Cultural Communication in Multilingual Europe". In: *Proceedings of the 12th Language Resources and Evaluation Conference (LREC 2020)*. Ed. by Nicoletta Calzolari, Frédéric Béchet, Philippe Blache, Christopher Cieri, Khalid Choukri, Thierry Declerck, Hitoshi Isahara, Bente Maegaard, Joseph Mariani, Asuncion Moreno, Jan Odijk, and Stelios Piperidis. Marseille, France: ELRA, pp. 3315–3325. URL: https://www.aclweb.org/anthology/2020.lrec-1.407/.

Rehm, Georg and Hans Uszkoreit, eds. (2012). *META-NET White Paper Series: Europe's Languages in the Digital Age*. 32 volumes on 31 European languages. Heidelberg etc.: Springer.

Rehm, Georg, Hans Uszkoreit, Ido Dagan, Vartkes Goetcherian, Mehmet Ugur Dogan, Coskun Mermer, Tamás Váradi, Sabine Kirchmeier-Andersen, Gerhard Stickel, Meirion Prys Jones, Stefan Oeter, and Sigve Gramstad (2014). "An Update and Extension of the META-NET Study "Europe's Languages in the Digital Age"". In: *Proceedings of the Workshop on Collaboration and Computing for Under-Resourced Languages in the Linked Open Data Era (CCURL 2014)*. Ed. by Laurette Pretorius, Claudia Soria, and Paola Baroni. Reykjavik, Iceland, pp. 30–37. URL: http://georg-re.hm/pdf/CCURL-2014-META-NET.pdf.

Rehm, Georg and Andy Way, eds. (2023). *European Language Equality: A Strategic Agenda for Digital Language Equality*. Cognitive Technologies. Forthcoming. Springer.

Soria, Claudia, Núria Bel, Khalid Choukri, Joseph Mariani, Monica Monachini, Jan Odijk, Stelios Piperidis, Valeria Quochi, and Nicoletta Calzolari (2012). "The FLaReNet Strategic Language Resource Agenda". In: *Proceedings of the Eighth International Conference on Language Resources and Evaluation (LREC 2012)*. Istanbul, Turkey: ELRA, pp. 1379–1386. URL: http://www.lrec-conf.org/proceedings/lrec2012/pdf/777_Paper.pdf.

STOA (2018). *Language equality in the digital age – Towards a Human Language Project*. STOA study (PE 598.621), IP/G/STOA/FWC/2013-001/Lot4/C2. URL: https://data.europa.eu/doi/10.2861/136527.

Straňák, Pavel, Ondřej Košarko, and Jozef Mišutka (2019). "CLARIN-DSpace repository at LIN-DAT/CLARIN : LINDAT/CLARIN FAIR repository for language data". In: *The grey Journal – International Journal on Grey Literature* 16, pp. 52–61.

Wilkinson, Mark D., Michel Dumontier, IJsbrand Jan Aalbersberg, Gabrielle Appleton, Myles Axton, Arie Baak, Niklas Blomberg, Jan-Willem Boiten, Luiz Bonino da Silva Santos, Philip E. Bourne, Jildau Bouwman, Anthony J. Brookes, Tim Clark, Mercè Crosas, Ingrid Dillo, Olivier Dumon, Scott Edmunds, Chris T. Evelo, Richard Finkers, Alejandra Gonzalez-Beltran, Alasdair J.G. Gray, Paul Groth, Carole Goble, Jeffrey S. Grethe, Jaap Heringa, Peter A.C 't Hoen, Rob Hooft, Tobias Kuhn, Ruben Kok, Joost Kok, Scott J. Lusher, Maryann E. Martone, Albert Mons, Abel L. Packer, Bengt Persson, Philippe Rocca-Serra, Marco Roos, Rene van Schaik, Susanna-Assunta Sansone, Erik Schultes, Thierry Sengstag, Ted Slater, George Strawn, Morris A. Swertz, Mark Thompson, Johan van der Lei, Erik van Mulligen, Jan Velterop, Andra Waagmeester, Peter Wittenburg, Katherine Wolstencroft, Jun Zhao, and Barend Mons (2016). "The FAIR Guiding Principles for Scientific Data Management and Stewardship". In: *Scientific Data* 3. DOI: 10.1038/sdata.2016.18. URL: http://www.nature.com/articles/sdata201618.

Wittenburg, Peter, Nuria Bel, Lars Borin, Gerhard Budin, Nicoletta Calzolari, Eva Hajicova, Kimmo Koskenniemi, Lothar Lemnitzer, Bente Maegaard, Maciej Piasecki, Jean-Marie Pierrel, Stelios Piperidis, Inguna Skadina, Dan Tufis, Remco van Veenendaal, Tamas Váradi, and Martin Wynne (2010). "Resource and Service Centres as the Backbone for a Sustainable Service Infrastructure". In: *Proceedings of the Seventh International Conference on Language Resources and Evaluation (LREC 2010)*. Valletta, Malta: ELRA. URL: http://www.lrec-conf.org/proceedings/lrec2010/pdf/679_Paper.pdf.

Wolf, Thomas, Lysandre Debut, Victor Sanh, Julien Chaumond, Clement Delangue, Anthony Moi, Pierric Cistac, Tim Rault, Rémi Louf, Morgan Funtowicz, Joe Davison, Sam Shleifer, Patrick von Platen, Clara Ma, Yacine Jernite, Julien Plu, Canwen Xu, Teven Le Scao, Sylvain Gugger, Mariama Drame, Quentin Lhoest, and Alexander M. Rush (2020). "Transformers: State-of-the-art Natural Language Processing". In: *Proceedings of the 2020 Conference on Empirical Methods in Natural Language Processing: System Demonstrations*. ACL, pp. 38–45. DOI: 10.18653/v1/2020.emnlp-demos.6. URL: https://aclanthology.org/2020.emnlp-demos.6.

Zeng, Marcia Lei and Lois Mai Chan (2006). "Metadata Interoperability and Standardization - A Study of Methodology Part II: Achieving Interoperability at the Record and Repository Levels". In: *D-Lib Magazine* 12.6. DOI: 10.1045/june2006-zeng. URL: http://www.dlib.org/dlib/june06/zeng/06zeng.html.

Part II
ELG Inventory of
Technologies and Resources

Chapter 7
Language Technology Tools and Services

Ian Roberts, Andres Garcia Silva, Cristian Berrìo Aroca, Jose Manuel
Gómez-Pérez, Miroslav Jánošík, Dimitris Galanis, Rémi Calizzano, Andis
Lagzdiņš, Milan Straka, and Ulrich Germann

Abstract At the time of writing, the European Language Grid includes more than
800 LT services of varied types, including machine translation (MT), automatic
speech recognition (ASR), text-to-speech synthesis (TTS), and text analysis ranging from simple tokenisers and part-of-speech taggers through to complete named
entity recognition and sentiment analysis systems. This chapter gives a high-level
summary of the development of the ELG service catalogue over time and digs deeper
to discuss the process of service integration by looking at a few example services.

1 Introduction

The European Language Grid platform is able to support a wide variety of different
types of Language Technology tools and services (see Chapter 3 for a more detailed
description). Service types are classified based on the type of data they process as

Ian Roberts
University of Sheffield, UK, i.roberts@sheffield.ac.uk

Andres Garcia Silva · Cristian Berrìo Aroca · Jose Manuel Gómez-Pérez
Expert AI, Spain, agarcia@expert.ai, cberrio@expert.ai, jmgomez@expert.ai

Miroslav Jánošík
HENSOLDT Analytics GmbH, Austria, miroslav.janosik@hensoldt-analytics.com

Dimitris Galanis
Institute for Language and Speech Processing, R. C. "Athena", Greece, galanisd@athenarc.gr

Rémi Calizzano
Deutsches Forschungszentrum für Künstliche Intelligenz GmbH, Germany,
remi.calizzano@dfki.de

Andis Lagzdiņš
Tilde, Latvia, andis.lagzdins@tilde.lv

Milan Straka
Charles University, Czech Republic, straka@ufal.mff.cuni.cz

Ulrich Germann
University of Edinburgh, UK, ulrich.germann@ed.ac.uk

© The Author(s) 2023

G. Rehm (ed.), *European Language Grid*, Cognitive Technologies,
https://doi.org/10.1007/978-3-031-17258-8_7

131

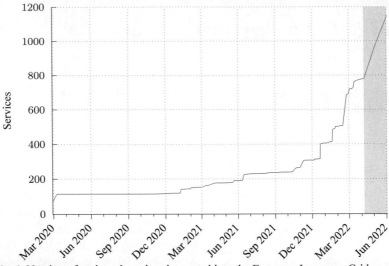

Fig. 1 Number of tools and services integrated into the European Language Grid over time; the grey shaded area denotes services whose integration is in progress at the time of writing and will be complete by the time of publication

input – text, audio, image data, etc. – and what they produce as *output* – annotations, text, audio, etc. This covers all the well-known service types such as Machine Translation (MT – text in, text out), Automatic Speech Recognition (ASR – audio in, text out), and Information Extraction/Text Analysis (IE – text in, annotations out), but also allows for services such as entity detection in *audio* data (audio in, annotations out), text-to-speech synthesis (TTS – text in, audio out), or optical character recognition (OCR – images in, text out).

Over the course of the original ELG EU project (Figure 1) the platform has grown from around 100 services available in the initial alpha release in 2020 to over 500 at the start of 2022 and almost 800 at the time of writing, with more being added all the time. The early stages of the project concentrated on services supplied by the ELG project consortium partners – such as ASR from HENSOLDT Analytics, MT from the University of Edinburgh and Tilde, TTS from Tilde, and a wide variety of Text Analysis services from Expert.AI, the University of Sheffield and DFKI (Roberts et al. 2020). More recently, an increasing number of services have been supplied by the ELG-funded pilot projects (see Part IV) and the platform has also begun to see contributions from third parties with no direct connection to the ELG consortium itself (Roberts et al. 2021, 2022). Of particular note is a set of over 500 MT services covering all pairs of EU official languages from the Neural Translation for the EU project, discussed in more detail in Section 2.[1] One third of these services have been integrated to date, with the remaining two thirds scheduled for integration during April and May 2022 (the grey shaded region in the graph), bringing the total number

---

[1] https://nteu.eu

		English	German	Italian	Spanish	French	Dutch	Swedish	Finnish	Polish	Czech	Greek	Portuguese	Danish	Bulgarian	Romanian	Estonian	Latvian	Slovenian	Croatian	Lithuanian	Slovak	Hungarian	Maltese	Irish	Total A	Total B (24 langs.)	Others (69 langs.)	Total
Linguistic pre-processing	Part-of-Speech Tagging	8	3	3	3	3	4	3	3	3	2	2	3	3	2	2	2	2	2	2	2	2	2	1	1	**60**	15	34	**109**
	Morphology	5	2	2	2	2	2	2	3	3	2	1	2	3	3	2	5	1	1	1	1	2	1	1	1	**43**	13	27	**83**
	Lemmatization	3	2	2	2	2	2	2	3	1	1	1	1	2	1	2	2	2	1	1	1	1	1	1	1	**36**	11	32	**79**
	Tokenization	6	4	3	2	2	3	1	2	1	1	1	1	1	1	2	2	1						1	1	**39**	10	27	**76**
	Sentence splitting	1	1				1																			**3**			**3**
	Chunking	1										1														**2**			**2**
Text analysis	**Total pre-processing**	**24**	**12**	**10**	**9**	**9**	**12**	**9**	**9**	**5**	**5**	**6**	**7**	**9**	**5**	**5**	**11**	**5**	**5**	**5**	**4**	**5**	**4**	**5**	**4**	**183**	**49**	**120**	**352**
	+ Classification	16	6	16	5	4	4	3	3	3	2	4	3	2	2	2	1	1	1	1	2	2	2			**83**	8	40	**131**
	+ Entity annotation	17	7	7	4	6	5	5	2	2	2	3	2	1	1	2		1	1	1	1	1	1			**65**	14	16	**95**
	+ Linking & disambiguation	7	2	3	4	4							1													**22**	2	5	**29**
	+ Sentiment/Opinion mining	13	3	2	2	2	1	1		1			2						1	1						**30**		10	**40**
	+ Text transformation	5	1	1			1						1													**15**	1	5	**21**
	+ Parsing	1	2	1	1	1	1			1	1	2	1	1										1		**26**	10	27	**63**
	+ Other text analysis	14	8	2	3	1	2	6	6			3		2										1		**48**	4	5	**57**
	Total Text Analysis	**97**	**43**	**39**	**30**	**29**	**26**	**25**	**20**	**11**	**10**	**19**	**18**	**15**	**9**	**10**	**13**	**7**	**8**	**10**	**6**	**9**	**8**	**5**	**5**	**472**	**88**	**228**	**788**
	+ Machine Translation into …	90	42	27	31	29	35	32	33	36	36	24	27	27	32	29	26	26	28	25	26	26	24	24	24	**760**	88	83	**931**
	+ Speech recognition & analysis	2	2	2	3	2	2	1	1	2	1	1	2	1	2	1	2	1	1	1	1	1	2	2	1	**27**	9	21	**57**
	+ Other services	11	7	5	4	8	4	2	1	4	2	3	2	2	4	3	4	2	2	2	2	2	2	1		**85**	10	77	**172**
	Grand Total	**200**	**94**	**73**	**68**	**68**	**67**	**60**	**56**	**53**	**49**	**48**	**47**	**46**	**45**	**43**	**43**	**39**	**38**	**37**	**37**	**36**	**36**	**31**	**30**	**1344**	**195**	**409**	**1948**

Table 1 A snapshot of all services in the ELG platform, grouped by function and supported language. This includes all services integrated as at the end of March 2022, plus 368 additional MT services whose integration is ongoing. EU official languages (type A) are listed individually; type B represents other languages used in the EU, accession candidate countries, or EEA/EFTA members; "others" refers to languages from the rest of the world. For Machine Translation, the columns in this table represent the *target* language. For a breakdown by *source* language, see Table 2 for a breakdown by *source*.

of integrated service entries in ELG up to at least 1,148 by June 2022. We hope this trend will accelerate now that the third platform release is complete.

Furthermore, the figure of 1,148 hides the fact that a number of services combine several different functions (such as tokenisation, sentence splitting, part-of-speech tagging, entity detection, linking and disambiguation) into a single process and/or offer the same function in more than one language. Counting each language/function pair individually gives a more informative picture of the scope and coverage of ELG. For example, the platform currently provides one service that does dependency parsing for Portuguese; it also provides one service that does lemmatisation for Portuguese. The user who is looking for these two functions does not care whether they are implemented by one service or by two, only whether or not the European Language Grid can meet their needs.

By this measure, as of the end of March 2022, ELG offers 1,576 distinct service function/language combinations – already exceeding the 1,300 predicted by the project in mid-2021 (Rehm et al. 2021) – and is on track to offer at least 1,948 by June, which are summarised in Table 1. Reading from the bottom up, the 1,948 total breaks down into 931 MT (47.7% of the total), 788 text analysis (40%), 57 speech recognition and audio analysis, and 172 services of other types such as text to speech and OCR. The middle section of Table 1 breaks the 788 text analysis services down into broad sub-categories, and the top section breaks the largest sub-category (linguistic pre-processing) down into individual functions.

The largest *single* category of services is MT, with 770 catalogue entries representing 931 actual translation services (since some of the models are multilingual, with the same endpoint accepting input in several different languages and translating them all to the same target). The available text analysis services range from low-level text processing tasks such as tokenisation, part-of-speech tagging or morphological analysis, through named entity annotation and on to higher-level services such as parsing, sentiment analysis and entity linking against knowledge bases. Dependency parsing in particular is supported for 60 languages courtesy of the UD-Pipe parser from Charles University in Prague. For speech, the platform currently supports speech transcription for 31 languages thanks to tools from HENSOLDT Analytics and Tilde, alongside other speech processing tools such as the keyword spotting tool described in Section 3.

Breaking the numbers down on another dimension, the ELG platform now hosts at least one service providing support for each of 114 distinct languages. English is unsurprisingly the most highly represented, but there is good support for other major EU languages – German, French, Spanish, and Italian all have support for at least 20 service functions aside from machine translation – and in total 28 languages have support for at least ten functions.

Of course there is a long tail on both axes, with 16 of the 48 distinct service functions available in only one language each and 25 in fewer than five languages. On the other hand 39 out of the 114 languages are supported by only one function, and 51 by fewer than three. Full multilinguality is still in the future, but for the languages with larger numbers of speakers at least, significant progress has been and is being made.

Target → / Source ↓	English	German	Czech	Polish	Dutch	Finnish	Swedish	Bulgarian	Spanish	Romanian	French	Slovenian	Italian	Danish	Portuguese	Latvian	Estonian	Lithuanian	Hungarian	Croatian	Slovak	Greek	Irish	Maltese	Total A	Total B (20)	Total Other (7)	Total
English		7	4	4	3	4	5	3	3	4	3	2	2	3	3	3	3	2	2	2	2	2	2	2	71	20	11	102
German	6		1	1	2	3	1	1	1	2	1	1	1	1	1	1	1	1	1	2	2	1	1	1	34	7	3	44
Czech	5	1		2	1	1	1	2	1	1	1	2	1	1	1	1	1	1	1	1	1	1	1	1	30	2	5	37
Polish	4	1	2		1	1	1	2	1	1	2	1	1	1	1	1	1	1	1	1	1	1	1	1	29	2	6	37
Dutch	2	2	1	1		1	1	1	1	1	1	1	1	1	1	1	1	1	1	1	1	1	1	1	25	4	2	31
Finnish	4	3	1	1	1		3	1	1	1	2	1	1	1	1	1	1	1	1	1	1	1	1	1	31	1	1	33
Swedish	4	1	1	1	1	3		1	1	1	1	1	1	2	1	1	1	1	1	1	1	1	1	1	29	5	1	35
Bulgarian	3	1	2	2	1	1	1		1	1	1	1	1	1	1	1	1	1	1	1	1	1	1	1	27	2	3	32
Spanish	3	1	1	1	1	1	1	1		1	1	1	1	1	1	1	1	1	1	1	1	1	1	1	25	3	1	29
Romanian	2	1	1	1	1	1	1	1	1		1	1	1	1	1	1	1	1	1	1	1	1	1	1	24		1	25
French	3	1	1	1	1	2	1	1	1	1		1	1	1	1	1	1	1	1	1	1	1	1	1	26	1	4	31
Slovenian	2	1	2	2	1	1	1	1	1	1	1		1	1	1	1	1	1	1	1	1	1	1	1	26		2	28
Italian	2	1	1	1	1	1	1	1	1	1	1	1		1	1	1	1	1	1	1	1	1	1	1	24		4	28
Danish	2	1	1	1	1	2	1	1	1	1	1	1	1		1	1	1	1	1	1	1	1	1	1	25	4	1	30
Portuguese	3	1	1	1	1	1	1	1	1	1	1	1	1	1		1	1	1	1	1	1	1	1	1	25		1	26
Latvian	3	1	1	1	1	1	1	1	1	1	1	1	1	1	1		1	1	1	1	1	1	1	1	25		2	27
Estonian	3	1	1	1	1	1	1	1	1	1	1	1	1	1	1	1		1	1	1	1	1	1	1	25		1	26
Lithuanian	2	1	1	1	1	1	1	1	1	1	1	1	1	1	1	1	1		1	1	1	1	1	1	24		2	26
Hungarian	2	1	1	1	1	1	1	1	1	1	1	1	1	1	1	1	1	1		1	1	1	1	1	24		1	25
Croatian	2	1	1	1	1	1	1	1	1	1	1	1	1	1	1	1	1	1	1		1	1	1	1	24			24
Slovak	2	1	1	1	1	1	1	1	1	1	1	1	1	1	1	1	1	1	1	1		1	1	1	24			24
Greek	2	1	1	1	1	1	1	1	1	1	1	1	1	1	1	1	1	1	1	1	1		1	1	24			24
Irish	2	1	1	1	1	1	1	1	1	1	1	1	1	1	1	1	1	1	1	1	1	1		1	24			24
Maltese	2	1	1	1	1	1	1	1	1	1	1	1	1	1	1	1	1	1	1	1	1	1	1		24			24
Total A	65	32	29	29	26	31	30	27	25	27	26	26	24	26	25	25	25	25	25	24	24	24	24	24	669	51	52	772
Total B	16	4	2	3	4	1	1	2	3																	36	20	12	68
Total Other	9	6	5	4	5	1	1	3	3	2	3	2	3	1	2	1	1	1	1		1				55	17	19	91
Grand Total	90	42	36	36	35	33	32	32	31	29	29	28	27	27	27	26	26	26	26	25	25	24	24	24	760	88	83	931

Table 2 A snapshot of supported MT language pairs as at the end of March 2022, with the addition of the remaining NTEU services for all pairs of EU official languages

2 Machine Translation

The ELG platform includes MT tools for 781 individual source/target language pairs, totalling 931 distinct services. Table 2 shows the breakdown; while English still dominates, it is much less ubiquitous than in the past, with only 21% of services involving English (102 from English, 90 into English, for a total of 192 out of the 931 available services). All pairs of EU official languages ("type A" in Table 2) are supported. In addition there is support for unofficial or regional European languages such as Basque, Galician and Luxembourgish and languages of accession candidates or free trade partners such as Icelandic, Norwegian[2] and Serbian[3] as well as languages important for trade and political reasons such as Modern Standard Arabic, Hindi, Ukrainian and Russian.

---

[2] Both Nynorsk and Bokmål varieties.

[3] Both Latin and Cyrillic script.

In addition to the MT services contributed by the ELG consortium partners Tilde (Pinnis and Bergmanis 2020) and University of Edinburgh (Junczys-Dowmunt et al. 2018; Germann et al. 2020; Germann 2020), two contributors in particular deserve a special mention here: the OPUS-MT ELG pilot project and the EU project Neural Translation for the European Union (NTEU).

The OPUS-MT ELG pilot project (Chapter 24, p. 325 ff., also see Tiedemann and Thottingal 2020) is responsible for 312 of the total 931 translation service options. To reduce the overall load on the ELG computing infrastructure, many of these language pairs are supported by multilingual models, where a single Docker container can accept input and/or produce output in many related languages. For example, there is a single OPUS model for "West Germanic", which can translate either way between any pair of English, German, Dutch, Luxembourgish, Afrikaans, Low Saxon, Gronings and Hunsrik. Some language pairs are supported by multiple models with different performance characteristics, for example, English to German is supported by a monolingual English-German model, a one-to-many "English to West Germanic", and the aforementioned many-to-many West Germanic model. Which model is most appropriate for a given task will vary, for example, if the input is known to be good-quality English then the monolingual model may be best, but if the input is a mix of languages, or English written by native speakers of other Germanic languages, then the multilingual model may be more accurate. Enabling users to test out different services on their own real data and switch between them with no technical changes to their code is one of the greatest benefits of the ELG approach.

NTEU is a project with a different focus, it was funded to produce high-quality translation tools for *all* possible pairs of EU official languages, to reduce the need for relay translation through a better-resourced language such as English (Bié et al. 2020; García-Martínez et al. 2021). This gives a total of 552 translation models (24 source languages each translating into the other 23 targets), so to spread the load of developing the models, NTEU involved three partner organisations, each responsible for models translating into eight target languages (one third of the total EU24). At the time of writing, one of the three sets of models has been published as ELG-integrated services and the other two sets are expected to be available by the time this book is published. The inclusion of these services marks an important milestone for ELG for two key reasons. First it shows the strong commitment of ELG to full multilinguality in the European Digital Single Market, and second it is the single largest contribution to the ELG platform originating outside the original ELG project consortium and pilot project ecosystem, demonstrating that ELG truly is a platform for the whole EU language technology community.

3 Automatic Speech Recognition

For automatic speech recognition, ELG currently hosts 48 services covering 30 languages and dialects. The majority of these have been provided by HENSOLDT Analytics, the speech recognition specialist in the ELG project consortium. In addition, there have also been important contributions from Tilde for the Baltic languages, and from two of the pilot project organisations: Elhuyar for Basque (see Chapter 15, p. 271 ff.) and Lingsoft for Scandinavian languages (see Chapter 20, p. 301 ff.). Lingsoft have also begun to deliver *domain-specific* ASR services, for example a service tuned to recognise clinical speech in Finnish. As general purpose ASR systems increasingly become commodities, the creation and provision of domain-specific models provides an important niche for smaller ASR providers.

These organisations are all commercial service providers; though the tools themselves are based on open source frameworks such as Kaldi[4], the models are the proprietary intellectual property of the respective provider.

3.1 Case Study: Speech Tools from HENSOLDT

In addition to the actual ASR, the components provided by HENSOLDT also perform several preprocessing steps: audio is downsampled and converted to the native format of the respective models (typically 16kHz, 16 bit, mono, signed). Segmentation and classification of the input audio is carried out next. Any segment classified as containing an insufficient amount of speech is discarded and not processed by the ASR. Disfluencies and non-speech within segments identified as audio-segments are processed by the ASR system via specific non-speech models. Segmentation as well as classification are parameterised and can be adapted to specific audio conditions (the components provided within ELG use standard settings). Processing within the HENSOLDT ASR is staged in a pipelined manner for optimal throughput. Processing parameters can be employed to balance processing speed and accuracy. Like Lingsoft, HENSOLDT also provides *domain-specific* models which can be included in the respective Docker components. The ASR engine itself is *aware* of processing throughput as well as of the various models used. It can be adjusted to provide realtime processing as well as to reload different sub-models as soon as they become available. While the current services use one standard model, this allows for future updates of vocabularies and language models in a transparent manner. Output of the HENSOLDT ASR component can be provided in 1-best, n-best or lattice formats. The former is currently used in the deployed components, however, lattice-based output is used indirectly for use of the ASR component for keyword-spotting (KWS) applications only. A sample result of the detection of keywords via ASR can be seen in Figure 2.

---

[4] http://kaldi-asr.org

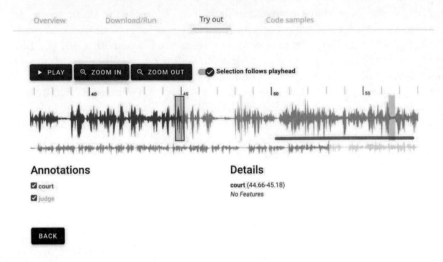

Fig. 2 Example of the word "court" having been detected as a keyword using HENSOLDT ASR

4 Text Analytics

After the set of MT services, the second largest group of services in the ELG platform are concerned in one way or another with the analysis and annotation of text, as discussed in Section 1. These cover a wide range from low-level text pre-processing tasks such as tokenisation and sentence splitting, through named entity annotation and linking tools (in many languages and domains), to dependency parsing, summarisation, sentiment analysis, and special purpose services such as the detection of misinformation or hate speech, and spelling and grammar checking.

Text analysis services have been provided by most members of the ELG project consortium, Expert.AI contributing their Cogito Discover toolkit, the University of Sheffield providing many services based on their GATE framework, Charles University providing their UDPipe dependency parser and other tools (e. g., Straka and Straková 2020; Straka et al. 2019b; Straka 2018; Straková et al. 2019; Straka et al. 2019a) and HENSOLDT (Dikici et al. 2019), ILSP (e. g., Prokopis and Piperidis 2020; Pontiki et al. 2018; Papanikolaou et al. 2016; Pontiki and Papageorgiou 2015) and DFKI (e. g., Schulz et al. 2022; Aksenov et al. 2021; Leitner et al. 2019) providing a variety of tools from their respective inventories. In addition, several of the pilot projects have contributed services in this class, notably

- *European Clinical Case Corpus* (Chapter 17, p. 283 ff.) – Fondazione Bruno Kessler. Clinical named entity recognisers in six languages.

- *Italian EVALITA Benchmark Linguistic Resources, NLP Services and Tools* (Chapter 19, p. 295 ff.) – University of Turin. A variety of services based on systems that participated in the various EVALITA shared tasks throughout the years such as misogyny and hate speech detection and gender prediction, all in the Italian language.

- *Lingsoft Solutions as Distributable Containers* (Chapter 20, p. 301 ff.) – Lingsoft. General text analysis, proofing tools (spelling and grammar checking) and morphology analysis, in English and Scandinavian languages. This includes regional variations, such as distinct services for Swedish as used in Sweden and Swedish as used in Finland, and domain variations with specific services for medical domain text.

- *Universal Semantic Annotator* (Chapter 28, p. 349 ff.) – Sapienza University of Rome. This service performs word sense disambiguation, semantic role labelling and parsing for a wide variety of different languages.

4.1 Case Study: Cogito Discover from Expert.AI

Cogito Discover is Expert.AI's scalable software platform for automatic semantic metadata generation and auto-classification that can be easily integrated in the production environment of document-processing applications or workflows. It can be deployed on premise and in cloud environments and is available for both Linux and Windows systems. Cogito Discover services that are included in ELG are:

- Language detection: Identify the main language used in a text.
- Part-of-speech annotation: Annotations at different levels (token, word/compound word, group, clause, sentence) with grammatical types.
- Named Entity Recognition: Annotation of entities, i.e., people, organisations, places, known concepts, unknown concepts and also tags, i.e., URLs, email addresses, phone numbers, addresses, dates, time, measures, money, percentage, file folder.
- Semantic annotation: This service returns the concepts spotted in a text which are modelled in the Cogito Discover knowledge graph.
- Lemmatisation: This service returns the lemma of each concept spotted in the text that is modelled in the Cogito Discover knowledge graph.
- Keyword extraction: Annotation of the most relevant information, i.e., main syncons, main lemmas, main multiword expressions.
- Sentiment analysis: Provides a sentiment score (positive or negative) for the entities recognised in the text, and an overall score for the whole set of entities in the document.
- Summarisation: Annotation of the most relevant information, i.e., main syncons, main lemmas, main multiword expressions, main sentences and main domains.
- Categorisation: Classify documents using the IPTC taxonomy.

Most services are available in 12 languages: English, Italian, Spanish, German, French, Dutch, Portuguese, Chinese, Arabic, Russian, Japanese and Korean.

For its deployment in ELG, Expert.AI generated a Docker image containing a Cogito Discover installation, the linguistic packages, and a general adapter that manages the communication between the ELG platform and Cogito Discover. The general adapter was developed using the ELG Spring Boot Starter described in Chapter 4 (Part I, p. 67 ff.)[5], which makes it as easy as possible to create ELG-compliant tools in Java using Spring Boot.

4.2 Case Study: GATE from University of Sheffield

The University of Sheffield has been developing and maintaining the GATE framework for Natural Language Processing[6] for over 20 years. The basic framework is open source software written in Java and comes with a wide variety of plugins, some implementing specific NLP algorithms and some providing the generic base on which other specific rule-based and machine learning-based tools can be built.

The GATE ecosystem includes its own software-as-a-service platform called GATE Cloud (Tablan et al. 2013). An early focus of Sheffield's work in the ELG project was to develop a bridge to GATE Cloud, i. e., a proxy that accepts ELG API requests and dispatches them to a service endpoint on GATE Cloud, translating the resulting annotations into the ELG API response format. The development of this bridge has enabled the rapid deployment of many GATE Cloud hosted services into the ELG catalogue with little demand on the computing capacity of the ELG platform itself. At the time of writing, there are 66 GATE-based services integrated in ELG via the bridging proxy.

However, GATE Cloud itself has rate limits, so alongside the bridge component, Sheffield has developed a generic tool that can take any NLP application built against the GATE framework and bundle the application and all the plugins on which it depends as a Docker image that can run the application in-process within the ELG infrastructure. This mechanism has been used to wrap up certain particularly significant GATE-based applications so they can run directly in the ELG Kubernetes cluster and take advantage of the ELG platform's auto-scaling capabilities (see Chapter 5).

As the ELG EU project draws to a close, things have started to come full circle, as a number of recent additions *to* GATE Cloud have in fact been implemented as ELG-compatible Docker images, with a bridge in the other direction to enable a GATE application to call out to an endpoint that exposes the ELG internal LT service API. Some of these ELG-compatible images have been contributed back to ELG.

In addition, Sheffield has promoted the use of ELG-compatible services and Docker images in a number of other projects, notably the Horizon 2020 projects WeVerify[7] and RISIS2[8]. Many of Sheffield's contributions to these projects have

---

[5] https://gitlab.com/european-language-grid/platform/elg-spring-boot-starter

[6] General Architecture for Text Engineering, https://gate.ac.uk, see Cunningham et al. (2013).

[7] Wider and Enhanced Verification For You, https://weverify.eu, see Marinova et al. (2020).

[8] Research Infrastructure for Science and Innovation Policy Studies, https://www.risis2.eu, see Reale et al. (2019).

been implemented as ELG-compatible Docker images, with bridging components written for those projects to act as clients of the ELG API. The same mechanism has been used as part of a long-term collaboration between the University of Sheffield and King's College London, to integrate medical domain LT services developed in Python at King's into an existing GATE-based processing workflow. The use of the ELG standardised API makes it easy to integrate a variety of services implemented in different programming languages in a minimally-invasive way.

4.3 Case Study: Microservices At Your Service

With the third release in 2022, the ELG platform has begun to see contributions from third parties beyond the initial ELG consortium and pilot projects. One notable source is the project Microservices At Your Service[9], funded by the European Commission's Connecting Europe Facility (CEF) programme and led by Lingsoft (one of the organisations funded for a pilot project in the first ELG open call, see Chapter 20, p. 301 ff.). The project describes its mission as "bridging the gap between NLP research and industry" and it aims to identify open source text analysis tools that could benefit the community, package them as Docker images, and publish them for wider use. The project has selected the ELG platform as its primary vehicle for publication of the tools, and uses the ELG API as its standard specification for interoperability.

The project concentrates primarily on Finnish, Estonian, Icelandic, Spanish and Portuguese, plus some tools for minority languages from the same regions such as Faroese, Galician and Catalan. So far more than 14 services have been published, including:

- A proxy to the Finto-AI subject indexing service[10], in Finnish, Swedish and English (Suominen et al. 2022)
- Named entity recognition tools for Swedish and Norwegian, originally from the respective national libraries of the two countries (Kummervold et al. 2021)
- A tokeniser and morphological analysis tool for Estonian (Kaalep and Vaino 2001)
- A variety of tools for Icelandic from the University of Reykjavík, including a tokeniser, part-of-speech tagger, shallow parser and named entity recogniser, as well as machine translation models between Icelandic and English

One of the Icelandic services, a part-of-speech tagger and lemmatizer, is shown in Figure 3.

---

[9] https://www.lingsoft.fi/en/microservices-at-your-service-bridging-gap-between-nlp-research-and-industry

[10] https://ai.finto.fi

Fig. 3 Icelandic lemmatizer and part-of-speech tagger from Microservices At Your Service

5 Other Service Types

Right from the start of the ELG project, it was clear that the three principal service classes (ASR, MT, Text Analytics), while significant, would never be exhaustive. An important goal of ELG was to remain flexible enough to be able to easily integrate new classes of services and tools that had not been foreseen in the original proposal. The API specifications were designed with this flexibility in mind, being based solely on the kinds of data each service expects and returns, rather than placing any requirements on what the service *does* with that data.

Three classes of "other" services have emerged since the beginning of the project:

- *Text-to-speech* services that take text and synthesise audio.
- *Audio analysis* services that take audio input and return standoff annotations over time segments of the audio stream.
- *Image analysis* services, in particular optical character recognition (OCR).

Text-to-speech services have been provided by Tilde within the ELG project consortium (for Latvian and Lithuanian), and by the Elhuyar pilot project (for Basque). The audio analysis services are the keyword spotting tools from HENSOLDT Analytics described along with their speech recognition systems in Section 3.

The University of Sheffield has contributed a multilingual image OCR service developed as part of the Horizon 2020 EU project WeVerify. The service is based on a multi-step pipeline of neural models, first running a segmentation model to identify regions within the image that contain text, then a classifier to identify the writing system and language of each text block, and finally an appropriate text recognition model on each block depending on the identified script (Arabic, Bengali-Assamese, Chinese, Latin, Devanagari, Kanna, Hangul or Cyrillic). An example can be seen in Figure 4. The models have been deliberately designed *not* to use the "attention" mechanism typical of other deep neural models, as this was found to give only marginal improvements in performance at the cost of significantly increased memory and compute requirements.

Part of the reason for ELG funding the open call for pilot projects was precisely to elicit suggestions of new classes of services that were not previously known to the project consortium. Two pilots in particular delivered on this: Text2TCS (Section 5.1) and Coreon's MKS as LLOD (Section 5.2).

Fig. 4 The Multilingual OCR service showing detection of two blocks of text in different scripts (the bounding boxes *are* part of the "try out" UI, they have not been added to this figure)

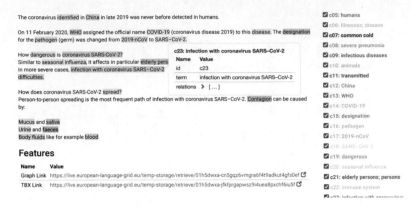

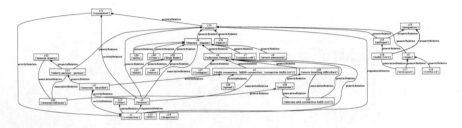

Fig. 5 Text2TCS service results in the "try out" GUI, showing links to the termbase and graph

Fig. 6 The termbase graph generated from the sample input text (Figure 5)

5.1 Pilot Project: Terminological Concept Systems from Natural Language Text from University of Vienna

The Text2TCS project (see Chapter 18, Part IV, p. 289 ff.) aimed to develop a tool for deriving terminological concept systems from natural language text. This required the generation not only of typical standoff annotations representing the mentions of the detected terms in the source text, but also two additional output files for the termbase in TBX format[11] and a visualisation of the terminology as a PNG image.

These additional outputs did not naturally fit the JSON-based data interchange formats of the ELG API. It would have been possible to force them into this format by, for example, encoding the PNG data in base 64 encoding, but instead the ELG team took this as the impetus to introduce the "temporary storage" helper service for use by LT service containers. The operation of the temporary storage service is very simple. LT services can send arbitrary binary data to a well-known URL `http://storage.elg/store` (a private host name that resolves only within the ELG Kubernetes cluster), and will receive in return a publicly-resolvable URL which can be returned to the caller of the LT service for them to use to retrieve the same

---

[11] https://www.tbxinfo.net

data. Storage URLs include a cryptographically-secure random token to make them un-guessable, and they expire by default 15 minutes from their generation, at which time the stored data is permanently deleted.

Figures 5 and 6 show how this appears in the ELG portal when a user tests the Text2TCS service using the "try out" mechanism.

The temporary storage service provides an elegant solution to the problem of allowing LT services to return binary data without introducing additional complexity for the majority of services that do not have this requirement.

5.2 Pilot Project: MKS as Linguistic Linked Open Data from Coreon

The pilot project MKS as LLOD by knowledge management company Coreon (see Chapter 23, Part IV, 319 ff.) is an interesting case that in some ways sits at the boundary between services and resources. The aim of the project was to take Coreon's existing knowledge representation systems, known as MKS for Multilingual Knowledge System, and expose them as Linguistic Linked Open Data (LLOD). There is already a (de jure *and* de facto) standard API for querying linked (open) data resources, i. e., the SPARQL query language[12], so rather than defining a new format under the ELG umbrella, we decided to adopt the existing standard.

For ELG, the question was how best to represent this kind of resource in the ELG metadata scheme. On the one hand, the object that was being provided by Coreon was conceptually a data resource, albeit one accessed via a query API rather than via direct download, but on the other hand the technical method of integration would be through providing a SPARQL *service* for users to query. The eventual solution was in fact a mixture of both.

The Coreon SPARQL endpoint was integrated into the ELG infrastructure and set up so that SPARQL queries could be authenticated using access tokens issued by the ELG Keycloak identity provider, exactly as for other ELG LT services. In parallel, Coreon developed a "try out" UI to allow users to make test queries through the ELG catalogue interface. The two were then tied together as follows:

1. The "try out" UI was registered in its own right as a "service" in the ELG catalogue, whose function is "resource access".
2. Each SPARQL endpoint was then registered as an individual "ELG-compatible Lexical or Conceptual Resource" (LCR), with a link to the "try out" UI as "this resource is queried by that service".

Logic was introduced in the ELG catalogue to recognise when a user visits an ELG-compatible LCR that has an associated query service, and to inject the query UI as a "try out" tab which is configured with the necessary information and access token to be able to query the SPARQL endpoint (see Figure 7 for the final result).

---

[12] https://www.w3.org/TR/sparql11-overview/

Fig. 7 Coreon SPARQL endpoint as an ELG-compatible Lexical/Conceptual Resource

6 Conclusions

Overall, the ELG project has succeeded in its aim to offer a broad variety of different service types covering many languages, and supplied by a range of different providers both academic and industrial. All the major classes of LT services are well represented in the ELG catalogue including ASR, MT and text analysis, with further classes of interest emerging during the course of the project. The generic design of the LT service execution APIs means that even services that do not exactly fit an existing class can be easily accommodated in the ELG platform, for example the HENSOLDT services for keyword spotting in audio required no API changes at all, only an adaptation of the "try out" GUI mechanism.

Inevitably, the majority of early contributions to the ELG platform were from the original ELG project consortium members. This was expected and planned for in the original project proposal, and the pilot project funding system was designed to help broaden the contributor pool more quickly by incentivising providers to adopt the ELG formats and specifications. It has succeeded in this aim, and many more details can be found in the various pilot project chapters in Part IV. As the funded project draws to a close and the ELG platform begins to transition to its long term sustainable mode of operation, we are seeing an increasing number of third-party contributions from beyond the original consortium and pilot projects, which stands the ELG in good stead for its sustainability as a platform over the coming years.

References

Aksenov, Dmitrii, Peter Bourgonje, Karolina Zaczynska, Malte Ostendorff, Julián Moreno-Schneider, and Georg Rehm (2021). "Fine-grained Classification of Political Bias in German News: A Data Set and Initial Experiments". In: *Proceedings of the 5th Workshop on Online Abuse and Harms (WOAH 2021)*. Ed. by Aida Mostafazadeh Davani, Douwe Kiela, Mathias Lambert, Bertie Vidgen, Vinodkumar Prabhakaran, and Zeerak Waseem. Bangkok, Thailand: ACL, pp. 121–131. URL: https://aclanthology.org/2021.woah-1.13.pdf.

Bié, Laurent, Aleix Cerdà-i-Cucó, Hans Degroote, Amando Estela, Mercedes García-Martínez, Manuel Herranz, Alejandro Kohan, Maite Melero, Tony O'Dowd, Sinéad O'Gorman, Mārcis Pinnis, Roberts Rozis, Riccardo Superbo, and Artūrs Vasiļevskis (2020). "Neural Translation for the European Union (NTEU) Project". In: *Proceedings of the 22nd Annual Conference of the European Association for Machine Translation*. Lisboa, Portugal: European Association for Machine Translation, pp. 477–478. URL: https://aclanthology.org/2020.eamt-1.60.

Cunningham, Hamish, Valentin Tablan, Angus Roberts, and Kalina Bontcheva (2013). "Getting More Out of Biomedical Documents with GATE's Full Lifecycle Open Source Text Analytics". In: *PLOS Computational Biology* 9.2, pp. 1–16. DOI: 10.1371/journal.pcbi.1002854.

Dikici, Erinç, Gerhard Backfried, and Jürgen Riedler (2019). "The SAIL LABS Media Mining Indexer and the CAVA Framework". In: *Interspeech 2019, 20th Annual Conference of the International Speech Communication Association*. Ed. by Gernot Kubin and Zdravko Kacic. Graz, Austria: ISCA, pp. 4630–4631. URL: https://researchr.org/publication/DikiciBR19.

García-Martínez, Mercedes, Laurent Bié, Aleix Cerdà, Amando Estela, Manuel Herranz, Rihards Krišlauks, Maite Melero, Tony O'Dowd, Sinead O'Gorman, Marcis Pinnis, Artūrs Stafanovič, Riccardo Superbo, and Artūrs Vasiļevskis (2021). "Neural Translation for European Union (NTEU)". In: *Proceedings of Machine Translation Summit XVIII: Users and Providers Track*. Association for Machine Translation in the Americas, pp. 316–334. URL: https://aclanthology.org/2021.mtsummit-up.23.

Germann, Ulrich (2020). "The University of Edinburgh's submission to the German-to-English and English-to-German Tracks in the WMT 2020 News Translation and Zero-shot Translation Robustness Tasks". In: *Proceedings of the Fifth Conference on Machine Translation*. ACL, pp. 197–201. URL: https://aclanthology.org/2020.wmt-1.18.

Germann, Ulrich, Roman Grundkiewicz, Martin Popel, Radina Dobreva, Nikolay Bogoychev, and Kenneth Heafield (2020). "Speed-optimized, Compact Student Models that Distill Knowledge from a Larger Teacher Model: the UEDIN-CUNI Submission to the WMT 2020 News Translation Task". In: *Proceedings of the Fifth Conference on Machine Translation*. ACL, pp. 191–196. URL: https://aclanthology.org/2020.wmt-1.17.

Junczys-Dowmunt, Marcin, Roman Grundkiewicz, Tomasz Dwojak, Hieu Hoang, Kenneth Heafield, Tom Neckermann, Frank Seide, Ulrich Germann, Alham Fikri Aji, Nikolay Bogoychev, André F. T. Martins, and Alexandra Birch (2018). "Marian: Fast Neural Machine Translation in C++". In: *Proceedings of ACL 2018, System Demonstrations*. Melbourne, Australia: ACL, pp. 116–121. URL: http://www.aclweb.org/anthology/P18-4020.

Kaalep, Heiki-Jaan and Tarmo Vaino (2001). "Complete Morphological Analysis in the Linguist's Toolbox". In: *Congressus Nonus Internationalis Fenno-Ugristarum Pars V*, pp. 9–16.

Kummervold, Per E, Javier De la Rosa, Freddy Wetjen, and Svein Arne Brygfjeld (2021). "Operationalizing a National Digital Library: The Case for a Norwegian Transformer Model". In: *Proceedings of the 23rd Nordic Conference on Computational Linguistics (NoDaLiDa)*. Reykjavik, Iceland: Linköping University Electronic Press, Sweden, pp. 20–29. URL: https://aclanthology.org/2021.nodalida-main.3.

Leitner, Elena, Georg Rehm, and Julián Moreno-Schneider (2019). "Fine-grained Named Entity Recognition in Legal Documents". In: *Semantic Systems. The Power of AI and Knowledge Graphs. Proceedings of the 15th International Conference (SEMANTiCS 2019)*. Ed. by Maribel Acosta, Philippe Cudré-Mauroux, Maria Maleshkova, Tassilo Pellegrini, Harald Sack, and York Sure-Vetter. Lecture Notes in Computer Science 11702. Karlsruhe, Germany: Springer, pp. 272–287. URL: https://link.springer.com/content/pdf/10.1007%2F978-3-030-33220-4_20.pdf.

Marinova, Zlatina, Jochen Spangenberg, Denis Teyssou, Symeon Papadopoulos, Nikos Sarris, Alexandre Alaphilippe, and Kalina Bontcheva (2020). "Weverify: Wider and Enhanced Verification for You Project Overview and Tools". In: *2020 IEEE International Conference on Multimedia Expo Workshops (ICMEW)*, pp. 1–4. DOI: 10.1109/ICMEW46912.2020.9106056.

Papanikolaou, Konstantina, Harris Papageorgiou, Nikos Papasarantopoulos, Theoni Stathopoulou, and George Papastefanatos (2016). ""Just the Facts" with PALOMAR: Detecting Protest Events in Media Outlets and Twitter". In: *Tenth International AAAI Conference on Web and Social Media*. Vol. 10. 2, pp. 135–142.

Pinnis, Mārcis and Toms Bergmanis (2020). "Tilde's Neural Machine Translation Technology". In: *Latvian Academy of Sciences Yearbook 2020*. Latvian Academy of Sciences, pp. 85–89.

Pontiki, Maria and Harris Papageorgiou (2015). "Opinion Mining and Target Extraction in Greek Review Texts". In: *Proceedings of the 12th International Conference on Greek Linguistics (ICGL 12)*. Vol. 2. Freie Universität. Berlin, Germany, pp. 871–883.

Pontiki, Maria, Konstantina Papanikolaou, and Haris Papageorgiou (2018). "Exploring the Predominant Targets of Xenophobia-motivated Behavior: A Longitudinal Study for Greece". In: *Proceedings of the Natural Language Processing meets Journalism Workshop (NLPJ 2018)*. Ed. by Octavian Popescu and Carlo Strapparava. ELRA.

Prokopis, Prokopidis and Stelios Piperidis (2020). "A Neural NLP toolkit for Greek". In: *11th Hellenic Conference on Artificial Intelligence*, pp. 125–128. URL: http://nlp.ilsp.gr/setn-2020/3411408.3411430.pdf.

Reale, Emanuela, Grazia Battiato, and Serena Fabrizio (2019). "RISIS2: an innovative research infrastructure as a support for STI research community". In: *ISSI*, pp. 2658–2659. DOI: 10.5281/zenodo.3478408.

Rehm, Georg, Stelios Piperidis, Kalina Bontcheva, Jan Hajic, Victoria Arranz, Andrejs Vasiļjevs, Gerhard Backfried, José Manuel Gómez Pérez, Ulrich Germann, Rémi Calizzano, Nils Feldhus, Stefanie Hegele, Florian Kintzel, Katrin Marheinecke, Julian Moreno-Schneider, Dimitris Galanis, Penny Labropoulou, Miltos Deligiannis, Katerina Gkirtzou, Athanasia Kolovou, Dimitris Gkoumas, Leon Voukoutis, Ian Roberts, Jana Hamrlová, Lukáš Kačena, Khalid Choukri, Valérie Mapelli, Mickaël Rigault, Jūlija Meļņika, Miro Janosik, Katja Prinz, Andres Garcia-Silva, Cristian Berrio, Ondrej Klejch, and Steve Renals (2021). "European Language Grid: A Joint Platform for the European Language Technology Community". In: *Proceedings of the 16th Conference of the European Chapter of the Association for Computational Linguistics: System Demonstrations (EACL 2021)*. Kyiv, Ukraine: ACL, pp. 221–230. URL: https://www.aclweb.org/anthology/2021.eacl-demos.26.pdf.

Roberts, Ian, Andres Garcia Silva, Miroslav Janosik, Nils Feldhus, Dimitris Galanis, Andis Lagzdiņš, and Rémi Calizzano (2022). *Deliverable D4.3 Services, Tools and Components (Final Release)*. Project deliverable; EU project European Language Grid (ELG); Grant Agreement no. 825627 ELG. URL: https://www.european-language-grid.eu/wp-content/uploads/2022/04/ELG-Deliverable-D4.3-final.pdf.

Roberts, Ian, Andres Garcia Silva, Miroslav Janosik, Andis Lagzdiņš, Nils Feldhus, Georg Rehm, Dimitris Galanis, Dusan Varis, and Ulrich Germann (2020). *Deliverable D4.1 Services, Tools and Components (First Release)*. Project deliverable; EU project European Language Grid (ELG); Grant Agreement no. 825627 ELG. URL: https://www.european-language-grid.eu/wp-content/uploads/2021/02/ELG-Deliverable-D4.1-final.pdf.

Roberts, Ian, Andres Garcia Silva, Miroslav Janosik, Andis Lagzdiņš, Nils Feldhus, Georg Rehm, Dimitris Galanis, Dusan Varis, and Ulrich Germann (2021). *Deliverable D4.2 Grid Content: Services, Tools and Components (Interim Release)*. Project deliverable; EU project European Language Grid (ELG); Grant Agreement no. 825627 ELG. URL: https://www.european-language-grid.eu/wp-content/uploads/2022/04/ELG-Deliverable-D4.2-final.pdf.

Schulz, Konstantin, Jens Rauenbusch, Jan Fillies, Lisa Rutenburg, Dimitrios Karvelas, and Georg Rehm (2022). "User Experience Design for Automatic Credibility Assessment of News Content About COVID-19". In: *Proceedings of HCI International 2022 – Late Breaking Papers*. Accepted for publication. 26 June-01 July 2022.

Straka, Milan (2018). "UDPipe 2.0 Prototype at CoNLL 2018 UD Shared Task". In: *Proceedings of CoNLL 2018: The SIGNLL Conference on Computational Natural Language Learning*. Stroudsburg, PA, USA: ACL, pp. 197–207.

Straka, Milan and Jana Straková (2020). "UDPipe at EvaLatin 2020: Contextualized Embeddings and Treebank Embeddings". In: *Proceedings of LT4HALA 2020 – 1st Workshop on Language Technologies for Historical and Ancient Languages*. Marseille, France: ELRA, pp. 124–129.

Straka, Milan, Jana Straková, and Jan Hajič (2019a). "Czech Text Processing with Contextual Embeddings: POS Tagging, Lemmatization, Parsing and NER". In: *Proceedings of the 22nd International Conference on Text, Speech and Dialogue (TSD 2019)*. Cham, Heidelberg, New York etc.: Springer, pp. 137–150.

Straka, Milan, Jana Straková, and Jan Hajič (2019b). "UDPipe at SIGMORPHON 2019: Contextualized Embeddings, Regularization with Morphological Categories, Corpora Merging". In: *Proceedings of the 16th SIGMORPHON Workshop on Computational Research in Phonetics, Phonology, and Morphology*. Stroudsburg, PA, USA: ACL, pp. 95–103.

Straková, Jana, Milan Straka, and Jan Hajič (2019). "Neural Architectures for Nested NER through Linearization". In: *Proceedings of the 57th Annual Meeting of the Association for Computational Linguistics*. Stroudsburg, PA, USA: ACL, pp. 5326–5331.

Suominen, Osma, Mona Lehtinen, and Juho Inkinen (2022). *Annif and Finto AI: Developing and Implementing Automated Subject Indexing*. Macerata. DOI: 10.4403/jlis.it-12740.

Tablan, Valentin, Ian Roberts, Hamish Cunningham, and Kalina Bontcheva (2013). "GATECloud.net: A Platform for large-scale, Open-Source Text Processing on the Cloud". In: *Philosophical Transactions of the Royal Society A: Math., Phys. and Eng. Sciences* 371.20120071.

Tiedemann, Jörg and Santhosh Thottingal (2020). "OPUS-MT – Building open translation services for the World". In: *Proceedings of the 22nd Annual Conference of the European Association for Machine Translation (EAMT)*. Lisboa, Portugal: European Association for Machine Translation, pp. 479–480. URL: https://helda.helsinki.fi/bitstream/handle/10138/327852/2020.eamt_1_499.pdf.

Chapter 8
Datasets, Corpora and other Language Resources

Victoria Arranz, Khalid Choukri, Valérie Mapelli, Mickaël Rigault, Penny Labropoulou, Miltos Deligiannis, Leon Voukoutis, and Stelios Piperidis

Abstract This chapter provides an overview of what is available in ELG in terms of datasets, corpora and other language resources (LRs) and how this has been achieved. We look at the procedures and steps that have been followed to complete the full resource ingestion cycle, which goes from repository and LR identification to metadata description and ingestion. We explain the approaches, priorities and methodology. The chapter also outlines the repositories that have been integrated into ELG, discussing the different procedures followed (metadata conversion, extraction, and completion, as well as harvesting) and the reasons behind these choices. Furthermore, the ELG catalogue content is described, with details on key elements and features as well as accomplishments. The last two sections are devoted to the crucial legal issues behind such a complex platform and its data management plan, respectively.

1 Introduction

As introduced in Part I, one of the ELG platform's primary functions is enabling sharing, distribution and deployment of Language Resources and Technologies (LRT). ELG provides access to thousands of datasets, by far the largest collection of relevant datasets for the European Language Technology community. Users can search for, download as well as provide different types of resources. As can be seen further down, ELG has identified, filtered, described and centralised a vast amount of datasets and other resources from different inventories and repositories, providing an easy to use point of search for the LT community. Its aim is to become the "yellow pages" and the primary platform for the European Language Technology community (see Chapter 9). Our work in terms of curating and further enriching ELG is ongoing, with new ingestions and collaborations at the time of writing.

Victoria Arranz · Khalid Choukri · Valérie Mapelli · Mickaël Rigault
ELDA, France, arranz@elda.org, choukri@elda.org, mapelli@elda.org, mickael@elda.org

Penny Labropoulou · Miltos Deligiannis · Leon Voukoutis · Stelios Piperidis
Institute for Language and Speech Processing, R. C. "Athena", Greece,
penny@athenarc.gr, mdel@athenarc.gr, leon.voukoutis@athenarc.gr, spip@athenarc.gr

© The Author(s) 2023
G. Rehm (ed.), *European Language Grid*, Cognitive Technologies,
https://doi.org/10.1007/978-3-031-17258-8_8

This chapter describes the work carried out so far as well as currently ongoing efforts towards the population of the ELG catalogue with Language Resources (datasets and language models). This work has consisted in 1. the identification of sources (inventories and repositories), language resources and models, 2. their analysis, 3. the selection of elements to be ingested, as well as 4. the conversion or harvesting of their metadata descriptions and 5. the ingestion of these descriptions, and actual LRs, if relevant. All these steps are complex and intertwined tasks that are operationalised in a collaborative manner.

As a core element of ELG, the term "Language Resource" (LR, LRs) is used for resources composed of linguistic material used in the development, improvement or evaluation of Language Technologies (LT, LTs), but also, in a broader sense, in language and language-mediated research studies and applications; examples include datasets of various types, such as textual, multimodal or multimedia corpora, lexical data, grammars, language models, etc. In related initiatives and the literature, the term is often used with a broader meaning, encompassing also tools and services used for the processing and management of datasets, and standards, guidelines and similar documents that support the research, development and evaluation of LTs. In the ELG metadata model (see Labropoulou et al. 2020, and also Chapter 2), we use the term as first defined for the META-SHARE metadata model (Gavrilidou et al. 2012), i. e., including both data resources and LT tools/services. The alternative term Language Resource/Technology (LRT) is also used in the context of ELG (Rehm et al. 2021). However, in this chapter we use LR as referring to datasets and language models only; tools and services in ELG are discussed in Chapter 7.

2 Identification of Language Resources and Repositories

ELG aims to become the primary marketplace for the European LT community. The organisations making use of it range from commercial to non-commercial, including research centres and companies, as well as initiatives and infrastructures, among others. Linking all these players and supporting them in their interaction is a two-fold mission, which involves helping them make their tools, services and data available and also establishing the means for them to find and have access to those they may require in their work.

To cover all relevant existing language resource repositories, ELG defined an identification and collection methodology. First, the ELG project consortium members performed a round of identification and analysis contributing their own resources. Second, we reached out to the ELG National Competence Centres (NCCs, see Chapter 11) to gather more input and pointers to additional existing repositories and resource inventories. This identification task has been run in parallel with a priority definition task, which has been adjusted regularly according to achievements and to the community's needs and demands.

2.1 Identification by the Consortium

ELG examined the available inventories and repositories of all potential LT/LR providers and users. The initial results have been completed with further collaborative input from the NCCs (see Section 2.2) and ELG's sister project European Language Equality (ELE, see Section 2.3.2). With regard to the typology of LRs searched for, all types and modalities deemed useful for some sort of LT application were considered. These comprise corpora, lexicons, terminologies, and derived resources (such as language models for ASR or TMX models for MT), and also focus on media such as speech/audio, text, video/audio-visual, images, OCR and sign language datasets (images, videos). The identification strategy was adjusted following initial findings. For example, users' needs guided us to take into account high-priority dataset types such as language models, and has led us to look into repositories which contain and even focus on such types of resources (see Section 4.2).

2.2 Identification by the National Competence Centres

In addition to the work described above (Section 2.1), a survey was carried out to gather more input from the NCCs and from other collaborators, often related to their local and regional repositories (Rehm and Marheinecke 2019). This way we have been able to identify new repositories and, moreover, we were also provided with extensive documentation by the NCCs (content, contacts, etc.). The collaboration with the NCCs has been valuable. We plan to continue the joint work to maximise ELG's coverage.

2.3 Collaboratively Filling the Gaps

With its (at the time of writing) 8,873 dataset descriptions and following the ingestion of several repositories, ELG is at a compelling stage for taking the next steps in its dataset provision strategy. It must be stressed that our collaboration with other initiatives has also had an impact on these numbers. Bearing that in mind, the population of ELG now follows the analysis and identification of gaps from several perspectives:

1. The ELG consortium members' analysis of contributions and ingestion statistics in the platform.
2. The analysis of gaps carried out under a joint strategy, such as the ELE project and the ELG pilot projects (see Part IV), which have contributed datasets and also shared their own needs with regard to ELG, thus supporting ELG on its LRT collection venture from the point of view of the provider and the user.

3. The analysis of feedback received from technology developers and data users who shared their needs with us.

2.3.1 Contributions from the ELG Pilot Projects

The ELG pilot projects were intended to demonstrate the usefulness of ELG by contributing datasets or services to the platform or by making use of existing datasets or services for the development of innovative LT applications. These contributions provided by the pilot projects benefit both the community that will have access to the assets provided as well as the pilot projects themselves that will gain visibility with their work and by displaying it in ELG. These projects are an excellent proof of concept for the ELG platform and those pilot projects that provide datasets often target – and fill – specific gaps. At the time of writing, the already concluded pilot projects have finished their work, which has resulted in a set of 52 datasets available through ELG. The pilot projects are described in detail in Part IV of this book.

2.3.2 Contributions from the European Language Equality Project

ELG collaborates with the European Language Equality (ELE) project[1] to promote digital language equality in Europe. In 2021, ELE organised an online survey addressed primarily to the more than 30 language experts of the consortium to collect information on language resources and technologies available for the languages[2] under investigation (see Chapter 6 for more details). Through a web form, the ELE consortium partners responsible for one or more of the languages addressed by the project were able to record and report new language resources and also new resource repositories. This additional and collaborative collection procedure resulted in approx. 6,300 records (Arranz et al. 2022), which have already been cleaned up, normalised and curated and finally ingested into ELG (4,127 metadata records for data resources and 2,215 metadata records for tools). Just like ELG organisation pages, metadata records can be claimed by the resource creators or other rightful owners (see Chapter 9, Section 3.3, p. 179) and enriched with further information. This is why all contact persons included in these metadata records have been notified of their publication in ELG; we encouraged them to claim their resources and enrich the descriptions. Complete metadata descriptions are an important aspect of ensuring findability and future reuse of the resources (see Chapter 2, Section 7).

---

[1] https://european-language-equality.eu
[2] https://european-language-equality.eu/languages/

2.3.3 Platform Users

Finally, users of the ELG platform can also provide feedback about their interaction with ELG or about unmet expectations with regard to the availability of datasets or LT services. With regard to the latter, if users raise a certain need for specific datasets in relation to specific technologies, the ELG team can investigate whether relevant datasets or resources exist.

3 Integrating Repositories into ELG

The individual ELG releases follow an evolutionary strategy with regard to the population of the catalogue. This strategy has evolved as procedures have been put in place and new priorities and needs identified. ELG Release 1 (R1) followed a rather pragmatic approach, exploring procedures while targeting large repositories under the management of ELG consortium members. This allowed us to set up procedures, locate flaws and address problems (e. g., pending legal issues). ELG Release 2 (R2) launched an ambitious acquisition of very large catalogues which were not compliant with ELG's structure and metadata schema. This was the case, for instance, for Quantum Stat and Zenodo (see Section 4 and Arranz et al. 2021). Repositories like Zenodo are extremely large digital libraries in which many different research artefacts are published, which is why it requires a certain amount of effort to find and extract artefacts that are relevant for ELG. Despite these challenges, the overall result is rewarding as it provides access to many LT-related datasets, which have not been directly discoverable so far and which are now made available to the community through ELG as a one-stop-shop. The LR provision strategy for ELG Release 3 (R3) has built on top of the processes firmly established in R2. It continued and finished up the integration of the already initiated repositories, it set up harvesting procedures for as many ingested repositories as possible and added further repositories.

3.1 Priorities in the Ingestion Work

The list of identified repositories comprised different types of portals, such as those storing data from evaluation campaigns or shared tasks (e. g., WMT resources, Yeganova et al. 2021), large catalogues of language resources (e. g., ELRA, Mapelli et al. 2022), networks of LR repositories (e. g., various META-SHARE nodes, Piperidis et al. 2014), databanks, initiatives supporting the collection of language data, etc. This initial list was prioritised by taking into account the following dimensions of the different repositories:

- Relevance of their content for ELG, its services and users.
- Access information (conditions of use, prioritising open licensing schemes).
- Languages covered (covering multiple different languages, filling detected gaps).

- LR typology (covering different modalities, filling detected gaps).
- Number of resources (prioritising repositories with larger numbers of resources).
- Metadata schema (prioritising schemas that allow automated conversions).

Following this prioritisation strategy, three repositories – all of which are run by members of the ELG project consortium – were initially selected for ingestion in ELG Release 1: ELRA[3], ELRC-SHARE[4] and the three META-SHARE nodes managed by DFKI[5], ELDA[6] and ILSP[7]. This choice was strategic, as a proof of concept for resource availability and metadata conversion, given that the involved partners were familiar with the content and metadata schemas of these repositories. All the datasets selected for metadata ingestion were filtered down for legal compliance to ensure that licensing or distribution conditions that could not be addressed by ELG at this early stage could be taken care of for a later release. ELG Release 2 continued with additional repositories under the management of ELG project consortium partners (ELRA-SHARE-LRs 2014, 2016, 2018 and 2020[8], and LINDAT/CLARIAH-CZ[9]) but also by extending its work on the META-SHARE network and looking into very large digital inventories such as Quantum Stat and Zenodo. The reasons behind these choices combined strategy and diversity, which were also the goal with repositories such as Hugging Face for ELG Release 3 (see Section 4.2.4).

3.2 Contributing Language Resources

Interested institutions or individuals can make datasets available for download, i. e., hosting datasets in the ELG platform, or they can simply point ELG users to external download locations. In both cases, a description of the resource in the form of a metadata record is needed that can be discovered through the ELG catalogue. Such metadata descriptions can be manually created in ELG using the corresponding editor, they can be prepared as an XML file, which is then uploaded and imported into ELG, or they can be automatically converted from existing metadata records that use a different schema and imported into ELG afterwards. The flexibility behind these different options to populate the ELG catalogue makes contributions very easy, they can be done according to the provider's needs and preferences.

ELRC-SHARE follows the metadata-only option; this repository is financed by the European Commission under the ELRC initiative (Lösch et al. 2021), datasets will be available through ELRC-SHARE for at least the duration of the ELRC contracts. For that reason, the master copies of the LRs provided to ELG remain within

---

[3] http://catalogue.elra.info

[4] https://elrc-share.eu

[5] http://metashare.dfki.de

[6] http://metashare.elda.org

[7] http://metashare.ilsp.gr:8080

[8] LRs contributed by LREC participants, see http://www.elra.info/en/lrec/shared-lrs/.

[9] LINDAT is the CLARIN Centre for Language Research Infrastructure in the Czech Republic.

ELRC-SHARE but corresponding metadata records are available through ELG, enabling their discovery through ELG and their download via a redirect to the corresponding ELRC-SHARE page. In addition to contractual reasons, some repositories prefer to host their LRTs themselves, such as the ELRA catalogue, which distributes its LRs under a typology of licences that cannot be fully covered or recreated by the ELG metadata schema for the time being. Repositories like Zenodo or Quantum Stat mostly provide links to the locations of their datasets, very often these are links to Github or Gitlab pages. Again, only metadata records with the links to the dataset locations have been ingested into ELG. Likewise, harvested repositories only export metadata records (e. g., different CLARIN nodes or Hugging Face).

4 Procedures to Ingest Language Resources

Different repositories need to be approached differently with the goal of extracting metadata records and ingesting them into ELG. This relates to a number of dimensions that have allowed us to categorise repositories and, thus, to set up procedures to process them. These relate to the *conversion, extraction and completion* as well as *harvesting* of LR metadata, further described in Sections 4.1, 4.2 and 4.3 below.

4.1 Metadata Conversion

We converted (through mapping) the metadata records of several repositories so that we could import them into the ELG catalogue, which follows the ELG metadata schema (Labropoulou et al. 2020). This was the case for the ELRA catalogue, the META-SHARE nodes and the initial ingestion of the ELRC-SHARE repository (managed through harvesting now, see below). This conversion work is complex, but it has paved the way for improvements and updates on both sides of the conversion line, on both the source and target metadata elements and descriptions.

4.1.1 From ELRA Catalogue to ELG

The conversion of the LR metadata entries in the ELRA catalogue into the ELG metadata format followed several steps:

- *Updating the ELRA catalogue XML Schema Definition (XSD):* The ELRA catalogue is based upon the META-SHARE structure, it has been adapted to ELRA's specific distribution requirements. Before proceeding with the metadata conversion, an analysis of discrepancies between the META-SHARE XSD and the ELRA catalogue XML files was performed. This allowed us to update the ELRA catalogue XSD and to export the XML files in META-SHARE 3.1 format.

- *Mapping between META-SHARE 3.1 and ELG-SHARE 1.0.2:* Once exported, the ELRA XML files were mapped to the ELG metadata schema 1.0.2. This mapping allowed us to adapt the validated ELRA XML files (in META-SHARE 3.1 format) and to make them compliant with the ELG-SHARE model. Several elements had to be adapted for that purpose.
- *Conversion from META-SHARE 3.1 to ELG Metadata Model 1.0.2:* Once the mapping between the ELRA catalogue and ELG was completed, we implemented an XSLT stylesheet to transform the META-SHARE 3.1 format to the ELG metadata model.

While the implementation of this first tool required quite a bit of effort, the experience gained was valuable for the subsequent implementation of other converters.

4.1.2 From META-SHARE to ELG

META-SHARE's DKFI, ELDA and ILSP nodes are based on META-SHARE XSD 3.0. An already existing XSLT stylesheet was used to convert from META-SHARE XSD 3.0 to 3.1. We implemented a second XSLT stylesheet to convert META-SHARE 3.1 XML files into ELG metadata 1.0.2 (as for the ELRA-SHARE conversion into ELG). This modular approach allowed us to use META-SHARE v3.1 as pivot schema, reusing the implemented XSLTs stylesheets for further conversions (such as ELRC-SHARE's below).

4.1.3 From ELRC-SHARE to ELG

ELRC-SHARE is also based on META-SHARE. The initial ingestion was carried out through conversion, a harvesting protocol was put in place later (see Section 4.3 and Chapter 6 in Part I). To benefit from the ELRA to ELG metadata converter, a subset of ELRC-SHARE LRs was converted first into the ELRA and then into the ELG format.

4.1.4 Import into ELG

The XML files converted from the metadata of the different repositories were then imported into ELG using the API developed for this purpose. Some inconsistencies remained that led to corrections both in the XML files and the ELRA catalogue.

4.2 Metadata Extraction and Completion

Now we look into those repositories that did not allow for a straightforward conversion or for which building converters was not a feasible option.

4.2.1 Zenodo

Zenodo[10] is a digital library launched in May 2013 within the OpenAire[11] project, to enable the compilation of research artefacts, such as publications, images, datasets, software, etc. A good number of those artefacts consists of LRs that may be of interest to the LT community. However, the extremely high number of artefacts in Zenodo together with the incompatibility of the Zenodo and ELG metadata schemes made the identification of relevant LRs a big challenge. We opted for a semi-automatic approach to collect what ELG considers as LRs, using a combination of Python and directly querying the Zenodo database, among others.[12] However, the compilation of metadata information still required manual intervention to ingest our selection of actual LRs as well as to add the minimal set of metadata elements which are mandatory for ELG and which do not exist in the Zenodo records. This semi-automated process required a lot of manual effort. We currently work on an automated harvesting-oriented approach (see Section 4.3 and Chapter 6 in Part I).

4.2.2 ELRA-SHARE-LRs

The ELRA-SHARE-LRs are provided by participants attending the Language Resources and Evaluation Conference (LREC). Participants can share the LRs they present at the conference either by uploading them in a special LREC repository or by linking them to their original download location using an online form. We selected a subset of these LRs by checking the compliance of licences with the ones accepted in ELG. Licences that are too vague were left aside (e. g., "Open Source", "Creative Commons" without further specification). Given that the original metadata was available as a spreadsheet, the sheet and conversion tool produced to gather Zenodo metadata (see above) was adapted. As the ELRA-SHARE-LRs metadata contained only a minimal set of information, missing but required information was added manually into the spreadsheet to comply with the mandatory ELG metadata (e. g., type of LR, linguality, annotation, data format, licence, etc.). Finally, the spreadsheet was converted into XML and ingested into ELG.

4.2.3 Quantum Stat

Quantum Stat enables LR producers to register datasets in the "Big Bad NLP Database".[13] The procedure for identifying, describing and ingesting datasets into ELG is as follows: first, an initial table with 481 datasets was exported and analysed for relevance to ELG by checking licensing information (whether licences are well

---

[10] https://zenodo.org

[11] https://www.openaire.eu

[12] https://developers.zenodo.org/#records

[13] https://datasets.quantumstat.com

identified), dataset type, and whether the resource can be downloaded. The datasets not complying to the LR description requirements were discarded and only compliant metadata information was kept. Then, as for ELRA-SHARE-LRs and Zenodo, the minimal set of metadata information was compiled, while also adding missing information before the actual conversion into XML and ingestion into ELG.

4.2.4 Hugging Face

Often described as a "model zoo", the Hugging Face[14] repository includes a large collection of machine learning models and datasets that can be used for training new models, with a focus on the Transformers architecture (Wolf et al. 2020). ELG collaborates with Hugging Face regarding the import of Hugging Face metadata records into ELG. One challenge relates to the fact that the description of resources in Hugging Face does not follow a specific methodology. To begin with, adding descriptions to resources is encouraged but not mandatory. Furthermore, the suggested metadata elements do not follow a standard schema. The manual work needed to process the filtered entries was considerable in order to enrich the information available. A conversion process was applied based on mapping the elements (see Chapter 6 for more details).

4.3 Metadata Harvesting

We implemented metadata harvesting solutions for ELRC-SHARE, LINDAT/CLA-RIAH-CZ, CLARIN-PL and CLARIN-SI as well as Zenodo, as described below.

4.3.1 ELRC-SHARE

Three groups of datasets were originally selected from the three prioritised repositories to be converted and ingested into ELG Release 1 (see Section 4.1). Of these, only ELRC-SHARE allowed for the import of the whole list given that its resources met the following conditions: their licensing conditions allowed it (all data were shared under CC-BY licences, they were open under the directive on the re-use of public sector information, or they belong to the public domain), and their metadata elements were compatible and fully covered by the ELG metadata schema. We have implemented an OAI-PMH[15] client that harvests metadata records compliant with the ELG metadata schema, and we use this for regular harvesting from ELRC-SHARE.

---

[14] https://huggingface.co
[15] Open Archives Initiative Protocol for Metadata Harvesting (2015).

4.3.2 LINDAT/CLARIAH-CZ

The LINDAT/CLARIAH-CZ repository makes its metadata available for harvesting through its OAI-PMH end-point.[16] Means for ingesting metadata complying to the META-SHARE schema[17] were already in place in ELG and the repository did provide a mapping from its internal metadata storage to META-SHARE. An attempt was made at reusing this conversion, but the result was deemed unacceptable as not all of the available metadata was mapped. After a few iterations we arrived at a mapping between concepts that are important and required in the ELG schema and the metadata stored in LINDAT/CLARIAH-CZ. LINDAT updated the metadata for several of its resources following the feedback received from ELG. Also, based on the feedback from LINDAT/CLARIAH-CZ, some changes were applied to the ELG schema. The implementation of this mapping represents around 1,200 changed lines of code, including some tooling to reflect some of the metadata issues discovered.[18]

4.3.3 CLARIN-PL and CLARIN-SI

The LINDAT/CLARIAH-CZ repository makes available an OAI-PMH endpoint which exposes ELG-compatible metadata records. The repository software developed by the LINDAT/CLARIAH-CZ team, based on DSpace, is also used by several other CLARIN centres for their repositories, i. e., their metadata records are ready to be imported into ELG using the same harvesting procedure. For ELG Release 3, this collaboration has resulted in the regular harvesting of the CLARIN centres in Slovenia (CLARIN-SI) and Poland (CLARIN-PL).[19]

4.3.4 Zenodo

As described in Chapter 6 (Part I), Zenodo is a particularly interesting catalogue for ELG purposes. Zenodo exposes its metadata records through a REST API[20] as JSON data and through an OAI-PMH API[21] in a set of standard metadata formats, i. e., DC[22], DataCite[23], MARC21[24] and DCAT[25]. Work is currently ongoing to replace the semi-manual import of Zenodo metadata records that started for ELG Release

---

[16] http://lindat.mff.cuni.cz/repository/oai/request?verb=Identify

[17] http://www.meta-share.org/p/93/Documentation

[18] https://github.com/ufal/clarin-dspace/pull/930

[19] http://www.clarin.si and https://clarin-pl.eu

[20] https://developers.zenodo.org/#rest-api

[21] https://developers.zenodo.org/#oai-pmh

[22] https://www.dublincore.org/specifications/dublin-core/dcmi-terms/

[23] https://schema.datacite.org/meta/kernel-4.4/

[24] https://www.loc.gov/marc/bibliographic/

[25] https://www.w3.org/TR/vocab-dcat-3/

2 with a more automated process taking advantage of the standard protocols and schemas offered by Zenodo. This task involves a number of challenges that we are currently addressing with regard to the selection of the source API, the selection and conversion of metadata, the selection of a subset of the downloaded metadata records and the setting-up of an automated procedure for regular harvesting.

5 Language Resources in the ELG Catalogue

After the most recent ingestions of datasets as well as the contributions from the pilot projects and ELE, the ELG catalogue has reached a total of 8,873 metadata entries in April 2022, far exceeding our expectations when we started the project. The majority of these are description records without the data being hosted in ELG (103 resources are fully available through ELG). However, even if not available through ELG directly, most datasets are available through the referenced repository page, often available for download, which is reflected in the ELG catalogue too. Figures 1 and 2 illustrate the breakdown of repository sources ingested so far together with the breakdown of the current numbers per source.

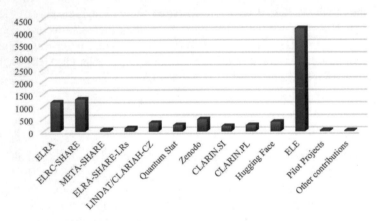

Fig. 1 Repository sources of the 8,873 datasets available in ELG in April 2022

Regarding resource types and their linguality, Figure 3 illustrates the numbers. As expected, the highest numbers apply to corpora (6,236 available in ELG), with twice as many monolingual corpora as bilingual ones (which in turn are three times as many as the multilingual ones). Lexical/Conceptual resources are also very well represented with 2,229 entries.

One of our bigger concerns at the time of Release 2 was the fact that there were barely any language descriptions (there were only 7). This has changed with the work towards ELG Release 3: at the time of writing, we count 408 language descriptions with the majority being monolingual. Further regarding language descriptions, the

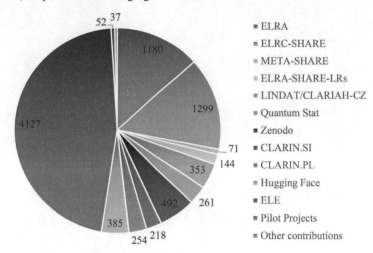

ELRA
ELRC-SHARE
META-SHARE
ELRA-SHARE-LRs
LINDAT/CLARIAH-CZ
Quantum Stat
Zenodo
CLARIN.SI
CLARIN.PL
Hugging Face
ELE
Pilot Projects
Other contributions

Fig. 2 Repository sources of the 8,873 datasets available in ELG in April 2022

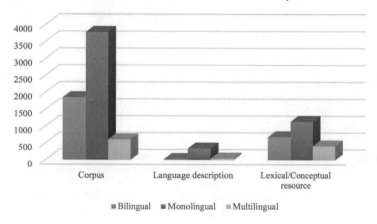

Bilingual   Monolingual   Multilingual

Fig. 3 Types of resources according to linguality

number of its "language models" subclass has increased to 358. This is good news as models are a popular and highly demanded resource type, currently providing the state of the art for many LT/NLP tasks. ELG is actively encouraging the use of its platform for the creation of models. The pilot projects have supported this resource type as well by contributing their models, too.

ELG also offers a very broad language coverage, with 450 languages represented by lexical/conceptual resources, and with corpora available in 438 languages, at the time of writing. The language models cover 156 languages, grammars are available for 25 languages. These are either monolingual or multilingual resources. Figure 4 shows the language resource type distribution for the EU official languages.

Finally, different media types are also represented in ELG. As expected, the largest number of resources belongs to the type "text" with more than 7,000 datasets.

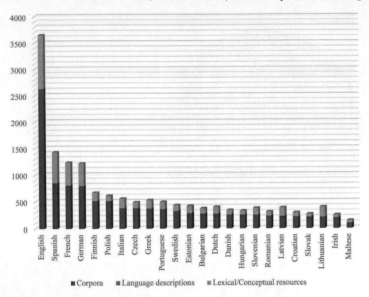

Fig. 4 Language resource type distribution for the official EU languages

Nonetheless, the type "audio" already offers more than 1,200 resources while currently 385 image and video resources are available.

6 Language Resources and Legal Issues

Managing legal issues in a large platform such as ELG implies taking care of a wide variety of legal aspects, often regarding licensing. It also implies taking into account processes that may differ from one provider to another. A provider may choose to distribute resources either through implicit or explicit licences, through specific conditions of use, or through considering a particular user status such as profiles or membership status. Moreover, the need to ensure GDPR compliance requires certain monitoring processes. For the development of the platform, the project has benefited from the support and advice of a dedicated team of legal experts who helped deploy the platform in a manner that is legally sound. This ranges from establishing the necessary legal context (e. g., Privacy Policy and Terms of Use) to stepping in for consultations. The legal team has also contributed to the preparation of a Data Management Plan (see Section 7). Below, we briefly describe some of the specific issues the ELG legal team has taken care of.

Advice on implicit versus explicit licences: One main distinction to make is the management of implied (or implicit) versus expressed (or explicit) licences. For implied licences, it has become a commonly and widely used practice to grant users access when they click on the licence terms acceptance button indicated on the repository pages.

Advice on conditions and terms of use: The conditions of use of a resource are another factor that has been defined and which may require further discussion and interaction between the provider and the user. Among the various elements to consider in licensing data or tools, we need to review the purpose of use (which could be commercial, for research, etc.), as well as the profile of the licencee (this is the type of institution, some resources may be restricted to particular types of institutions, e. g., *academic* or *commercial*)[26].

Financial and distributional issues: Not only legal issues may condition the delivery of resources to a user, but also the financial and distribution policies of the provider. Such policies involve a dedicated team, with expertise in technical, legal and financial domains. Parameters like the legal profile of the licencee, the purpose of use and the pricing policy need to be clearly displayed.

META-SHARE licensing: The selection of LRs for ingestion done for the three META-SHARE nodes needed to be revised due to licensing restrictions. These involved proprietary licences (e. g., MS-C-NoReD, MS-NC-NoReD and MS-Commons-BY-SA), as well as licences that required negotiations with providers. To address this, a study of the licences was performed by the ELG legal team for discussion with node managers. A proposal for licence mapping was drafted where non-restrictive licences were invited to move to Creative Commons licences. Restrictive licences were encouraged to move to more open licences, too.

Legal checking: The identification of various repositories demonstrated the importance of legal checking all throughout the information compilation process. In some cases (e. g., Zenodo), licences were well identified and could usually be integrated in the ELG metadata without further analysis. However, for other cases (e. g., ELRA-SHARE-LRs, Quantum Stat), legal information did not always comply with ELG requirements or was simply missing. Consequently, legal expertise was needed to either check and confirm the accuracy of present legal information, or to search for and gather the appropriate legal information.

Improvement of the licence list: When we processed the Zenodo datasets, we realised that several licences were not part of the ELG metadata values. Thus, the ELG legal expert was asked to compare the Zenodo list with the ELG list and make suggestions to integrate some of those licences into the ELG metadata. A list of 68 licences that did not correspond to ELG values was checked, out of which 40 could be added to the ELG licence list, whereas the other 28 did not need to be added because they were already used within ELG using other labels, they were not used, or they had no link.

Addition of conditions of use in the ELG metadata: We decided to add a new metadata field corresponding to the "conditions of use" associated to each identified licence to improve the search functionality for resources based on their licensing conditions. For "standard" licences, the conditions of use were added by the ELG team, based on information gathered from Creative Commons licences,

---

[26] https://live.european-language-grid.eu/terms-of-use

values from the CLARIN licencing framework[27], META-SHARE licences, and the ELRA licence wizard[28]. For all other LRs, a thorough analysis of over 300 licences (all licences in the SPDX list[29]) was done by our legal team who went through the different conditions of use such as the intellectual property rights granted by the licences, the requirements on redistribution imposed by the licence, the requirements on use of the data and, finally, the requirements imposed on users (Rigault et al. 2022b).

7 Language Resources and Data Management

ELG is a platform for commercial and non-commercial Language Technologies, both functional (running services and tools) and non-functional (datasets, resources, models). In order to achieve this, the consortium in charge of the ELG platform has enacted several priorities that include the processing of massive amounts of data and of different types. These large amounts of data derive from partners' contributions, external providers willing to share their datasets through ELG, our harvesting of other repositories as well as different kinds of resource and repository identification work. As can be expected, such a data intensive project requires clear data management policies, in particular considering GDPR constraints. For that purpose, we implemented a Data Management Plan (DMP) as a concrete necessity for organisational, technical and legal management of all data types processed in the course of the project (Rigault et al. 2022a). The DMP documents the variety of data types collected, received and/or processed in the course of the project and reports on how the data is going to be managed with regard to technical, organisational and legal aspects. The DMP also complies with best practices and, in particular, with the requirements of Horizon 2020 as well as GDPR obligations. It defines useful practices to enhance compatibility with the FAIR principles (see Section 7 in Chapter 2 and Wilkinson et al. 2016)[30], as endorsed and specified for Horizon 2020. Moreover, the DMP provides advice in terms of best practices for language resource creation in all steps of an LR life cycle (Choukri and Arranz 2012; Rehm 2016).

8 Conclusions

We integrated more than 10,000 metadata records for datasets, models and other classes of language resources into the ELG platform. These LRTs have been carefully described so as to ease their findability (following the FAIR principles) and to

---

[27] See https://www.clarin.eu/content/licenses-and-clarin-categories#res and https://www.clarin.eu/content/clarin-license-category-calculator

[28] http://wizard.elra.info/principal.php

[29] https://spdx.org/licenses/

[30] https://www.go-fair.org

ensure compliance with the ELG metadata schema while advocating for interoperability. A series of steps and best practices has been followed with the objective of establishing procedures for resource identification, description and ingestion. The work carried out during the ELG project has allowed us to consider expertise and lessons learned to improve protocols and principles. This has been the reason for updating the integration approach of some repositories (e. g., ELRC-SHARE and Zenodo). The strategy behind the choice of repositories has also been planned carefully, following technical and strategic priorities, as well as evolutionary needs and demands. ELG users can now either access thousands of resources or contribute resources through the different means provided. Legal issues have also been considered with a special focus on licensing. Moreover, a Data Management Plan has been conceived to address the handling of all types of data (including sensitive data) within ELG as well as guiding the production and life cycle aspects of LRs.

References

Arranz, Victoria, Khalid Choukri, Valérie Mapelli, Mickaël Rigault, Jan Hajic, Ondrej Kosarko, Cristian Berrio, Andrés Garcia-Silva, Rémi Calizzano, Nils Feldhus, Miltos Deligiannis, Penny Labropoulou, Stelios Piperidis, and Ulrich Germann (2021). *Deliverable D5.2 Data Sets, Identified Gaps, Produced Resources and Models (Version 2)*. Project deliverable; EU project European Language Grid (ELG); Grant Agreement no. 825627 ELG. URL: https://www.european-language-grid.eu/wp-content/uploads/2022/04/ELG-Deliverable-D5.2-final.pdf.

Arranz, Victoria, Khalid Choukri, Valérie Mapelli, Mickaël Rigault, Penny Labropoulou, Miltos Deligiannis, Leon Voukoutis, Stelios Piperidis, and Ulrich Germann (2022). *Deliverable D5.3 Data Sets, Models, Identified Gaps, Produced Resources and their Exploitation within ELG (Version 3)*. Project deliverable; EU project European Language Grid (ELG); Grant Agreement no. 825627 ELG. URL: https://www.european-language-grid.eu/wp-content/uploads/2022/04/ELG-Deliverable-D5.3-final.pdf.

Choukri, Khalid and Victoria Arranz (2012). "An Analytical Model of Language Resource Sustainability". In: *Proceedings of the Eighth International Conference on Language Resources and Evaluation (LREC 2012)*. Istanbul, Turkey: ELRA, pp. 1395–1402. URL: http://www.lrec-conf.org/proceedings/lrec2012/pdf/846_Paper.pdf.

Gavrilidou, Maria, Penny Labropoulou, Elina Desipri, Stelios Piperidis, Haris Papageorgiou, Monica Monachini, Francesca Frontini, Thierry Declerck, Gil Francopoulo, Victoria Arranz, and Valerie Mapelli (2012). "The META-SHARE Metadata Schema for the Description of Language Resources". In: *Proceedings of the Eighth International Conference on Language Resources and Evaluation (LREC 2012)*. Istanbul, Turkey: ELRA, pp. 1090–1097. URL: http://www.lrec-conf.org/proceedings/lrec2012/pdf/998_Paper.pdf.

Labropoulou, Penny, Katerina Gkirtzou, Maria Gavriilidou, Miltos Deligiannis, Dimitris Galanis, Stelios Piperidis, Georg Rehm, Maria Berger, Valérie Mapelli, Michael Rigault, Victoria Arranz, Khalid Choukri, Gerhard Backfried, José Manuel Gómez Pérez, and Andres Garcia-Silva (2020). "Making Metadata Fit for Next Generation Language Technology Platforms: The Metadata Schema of the European Language Grid". In: *Proceedings of the 12th Language Resources and Evaluation Conference (LREC 2020)*. Ed. by Nicoletta Calzolari, Frédéric Béchet, Philippe Blache, Christopher Cieri, Khalid Choukri, Thierry Declerck, Hitoshi Isahara, Bente Maegaard, Joseph Mariani, Asuncion Moreno, Jan Odijk, and Stelios Piperidis. Marseille, France: ELRA, pp. 3421–3430. URL: https://www.aclweb.org/anthology/2020.lrec-1.420/.

Lösch, Andrea, Valérie Mapelli, Khalid Choukri, Maria Giagkou, Stelios Piperidis, Prokopis Prokopidis, Vassilis Papavassiliou, Miltos Deligiannis, Aivars Berzins, Andrejs Vasiljevs, Eileen
Schnur, Thierry Declerck, and Josef van Genabith (2021). "Collection and Curation of Language Data within the European Language Resource Coordination (ELRC)". In: *Proceedings
of the Conference on Digital Curation Technologies (QURATOR 2021)*. Ed. by Adrian Paschke,
Georg Rehm, Jamal Al Qundus, Clemens Neudecker, and Lydia Pintscher. Vol. 2836. CEUR
Workshop Proceedings. Berlin, Germany: CEUR-WS.org. URL: http://ceur-ws.org/Vol-2836
/qurator2021_paper_6.pdf.
Mapelli, Valérie, Victoria Arranz, Hélène Mazo, and Khalid Choukri (2022). "Language Resources
to Support Language Diversity – the ELRA Achievements". In: *Proceedings of the 13th Language Resources and Evaluation Conference (LREC 2022)*. Ed. by Nicoletta Calzolari, Frédéric
Béchet, Philippe Blache, Christopher Cieri, Khalid Choukri, Thierry Declerck, Hitoshi Isahara,
Bente Maegaard, Joseph Mariani, Jan Odijk, and Stelios Piperidis. Marseille, France: ELRA,
pp. 551–558. URL: http://www.lrec-conf.org/proceedings/lrec2022/pdf/2022.lrec-1.58.pdf.
Piperidis, Stelios, Harris Papageorgiou, Christian Spurk, Georg Rehm, Khalid Choukri, Olivier Ha-
mon, Nicoletta Calzolari, Riccardo del Gratta, Bernardo Magnini, and Christian Girardi (2014).
"META-SHARE: One year after". In: *Proceedings of the 9th Language Resources and Evalu-
ation Conference (LREC 2014)*. Ed. by Nicoletta Calzolari, Khalid Choukri, Thierry Declerck,
Hrafn Loftsson, Bente Maegaard, Joseph Mariani, Asuncion Moreno, Jan Odijk, and Stelios
Piperidis. Reykjavik, Iceland: ELRA, pp. 1532–1538. URL: http://www.lrec-conf.org/proceed
ings/lrec2014/pdf/786_Paper.pdf.
Rehm, Georg (2016). "The Language Resource Life Cycle: Towards a Generic Model for Creat-
ing, Maintaining, Using and Distributing Language Resources". In: *Proceedings of the 10th
Language Resources and Evaluation Conference (LREC 2016)*. Ed. by Nicoletta Calzolari,
Khalid Choukri, Thierry Declerck, Marko Grobelnik, Bente Maegaard, Joseph Mariani, Asun-
cion Moreno, Jan Odijk, and Stelios Piperidis. Portorož, Slovenia: ELRA, pp. 2450–2454. URL:
https://aclanthology.org/L16-1388.pdf.
Rehm, Georg and Katrin Marheinecke (2019). *Deliverable D7.2 National Competence Centres
and Language Technology Council*. Project deliverable; EU project European Language Grid
(ELG); Grant Agreement no. 825627 ELG. URL: https://www.european-language-grid.eu/wp-
content/uploads/2021/02/ELG-Deliverable-D7.2-final.pdf.
Rehm, Georg, Stelios Piperidis, Kalina Bontcheva, Jan Hajic, Victoria Arranz, Andrejs Vasiļjevs,
Gerhard Backfried, José Manuel Gómez Pérez, Ulrich Germann, Rémi Calizzano, Nils Feldhus,
Stefanie Hegele, Florian Kintzel, Katrin Marheinecke, Julian Moreno-Schneider, Dimitris Gala-
nis, Penny Labropoulou, Miltos Deligiannis, Katerina Gkirtzou, Athanasia Kolovou, Dimitris
Gkoumas, Leon Voukoutis, Ian Roberts, Jana Hamrlová, Dusan Varis, Lukáš Kačena, Khalid
Choukri, Valérie Mapelli, Mickaël Rigault, Jūlija Meļņika, Miro Janosik, Katja Prinz, Andres
Garcia-Silva, Cristian Berrio, Ondrej Klejch, and Steve Renals (2021). "European Language
Grid: A Joint Platform for the European Language Technology Community". In: *Proceedings
of the 16th Conference of the European Chapter of the Association for Computational Linguis-
tics: System Demonstrations (EACL 2021)*. Kyiv, Ukraine: ACL, pp. 221–230. URL: https://w
ww.aclweb.org/anthology/2021.eacl-demos.26.pdf.
Rigault, Mickaël, Victoria Arranz, Khalid Choukri, Valérie Mapelli, Pawel Kamocki, and Lucille
Blanchard (2022a). *Deliverable D5.6 Data Management Plan (Version 3)*. Project deliverable;
EU project European Language Grid (ELG); Grant Agreement no. 825627 ELG. URL: https:
//www.european-language-grid.eu/wp-content/uploads/2022/04/ELG-Deliverable-D5.6-final
.pdf.
Rigault, Mickaël, Victoria Arranz, Valérie Mapelli, Penny Labropoulou, and Stelios Piperidis
(2022b). "Categorizing Legal Features in a Metadata-Oriented Task: Defining the Conditions
of Use". In: *Proceedings of the Legal and Ethical Issues Workshop (LREC 2022)*. Ed. by Nicoletta Calzolari, Frédéric Béchet, Philippe Blache, Christopher Cieri, Khalid Choukri, Thierry
Declerck, Hitoshi Isahara, Bente Maegaard, Joseph Mariani, Jan Odijk, and Stelios Piperidis.
Marseille, France: ELRA, pp. 22–26.

Wilkinson, Mark D., Michel Dumontier, IJsbrand Jan Aalbersberg, Gabrielle Appleton, Myles Axton, Arie Baak, Niklas Blomberg, Jan-Willem Boiten, Luiz Bonino da Silva Santos, Philip E. Bourne, Jildau Bouwman, Anthony J. Brookes, Tim Clark, Mercè Crosas, Ingrid Dillo, Olivier Dumon, Scott Edmunds, Chris T. Evelo, Richard Finkers, Alejandra Gonzalez-Beltran, Alasdair J.G. Gray, Paul Groth, Carole Goble, Jeffrey S. Grethe, Jaap Heringa, Peter A.C 't Hoen, Rob Hooft, Tobias Kuhn, Ruben Kok, Joost Kok, Scott J. Lusher, Maryann E. Martone, Albert Mons, Abel L. Packer, Bengt Persson, Philippe Rocca-Serra, Marco Roos, Rene van Schaik, Susanna-Assunta Sansone, Erik Schultes, Thierry Sengstag, Ted Slater, George Strawn, Morris A. Swertz, Mark Thompson, Johan van der Lei, Erik van Mulligen, Jan Velterop, Andra Waagmeester, Peter Wittenburg, Katherine Wolstencroft, Jun Zhao, and Barend Mons (2016). "The FAIR Guiding Principles for Scientific Data Management and Stewardship". In: *Scientific Data* 3. DOI: 10.1038/sdata.2016.18. URL: http://www.nature.com/articles/sdata201618.

Wolf, Thomas, Lysandre Debut, Victor Sanh, Julien Chaumond, Clement Delangue, Anthony Moi, Pierric Cistac, Tim Rault, Rémi Louf, Morgan Funtowicz, Joe Davison, Sam Shleifer, Patrick von Platen, Clara Ma, Yacine Jernite, Julien Plu, Canwen Xu, Teven Le Scao, Sylvain Gugger, Mariama Drame, Quentin Lhoest, and Alexander M. Rush (2020). "Transformers: State-of-the-art Natural Language Processing". In: *Proceedings of the 2020 Conference on Empirical Methods in Natural Language Processing: System Demonstrations*. ACL, pp. 38–45. DOI: 10.1865 3/v1/2020.emnlp-demos.6. URL: https://aclanthology.org/2020.emnlp-demos.6.

Yeganova, Lana, Dina Wiemann, Mariana Neves, Federica Vezzani, Amy Siu, Inigo Jauregi Unanue, Maite Oronoz, Nancy Mah, Aurélie Névéol, David Martinez, Rachel Bawden, Giorgio Maria Di Nunzio, Roland Roller, Philippe Thomas, Cristian Grozea, Olatz Perez-de-Viñaspre, Maika Vicente Navarro, and Antonio Jimeno Yepes (2021). "Findings of the WMT 2021 Biomedical Translation Shared Task: Summaries of Animal Experiments as New Test Set". In: *Proceedings of the Sixth Conference on Machine Translation*. ACL, pp. 664–683. URL: https://aclanthology.org/2021.wmt-1.70.

Chapter 9
Language Technology Companies, Research Organisations and Projects

Georg Rehm, Katrin Marheinecke, Rémi Calizzano, and Penny Labropoulou

Abstract The European Language Grid is meant to develop into the primary platform of the European Language Technology community. In addition to LT tools and services (Chapter 7) and Language Resources (Chapter 8), ELG represents the actual members of this community, i. e., the companies and research organisations that develop language technologies and that are engaged in related activities. The goal of becoming the primary platform for LT in Europe implies that ELG should ideally represent *all* European companies and *all* European research organisations with corresponding metadata records in the ELG catalogue, which are interlinked with the respective LT tools and services as well as language resources they offer. This chapter describes the European stakeholders and user groups that are relevant for the ELG initiative, the composition of the community and the locations of the companies and research groups as currently listed in ELG. Furthermore, we describe a number of technical and organisational challenges involved in the preparation of our list of stakeholders, and outline the process of catalogue population.

1 Introduction

The European Language Grid is meant to develop into the primary platform of the European LT community. This is why, in addition to functional LT tools and services and more static Language Resources (LRs), ELG also represents the actual members of this community, i. e., the companies and research organisations that develop LTs and that are engaged in related activities such as the integration of LT into existing systems or support services such as data annotation at scale. This overall goal of eventually establishing ELG as the primary platform for LT in Europe implies that ELG should ideally represent *all* European companies and *all* European research

Georg Rehm · Katrin Marheinecke · Rémi Calizzano
Deutsches Forschungszentrum für Künstliche Intelligenz GmbH, Germany, georg.rehm@dfki.de, katrin.marheinecke@dfki.de, remi.calizzano@dfki.de

Penny Labropoulou
Institute for Language and Speech Processing, R. C. "Athena", Greece, penny@athenarc.gr

© The Author(s) 2023
G. Rehm (ed.), *European Language Grid*, Cognitive Technologies,
https://doi.org/10.1007/978-3-031-17258-8_9

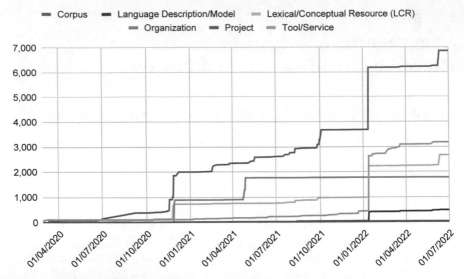

Fig. 1 Evolution of resources in ELG over time broken down by resource type

organisations in the ELG catalogue, which are interlinked with the respective LT tools and services as well as language resources these organisations offer on and through the European Language Grid. In other words, the European Language Grid also functions as the "yellow pages" of the European LT community, ideally listing and promoting *all* relevant members of this community, i. e., small and medium-sized companies as well as large enterprises, research centers, universities and other academic institutions that develop LT but also organisations in the periphery of this core, e. g., integrators and annotation service providers (Rehm et al. 2020, 2021).[1]

In addition to serving as the central directory for members of the European LT community, ELG also includes information about relevant projects in the area.[2] The reasoning behind this is the way many LTs are typically developed, i. e., through publicly funded project consortia in which academic or commercial organisations participate. Such projects often result in concrete tools and technologies as well as language resources, which can then be made available, among others, through ELG, which allows representing and interlinking these project artefacts (LTs, LRs), the projects that helped create these artefacts and the members of the respective project consortia. Technically, project consortia can provide relevant metadata to create and later edit and update their own project pages in ELG ensuring more visibility as well as an additional dissemination channel for their projects' outputs.

In the second half of the ELG project's runtime, corresponding activities in terms of populating the ELG catalogue with information about companies, academic organisations and projects have been drastically increased so that, towards the end of the project, ELG now includes convincing figures in terms of community members,

---

[1] https://live.european-language-grid.eu/catalogue/?entity_type__term=Organization

[2] https://live.european-language-grid.eu/catalogue/?entity_type__term=Project

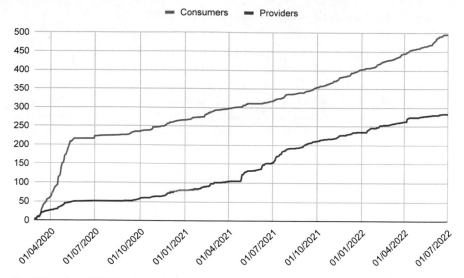

Fig. 2 Number of ELG consumer and provider accounts over time

projects and also active users of the platform. At the time of writing, ELG lists more than 13,000 metadata records on tools and services, resources, organisations and projects. Figure 1 shows the corresponding development of the ELG catalogue and its population over time, differentiated by type of entry.

Not only the number of resources and organisations listed in ELG is constantly growing. In addition, the number of users is rising continuously. The number of ELG users of the consumer category who have a registered a user account went up significantly at the end of April 2020, after the first official release to the public, and has grown further ever since. The number of ELG users of the provider category, i. e., users with the right to integrate metadata, tools and resources in ELG, is also increasing continuously, albeit more slowly, as can be expected (see Figure 2).

As encouraging as this development is, ELG is still at the beginning. The platform has been designed in such a way that it can be actively used by the community and that it can grow. To achieve this goal of a true one-stop shop for the whole European LT community, it is necessary to steadily expand the consumer and provider base and monitor as well as reflect all changes and new developments in the European LT landscape. Only with this momentum will the desired snowball effect be generated eventually, which ultimately helps ELG to achieve sustainable success from which all stakeholders can benefit.

2 The European Language Technology Landscape

One key characteristic of the European Language Technology landscape is its extreme fragmentation, which has been mentioned repeatedly throughout the years, as, for example, in the META-NET White Paper Series (Rehm and Uszkoreit 2012), in the META-NET Strategic Research Agenda (Rehm and Uszkoreit 2013; Rehm et al. 2016), in the *Final study report on CEF automated translation value proposition in the context of the European LT market/ecosystem* (Vasiljevs et al. 2019) or in the various reports of the European Language Equality project (especially see Aldabe et al. 2022). In fact, this extreme fragmentation is one of the main reasons why the ELG platform has been developed in the first place because the fragmentation is generally perceived as one of the main reasons why the European LT community has been unable to unleash its full potential.

The analysis in the CEF LT Market study (Vasiljevs et al. 2019) shows that European LT vendors are often SMEs with local or regional, often highly specialised solutions. In the study, 473 companies were collected that are active in EU member states in the domain of LT and that fully qualify as LT vendors. According to the research, the total size of the LT industry within the EU member states (plus Iceland and Norway) was estimated at approx. 800M€ in the year 2017. In the study sample investigated, only 14% of the LT vendors had a revenue of more than €10M, whereas almost half of them (48%) had a revenue below €1M. In terms of size, 52% of the companies had between 10 and 99 employees, and 26% had less than 10 employees, both combined representing nearly 80% of the 473 companies studied. Only 44% of the EU companies in this sample received external funding or venture capital.

Consequently, the global LT and NLP market continues to be dominated by large technology enterprises from the United States and Asia which establish "data-driven intellectual monopolies" (Rikap and Lundvall 2020) – in that regard, large companies are the exception in Europe. However, these big non-European LT providers have certain deficiencies regarding under-resourced languages, customisation needs, as well as security and privacy requirements which is a frequently expressed demand from corporate clients and European administrations (Overton 2017).

Despite the fact that the LT market is relatively small when compared to the general IT market at large, it is a market with strong competition, which is one of the reasons why many LT developing companies tend to focus on highly specialised niche markets with less intense competition. This, however, affects profitability, which is, on average, rather low and margins are compressed. On the other hand, LT can also be considered a growing market: today, (potential) customers have more awareness of the benefits of LT, which is also due to marketing activities of large international players. From a local vendors' point of view, the large technology enterprises help create a market awareness that simply did not exist ten years ago. Nevertheless, these companies are also the toughest competition of the European LT community as they tend to offer high-quality LT software free of charge or for very low prices, which European SMEs usually cannot afford to do.

The STOA study *Language equality in the digital age – Towards a Human Language Project* (STOA 2018), which examines the causes of language barriers in

Europe and formulates recommendations for policies to overcome these barriers, mentions among its 11 key recommendations the need for a pan-European LT Platform of resources and services and ELG has stepped up to solve this problem (also see European Parliament 2018). ELG not only brings together LT resources from all over Europe supporting almost all European languages (although ELG is not limited to European languages) but ELG also has the ambition to unite the European LT community behind these services, tools and resources using one shared umbrella platform to create a common access point and marketplace from which all languages and members of the community will eventually benefit (see Part III of this book).

At the time of writing, ELG contains approx. 1,800 organisations operating in the European LT sphere. One half of these organisations consists of companies, the other half of universities and research groups (Figure 3).[3]

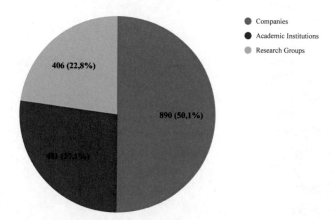

Fig. 3 Distribution of organisations listed in ELG per type

The quantitative distribution of LT developing organisations among the respective countries in Europe already hints at a strongly varying coverage of LT resources for their respective national and regional languages. Whereas countries like the UK, Germany or Spain are well or relatively well equipped with LT developing companies, smaller countries like Malta or Cyprus have only little representation in the European LT community (see Figure 4).[4] Figure 5 shows the geographical distribution in Europe of organisations listed in ELG.

---

[3] Companies are commercial organisations, academic institutions are universities and research centers, research groups are sub-groups of academic institutions, e. g., faculties or departments.

[4] In Figure 4, countries are ordered by decreasing number of organisations. The country with the head office of the respective organisation is used as the organisation's country.

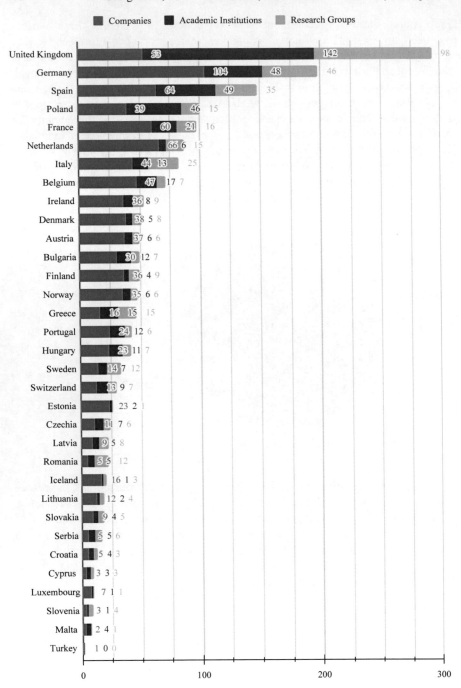

Fig. 4 Distribution of organisations listed in ELG per type and country

Fig. 5 Organisations listed in ELG per country

3 Organisations in the European Language Grid

To bootstrap the ELG catalogue with as many LT developing European companies and academic organisations as possible, we decided on the following procedure. First, together with the ELG National Competence Centres (see Chapter 11, p. 205 ff.), we collected LT developing organisations semi-automatically and in a decentralised way, i. e., on the national level (Section 3.1). Second, based on the results of this collection, metadata records were prepared that could be automatically ingested into the ELG catalogue (Section 3.2). This resulted in the ELG catalogue being populated with approx. 1,800 metadata records, i. e., pages, each of which describes one LT developing organisation with a basic profile. These organisation profiles can then be claimed by the rightful owners (Section 3.3), i. e., an organisation described in such an ELG page can take over the maintenance of its own page and enrich it with additional information, e. g., upload a logo, associate resources with their organisation etc. (Section 3.4). This bootstrapping procedure enables members of the European LT community to participate actively in ELG with their own organisation within minutes. As a positive side effect, it enabled ELG – including its sister project ELE – to produce a fairly detailed picture of the European LT landscape.

3.1 Collecting the Members of the European LT Community

In order to populate ELG with organisations, we used our own databases, carried out desk research and, most importantly, we involved the 32 National Competence Centres (NCCs) to tap into their detailed knowledge of their respective countries' LT communities. Our general goal was to identify and to record, in a machine-readable format, as many national and regional members of the European LT community as possible so that ELG can eventually provide as complete and up to date a picture as possible. In September 2020, this data collection task was conducted with NCC Leads representing their countries and regions to ideally identify all companies and academic organisations in the European LT community to be listed in ELG.

To streamline the process, based on data gathered in various workshops, conferences and other events over the last ten years, the ELG project team created lists of organisations involved in LT activities in all European countries. Each entry in the list contained, among others, the following information: organisation name, department name, website, address (region, ZIP code, city, country) and LT areas in which they are active. Each NCC Lead received the data records for their country, along with detailed guidelines, and they were asked to check the data included in the list, to correct the data if necessary (e. g., remove duplicates with similar names, correct wrong names of organisations) and to complete them where possible, i. e., to fill in blanks. Furthermore, the NCCs were asked to do their own research and provide new, unlisted organisations. The goal was to find all relevant organisations of each country that develop, market or sell LT in their countries. This way, the ELG consortium wanted to ensure that in addition to well-known orgnaisations also start-ups andyoung research groups are included in ELG.

The feedback received from the NCCs was submitted to a comprehensive internal quality review by the ELG team, which resulted in the final dataset that reflects a fairly complete representation of the relevant stakeholders and providers of Language Technology and language-centric AI in Europe.[5]

3.2 Preparation and Integration of Metadata Records

The efforts of the NCCs and the ELG team for the collection of data regarding LT organisations relevant for ELG resulted in two spreadsheets per country containing companies and research groups respectively. All entries were automatically converted into XML files that are compliant with the ELG metadata schema as described in Chapter 2. Furthermore, for columns corresponding to metadata elements that take values from controlled vocabularies (e. g., LT area), we mapped the input to the values in the controlled vocabulary. This process also served as a sanity check during

---

[5] In this procedure, the regulations of the Data Protection Act were adhered to at any time and no personal data have been published without the consent of the data owners.

which errors were identified and resolved. The procedure resulted in 1,740 XML files, 867 for companies and 873 for research groups.

The ELG life-cycle for the publication of individual resources includes a validation process aiming to ensure the quality of the metadata published in ELG (see Chapter 2). For the import of the organisation-related XML files, we applied a different procedure that involved their bulk import with the assignment of the tag "imported by ELG". Metadata records marked as such do not go through a validation process and are immediately published on ELG.

3.3 Claiming and Enriching Organisation Pages

Once the population of ELG with these entries was completed, a campaign was launched inviting (via email) legitimate owners to claim, edit and curate the entries of their own organisations. Since the pages created by the ELG team contained only minimal information, the representatives of the organisations were invited to enrich these pages with reliable and accurate content and also to start providing tools, services and resources. In several email campaigns, we reached out to contact persons identified by the NCCs and we informed them about the existence of their organisations' pages on ELG, also inviting them to take over the pages. To do so, the legitimate owner can "claim" their organisation's page as their own by clicking the "Claim" button on the page (see Figure 6).

Fig. 6 Imported organisation page with a "Claim" button

The claiming process can only be triggered by persons signed in with an ELG account (with provider role). This step serves as a security mechanism ensuring correct and rightful authorisation of eligible persons. Once a request is made, the ELG team checks its validity, which also includes checking the email address used to register the ELG account, making sure that it belongs to the organisation, the page of which is being claimed. Approval of the request entails that the entry is assigned to the claimant and returns to a status that it can be edited. The claiming person is prompted by email that they can now start editing the metadata entry and ELG page. Once edited, the page needs to be submitted to publication and the usual ELG validation process starts, i. e., the changes made to the resource are reviewed by the ELG team and the entry is made publicly available again.

3.4 Organisation Pages in the European Language Grid

Organisation pages can include different tabs. The "Overview" tab includes a description of the organisation as well as an info box on the right with data such as postal address and contact email as well as a link to the organisation's own website. This tab can also include keywords that describe the general domain and LT areas an organisation addresses. ELG pages can also be exported in XML format. The tab "Related LRTs & projects" lists all resources and technologies the respective organisation has made available on ELG and the projects they are involved in. This helps companies to promote their tools and resources and to show connections between companies or research organisations and their research projects and corresponding results. The "Related organisations" tab is especially important for academic institutions and universities to reflect their relationship to other departments, faculties or the umbrella organisation (usually the university). Figure 7 provides an example for a page of an academic organisation. Figure 8 (p. 182) shows a company page.

4 Projects in the European Language Grid

ELG is also able to represent research projects, especially for the purpose of acknowledging the funding that made the development of a technology or resource possible and also to interlink projects with organisations and resources.[6] ELG project pages are structured in a similar way, but they are especially adapted to the characteristics and metadata of a typical research project. In addition to information regarding the start and end of the project, the info box also contains details on the funding agency, the funding country, the type of project and the amount of funding provided. Besides the project description and keywords, the "Overview" tab contains the list of consortium partners, that are linked to their respective ELG pages if they exist. Again, the tab "Related LRTs" lists all technologies and resources associated with or resulting from the project. Two examples are shown in Figures 9 (p. 183) and 10 (p. 184).

---

[6] At the time of writing, we are preparing a list with more than 500 projects that will be imported into the ELG catalogue in the second half of 2022; this list was put together in a similar manner as the list of organisations described in Section 3.1.

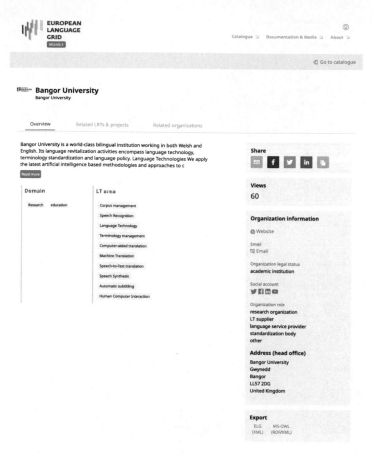

Fig. 7 Example ELG organisation page: Bangor University

5 Conclusions

The European Language Grid is meant to develop into the primary platform of the European LT community. In addition to the technical resources, ELG also represents the actual members of this community: companies and research organisations that develop LTs and related organisations. Our ambition is for ELG eventually to represent *all* companies and *all* research organisations active in the European LT community. In order for ELG to function as a marketplace for European LT, it also needs to provide core information about the European LT community (i. e., "yellow pages" functionalities).

ELG currently contains approx. 1,800 organisations active in the European LT community. Like every similar repository or digital catalogue with certain artefacts, one of the key challenges is the maintenance of the records and metadata entries, i. e., keeping the entries up to date and also making sure that the community is fully

Fig. 8 Example ELG organisation page: Code Runners

represented. Our long-term vision for ELG is to become the primary platform of the European LT community, which entails that *all* members of the European LT community, both commercial and academic, immediately recognise the value, importance and relevance of ELG and, thus, actively want to participate in ELG, keeping their pages up to date, sharing technologies and resources, benefiting from this European marketplace. Until this intended snowball effect is fully in place, i. e., all stakeholders recognise the benefit ELG brings about and participate actively, we will perform, even if time-consuming and logistically challenging, manual updates of the ELG catalogue, we will continue to convert as many members of the community as possible into active users and also active providers of ELG and we will increase our our outreach activities, encouraging more organisations to claim their ELG pages. As soon as the snowball effect is in place and ELG is accepted as the primary platform of the European LT community, all participating organisations will have a sufficient amount of intrinsic motivation to maintain their ELG pages and to keep their information, technologies and resources up to date. At this time, ELG strives to be an established player, which is known throughout the community so

Fig. 9 Example ELG project page: EMBEDDIA (Overview)

that also new companies are attracted by and to ELG. In addition to simplifying the claim process, the attractiveness of ELG will be further enhanced through increased community-related promotions, new features and improved offerings.

Fig. 10 Example ELG project page: EMBEDDIA (Related LRTs)

References

Aldabe, Itziar, Georg Rehm, German Rigau, and Andy Way (2022). *Deliverable D3.1 Report on existing strategic documents and projects in LT/AI (second revision)*. Project deliverable; EU project European Language Equality (ELE); Grant Agreement no. LC-01641480 – 101018166 ELE. URL: https://european-language-equality.eu/wp-content/uploads/2022/06/ELE___Deliv erable_D3_1__second_revision_2.pdf.

European Parliament (2018). *Language Equality in the Digital Age. European Parliament resolution of 11 September 2018 on Language Equality in the Digital Age (2018/2028(INI))*. URL: http://www.europarl.europa.eu/doceo/document/TA-8-2018-0332_EN.pdf.

Overton, David (2017). *Next Generation Internet Initiative – Consultation*. URL: https://ec.europ a.eu/futurium/en/system/files/ged/ec_ngi_final_report_1.pdf.

Rehm, Georg, Katrin Marheinecke, Stefanie Hegele, Stelios Piperidis, Kalina Bontcheva, Jan Hajic, Khalid Choukri, Andrejs Vasiļjevs, Gerhard Backfried, Christoph Prinz, José Manuel Gómez Pérez, Luc Meertens, Paul Lukowicz, Josef van Genabith, Andrea Lösch, Philipp Slusallek, Morten Irgens, Patrick Gatellier, Joachim Köhler, Laure Le Bars, Dimitra Anastasiou, Albina Auksoriūtė, Núria Bel, António Branco, Gerhard Budin, Walter Daelemans, Koenraad De Smedt, Radovan Garabík, Maria Gavriilidou, Dagmar Gromann, Svetla Koeva, Simon Krek, Cvetana Krstev, Krister Lindén, Bernardo Magnini, Jan Odijk, Maciej Ogrodniczuk, Eiríkur Rögnvaldsson, Mike Rosner, Bolette Pedersen, Inguna Skadina, Marko Tadić, Dan Tufiş, Tamás Váradi, Kadri Vider, Andy Way, and François Yvon (2020). "The European Language Technology Landscape in 2020: Language-Centric and Human-Centric AI for Cross-Cultural Communication in Multilingual Europe". In: *Proceedings of the 12th Language Resources and Evaluation Conference (LREC 2020)*. Ed. by Nicoletta Calzolari, Frédéric Béchet, Philippe Blache, Christopher Cieri, Khalid Choukri, Thierry Declerck, Hitoshi Isahara, Bente Maegaard, Joseph Mariani, Asuncion Moreno, Jan Odijk, and Stelios Piperidis. Marseille, France: ELRA, pp. 3315–3325. URL: https://www.aclweb.org/anthology/2020.lrec-1.407/.

Rehm, Georg, Stelios Piperidis, Kalina Bontcheva, Jan Hajic, Victoria Arranz, Andrejs Vasiļjevs, Gerhard Backfried, José Manuel Gómez Pérez, Ulrich Germann, Rémi Calizzano, Nils Feldhus, Stefanie Hegele, Florian Kintzel, Katrin Marheinecke, Julian Moreno-Schneider, Dimitris Galanis, Penny Labropoulou, Miltos Deligiannis, Katerina Gkirtzou, Athanasia Kolovou, Dimitris Gkoumas, Leon Voukoutis, Ian Roberts, Jana Hamrlová, Dusan Varis, Lukáš Kačena, Khalid Choukri, Valérie Mapelli, Mickaël Rigault, Jūlija Meļņika, Miro Janosik, Katja Prinz, Andres Garcia-Silva, Cristian Berrio, Ondrej Klejch, and Steve Renals (2021). "European Language Grid: A Joint Platform for the European Language Technology Community". In: *Proceedings of the 16th Conference of the European Chapter of the Association for Computational Linguistics: System Demonstrations (EACL 2021)*. Kyiv, Ukraine: ACL, pp. 221–230. URL: https://www.aclweb.org/anthology/2021.eacl-demos.26.pdf.

Rehm, Georg and Hans Uszkoreit, eds. (2012). *META-NET White Paper Series: Europe's Languages in the Digital Age*. 32 volumes on 31 European languages. Heidelberg etc.: Springer.

Rehm, Georg and Hans Uszkoreit, eds. (2013). *The META-NET Strategic Research Agenda for Multilingual Europe 2020*. Heidelberg, New York, Dordrecht, London: Springer. URL: http://www.meta-net.eu/vision/reports/meta-net-sra-version_1.0.pdf.

Rehm, Georg, Hans Uszkoreit, Sophia Ananiadou, Núria Bel, Audronė Bielevičienė, Lars Borin, António Branco, Gerhard Budin, Nicoletta Calzolari, Walter Daelemans, Radovan Garabík, Marko Grobelnik, Carmen García-Mateo, Josef van Genabith, Jan Hajič, Inma Hernáez, John Judge, Svetla Koeva, Simon Krek, Cvetana Krstev, Krister Lindén, Bernardo Magnini, Joseph Mariani, John McNaught, Maite Melero, Monica Monachini, Asunción Moreno, Jan Odjik, Maciej Ogrodniczuk, Piotr Pęzik, Stelios Piperidis, Adam Przepiórkowski, Eiríkur Rögnvaldsson, Mike Rosner, Bolette Sandford Pedersen, Inguna Skadiņa, Koenraad De Smedt, Marko Tadić, Paul Thompson, Dan Tufiş, Tamás Váradi, Andrejs Vasiļjevs, Kadri Vider, and Jolanta Zabarskaite (2016). "The Strategic Impact of META-NET on the Regional, National and International Level". In: *Language Resources and Evaluation* 50.2, pp. 351–374. DOI: 10.1007/s10579-015-9333-4. URL: http://link.springer.com/article/10.1007/s10579-015-9333-4.

Rikap, Cecilia and Bengt-Åke Lundvall (2020). "Big Tech, Knowledge Predation and the Implications for Development". In: *Innovation and Development*, pp. 1–28. DOI: 10.1080/2157930X.2020.1855825.

STOA (2018). *Language equality in the digital age – Towards a Human Language Project*. STOA study (PE 598.621), IP/G/STOA/FWC/2013-001/Lot4/C2. URL: https://data.europa.eu/doi/10.2861/136527.

Vasiļjevs, Andrejs, Khalid Choukri, Luc Meertens, and Stefania Aguzzi (2019). *Final study report on CEF Automated Translation value proposition in the context of the European LT market/ecosystem*. DOI: 10.2759/142151. URL: https://op.europa.eu/de/publication-detail/-/publication/8494e56d-ef0b-11e9-a32c-01aa75ed71a1/language-en.

Chapter 10
European Language Technology Landscape: Communication and Collaborations

Georg Rehm, Katrin Marheinecke, and Jens-Peter Kückens

Abstract The European Language Technology community is a diverse group of stakeholders that is characterised by severe fragmentation. This chapter provides an overview of the stakeholders that are relevant for the European Language Grid. We also briefly describe our communication channels and strategies with regard to the promotion of ELG. Furthermore, we highlight a few of the current projects and initiatives and their relationship to and relevance for ELG, especially with regard to collaborations. The overall goal of the target group-specific communication strategy we developed is to create more and more uptake of ELG in the European LT community, eventually creating a snowball effect.

1 Introduction

A key challenge to which ELG aims to respond is the ubiquitous fragmentation of the European LT landscape. ELG addresses this problem by bringing together all European stakeholders under one umbrella platform (European Parliament 2018). While Chapter 9 (p. 171 ff.) provides a high-level description of the LT companies, research organisations and projects registered in ELG at the time of writing (including statistics etc.), the present chapter focuses upon the stakeholder groups themselves. The challenge of severe fragmentation (STOA 2018) has been taken up in ELG from the very beginning on different levels by implementing various communication and cooperation activities. Their aim has been to make ELG known in all relevant communities within a short time in such a way that companies and research organisations develop an active interest in ELG: the more providers offer high quality and attractive services and datasets, the faster ELG will become a central marketplace, which in turn will benefit providers and users alike. This is why the ELG consortium pursued a strategy through which the communication activities in combination with the high quality of the platform and its services and resources, as well as fast and reliable

Georg Rehm · Katrin Marheinecke · Jens-Peter Kückens
Deutsches Forschungszentrum für Künstliche Intelligenz GmbH, Germany, georg.rehm@dfki.de, katrin.marheinecke@dfki.de, jens_peter.kueckens@dfki.de

© The Author(s) 2023
G. Rehm (ed.), *European Language Grid*, Cognitive Technologies,
https://doi.org/10.1007/978-3-031-17258-8_10

support services, produce this desired snowball effect. Some of the communication
and cooperation areas and activities were:

National Competence Centres (NCCs)   Establish a network of 32 carefully selected National Competence Centres (see Chapter 11, p. 205 ff.).

ICT-29b) Projects   Cooperate with the six EU projects funded through the call
ICT-29b), i. e., Bergamot[1], Comprise[2], ELITR[3], Embeddia[4], GoURMET[5], Prêt-
à-LLOD[6] and their consortia and networks.

Major European Initiatives   Collaborate with all relevant major European initiatives including, among others, the European AI on Demand Platform[7], CLAIRE[8],
HumanE AI Net[9], CLARIN[10] and others (see Chapter 2, Section 8, p. 27 ff., as
well as Chapter 6, p. 107 ff.). These collaborations are described in more detail in
Section 4 (p. 199 ff.) of the present chapter.

Events   Organise local, regional and national events together with the ELG National Competence Centres (see Chapter 11, p. 205 ff.).

Talks and Presentations   Give talks and presentations, especially at networking
and outreach events, to decision-makers and multipliers, both in the industrial
sector but also in scientific European conferences.

Open Calls and Pilot Projects   Selected 15 pilot projects, with which we also collaborated in terms of communication activities on their respective regional and
local levels (see Part IV, p. 256 ff., of this book).

Next up, Section 2 describes the European Language Technology community in
more detail, focusing upon the different stakeholder groups. A key driver of success
of the ELG initiative is this support and buy-in from the stakeholder community
including the uptake of the platform. In addition to these networking activities in
the project, several public communication channels have been established. Under
the umbrella brand "European Language Technology", ELG and its sister project
European Language Equality (ELE, see Rehm and Way 2023) have started addressing the stakeholders and initiatives listed above, community members outside these
networks and the wider public in order to provide them with news about relevant
project developments, events and updates on ELG features, among others. For this
purpose, social media profiles on Twitter and LinkedIn were established. We also set
up an email newsletter, which was initially published on a monthly basis and later
on changed to a biweekly schedule. These communication channels, their purpose,
effectiveness and the content shared through them is further detailed in Section 3.

---

[1] https://browser.mt

[2] https://www.compriseh2020.eu

[3] https://elitr.eu

[4] http://embeddia.eu

[5] https://gourmet-project.eu

[6] https://pret-a-llod.github.io

[7] https://www.ai4europe.eu

[8] https://claire-ai.org

[9] https://www.humane-ai.eu/workpackages/

[10] https://www.clarin.eu

2 Stakeholders of the European Language Grid

For our main groups of stakeholders we defined their specific relationships with ELG and how we will communicate and engage with them in terms of communication channels but also in terms of messages, considering our overall communication goals. Most target groups also interact with ELG in one way or another, which is why they are, in most cases, not just passive audiences but also immediate stakeholders within the ELG community (Rehm et al. 2020c, 2021). In the following, all stakeholder groups are defined including aspects relating to communication.

2.1 Language Technology Providers

The interests of LT *providers* (see Chapter 9 for specific numbers) are different from those of LT *users*, which is why specific communication formats need to be applied. Typically, commercial providers of LT (also see Vasiljevs et al. 2019) want to showcase their products and promote their solutions and services or their company and – on a more abstract level – they look for an appropriate marketplace in which they can participate. In contrast to other target groups, their interactions with ELG are active and direct. In order to upload or offer a service or tool via ELG, they need specific technical information and an understanding of how ELG works. This demand is met through various forms of communication, including a technical documentation with clear and in-depth explanations of ELG's functionalities, based on which video tutorials were prepared. These videos are shared through all communication channels. Furthermore, blog articles explain specific ELG features to LT providers and short announcements of new features are included in the newsletter.

The more ELG meets business requirements, the more likely LT providers are to actively use and promote it and to exploit it as an additional or sales channel or even as their preferred marketplace. Our communication activities addressing LT providers uses a marketing tonality and promotes the advantages of the ELG initiative. We have also reached out repeatedly to LT providers, inviting them to send in their questions or feedback with regard to their experience with ELG, including missing features or suggestions for improvement.

In many cases research centres and universities are also LT providers, but their interest is usually not a monetary but a research-driven one. This stakeholder group provides larger or smaller datasets or perhaps tools or rudimentary, experimental services that have evolved from research projects rather than robust, production-ready services that can be directly monetised. For researchers, sharing their results, the further development of tools and the exchange with other researchers is the main driver to use ELG. Finding datasets and tools bundled in one place, they can test functionalities in the development phase and provide feedback. Ideally, they spread the word about ELG in scientific articles or in academic conferences, and they can be approached most easily through these channels. Public communication about the usefulness of an easy-to-use platform for hosting, sharing and making available LT services has proven an effective measure to attract researchers and initiate direct communication about ELG.

2.1.1 Participants in the Open Calls – Pilot Projects

ELG tested the platform and demonstrated its usefulness with the help of 15 pilot projects that it supported financially (see Part IV for more details). After their completion, the results were fed back into the ELG platform and community. To attract companies or research centres to submit proposals and to make the selected pilot projects known, communication activities were necessary. The open calls were published and advertised through email campaigns, through the ELG website and on multiple events. META-FORUM 2019 was the first public occasion where the open calls have been publicly presented. This target group had a high demand for information, therefore different channels like online trainings, videos, fact sheets and news articles were implemented. The pilot projects were an important measure and instrument to make ELG known to a wider audience, communication in this area had to be especially effective. The overwhelming response with more than 200 project proposals in total proves that this strategy has worked out and the successful completion of all 15 selected pilot projects is evidence of successful communication (and a thorough evaluation of the proposals). The results of the pilot projects were also presented in the virtual project expos at META-FORUM 2020, 2021 and 2022 and also in a number of sessions and presentations.[11]. Several pilot projects were showcased on the ELG blog, presenting their activities but also the greater implementations of making use of a pan-European LT platform, while the promotional videos created for META-FORUM 2021 were featured in the newsletter and on social media.

2.2 Language Technology Users

The users of Language Technology are the most diverse and also, by a margin, the biggest target group. Users include almost everyone – from students doing research for a paper to job seekers in the LT field, to companies looking for a machine translation solution for the corporate website, just to mention a few examples. Members of this group can look for information, try to find certain LT services or datasets or they can be potential buyers or integrators of LT. This enormous group interacts with ELG in the form of a user, consumer or potential customer (Rehm et al. 2021). This stakeholder group is addressed by a communication strategy that treats this highly heterogeneous audience as a homogeneous entity. The strategy involves focusing on what is common in terms of customer needs and preferences instead of focusing upon the differences of individual subgroups. Communication-wise, messages promoting ELG are designed to have a general appeal, transmitting communication

---

[11] https://www.european-language-grid.eu/meta-forum-2021/project-expo/

primarily concentrated on the common needs such as information (ELG as an information hub), match-making (a digital marketplace where supply meets demand) and elimination of language barriers. The main communication channels include email campaigns, social media posts, regular newsletter editions and the ELG website, but also presentations and booths at industry events and conferences. For the target group of LT users, we emphasised the possibilities of modern LT and its various application areas. With this aim at stressing the importance of LT, for instance in terms of cross-language communication, information access and automation in fields such as research and the information industry, ELG intends to include both experienced and potential LT users and informs about the important role LT plays in the digital world.

2.2.1 Public Administrations and NGOs

As an EU-funded project, ELG can also provide technologies to public administrations, e. g., to the European institutions or national or regional administrations. For example, ELG offers the language resources provided by ELRC, which were collected and prepared to serve the needs of public services and administrations across the EU, Norway and Iceland. At the same time, ELG wants to offer solutions to non-governmental organisations that often have to pursue their goals with limited financial resources. They can benefit from ELG as users of LT because they typically do not have the funding or technological know-how to find LT services or tools that would suit their needs. Apart from more general forms of communication like email campaigns or press releases, representatives of public administrations as well as NGOs were invited to conferences like META-FORUM, where traditionally one of the keynotes or opening addresses is given by a representative of the EU.

2.2.2 European Citizens – Members of the European Language Communities

This stakeholder group also includes the members of the European language communities, i. e., all citizens of Europe, speaking and representing the official EU languages, regional or minority languages or any of the other languages spoken in Europe. Communication, networking and surveying activities have primarily taken place in the EU project European Language Equality (ELE). Through the tight collaboration between ELG and ELE we have been able to identify and exploit a number of synergies, such as, among others, the EU Citizen Survey, through which we have been able to learn more about how Europe's citizens perceive Language Technology and what kind of preconceptions and demands they have.

2.3 Additional Horizon 2020 EU Projects

The projects supported through the Horizon 2020 call ICT-29-2018 (see Section 1) are a special stakeholder group, as their consortia consist of research centres and universities as well as several industry partners. All projects dealt with domain-specific, challenge-oriented LT and provided services, tools and datasets which are also showcased in ELG. As the projects were especially featured, they benefited from a higher level of promotion (Rehm et al. 2021). Furthermore, they could make use of the various features as well as of the vast community connected with ELG. Due to their outreach into industry and academia, they functioned as excellent multipliers on multiple occasions. This target group proved to be very dynamic. We were engaged in active, bi-directional communication with all consortia, e.g., via online meetings, mutual invitations to each other's events, or by advertising our projects on our websites. Communication activities with this group had started in early 2019 and turned out to be successful and vivid.

2.4 Major European Projects and Initiatives

An overarching platform like ELG can only be successful if it is recognised in and used by the whole LT community. To establish ELG within the LT scene and to avoid silo-thinking, we communicated closely and in a targeted manner with other major projects and initiatives in the field including neighbouring areas, in an attempt to establish collaborations to create synergies and to share best practices. The ELG consortium has cooperated directly with projects active in similar areas, with a similar scope or working on similar topics, for example, the European AI on Demand Platform (i.e., the AI4EU EU project), CLAIRE, CLARIN and various other projects and initiatives. In addition to meetings, conferences like META-FORUM are an appropriate format to share information and knowledge about each other's activities. At META-FORUM 2019, 2020, 2021 and 2022, many relevant projects and initiatives showcased their plans and missions with the help of (virtual) expo booths, presentations or panel discussions. Members of the ELG consortium took every opportunity to present ELG at conferences and public events to make the ELG concept and approach known in different sectors and industries. Existing networks like ELRC (European Language Resource Coordination) and META-NET were tapped regularly with regards to knowledge transfer and information exchange. Section 4 presents these collaborations in more detail.

2.5 National Competence Centres

The National Competence Centres (NCC) played a crucial role for ELG's communication and promotion activities (see Chapter 11). This stakeholder group also functioned as an abstract communication channel (Rehm et al. 2021). The NCCs were and still are an important target group included in our communication channels, they also served as multipliers of the ELG mission in their own regions and networks, through mailings, social media posts, newsletter features, face-to-face meetings, conferences, tutorials, training sessions and promotion events.

2.6 Public at Large

ELG is a public and inclusive platform that also attempts to address citizens interested in Language Technology. Members of civil society who browse the web and visit ELG with no specific intention, also need to be addressed adequately. ELG wants to promote the purpose and usability of LT beyond the borders of tech-savvy stakeholders. Our communication activities aim not only at experts, but also at the public at large. Appropriate communication channels are news and blog posts on the website or videos on platforms such as YouTube. Social media channels, especially Twitter, are used to communicate updates and project results in a style that intends to make them interesting and comprehensible to audiences beyond the core LT community. Of interest are especially those ELG features that have broader social implications due to related topics in the news, which are perceived positively by followers and readers with diverse professional and personal backgrounds.

3 Communication and Outreach Activities

As a project with several objectives, addressing various gaps in the European Language Technology landscape and serving as a marketplace for research and industry, ELG depends on the reputation and brand it has established. In addition to the platform's functionality and positive experience of users and providers interacting with ELG, another relevant aspect is the ease of access with regard to content and information served by the platform. This refers to the information architecture of the website, structure and quality of the technical documentation, responses to requests directed at the ELG technical team as well as the overall communication strategy.

3.1 Communication Strategy

A communication strategy enables effective communication, in the case of ELG, this relates to informing specific target audiences and the broad public about the project and its results, gaining users and providers for ELG and representing ELG as a brand for pan-European, multilingual and all-encompassing LT. The key elements of the communication strategy are the stakeholders, the overall goals of the communication, the messages to communicate, the communication channels and the timing.

We have two main communication goals that are closely aligned with our Unique Selling Propositions (USP), which are the key differentiators from existing platforms and offerings on the market. The success of the project and the ELG legal entity depend on these two USPs to be widely known by all relevant stakeholders. This is why the USPs became central messages for communication related to the uptake and popularity of ELG directed at potential users, participating organisations or stakeholders to be won over.

ELG is the primary platform for Language Technologies in Europe.

ELG strives to become the most important and most relevant marketplace for Language Technology in Europe – a one-stop LT shop in which all kinds of stakeholders can find what they are looking for in terms of services, tools or resources provided by research or industry. ELG is not only a directory of companies, universities and research centres, but also contains a repository of thousands of datasets as well as hundreds of functional tools and services. To make ELG useful and efficient for its users, visibility and completeness are crucial. Moreover, to include as many relevant players as possible, one of the main objectives is wide outreach.

ELG provides Language Technology for *Europe built* in *Europe.*

The second USP relates to the fact that LT from other continents or large global technology corporations do not have intimate linguistic knowledge of Europe's languages including their varieties (i. e., European developers of LT can serve European demand in a better and more adequate way) and that legal aspects such as copyright law, the General Data Protection Regulation (GDPR) and other policies are well considered by European players. The same goes for core European values like privacy, confidentiality and trustworthiness. Users of ELG do not have to fear their data being sold to third parties when using or offering services or resources on the platform.

3.2 Communication Campaign

The ELG communication campaign was developed and operationalised with communication experts and continuously revised and expanded to meet the changing conditions in the project and initiative. The initial situation was thoroughly analysed and then appropriate marketing measures were planned using various communication channels including social media.

3.2.1 Communication Objectives

In addition to communicating the overall USPs of ELG to the relevant stakeholders, all ELG communication activities are also geared towards supporting and realising

ELG's overall objectives. We distilled the overall objectives into three main messages, which are the underlying drivers in all ELG communication activities:

- *Support the Multilingual Digital Single Market* by providing technologies for all European languages, which can be used by LT user stakeholders in all European countries to provide digital offerings, products and solutions that support all European languages relevant for the respective LT user stakeholder.
- *Establish and grow a vibrant community and help coordinate all European LT activities* by becoming the primary platform for LT in Europe.
- *Develop and offer a powerful and scalable LT platform* through a novel technological approach, which enables innovations and synergies between commercial and non-commercial LT providers, buyers and users.

3.2.2 Communication Channels

For ELG, we selected four main areas of communication as the most relevant ones for informing the main stakeholders and for marketing the project and the platform. These four areas include the ELG website itself, the annual ELG conference (and other events), the ELG social media channels and the ELG newsletter. While the ELG website and the representation of the project at conferences and events was primarily connected to the ELG brand, a more flexible approach was chosen for social media and the newsletter.

For the duration of the project, we maintained, in addition to the actual European Language Grid, a separate ELG website for information, promotion and marketing purposes. This website served as the face to the public with all relevant information on the project itself and its wider setup, including, among others, the ELG architecture, NCCs, annual conferences, newsletter and many other topics. It also included a news section and a blog. This stand-alone website has been merged with the European Language Grid proper in the summer of 2022 so that all the relevant information and the European Language Grid itself are now available at the same address.[12]

From 2019 to 2022, ELG organised an annual conference (in 2022 in collaboration with the EU project ELE). At these conferences, all relevant aspects of ELG have been presented and discussed with relevant stakeholders. In addition, ELG participated in many other conferences, workshops, industry events and expos. For more details see Chapter 11, Section 3 (p. 210 ff.).

In terms of social media channels, ELG uses Twitter and LinkedIn, their main advantages are the potential to create a very wide reach and large number of followers, thus enabling the project to address exactly the right stakeholders. Instead of establishing dedicated channels for ELG, we decided to create one slightly more general online identity, namely the umbrella-brand "European Language Technology" (ELT), which serves as the name of the social media channels on Twitter[13]

---

[12] https://www.european-language-grid.eu.

[13] https://twitter.com/EuroLangTech

and LinkedIn[14]. This brand serves as the outlet and interaction channel for ELG and also for its sister project, European Language Equality. The ELT brand solves the problem of communicating about two related but different projects through a single channel, while tackling the topic of European Language Technology from a technological (ELG) and from a strategic perspective (ELE). The approach has proven successful, as the ELT channels quickly gathered several hundred followers each. Table 1 shows some key statistics on both platforms.

Channel	Twitter	LinkedIn
Followers (total)	666	818
Posts (total)	316	150
Posts per month (example: March 2022)	27	19
Followers gained per month (example: March 2022)	63	75
Profile visits per month (example: March 2022)	5,944	198
Impressions per month (example: March 2022)	40,300	9,248

Table 1 European Language Technology: social media statistics (July 2022)

The differences in the statistics of the two channels can be attributed to the fact that while Twitter generally sees more activity in interaction and content reception, LinkedIn follows more professional conventions and goals. Its user base has a slightly bigger overlap with the main target groups of ELG. This is why the LinkedIn channel gained more followers even though there was less activity in comparison to Twitter. Both channels are used for communicating a variety of contents in specified formats: 1. new ELG platform features and quotes from reports are shared in specifically designed images (known as shareables); 2. new blog articles are promoted through links and quotes from the text; 3. upcoming events are promoted using, e. g., summaries of the programme and links to the event website; 4. related news from other sources are shared through links or the retweet/sharing function, ideally with a comment regarding the relevance for ELG.

Following the concept of the ELT brand, a newsletter was established under the same name, sharing information from and about ELG and ELE with a total of approx. 4,000 subscribers as of July 2022.[15] We invited many of our existing contacts to subscribe to the newsletter, we invite visitors of the website to subscribe to the newsletter and we also share the newsletter on a regular basis through our other communication channels. At first the newsletter was published on a monthly, later on a bi-weekly basis. Each issue of the newsletter includes a general introduction to the latest edition, including a list of highlights from social media and an overview of press articles in relation to ELT, followed by dedicated sections on ELG and ELE. The ELG section contains general news from and about ELG, a summary of the latest ELG blog article, a few of the latest tools or services added to ELG and the latest organisation that joined ELG (short profile and link to their ELG entry).

---

[14] https://www.linkedin.com/company/74073406

[15] https://www.european-language-technology.eu/elt-newsletter-archive/

4 Collaborations with other Projects and Initiatives

ELG is a technology platform for the whole European LT community, which is why collaboration played and plays an important role for the success and uptake of the ELG initiative (Rehm et al. 2020c). While we are unable to list all projects and organisations we collaborated with during the ELG project's runtime, below we attempt to list the major ones (see Chapter 2, Section 8, p. 27 ff., as well as Chapter 6, p. 107 ff.).

European Language Equality   ELG and ELE[16] worked together on many different topics. ELE collected more than 6,000 LT and LR records, which were ingested in ELG, resulting in a substantial increase of the total number of available resources (Giagkou et al. 2022). The Digital Language Equality metric, developed by ELE (Gaspari et al. 2022; Grützner-Zahn and Rehm 2022), is based on the contents of the ELG catalogue and can be accessed through a dashboard developed by ELE and available on ELG.[17] While ELE prepares the strategic agenda and roadmap towards digital language equality in Europe, ELG offers the appropriate platform for sharing and deploying these Language Technologies. The synergies between the projects were communicated through blog articles and our shared social media channels as well as our shared newsletter.

Open Calls and Pilot Projects   ELG collaborated with the organisations behind the 15 selected pilot projects in terms of technical aspects and communication activities on their respective regional and local levels (see Part IV, p. 256 ff.).

ICT-29b) Projects   ELG collaborated with the six EU projects funded through the Horizon 2020 call ICT-29b), i. e., Bergamot[18], Comprise[19], ELITR[20], Embeddia[21], GoURMET[22], Prêt-à-LLOD[23] and their consortia and networks, especially with regard to outreach and communication, coordination and making project results available through ELG.

European AI on Demand Platform   ELG cooperated with the European AI on Demand Platform through the EU project AI4EU.[24] Topics include strategic and coordination aspects, the technical interoperability between both platforms (Rehm et al. 2020b), the preparation of an AI ontology and participation in outreach and promotion events.

HumanE AI Net   This EU network of excellence[25], which also belongs to the European AI on Demand Platform, aims at facilitating a European brand of trustwor-

---

[16] https://european-language-equality.eu

[17] https://live.european-language-grid.eu/catalogue/dashboard

[18] https://browser.mt

[19] https://www.compriseh2020.eu

[20] https://elitr.eu

[21] http://embeddia.eu

[22] https://gourmet-project.eu

[23] https://prct-a-llod.github.io

[24] https://www.ai4europe.eu

[25] https://www.humane-ai.eu/workpackages/

thy, ethical AI that enhances human capabilities and empowers citizens and society to effectively deal with the challenges of an interconnected globalised world. ELG supports this initiative as language is a core topic in human-oriented AI. Many organisations involved in ELG are also active in HumanE AI Net through specific microprojects that focus on certain research questions, funded by the initiative. HumanE AI Net and ELG collaborated with regard to joint outreach and promotion activities.

CLAIRE   ELG and the Confederation of Laboratories for AI Research in Europe[26], the world's largest network for AI research, collaborated with regard to strategic and coordination topics. ELG, representing the language-centric AI landscape, serves as a link between the LT and the AI communities. We also participated in various joint events.

CLARIN   ELG and the Common Language Resources and Technology Infrastructure[27] (Eskevich et al. 2020) collaborated with regard to strategic and technical aspects such as metadata harvesting (see Chapter 6) and events.

Microservices at your Service   This CEF-supported EU project collects and develops a larger number of functional services, develops ELG-compatible containers and makes these available through ELG.[28] Additionally, the two projects collaborated by participating in relevant outreach and training events.

NTEU and MAPA   The two CEF-supported EU projects Neural Translation for the EU (NTEU)[29] and Multilingual Anonymisation for Public Administrations (MAPA)[30] have contributed a large number of tools and services to ELG (García-Martínez et al. 2021). NTEU alone has provided hundreds of high quality machine translation models, which are now available through ELG.

WeVerify   This EU project develops tools and technologies for the identification and verification of various types of news and media (Marinova et al. 2020).[31] Internally, the WeVerify tools make use of several ELG services.

ELRC   The CEF-supported EU initiative European Language Resource Coordination (ELRC)[32] supports multilingual Europe, among others, by collecting publicly available language data from national public administrations and making them available to the European Union through the repository ELRC-SHARE (Lösch et al. 2018). ELG automatically harvests ELRC-SHARE, enabling the discovery of these resources through ELG. ELRC and ELG also collaborated in terms of joint communication and dissemination activities.

QURATOR   The German project QURATOR has developed a technology platform and large number of tools, services and resources for several digital con-

---

[26] https://claire-ai.org

[27] https://www.clarin.eu

[28] https://www.lingsoft.fi/en/microservices-at-your-service-bridging-gap-between-nlp-research-and-industry

[29] https://nteu.eu

[30] https://mapa-project.eu

[31] https://weverify.eu

[32] https://www.lr-coordination.eu

tent curation use cases (Rehm et al. 2020a).[33] Both projects, QURATOR and ELG worked together closely from the very beginning in terms of platform development, communication and dissemination, among others, through the annual QURATOR conferences. Many tools and resources created by QURATOR are available through ELG.

PANQURA   This sister project of QURATOR focuses upon the application of QURATOR technologies to the COVID-19 pandemic, striving for more transparency in times of a global crisis.[34] Among others, PANQURA has developed tools for the automated assessment of the credibility of online content, which are now available through ELG (Schulz et al. 2022).

OpenGPT-X and Gaia-X   The German project OpenGPT-X develops large language models for the German language.[35] The project is part of a group of AI projects that will test and deploy their project results through the emerging Gaia-X infrastructure.[36] In Gaia-X, representatives from business, politics, and science are working together to create a federated and secure data infrastructure for Europe, addressing the topic of data sovereignty in Europe. OpenGPT-X will not only make use of various resources available in and through ELG, the project will also extend ELG so that the platform is compatible with Gaia-X, i. e., OpenGPT-X will integrate the ELG platform into the emerging Gaia-X infrastructure.

NFDI4DS   The project NFDI for Data Science and AI[37] is part of the German NFDI initiative, which develops, with a total of approx. 20-25 projects, the national German research data infrastructure.[38] NFDI4DS will support all steps of the research data life cycle, including collecting or creating, processing, analysing, publishing, archiving, and reusing resources in Data Science and AI. In NFDI4DS, ELG will be integrated into the emerging NFDI infrastructure.

DataBri-X   The EU project Data Process and Technological Bricks for expanding digital value creation in European Data Spaces (DataBri-X), which will start in October 2022, will develop a toolbox for data processing, data handling and data curation. The ELG platform will be used and also extended as one technical infrastructure in this project.

SciLake   The EU project Democratising and Making Sense out of Heterogeneous Scholarly Content (SciLake), which will start in January 2023, will build upon the OpenAIRE ecosystem and European Open Science Cloud (EOSC) services to facilitate, among others, the creation, interlinking and maintenance of research-oriented knowledge graphs. In SciLake we will establish technical bridges between the ELG platform and EOSC.

---

[33] https://qurator.ai

[34] https://qurator.ai/panqura/

[35] https://opengpt-x.de

[36] https://gaia-x.eu

[37] https://www.nfdi4datascience.de

[38] https://www.nfdi.de

5 Conclusions

As a community platform and initiative, ELG does not operate in a vacuum without contact to other projects, groups or initiatives. On the contrary, it is of fundamental importance that ELG is tightly integrated into the community with active use of the ELG platform by many members of the community. To achieve this, ELG has defined its target groups and cooperates closely with a number of relevant projects to exploit existing synergies. These networking and collaboration efforts will be continued after the runtime of the ELG EU project, i.e., when the ELG legal entity is established and operational. This approach is based on a clear communication strategy with transparent goals that are pursued jointly with other key stakeholders.

While we have been able to establish a shared platform for the European LT community during the 42 months of the ELG project, we now need to concentrate on engaging with more and more stakeholders so that ELG is also utilised and expanded by more and more active users, resulting in a European Language Grid *from* the European LT community *for* the European LT community.

References

Eskevich, Maria, Franciska de Jong, Alexander König, Darja Fišer, Dieter Van Uytvanck, Tero Aalto, Lars Borin, Olga Gerassimenko, Jan Hajic, Henk van den Heuvel, Neeme Kahusk, Krista Liin, Martin Matthiesen, Stelios Piperidis, and Kadri Vider (2020). "CLARIN: Distributed Language Resources and Technology in a European Infrastructure". In: *Proc. of the 1st Int. Workshop on Language Technology Platforms (IWLTP 2020, co-located with LREC 2020)*. Ed. by Georg Rehm, Kalina Bontcheva, Khalid Choukri, Jan Hajic, Stelios Piperidis, and Andrejs Vasiljevs. Marseille, France: ELRA, pp. 28–34. URL: https://aclanthology.org/2020.iwltp-1.5.

European Parliament (2018). *Language Equality in the Digital Age. European Parliament resolution of 11 September 2018 on Language Equality in the Digital Age (2018/2028(INI))*. URL: http://www.europarl.europa.eu/doceo/document/TA-8-2018-0332_EN.pdf.

García-Martínez, Mercedes, Laurent Bié, Aleix Cerdà, Amando Estela, Manuel Herranz, Rihards Krišlauks, Maite Melero, Tony O'Dowd, Sinead O'Gorman, Marcis Pinnis, Artūrs Stafanovič, Riccardo Superbo, and Artūrs Vasiļevskis (2021). "Neural Translation for European Union (NTEU)". In: *Proceedings of Machine Translation Summit XVIII: Users and Providers Track*. Association for Machine Translation in the Americas, pp. 316–334. URL: https://aclanthology .org/2021.mtsummit-up.23.

Gaspari, Federico, Owen Gallagher, Georg Rehm, Maria Giagkou, Stelios Piperidis, Jane Dunne, and Andy Way (2022). "Introducing the Digital Language Equality Metric: Technological Factors". In: *Proceedings of the Workshop Towards Digital Language Equality (TDLE 2022; co-located with LREC 2022)*. Ed. by Itziar Aldabe, Begoña Altuna, Aritz Farwell, and German Rigau. Marseille, France, pp. 1–12. URL: http://www.lrec-conf.org/proceedings/lrec2022/wor kshops/TDLE/pdf/2022.tdle-1.1.pdf.

Giagkou, Maria, Stelios Piperidis, Penny Labropoulou, Miltos Deligiannis, Athanasia Kolovou, and Leon Voukoutis (2022). "Collaborative Metadata Aggregation and Curation in Support of Digital Language Equality Monitoring". In: *Proceedings of the Workshop Towards Digital Language Equality (TDLE 2022; co-located with LREC 2022)*. Ed. by Itziar Aldabe, Begoña Altuna, Aritz Farwell, and German Rigau. Marseille, France, pp. 27–35. URL: http://www.lrec-conf.o rg/proceedings/lrec2022/workshops/TDLE/pdf/2022.tdle-1.3.pdf.

Grützner-Zahn, Annika and Georg Rehm (2022). "Introducing the Digital Language Equality Metric: Contextual Factors". In: *Proceedings of the Workshop Towards Digital Language Equality (TDLE 2022; co-located with LREC 2022)*. Ed. by Itziar Aldabe, Begoña Altuna, Aritz Farwell, and German Rigau. Marseille, France, pp. 13–26. URL: http://www.lrec-conf.org/proceedings /lrec2022/workshops/TDLE/pdf/2022.tdle-1.2.pdf.

Lösch, Andrea, Valérie Mapelli, Stelios Piperidis, Andrejs Vasiļjevs, Lilli Smal, Thierry Declerck, Eileen Schnur, Khalid Choukri, and Josef van Genabith (2018). "European Language Resource Coordination: Collecting Language Resources for Public Sector Multilingual Information Management". In: *Proc. of the Eleventh International Conference on Language Resources and Evaluation (LREC 2018)*. Miyazaki, Japan: ELRA. URL: https://aclanthology.org/L18-1213.

Marinova, Zlatina, Jochen Spangenberg, Denis Teyssou, Symeon Papadopoulos, Nikos Sarris, Alexandre Alaphilippe, and Kalina Bontcheva (2020). "Weverify: Wider and Enhanced Verification for You Project Overview and Tools". In: *2020 IEEE International Conference on Multimedia Expo Workshops (ICMEW)*, pp. 1–4. DOI: 10.1109/ICMEW46912.2020.9106056.

Rehm, Georg, Peter Bourgonje, Stefanie Hegele, Florian Kintzel, Julián Moreno Schneider, Malte Ostendorff, Karolina Zaczynska, Armin Berger, Stefan Grill, Sören Räuchle, Jens Rauenbusch, Lisa Rutenburg, André Schmidt, Mikka Wild, Henry Hoffmann, Julian Fink, Sarah Schulz, Jurica Seva, Joachim Quantz, Joachim Böttger, Josefine Matthey, Rolf Fricke, Jan Thomsen, Adrian Paschke, Jamal Al Qundus, Thomas Hoppe, Naouel Karam, Frauke Weichhardt, Christian Fillies, Clemens Neudecker, Mike Gerber, Kai Labusch, Vahid Rezanezhad, Robin Schaefer, David Zellhöfer, Daniel Siewert, Patrick Bunk, Lydia Pintscher, Elena Aleynikova, and Franziska Heine (2020a). "QURATOR: Innovative Technologies for Content and Data Curation". In: *Proceedings of QURATOR 2020 – The conference for intelligent content solutions*. Ed. by Adrian Paschke, Clemens Neudecker, Georg Rehm, Jamal Al Qundus, and Lydia Pintscher. CEUR Workshop Proceedings, Volume 2535. 20/21 January 2020. Berlin, Germany. URL: http p://ceur-ws.org/Vol-2535/paper_17.pdf.

Rehm, Georg, Dimitrios Galanis, Penny Labropoulou, Stelios Piperidis, Martin Welß, Ricardo Usbeck, Joachim Köhler, Miltos Deligiannis, Katerina Gkirtzou, Johannes Fischer, Christian Chiarcos, Nils Feldhus, Julián Moreno-Schneider, Florian Kintzel, Elena Montiel, Víctor Rodríguez Doncel, John P. McCrae, David Laqua, Irina Patricia Theile, Christian Dittmar, Kalina Bontcheva, Ian Roberts, Andrejs Vasiļjevs, and Andis Lagzdiņš (2020b). "Towards an Interoperable Ecosystem of AI and LT Platforms: A Roadmap for the Implementation of Different Levels of Interoperability". In: *Proc. of the 1st Int. Workshop on Language Technology Platforms (IWLTP 2020, co-located with LREC 2020)*. Ed. by Georg Rehm, Kalina Bontcheva, Khalid Choukri, Jan Hajic, Stelios Piperidis, and Andrejs Vasiljevs. Marseille, France, pp. 96–107. URL: https://www.aclweb.org/anthology/2020.iwltp-1.15.pdf.

Rehm, Georg, Katrin Marheinecke, Stefanie Hegele, Stelios Piperidis, Kalina Bontcheva, Jan Hajic, Khalid Choukri, Andrejs Vasiļjevs, Gerhard Backfried, Christoph Prinz, José Manuel Gómez Pérez, Luc Meertens, Paul Lukowicz, Josef van Genabith, Andrea Lösch, Philipp Slusallek, Morten Irgens, Patrick Gatellier, Joachim Köhler, Laure Le Bars, Dimitra Anastasiou, Albina Auksoriūtė, Núria Bel, António Branco, Gerhard Budin, Walter Daelemans, Koenraad De Smedt, Radovan Garabík, Maria Gavriilidou, Dagmar Gromann, Svetla Koeva, Simon Krek, Cvetana Krstev, Krister Lindén, Bernardo Magnini, Jan Odijk, Maciej Ogrodniczuk, Eiríkur Rögnvaldsson, Mike Rosner, Bolette Pedersen, Inguna Skadina, Marko Tadić, Dan Tufiş, Tamás Váradi, Kadri Vider, Andy Way, and François Yvon (2020c). "The European Language Technology Landscape in 2020: Language-Centric and Human-Centric AI for Cross-Cultural Communication in Multilingual Europe". In: *Proceedings of the 12th Language Resources and Evaluation Conference (LREC 2020)*. Ed. by Nicoletta Calzolari, Frédéric Béchet, Philippe Blache, Christopher Cieri, Khalid Choukri, Thierry Declerck, Hitoshi Isahara, Bente Maegaard, Joseph Mariani, Asuncion Moreno, Jan Odijk, and Stelios Piperidis. Marseille, France: ELRA, pp. 3315–3325. URL: https://www.aclweb.org/anthology/2020.lrec-1.407/.

Rehm, Georg, Stelios Piperidis, Kalina Bontcheva, Jan Hajic, Victoria Arranz, Andrejs Vasiļjevs, Gerhard Backfried, José Manuel Gómez Pérez, Ulrich Germann, Rémi Calizzano, Nils Feldhus, Stefanie Hegele, Florian Kintzel, Katrin Marheinecke, Julian Moreno-Schneider, Dimitris Galanis, Penny Labropoulou, Miltos Deligiannis, Katerina Gkirtzou, Athanasia Kolovou, Dimitris Gkoumas, Leon Voukoutis, Ian Roberts, Jana Hamrlová, Dusan Varis, Lukáš Kačena, Khalid Choukri, Valérie Mapelli, Mickaël Rigault, Jūlija Meļņika, Miro Janosik, Katja Prinz, Andres Garcia-Silva, Cristian Berrio, Ondrej Klejch, and Steve Renals (2021). "European Language Grid: A Joint Platform for the European Language Technology Community". In: *Proceedings of the 16th Conference of the European Chapter of the Association for Computational Linguistics: System Demonstrations (EACL 2021)*. Kyiv, Ukraine: ACL, pp. 221–230. URL: https://www.aclweb.org/anthology/2021.eacl-demos.26.pdf.

Rehm, Georg and Andy Way, eds. (2023). *European Language Equality: A Strategic Agenda for Digital Language Equality*. Cognitive Technologies. Forthcoming. Springer.

Schulz, Konstantin, Jens Rauenbusch, Jan Fillies, Lisa Rutenburg, Dimitrios Karvelas, and Georg Rehm (2022). "User Experience Design for Automatic Credibility Assessment of News Content About COVID-19". In: *Proceedings of HCI International 2022 – Late Breaking Papers*. Accepted for publication. 26 June-01 July 2022.

STOA (2018). *Language equality in the digital age – Towards a Human Language Project*. STOA study (PE 598.621), IP/G/STOA/FWC/2013-001/Lot4/C2. URL: https://data.europa.eu/doi/10.2861/136527.

Vasiljevs, Andrejs, Khalid Choukri, Luc Meertens, and Stefania Aguzzi (2019). *Final study report on CEF Automated Translation value proposition in the context of the European LT market/ecosystem*. DOI: 10.2759/142151. URL: https://op.europa.eu/de/publication-detail/-/publication/8494e56d-ef0b-11e9-a32c-01aa75ed71a1/language-en.

Chapter 11
ELG National Competence Centres and Events

Katrin Marheinecke, Annika Grützner-Zahn, and Georg Rehm

Abstract The National Competence Centres (NCCs) in ELG are an international network of 32 regional and national networks, lead by one regional/national representative. The 32 NCCs play a crucial role in ELG, they support the project by bringing in their corresponding regional and national perspective and stakeholders, organising ELG workshops and functioning as regional/national representatives. The chapter explains why, despite a considerable coordination effort, it was worth putting this network together. One important task carried out by the NCCs was to conduct regional/national dissemination events and to participate in relevant regional/national events and also in the annual META-FORUM conferences, organised by ELG.

1 Introduction

The diverse *Multilingual Europe* community, consisting of multiple stakeholder groups, is an important component of our concept for the ELG (Rehm et al. 2020). This heterogeneous set of stakeholder groups includes LT provider companies, LT user/buyer companies, research centres and universities involved in LT research, development and innovation activities, language communities, politics and public administrations, national funding agencies, language service providers and translators as well as the European citizen at large (Rehm et al. 2021).

In this chapter we focus upon one specific part of the wider group of stakeholders involved in the ELG initiative, i. e., the National Competence Centres (NCCs). The ELG NCCs are an international network of 32 regional and national networks. Section 2 describes the NCCs as well as the activities carried out together with the NCCs. We also touch upon the setup procedure and the involvement of the NCCs. Conferences, workshops and other events play a crucial role in disseminating the mission and idea of the ELG initiative, as well as the platform itself. We involved the NCCs to help spread the word about ELG on the regional and national levels. A major part

---

Katrin Marheinecke · Annika Grützner-Zahn · Georg Rehm
Deutsches Forschungszentrum für Künstliche Intelligenz GmbH, Germany,
katrin.marheinecke@dfki.de, annika.gruetzner-zahn@dfki.de, georg.rehm@dfki.de

G. Rehm (ed.), *European Language Grid*, Cognitive Technologies,
https://doi.org/10.1007/978-3-031-17258-8_11

of their involvement was, thus, devoted to the organisation of and participation in conferences and events.

Section 3 provides a brief overview of the events and conferences ELG organised or participated in. We focus upon the four editions of the annual META-FORUM conference series, which were organised by the ELG project (2019 until 2022). Due to the impact of the COVID-19 pandemic, more than two thirds of all events planned under the umbrella of the project had to be organised as virtual events.

2 National Competence Centres

The ELG National Competence Centres comprises 32 colleagues from all over Europe who all have their own strong regional and national networks, which comprise both industry and also research. For the setup of the NCCs, we benefited from structures and instruments that have been set up by partners of the ELG consortium starting in 2010 and that have been in active use since then, including META-NET[1], META-SHARE (Piperidis et al. 2014)[2], CRACKER (Cracking the Language Barrier, Rehm 2017)[3], EFNIL (European Federation of National Institutions for Language)[4], ELRC (European Language Resource Coordination)[5] and the META-FORUM conference series (Rehm et al. 2016, 2020).

In ELG, we made use of this large set of collaborators, established infrastructures and communication instruments. The involvement in different projects and initiatives made it possible to set up a strong and representative network of National Competence Centres with broad reach into regional and national networks already during the ELG proposal preparation phase, i. e., before the project had actually started. We invited more than 30 experts from the field that met a number of criteria (participation in relevant initiatives, members of academic organisations, good connections to industry and research etc.) to participate in ELG as National Competence Centre Leads with a clearly defined set of tasks and responsibilities.

2.1 Tasks and Responsibilities

The NCCs support the ELG project and initiative in various ways. This international network of national networks not only significantly contributes to the population of the ELG cloud platform with services, resources and data sets, it also plays an important role for broadening the reach of the ELG project and initiative. Early in

---

[1] http://www.meta-net.eu

[2] http://www.meta-share.org

[3] http://www.cracker-project.eu

[4] http://www.efnil.org

[5] https://lr-coordination.eu

the project, the NCCs were asked to provide information and share their knowledge, e. g., on national/regional information about services, datasets, resources, tools, technologies, research centres, experts, communities, companies, initiatives, projects etc. Additionally, the NCCs have been crucial as multipliers who spread the word about ELG and inform regional and national stakeholders and organisations about ELG and its benefits. The NCCs also fed local needs, ideas and demands back to the ELG to make sure that the ELG development takes the requirements of their constituency into account. Moreover, the NCCs helped with general outreach and dissemination activities, e. g., promoting events like the ELG conferences (Section 3) or the ELG open calls (see Part IV) through their own established channels and networks.

Whereas some activities could be performed by the NCCs with sending emails and providing quickly accessible information, there are a number of tasks that required more effort. These included:

- Organisation of a regional/national ELG workshop including agenda preparation, advertising and promotion (web, social media, emails), identification of speakers and participants etc.
- Participation in regional/national events (both scientific and industry conferences and workshops) on behalf of ELG to promote ELG and to interest relevant stakeholders from research and industry.
- Participation in each of the annual ELG conferences (META-FORUM) in order to strengthen the LT community, support dissemination activities related to ELG and to foster discussion on current LT-related topics and trends.
- Desk research and information gathering: Collection of relevant regional/national information regarding funding programmes, national language (technology) development plans, AI strategies etc. with the overall goal of putting together a comprehensive picture of the European LT landscape.[6]

These tasks corresponded to the priorities of the ELG project consortium, but were to be understood as recommendations rather than mandatory activities. The actual selection of tasks to be organised by an NCC depended on the situation in their country and was determined individually.

We organised meetings with all NCC Leads approximately twice a year; originally at least one annual meeting was meant to be held as a face-to-face meeting co-located with the annual ELG conference in order to minimise travel efforts.[7] Due to the COVID-19 pandemic, further face-to-face meetings have been impossible, which is why all follow-up meetings were held virtually. In the NCC meetings, all NCCs Leads were asked to report briefly on the situation in their countries; furthermore, planned activities and tasks foreseen were discussed. Contractual and organisational matters could also be addressed.

---

[6] With regard to these desk research activities, many synergies with the project European Language Equality (ELE), which started in January 2021 and which included almost all NCCs as consortium partners, have been identified and made use of, see https://european-language-equality.eu.

[7] The first and, so far, only face-to-face meeting of all National Competence Centres took place on 7 October 2019, as a pre-conference meeting of META-FORUM 2019 in Brussels (see Figure 1).

Fig. 1 National Comptence Centre meeting in Brussels, Belgium (7 October 2019)

2.2 Role and Structure

The rationale behind setting up this international network of national networks was to broaden the reach of the ELG consortium, to provide input with regard to the linguistic situation in the different countries and to fuel the knowledge transfer and sharing between national programmes and initiatives on the one hand and ELG on the other. Since the EU Member States and other European countries have quite diverse situations and individual language policies, a "one-size-fits-all" approach would not have worked. It was crucial for ELG to have access to dedicated experts in all countries to turn to and ask for input. Due to their vast personal connections, the NCCs were ideally suited to make the ELG initiative known in the local markets and in the research spheres of their home countries. It was a deliberate decision to move forward only with academic organisations as NCCs in order to guarantee independence from any commercial interests.

The network of NCCs was compiled based on participation in existing structures and initiatives (META-NET, ELRC NAPs, CLARIN etc.), taking into account scientific standing and existing connections to industry and research. Table 1 lists the NCC Leads, their country and affiliation. Figure 1 shows the NCC Leads at the NCC kick-off meeting in October 2019 in Brussels, Belgium.

2.3 Visibility and Promotion

The NCCs provided valuable insights and feedback to the ELG project and initiative. In return, the project consortium helped increase the visibility of the NCCs and their institutions, for example, by promoting the NCCs and their organisations on the ELG

Name and Country		Institution
Dagmar Gromann	AT	Zentrum für Translationswissenschaft, Universität Wien
Walter Daelemans	BE	Comp. Ling. and Psycholing. Res. Centre (CLiPS), Univ. of Antwerp
Svetla Koeva	BG	Institute for Bulgarian Language, Bulgarian Academy of Sciences
Marko Tadić	HR	Inst. of Ling., Faculty of Hum. and Social Science, Univ. of Zagreb
Dora Loizidou	CY	Department French and Modern Languages, University of Cyprus
Jan Hajič*	CZ	Inst. of Formal and Applied Linguistics, Charles University
Bolette S. Pedersen	DK	Centre for Lang. Tech., Dpt. of Nordic Research, Univ. of Copenhagen
Susanna Oja	EE	Competence Centre for NLP at the Institute of the Estonian Language
Krister Lindén	FI	Department of Digital Humanities, University of Helsinki
François Yvon	FR	Laboratoire Interdisciplinaire des Sciences du Numérique, CNRS
Georg Rehm*	DE	Deutsches Forschungszentrum für Künstliche Intelligenz (DFKI)
Maria Gavriilidou*	EL	Institute for Language and Speech Processing (ILSP), R. C. "Athena"
Tamás Váradi	HU	Research Institute for Linguistics, Hungarian Academy of Sciences
Eiríkur Rögnvaldsson	IS	School of Humanities, University of Iceland
Andy Way	IE	ADAPT Centre, Dublin City University (DCU)
Bernardo Magnini	IT	Human Language Technology, Fondazione Bruno Kessler (FBK)
Inguna Skadina	LV	Institute of Mathematics and Computer Science, University of Latvia
Albina Auksoriūtė	LT	Institute of the Lithuanian Language
Dimitra Anastasiou	LU	Luxembourg Institute of Science and Technology (LIST)
Michael Rosner	MT	Department Intelligent Computer Systems, University of Malta
Vincent Vandeghinste	NL	Instituut voor de Nederlandse Taal (INT)
Kristine Eide	NO	Norwegian Language Council
Maciej Ogrodniczuk	PL	Institute of Computer Science, Polish Academy of Sciences
António Branco	PT	Department of Informatics, University of Lisbon
Dan Tufiş	RO	Research Institute for AI, Romanian Academy of Sciences
Cvetana Krstev	RS	Faculty of Mathematics, Belgrade University (UBG)
Radovan Garabík	SK	L'udovít Štúr Institute of Linguistics, Slovak Academy of Sciences
Simon Krek	SI	Jozef Stefan Institute (JSI)
Marta Villegas	ES	Barcelona Supercomputing Center (BSC)
Jens Edlund	SE	Royal Institute of Technology (KTH)
Hervé Bourlard	CH	Idiap Research Institute
Kalina Bontcheva*	UK	Department of Computer Science, University of Sheffield

Person belongs to the ELG consortium

Table 1 List of National Competence Centres

website.[8] At the ELG conferences, the organisers dedicated several sessions to the activities and concerns of selected NCCs and also addressed locally relevant aspects in the conference programme. Furthermore, the NCC meetings served as discussion platforms where the NCCs could promote their topics and exchange experience and knowledge with colleagues from other countries.

The fact that more than two thirds of the project's runtime took place during the global COVID-19 pandemic thwarted our collective plans for almost all face-to-face events and workshops and severely affected our dissemination activities. However, the shift to virtual formats has allowed interested people to attend conferences or workshops who might not have attended otherwise because of the effort and expenses

---

[8] https://www.european-language-grid.eu/ncc/

involved. In addition, online events have made it easier for the ELG team to provide presentations and platform demos because there was no travel component involved.

In June 2022, a new format was introduced for META-FORUM 2022, as this final project conference was planned and conducted as a hybrid event, combining the benefits of face-to-face and online conferences.

2.4 Operational Aspects

Operationally, DFKI as the coordinating partner of the ELG project prepared subcontracts that specified the details of the cooperation between ELG and the NCCs. The NCCs agreed to take over tasks in the interest of disseminating and promoting the European Language Grid in their countries with the activities described. In return, the ELG project reimbursed costs incurred for activities like:

- Organisation of a regional or national ELG workshop.
- Participation in the annual ELG conferences 2019 and 2022 (including costs for travel and accommodation).
- Participation in regional or national conferences or other events to promote ELG (including costs for travel, accommodation and conference fees, if applicable).
- Desk research, participation in surveys or questionnaires, communication and participation in virtual meetings.

3 Conferences and Workshops

ELG organised four annual conferences (META-FORUM 2019, 2020, 2021, 2022) to present, discuss and widely disseminate the idea of a joint technology cloud platform under the umbrella of the wider *Multilingual Europe* topic. While these conferences are described in more detail in Section 3.1, the more focused ELG workshops and additional events are described in Sections 3.2 and 3.3, respectively.

3.1 META-FORUM Conference Series

META-FORUM is the annual international conference on Language Technologies in Europe, organised by ELG together with the META-NET Network of Excellence, dedicated to fostering the multilingual European information society. Previous META-FORUM editions were organised and financially supported through the EU projects META-NET (T4ME; 2010, 2011, 2012, 2013) and CRACKER (2015, 2016, 2017). For the four editions 2019-2022, ELG took over the organisation of META-FORUM, which at the same time serves as the annual ELG conference (Section 3.1.1 to 3.1.4). Table 2 shows all META-FORUM conferences so far.

The two main goals of META-FORUM are community building and outreach to the wider European Language Technology community including research and industry. The ELG editions also had the goal of promoting the ELG initiative and also ELG as the primary platform for Language Technology in Europe. The conferences featured presentations and project expos with a special collaboration focus in order to attract users and providers of LT. As the conference also functions as a dissemination and promotion platform, the ambition was to attract a large and varied number of participants so that all relevant stakeholder groups were adequately covered.

Year	Conference Motto	Location	Date
2010	Challenges for Multilingual Europe	Brussels, BE	Nov. 17/18
2011	Solutions for Multilingual Europe	Budapest, HU	June 27/28
2012	A Strategy for Multilingual Europe	Brussels, BE	June 20/21
2013	Connecting Europe for New Horizons	Berlin, DE	Sept. 19/20
2015	Technologies for the Multilingual Digital Single Market	Riga, LV	April 27
2016	Beyond Multilingual Europe	Lisbon, PT	July 04/05
2017	Towards a Human Language Project	Brussels, BE	Nov. 13/14
2019	Introducing the European Language Grid	Brussels, BE	Oct. 08/09
2020	Piloting the European Language Grid	*online*	Dec. 01-03
2021	Using the European Language Grid	*online*	Nov. 15-17
2022	Joining the European Language Grid	Brussels, BE	June 08/09

Table 2 META-FORUM conference series

3.1.1 META-FORUM 2019

META-FORUM 2019 took place in October 2019 in Brussels.[9] Its motto was "Introducing the European Language Grid". The first session was dedicated to a presentation of the overall ELG project including a very first prototype of the platform, which was demonstrated live on stage to the LT community and stakeholders from the EU institutions for the very first time. After presentations of the three project areas (ELG Platform, ELG Content, ELG Community), the open calls for pilot projects were announced including overall procedures and timeline. Another session focused on the six LT research projects – ELITR, COMPRISE, Bergamot, EMBEDDIA, Gourmet and Prêt-à-LLOD – funded under the Horizon 2020 call ICT-29b-2018 "A multilingual Next Generation Internet". Moreover, panel discussions and presentations on LT and AI, on LT and digital public services, on news from the language communities as well as discussions with stakeholders from industry were organised. An expo featured LT and relevant AI projects. Interest in the ELG platform was very high during and after the conference, as evidenced by a high number of relevant discussions during the sessions and in the breaks. These discussions provided valuable feedback for the further development of the platform. All in all, feedback regarding the event

---

[9] https://www.european-language-grid.eu/meta-forum-2019/

was overwhelmingly positive. Among others, stakeholders from minority languages expect ELG to make significant breakthroughs, because they hope to find datasets more easily. After the conference, we received several enquiries from companies highly interested in including their services in the ELG platform.

3.1.2 META-FORUM 2020

Due to the global COVID-19 pandemic, META-FORUM 2020 had to be organised as a virtual event, it was held in early December 2020.[10] The motto of the conference was "Piloting the European Language Grid" and it consisted of three half days of presentations and panel discussions. META-FORUM 2020 received a lot of interest with many fruitful conversations. Once again, a strong focus was on presenting the wider landscape of currently funded projects in the area of LT and language-centric AI but also the industry perspective was taken into account.

Holding a conference that is supposed to foster community building and network-ing as an online event, is a technical challenge. At the same time, the year 2020, with many cancelled events, made it even more necessary to provide room for open ex-change among colleagues and (potential) collaborators. This is why we decided to organise a large project expo to enable in-depth discussions on different approaches in the various projects.[11] Like a face-to-face expo, not only the general idea of the respective project was presented but the virtual booths also allowed for technical de-mos, detailed explanations and profound exchange between visitors and the project representatives. The expo featured 35 projects, all of which had their own dedi-cated virtual meeting room. We also prepared web pages for each project with an abstract, project poster and other visual materials provided by the projects. Thus, visitors could study the material on the website or jump into the project meeting rooms (i. e., the virtual expo booths) and stay in the meetings as long as they liked. Apart from the first set of ten ELG pilot projects, the following projects participated in META-FORUM 2020 with project booths: AI4MEDIA[12], Bergamot[13], COM-PRISE[14], CURLICAT[15], DSDE[16], Elexis[17], ELG[18], ELITR[19], ELRC[20], EMBED-

---

[10] https://www.european-language-grid.eu/meta-forum-2020

[11] https://www.european-language-grid.eu/meta-forum-2020/meta-forum-2020-project-expo/

[12] https://ai4media.eu

[13] https://browser.mt

[14] https://www.compriseh2020.eu

[15] http://clip.ipipan.waw.pl/CURLICAT

[16] https://www.cjvt.si/rsdo/en/project/

[17] https://elex.is

[18] https://www.european-language-grid.eu

[19] https://elitr.eu

[20] http://www.lr-coordination.eu

DIA[21], EUCPT[22], FedTerm[23], Gourmet[24], Lynx[25], MAPA[26], MARCELL[27], Marian[28], MeMAD[29], MT4All[30], NexusLinguarum[31], NTEU[32], Prêt-à-LLOD[33], PRINCIPLE[34], PROVENANCE[35], QURATOR[36] and WeVerify[37]. In addition, members of the ELG consortium provided demos of the platform and discussed questions and ideas of (potential) users, providers and other interested parties.

Interest in the ELG platform and initiative was considerably stronger than in 2019, i. e., ELG was gaining more and more traction. META-FORUM has proven to be an effective marketing and information channel for ELG. Discussions that took place in the expo provided, again, a lot of valuable feedback and inspiration. This format worked also very well to advertise the work of the ELG pilot projects. Despite the challenging conditions, the conference was successful, while it is obvious that virtual events can only emulate certain parts of a face-to-face event while others – the often mentioned informal chats over coffee – are difficult to recreate in the virtual format. While not every participant attended each session, the online format made it possible for visitors to select only those sessions they are interested in and for which they had sufficient time capacities. The virtual format made it possible for all participants to attend including those with time and budget restrictions. A poll during the opening session showed that more than half of the participants attended META-FORUM for the first time in 2020. All META-FORUM 2020 sessions are available online.[38]

3.1.3 META-FORUM 2021

META-FORUM 2021 was the 10th edition of the conference series overall and the second to take place online, given the ongoing pandemic situation.[39] The motto of

---

[21] http://embeddia.eu

[22] https://www.presidencymt.eu

[23] https://www.eurotermbank.com

[24] https://gourmet-project.eu

[25] https://lynx-project.eu

[26] https://mapa-project.eu

[27] http://marcell-project.eu

[28] https://marian-project.eu

[29] https://memad.eu

[30] http://ixa2.si.ehu.eus/mt4all/

[31] https://nexuslinguarum.eu

[32] https://nteu.eu

[33] https://pret-a-llod.github.io

[34] https://principleproject.eu

[35] https://www.provenanceh2020.eu

[36] https://qurator.ai

[37] https://weverify.eu

[38] https://www.youtube.com/playlist?list=PLL1cFzaG0S5ghZz0HxO5TEUIdwrY7J8qJ

[39] https://www.european-language-grid.eu/meta-forum-2021/

the conference was "Using the European Language Grid" and it highlighted the first actual uses of the ELG platform. The setup of the conference was similar to the structure used in 2020. However, the project expo was organised using the virtual meeting space environment Gather.town to further stress the community aspect.[40]

As the motto implies, in 2021 using and benefiting from ELG was the main focus. To demonstrate this, five of the ten successfully finished pilot projects were featured with their results. Furthermore, representatives from the European LT industry took part in a panel to discuss their expectations towards and experiences with the ELG platform. In the more hands-on ELG integration tutorial, potential users who were considering to integrate their own tools and services into ELG had the chance to learn how. All META-FORUM 2021 sessions are available online.[41]

Overall interest in the conference was enormous and the number of participants significantly exceeded that of the previous year. The feedback collected in the session again proved to be a valuable source of information and was thoroughly evaluated after the conference in order to further enhance the platform development.

3.1.4 META-FORUM 2022

While the virtual editions of META-FORUM 2020 and 2021 were very successful, there are certain disadvantages of online-only events compared to face-to-face conferences. This is why META-FORUM 2022 was organised as a hybrid event, combining the advantages of flexibility and higher reach with the benefits of face-to-face discussions. The onsite conference in Brussels was held under appropriate COVID-19-safe conditions with approx. 100 participants from the European LT community and representatives of the European Institutions. Several hundred participants attended the conference online.

3.2 ELG Workshops

ELG is committed to community building and collaborating with relevant initiatives on the European level as well as forming its own network of networks (Section 2). The network of 32 NCCs acts as local and national bridges to the ELG initiative and cloud platform. Accordingly, dedicated workshops with and for the national LT communities have been a crucial task the NCCs were asked to fulfil.[42] These workshops were organised with the goal of making ELG known all over Europe.

Usually the workshops were organised as individual events by each NCC. In some cases, they were co-hosted by several NCCs together, e. g., the ELG workshop at SwissText 2020 (hosted by the ELG NCCs Austria, Switzerland and Germany) or

---

[40] https://www.european-language-grid.eu/meta-forum-2021/project-expo/

[41] https://www.youtube.com/playlist?list=PLL1cFzaG0S5iDaCg2SliyA-4axKY0LfiQ

[42] https://www.european-language-grid.eu/events/

National Competence Centre(s)	Location	Date
Switzerland, Austria, Germany	*online*	23 June 2020
Lithuania, Latvia, Estonia	Kaunas, LT	21 Sept. 2020
Poland	*online*	27 Oct. 2020
Finland	*online*	15 Dec. 2020
Germany	*online*	20 April 2021
Austria	*online*	11 May 2021
Switzerland, Austria, Germany	*online*	14 June 2021
Belgium, Luxembourg	*online*	08 July 2021
Spain	*online*	23 Sept. 2021
Czech Republic, Slovakia	*online*	18 Oct. 2021
Denmark	Copenhagen, DK	16 Nov. 2021
Netherlands	*online*	03 Dec. 2021
France	*online*	08 Feb. 2022
Bulgaria	*online*	11 Feb. 2022
Serbia	*online*	11 March 2022
Norway	Oslo, NO	16 March 2022
Romania	*online*	24 March 2022
Slovenia	*online*	27 May 2022
United Kingdom	*online*	17 June 2022

Table 3 Workshops organised by the National Competence Centres

the ELG workshop of the Baltic NCCs of Lithuania, Latvia and Estonia that was co-located with the Baltic HLT conference in 2020.

Since all workshops were held during the pandemic, almost all were online events that usually attracted between 25 and 100 participants. Depending on the country and target audience of the workshop, they either had a more informative or a more technical spin, or a combination of both. In an introductory talk by the project coordinator or a partner of the consortium, ELG and its history, its goals and current status was presented. In a separate presentation, the technical setup of the platform and its offerings were explained. After that, the NCCs either organised discussion panels or invited speakers from industry to emphasise the demands and expectations towards ELG. Especially these talks often spurred interesting and inspiring discussions and provided valuable feedback for the ELG consortium. In various workshops, a short hands-on tutorial session was included in which a member of the technical ELG team explained how to make available services or resources through ELG. Many of the ELG NCC workshops are available online.[43] Table 3 lists all NCC workshops.

3.3 Additional Conferences

Representatives of the ELG consortium took the opportunity to promote the platform and the initiative at numerous occasions throughout the run-time of the ELG project. In addition to local events, ELG was also present with talks and papers at

---

[43] https://www.youtube.com/channel/UCarEHmsWT2JslcvvWkbhL4A

more than 50 different European and international conferences, such as LT4ALL (2019), LREC 2020, AI Boost (2021), European Big Data Value Conference (2021), Fachtagung Maschinelle Verfahren in der Erschließung (Deutsche Nationalbibliothek, 2021) and Wales Academic Symposium on Language Technologies (2022).

4 Conclusions

The collaboration with the National Competence Centres was successful. The impact they have had in their countries to promote ELG cannot be overstated. Also, the NCCs' expert knowledge of language resources in their regions and their contacts to representatives from industry and research have been and continue to be extremely useful. Although the formal contracts with the NCCs will expire at the end of the project, we will make an effort to maintain good working relationships with these experts in the future and, if possible, to intensify the work again in future projects.

Under the umbrella of the ELG legal entity we will continue to organise events and workshops in the coming years to demonstrate new developments and to seek contact with the communities in the various European countries and regions in order to further promote networking. The annual META-FORUM conference is an established brand and will continue to be an important activity to bring stakeholders together and counteract the fragmentation of the European LT community. Experiences from the last years with different meeting formats have significantly extended the spectrum of what is possible.

References

Piperidis, Stelios, Harris Papageorgiou, Christian Spurk, Georg Rehm, Khalid Choukri, Olivier Hamon, Nicoletta Calzolari, Riccardo del Gratta, Bernardo Magnini, and Christian Girardi (2014). "META-SHARE: One year after". In: *Proceedings of the 9th Language Resources and Evaluation Conference (LREC 2014)*. Ed. by Nicoletta Calzolari, Khalid Choukri, Thierry Declerck, Hrafn Loftsson, Bente Maegaard, Joseph Mariani, Asuncion Moreno, Jan Odijk, and Stelios Piperidis. Reykjavik, Iceland: ELRA, pp. 1532–1538. URL: http://www.lrec-conf.org/proceedings/lrec2014/pdf/786_Paper.pdf.

Rehm, Georg, ed. (2017). *Language Technologies for Multilingual Europe: Towards a Human Language Project. Strategic Research and Innovation Agenda*. CRACKER and Cracking the Language Barrier federation. URL: http://cracker-project.eu/sria/.

Rehm, Georg, Katrin Marheinecke, Stefanie Hegele, Stelios Piperidis, Kalina Bontcheva, Jan Hajic, Khalid Choukri, Andrejs Vasiļjevs, Gerhard Backfried, Christoph Prinz, José Manuel Gómez Pérez, Luc Meertens, Paul Lukowicz, Josef van Genabith, Andrea Lösch, Philipp Slusallek, Morten Irgens, Patrick Gatellier, Joachim Köhler, Laure Le Bars, Dimitra Anastasiou, Albina Auksoriūtė, Núria Bel, António Branco, Gerhard Budin, Walter Daelemans, Koenraad De Smedt, Radovan Garabík, Maria Gavriilidou, Dagmar Gromann, Svetla Koeva, Simon Krek, Cvetana Krstev, Krister Lindén, Bernardo Magnini, Jan Odijk, Maciej Ogrodniczuk, Eiríkur Rögnvaldsson, Mike Rosner, Bolette Pedersen, Inguna Skadina, Marko Tadić, Dan Tufiş, Tamás Váradi, Kadri Vider, Andy Way, and François Yvon (2020). "The European Language Technology Landscape in 2020: Language-Centric and Human-Centric AI for Cross-Cultural Communication in Multilingual Europe". In: *Proceedings of the 12th Language Resources and Evaluation Conference (LREC 2020)*. Ed. by Nicoletta Calzolari, Frédéric Béchet, Philippe Blache, Christopher Cieri, Khalid Choukri, Thierry Declerck, Hitoshi Isahara, Bente Maegaard, Joseph Mariani, Asuncion Moreno, Jan Odijk, and Stelios Piperidis. Marseille, France: ELRA, pp. 3315–3325. URL: https://www.aclweb.org/anthology/2020.lrec-1.407/.

Rehm, Georg, Stelios Piperidis, Kalina Bontcheva, Jan Hajic, Victoria Arranz, Andrejs Vasiļjevs, Gerhard Backfried, José Manuel Gómez Pérez, Ulrich Germann, Rémi Calizzano, Nils Feldhus, Stefanie Hegele, Florian Kintzel, Katrin Marheinecke, Julian Moreno-Schneider, Dimitris Galanis, Penny Labropoulou, Miltos Deligiannis, Katerina Gkirtzou, Athanasia Kolovou, Dimitris Gkoumas, Leon Voukoutis, Ian Roberts, Jana Hamrlová, Dusan Varis, Lukáš Kačena, Khalid Choukri, Valérie Mapelli, Mickaël Rigault, Jūlija Meļņika, Miro Janosik, Katja Prinz, Andres Garcia-Silva, Cristian Berrio, Ondrej Klejch, and Steve Renals (2021). "European Language Grid: A Joint Platform for the European Language Technology Community". In: *Proceedings of the 16th Conference of the European Chapter of the Association for Computational Linguistics: System Demonstrations (EACL 2021)*. Kyiv, Ukraine: ACL, pp. 221–230. URL: https://www.aclweb.org/anthology/2021.eacl-demos.26.pdf.

Rehm, Georg, Hans Uszkoreit, Sophia Ananiadou, Núria Bel, Audronė Bielevičienė, Lars Borin, António Branco, Gerhard Budin, Nicoletta Calzolari, Walter Daelemans, Radovan Garabík, Marko Grobelnik, Carmen García-Mateo, Josef van Genabith, Jan Hajič, Inma Hernáez, John Judge, Svetla Koeva, Simon Krek, Cvetana Krstev, Krister Lindén, Bernardo Magnini, Joseph Mariani, John McNaught, Maite Melero, Monica Monachini, Asunción Moreno, Jan Odijk, Maciej Ogrodniczuk, Piotr Pęzik, Stelios Piperidis, Adam Przepiórkowski, Eiríkur Rögnvaldsson, Mike Rosner, Bolette Sandford Pedersen, Inguna Skadiņa, Koenraad De Smedt, Marko Tadić, Paul Thompson, Dan Tufiş, Tamás Váradi, Andrejs Vasiļjevs, Kadri Vider, and Jolanta Zabarskaite (2016). "The Strategic Impact of META-NET on the Regional, National and International Level". In: *Language Resources and Evaluation* 50.2, pp. 351–374. DOI: 10.1007/s10579-015-9333-4. URL: http://link.springer.com/article/10.1007/s10579-015-9333-4.

Chapter 12
Innovation and Marketplace: A Vision for the European Language Grid

Katja Prinz and Gerhard Backfried

Abstract This chapter provides a comprehensive overview of innovation and the ELG marketplace as core elements for the generation of value and the creation of an active, attractive and vibrant community surrounding the European Language Grid. Innovation is an essential element in making ELG a credible and sustainable undertaking. However, it does not happen by itself nor materialise in a vacuum. Consequently, ELG provides a habitat for various kinds of innovation and a home for the necessary community to put innovation into action. The marketplace is essential for attracting participants supplying and demanding services, resources, components and technologies on a European scale. Innovation and marketplace – as well as the overall business model – are tightly connected and need to be developed and managed in a joint manner. Clearly, this is not a one-off activity, but rather needs to be carried out continuously and extend into the future. ELG is designed and created to promote the excellence and growth of the European LT market, creating new jobs and business opportunities and supporting European digital sovereignty. Encompassing a wide array of technologies and resources for many languages spoken across Europe and in neighbouring regions, it contributes to the Multilingual Digital Single Market as a cross-European driver for innovation.

1 Introduction

The ELG marketplace and the kinds of innovations it enables form central elements of ELG and its goal to become the *one-stop-shop for Language Technology in Europe*. These aspects are closely interlinked with a series of further topics concerning the business aspects of ELG in a wider sense, none of which can be viewed in isolation but rather need to be approached in a connected and holistic manner.

Artificial Intelligence (AI), Natural Language Processing (NLP) and Natural Language Understanding (NLU) are highly active areas of research and development

Katja Prinz · Gerhard Backfried
HENSOLDT Analytics GmbH, Austria,
katja.prinz@hensoldt.net, gerhard.backfried@hensoldt.net

leading to novel applications on a continuous basis. Over time, new actors enter the stage and change the course of events. In this highly dynamic landscape it is imperative to constantly monitor progress, remain alert and be able to adapt to newly emerging trends. Consequently, any platform and strategy implemented on and by AI/NLP/NLU need to remain flexible and open to change. Fundamental concepts such as value-generation provide orientation across time and should form the base of any strategies developed.

Neither the marketplace nor innovation make sense without an underlying crowd of committed actors, which drive the cycles of supply and demand, form the ingredients of cooperation and consulting and are at the heart of creation and innovation. Establishing and fostering this community who will take LT one step further thus forms one of the most important tasks to be addressed by ELG.

2 Innovation

In today's agile, interconnected and virtualised world, the paradigm of open innovation (Chesbrough 2006), connecting many different disciplines, sectors and actors in a non-linear fashion has gained considerable traction. Under this paradigm, innovation takes place within as well as outside an organisation with knowledge flowing in both directions. It allows different actors to collaborate and experiment across organisational boundaries, across different sectors and disciplines, and enables them to dynamically produce innovation in a heterogeneous manner. Eco-systems like ELG form a natural habitat for such activities and a powerful environment for innovation. In this chapter, the concept of innovation is viewed from the angle of open innovation, forming the most appropriate and promising approach for a platform like ELG, rather than the silo'd and closed kind of innovation which is limited to individual organisations. For innovation to occur, two fundamental ingredients need to be combined: innovation = invention + adoption (Schrage 2004). Both of these factors must be present for innovation to take place and to put it into effect in order to generate new knowledge, to develop new products, services or processes. Any environment or innovation-strategy consequently has to reflect both factors, balance efforts and encourage and support both kinds of activities.

2.1 Significance of Innovation

Applications in the fields of AI, NLP or NLU reside in a highly competitive and dynamic landscape. As technology leaps are produced in rapid succession and markets and opportunities expand, organisations can and should make use of internal as well as external ideas and paths to market as they seek to advance their technology (Chesbrough 2006). Justin Rattner, Intel's former CTO evangelised the concept of 21st century industrial research where innovation is driven by teams of boundary spanners that possess multidisciplinary skills. Online platforms such as ELG provide ideal multi-sided ecosystems for such teams, offering the means to link up and collaborate and to unite a multitude of participants with the joint aim to create novel products and services ready for swift adoption. However, beyond providing the technical framework, resources and tools, such platforms also foster the sharing and exchange of knowledge and ideas between participants. As a result of the increased diversity and connectedness of actors, the generation of genuinely new knowledge and more radical innovation is possible. Whether and to what extent these goals also materialise in practice depends on a variety of factors, such as acceptance and openness to a culture of open innovation that also supports the useful and selective sharing of research results and data. If exercised successfully, open innovation has the potential to eliminate barriers in research and development and generates a dynamic environment that cannot be achieved with traditional methods.

2.2 Types of Innovation and Innovation Strategies

Innovation may span a wide spectrum concerning products, services, methods, business models and even entire organisations. Figure 1 depicts different dimensions and types of innovation and provides several examples for each kind.

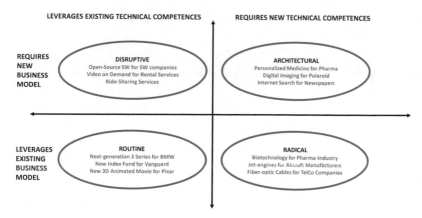

Fig. 1 Innovation landscape (Pisano 2015)

Routine innovation (or incremental innovation) builds on an organisation's existing technological competences and fits with its existing business model and customer base. Routine innovation aims at improving existing products (or services) continuously until the end of their life-cycles. It typically involves activities to improve features, reduce costs or expand production lines and mechanisms. Architectural innovation combines technological and business model disruptions. Disruptive innovation typically requires a new business model but not necessarily a technological breakthrough. For that reason, it also challenges, or *disrupts*, the business models of other actors. Breakthrough innovation can be regarded as the more radical version of disruptive innovation causing fundamental changes in the market through the introduction of new products, methods or business models. These categories are not clear-cut and overlap to some extent. However, the dimensions can serve to locate different types of innovation when designing an innovation strategy. Aside from these categories, innovation can also be characterised by the kinds and magnitude of impact caused by it.

Any innovation strategy needs to specify how the different types of innovation (as outlined above) fit into the overall business strategy. It must map an organisation's value proposition for the defined markets and at the same time set realistic boundaries. Furthermore, the strategy must be clearly communicated in order to assure a common goal for all participants involved, secure their commitment and to streamline activities between all partners. Innovation for innovation's sake or for generic goals such as *"we need to be innovative"* are neither sufficient nor effective. Pisano (2015) emphasises the importance of these inter-connections by defining the term "innovation strategy" as the "commitment to a set of coherent, mutually reinforcing policies or behaviours aimed at achieving a specific competitive goal, promoting alignment among diverse groups within an organisation, clarifying objectives and priorities, helping focus efforts around them and specifying how various functions will support it". Innovation – and an innovation strategy – can neither be developed nor executed in isolation, but need to be carried out in sync with the defined business strategies of an organisation to be successful.

2.3 Open Innovation in the ELG Platform and Marketplace

Innovation does not take place in a vacuum, but is tightly connected to the vision, business, marketplace and sustainability strategies aiming to establish and sustain ELG as the primary marketplace for LT in Europe. The platform and community are positioned at the centre around which these different strategies are aligned, supporting each other in the overall goal as depicted in Figure 2.

ELG is a multi-sided and integrated platform and envisoned to function as an innovation driver during the lifetime of the project as well as beyond. The platform itself is complemented by a vibrant and active community of users and stakeholders. These are a key ingredient in creating the critical mass required to make ELG an established marketplace. Building and strengthening this community consequently forms an essential element of the ELG innovation and communication strategies.

Placing the platform and community at the core allows us to adopt an open and collaborative approach to innovation, which needs to become an inherent element (a process) of ELG. The principles of Open Innovation as coined by Chesbrough (2006) form the over-arching theme of this continuous process. Figure 3 provides a schematic overview of the actors and interactions which need to be aligned for innovation and value creation. It is imperative that all groups are present and participate

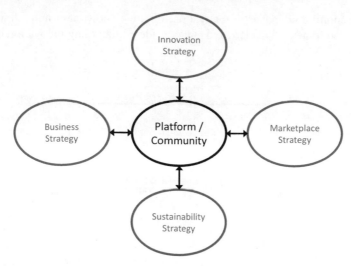

Fig. 2 Strategies centred around the ELG platform and community

actively in the process. To attract and motivate these groups, targeted communication is required.

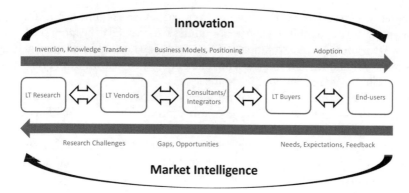

Fig. 3 ELG innovation cycle

In line with the overall approach of ELG, in Figure 3 the process of innovation spans the complete set of activities and actors from invention to adoption. The goal to generate value within the scope of the business model forms the central element. Continuous feedback regarding the needs, gaps, expectations and opportunities is collected via the community, leading to further cycles, which need to be carried out repeatedly and continuously. As a result of the continuous feedback mechanism, strategies can be updated and the speed of adoption increased over time, hence allowing for more rapid cycles of innovation. Figure 4 shows four main dimensions and associated issues to be addressed and considered regarding innovation in ELG.

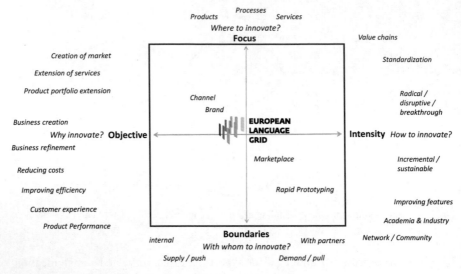

Fig. 4 Dimensions of innovation

For each dimension, several possible approaches are outlined. Together, they form a portfolio of possibilities and opportunities which need to be monitored continuously. Depending on the evolution of ELG, they may need to be adapted to changing conditions and (re-)prioritised. The innovation cycle shown in Figure 3 forms the blueprint for these continuous activities.

For the duration of the ELG project the most important element of innovation is the creation of ELG itself. The use of a platform in the scope of LT as a multisided marketplace, allowing participants to create value together by interacting with each other represents an innovative business model (Still et al. 2017). Beyond the platform itself, the creation of products (Section 2.3.1) and services (Section 2.3.2) form two further promising alleys for innovation activities.

2.3.1 Products

ELG provides a large set of technological components and resources which provide a broad basis for product offerings as individual products or product bundles. In terms of innovation potential, both bundles as well as individually improved and adapted LTs provide a wide range of opportunities. Different setups of where services are hosted and run are provided by ELG to optimise resource usage and adapt to the particular needs of customers. An extensive catalogue of tools and resources provides a single point of entry and access to these tools and LTs.

2.3.2 Services

Two kinds of services are provided by ELG: services in the sense of running components (technological services) and services in the sense of experts providing their expertise (human services). In terms of the former, the services can be used individually or in combination (as chains of services) to create value-chains. Combination and composition allow us to establish more complex workflows, enabling end-users to benefit from the capabilities of individual providers without having to worry about any inner workings or being locked in the products of an individual supplier. Corresponding mechanisms regarding billing, licensing and support will provide a single point of contact for customers. Regarding the latter, ELG provides a virtual agora, a business-space for connecting stakeholders developing or deploying (complex) solutions which require skills beyond that of individual actors. This includes services of consultants and integrators who are crucial elements in broadening the adoption (and hence boosting innovation) of LT. They are expected to act as enablers and multipliers for putting LT into practice, supporting their introduction into organisational as well as business processes.

2.3.3 Further Aspects of Innovation

Regarding the *intensity of innovation*, ELG is expected to mainly operate on a level of incremental, continuous innovation, improving existing features and extending the portfolio of features. Through this continuous extension, new combinations of services and products are expected to become available over time which allow the implementation of new features. Linking different services and thus producing value chains in a simple and transparent manner will allow for increased experimentation and thus for an agile environment for the creation of new features. Regarding the *boundaries of innovation*, ELG will focus on the community and stakeholders present on the platform. A catalogue of resources (services, corpora, datasets etc.) as well as of LT experts, consultants and integrators provides a prime resource for locating crucial resources for business. The strength, weight and activity of the community is one of the determining factors for the overall success and adoption of the ELG and hence one of the gate factors for innovation. Regarding the *objective of innovation*, the refinement as well as creation of business form viable alleys. The above-mentioned manner of gradual and incremental innovation lends itself to various kinds of business refinement such as reducing costs, improving the efficiency or product performance and improving customer experience.

Business creation may take place via the platform and community and through the creation of novel services or products via the combination of building blocks offered by ELG. The creation of standards for resources, processing services and interfaces can play an important role as it effectively decouples individual components and vendors. In combination with the technical environment of ELG, this enables increased resilience, scalability, composability and replaceability of components, avoiding vendor lock-in situations. Furthermore, standardisation of these elements will allow for a higher level of experimentation and show-casing and lower the risk of failure in the development of innovative solutions.

3 Multi-sided Marketplace Approach

To date, there is no general digital umbrella platform for LT in Europe. The ELG platform is designed to fill this gap: it is envisioned to serve as the comprehensive virtual marketplace, where value is created for all its members in Europe and beyond. Based on a multi-sided marketplace approach (see Figure 5), ELG will facilitate value and business creation and efficient transactions coupled with large developer ecosystems that build innovative technologies and services on top of a digital platform in an open and agile manner. The advantage of this approach lies in the nature of multi-sided marketplaces as enablers of transactions driving positive network externalities. They make it easier and more efficient for the participants from diverse markets to interact with each other, as the friction between different contact points is reduced. In addition, these interactions increase the value created together which almost comes naturally due to the network effects. A platform becomes more attractive to potential new users the more users meet and interact on it. In other words, value increases for all participants when more users actively use the platform (Sánchez-Cartas and León 2021). As a marketplace, ELG is designed to make it easy and efficient for participants to connect and exchange ideas and products. These can be as diverse as language resources, technologies, services, components, expertise, innovation or even information. The distinctive feature of the multi-sided approach is that the marketplace enables direct interactions between two or more sides, who can be both – product suppliers and demanders at the same time. In other words, value creation is two-way and continuous.

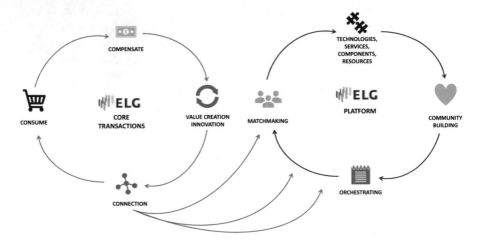

Fig. 5 ELG multi-sided marketplace approach

The core transactions of the multi-sided marketplace are represented by the left part in Figure 5 and are mainly concerned with creating value, establishing connections between supply and demand, and facilitating consumption and compensation of the products (technologies, services, components and resources) offered by ELG. *Connection* is a complex mechanism consisting of the elements portrayed in the right half of Figure 5. Various kinds of connections are supported and promoted by the platform, from matchmaking, to matching of technologies, resources and services vertically and horizontally in order to provide a more comprehensive offering, to orchestrating all interactions between, users, providers and innovators, as well as nurturing a vibrant and active community. The multi-sided marketplace approach encompasses the following principles.

Value Creation   ELG aims to be a platform for value creation which will be achieved by facilitating reciprocal exchanges between multiple marketplace participants. In addition, participants can create value by tapping into resources and capacities that they do not have to own. Any resource exchange handled via ELG will reduce transaction costs for each participant and enables access to externalised innovation. The cornerstone of the ELG marketplace positioning is the value it provides to its participants. As *the* European marketplace for LT, it connects previously unmatched supply-side and demand-side participants through innovative forms of value creation, capture and delivery. The value proposition depends on the components and services, their uniqueness, and the means of delivering value to target groups as well as on the right balance between the perceived value and the set price. Furthermore, ELG is the orchestrator to ensure value creation and high quality of participation on the platform. As such, the unique positioning as a marketplace will be based on the value generated and offered across verticals (see Figure 6). For example, a particular buyer receives a vertically packaged LT solution for their desired domain (e. g., the health industry) in the form of a unique combination of components and services from ELG. In addition, they can select the languages for the desired technologies, services and resources for the particular domain.

Connection, Gravity and Flow   Whereas traditional offline marketplaces tend to push products and technologies to the market, ELG will rather create a pull-effect. As a multi-sided marketplace it will be equipped to create network effects, i. e., effects that attract new users to enter the marketplace to be part of an ever-growing number of partners who are also part of the network. Together they engage in a mutual value exchange process which is orchestrated by the marketplace. ELG will enable easy access, meaning that participants can easily plug into the platform to share, transact and *connect*. ELG will function like a magnet in creating a pull that attracts participants to the platform with its *gravity*. Because it is both, a transaction and innovation platform, both LT providers and LT users (supply and demand) will be present to achieve critical mass. The *flow* of value will be fostered by matchmaking, i. e., making connections between LT providers and LT users. Rich data will be used for successful matchmaking and the co-creation of value.

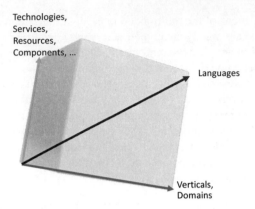

Technologies, Services, Resources, Components, ...

Languages

Verticals, Domains

Fig. 6 Value dimensions of the marketplace

Compound Growth   The marketplace aims at providing its participants a broad base that enables compound growth and scaling. Growth will be mainly driven by the network effects described above.

Visibility   ELG is designed to enhance the visibility of each of its participants, extending their reach and networking power. From the LT vendor perspective the main interest is to acquire customers. As an umbrella platform for European LT, the ELG aims at removing geographic boundaries and language barriers, thus fostering the European Digital Single Market.

Community Building   A very important aspect of this approach is to attract, grow and nurture a vibrant and active community around ELG thus promoting an interactive marketplace. The stakeholders include LT providers, academic research organisations, LT customers, EU institutions, public administrations, NGOs, policy makers, project consortia, research projects, as well as the ELG National Competence Centres (NCCs) in 32 European countries. This critical mass of active participants also generates the necessary market pull: an excellent case in point for this are the several pilot projects funded by ELG (see the chapters in Part IV), e. g., Lingsoft, Inc., Coreon GmbH and Elhuyar, among many others, have successfully enhanced the attractivity of the marketplace by contributing highly demanded services, technologies and languages to the platform.

3.1 Foundations for a Successful Marketplace

What are the key ingredients for a successful marketplace? The answer is not straightforward because the formation and growth of marketplaces depends on many factors such as the availability of capital, sufficient demand, talent, legal situation, tax systems, the innovation and startup culture of a country and many more. Nonetheless, there are certain elements successful marketplaces have in common which are equally important for ELG.

Attraction   Indisputably, success can only be achieved if enough participants are attracted to join the ecosystem. This *gravity*, which is one of the most important ingredients, will be supported by a well-balanced interplay of supply and demand all of which will be governed by ELG. It is vital for the marketplace to generate a market pull in order to fulfil the goals of self-sustainability. The more participants the marketplace attracts, the greater will be the network effect and compound value growth (a critical mass has to be reached, cf. Bonchek and Choudary 2013). The technical foundation to ensure that people are attracted to ELG is an innovative and state-of-the-art solution for containerised LT components, services and resources coupled with cloud solutions to enable fast and efficient interaction and speedy and scalable innovation.

Demand Economies of Scale   ELG will also rely on demand economies of scale, which take advantage of technological improvements on the demand side and are driven by demand aggregation, efficiencies in networks, and other phenomena (like crowd sourcing of software development) that make bigger networks more valuable to their users (Osterwalder and Pigneur 2010). Once the gravity of the marketplace is functioning, network effects will be the natural result. Growth via network effects leads to market expansion. New buyers enter the marketplace, attracted to ELG by the growing number of partners who are part of the network.

Time-to-Market   Strategically speaking, ELG will also focus on reduced time-to-market objectives: the corporate strategy of the future marketplace will be designed to truly fulfill the role as accelerator for business creation and will consider concepts like "lean management" and "just-in-time" supply chain delivery. Furthermore, the agile environment will provide a flexible test-bed for trying out new technologies and approaches.

Quality Standards   In order to be successful, the marketplace needs to facilitate the exchange of value which means that the components, services, resources provided through ELG require certain quality standards. In order to safeguard the quality of products (technologies, services, resources and components) provided, ELG standards and quality seals will eventually be implemented. In any case, the provision of high-quality state of the art LT, open architecture, reusable software, industry-grade robust components provide key ingredients for establishing confidence and trust in ELG as a whole. In addition, trust in the marketplace will be created through transparent product offering and by providing feedback and reviews of participants concerning their prior transactions.

Orchestration   Furthermore, a proper organisation and infrastructure have to be provided to guarantee that the platform smoothly works as enabler of transactions: ideally, the whole setup fosters the exchange and creation of value and supports doing business in an easy and smooth manner. A prerequisite for this is an attractive, simple and transparent licensing and pricing model, and a simple business processing scheme (Täuscher and Laudien 2018).

Ecosystem of Participants   Successful ecosystems have the ability to provide for *coopetition* (competition and cooperation) and value co-creation, which are ideally governed by structure and orchestration to work best. ELG will provide for the ideal environment to foster the structured creation and well-coordinated growth of the ecosystem. This principle is also reflected in the paradigm of open innovation adopted and encouraged by ELG.

3.2 ELG Ecosystem of Participants

One of the most important ingredients for a sustainable and successful marketplace rely on the ability of ELG to create, nurture and grow an ecosystem of participants. ELG is in the process of expanding and sustaining a unique ecosystem by attracting diverse stakeholder groups holding different roles – reaching from LT suppliers and demanders to networks and associations, industry members and academia, as well as policy makers and national competence centers (see Figure 7). By aligning itself with key associations and initiatives, ELG aims at establishing itself as a central element in a platform-of-platforms landscape.

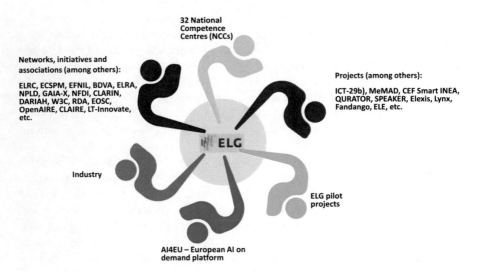

Fig. 7 ELG ecosystem of participants

The ecosystem is designed to connect people, foster an environment for open and two-way communication, create mutually beneficial relationships, and promote community building. In short, it is there to provide an umbrella platform for its participants enabling them to build relationships and to provide value to one another. The role of community building is very important because it is the driver of the marketplace. It is needed in order to reach a critical mass of active participants which eventually generate the intended market pull. From a business perspective, ELG will provide the infrastructure for an ecosystem allowing to match products, services, providers (supply) and users (demand), within a multi-sided setup. By orchestrating different stakeholders' needs, the ecosystem will allow for matchmaking of demand

and supply and the continuous multi-directional exchange of values. The technological and organisational infrastructure for this matchmaking as well as the interaction governance principles are key building blocks of ELG.

3.3 Technical and Practical Aspects

From a technical perspective, ELG will be the first large-scale LT platform applying containerisation through Kubernetes. This choice and combination of technnologies provides a scalable environment with an web user interface and corresponding back-end components and REST APIs. During the course of the project and beyond, it will provide access to a multitude of state-of-the-art technologies, services and components. Furthermore, it will include an overarching LT directory of stakeholders from research, innovation and technology, i. e., it will be the "yellow pages" or the "who's who" of the European Language Technology community.

On the provider side, ELG adheres to a number of standards in order to facilitate the integration of a large number of disparate tools:

1. Definition of common APIs for each class of tool, designed to be powerful enough to support the necessary use cases but lightweight and flexible enough to allow tools to expose their own specific parameters where this makes sense.
2. Containerisation to isolate tools from one another and to allow each tool to manage its own software dependencies. ELG uses the well-established Kubernetes system to manage the deployment, scaling and execution of containers in combination with Knative to handle auto-scaling of containers on demand.
3. Orchestration of services will become an important topic as the set of offered services grows and the demand for complex workflows becomes visible. This may potentially even concern workflows spanning multiple platforms.

With regard to the user interface, standards in user friendliness are adopted and marketplace-related features, such as upload/download, licensing, billing, payment as well as transparent pricing models will be used. In addition, ELG will promote direct contact to its participants which is important to create additional transparency and trust in the platform.

4 Conclusions

ELG has set its goal to become the *primary platform for Language Technologies in Europe* which incorporates many aspects in one setting: marketplace, business space and a scalable environment for innovation. With regard to innovation, an open innovation approach is adopted, putting the combination of creation and adoption at the centre. Different kinds and granularities of innovation (step-wise and gradual to disruptive) are enabled by ELG and the way the community behind it is set up and managed. Innovation, however, is not viewed in isolation but rather as a crucial element within the larger context of the ELG business model. The marketplace will focus on commercial aspects and communities, linking supply and demand and enabling reciprocal value exchange. In addition, ELG will form a business space and innovation platform in the sense of becoming a virtual agora, bringing researchers, experts, end-users, requirements and capabilities together in one forum. Moreover, it will serve as a promoter for open innovation, providing access to (external and internal) resources and ingredients for innovation. As *the* umbrella platform shared by the whole European LT community, it will support the bundling of efforts and forces and facilitate the reciprocal transaction of values for all participants to grow and benefit from this scaling.

References

Bonchek, Mark and Sangeet Paul Choudary (2013). "Three Elements of a Successful Platform Strategy". In: *Harvard Business Review* (January). URL: https://hbr.org/2013/01/three-elements-of-a-successful-platform.

Chesbrough, Henry (2006). *Open Innovation: Researching a New Paradigm*. Oxford University Press.

Osterwalder, Alexander and Yves Pigneur (2010). *Business Model Generation – A Handbook For Visionaries, Game Changers, And Challengers*. Wiley.

Pisano, Gary (2015). "You Need an Innovation Strategy". In: *Harvard Business Review* (June). URL: https://hbr.org/2015/06/you-need-an-innovation-strategy.

Sánchez-Cartas, Juan Manuel and Gonzalo León (2021). "Multisided Platforms and Markets: A Survey of the Theoretical Literature". In: *Journal of Economic Surveys* 35 (2). URL: https://doi.org/10.1111/joes.12409.

Schrage, Michael (2004). "Interview in Ubiquity". In: *ACM Ubiquity* (December). URL: http://ubiquity.acm.org.

Still, Kaisa, Heidi Korhonen, Miika Kumpulainen, Marko Seppänen, Arho Suominen, and Katri Valkokari (2017). "Business Model Innovation of Startups Developing Multisided Digital Platforms". In: *IEEE 19th Conference on Business Informatics*. Vol. 2. Thessaloniki, Greece: IEEE, pp. 70–75.

Täuscher, Karl and Sven Laudien (2018). "Understanding Platform Business Models: A Mixed Methods Study of Digital Marketplaces". In: *European Management Journal* 36 (3), pp. 319–329. DOI: 10.1016/j.emj.2017.06.005. URL: https://doi.org/10.1016/j.emj.2017.06.005.

Chapter 13
Sustaining the European Language Grid: Towards the ELG Legal Entity

Georg Rehm, Katrin Marheinecke, Stefanie Hegele, Stelios Piperidis, Kalina Bontcheva, Jan Hajič, Khalid Choukri, Andrejs Vasiļjevs, Gerhard Backfried, Katja Prinz, Jose Manuel Gómez-Pérez, and Ulrich Germann

Abstract When preparing the European Language Grid EU project proposal and designing the overall concept of the platform, the need for drawing up a long-term sustainability plan was abundantly evident. Already in the phase of developing the proposal, the centrepiece of the sustainability plan was what we called the "ELG legal entity", i. e., an independent organisation that would be able to take over operations, maintenace, extension and governance of the European Language Grid platform as well as managing and helping to coordinate its community. This chapter describes our current state of planning with regard to this legal entity. It explains the different options discussed and it presents the different products specified, which can be offered by the legal entity in the medium to long run. We also describe which legal form the organisation will take and how it will ensure the sustainability of ELG.

Georg Rehm · Katrin Marheinecke · Stefanie Hegele
Deutsches Forschungszentrum für Künstliche Intelligenz GmbH, Germany, georg.rehm@dfki.de, katrin.marheinecke@dfki.de, stefanie.hegele@dfki.de

Stelios Piperidis
Institute for Language and Speech Processing, R. C. "Athena", Greece, spip@athenarc.gr

Kalina Bontcheva
University of Sheffield, UK, k.bontcheva@sheffield.ac.uk

Jan Hajič
Charles University, Czech Republic, hajic@ufal.mff.cuni.cz

Khalid Choukri
ELDA, France, choukri@elda.org

Andrejs Vasiļjevs
Tilde, Latvia, andrejs@tilde.lv

Gerhard Backfried · Katja Prinz
HENSOLDT Analytics GmbH, Austria, katja.prinz@hensoldt.net, gerhard.backfried@hensoldt.net

Jose Manuel Gómez-Pérez
Expert AI, Spain, jmgomez@expert.ai

Ulrich Germann
University of Edinburgh, UK, ulrich.germann@ed.ac.uk

© The Author(s) 2023
G. Rehm (ed.), *European Language Grid*, Cognitive Technologies,
https://doi.org/10.1007/978-3-031-17258-8_13

1 Introduction

One of the challenges the European Language Grid initiative aims to address is the fragmentation of the European Language Technology landscape, with regard to academia, research institutions and commercial entities. ELG aims to bring together all stakeholders, currently scattered all over Europe, under the European Language Grid platform as a common umbrella (Rehm et al. 2021; Vasiljevs et al. 2019). However, the efforts taken within the project can only be translated into a large-scale success if ELG continues to exist beyond the project runtime of 42 months. This is why it had already been foreseen in the ELG project proposal to develop a long-term sustainability plan during the project. Its centrepiece is the idea of establishing, in the second half of 2022, a dedicated ELG legal entity, which is meant to take over operations, maintenance, extension and governance of the European Language Grid platform as well as managing and helping to coordinate its community. Only with such a sustainable, long-term activity can the overarching goal of strengthening, harmonising and bringing together the European LT business and research community be met. In other words, the sustainability plan and the legal entity are mission-critical for the success of the project.

After a brief presentation of the long-term vision of ELG (Section 2), this chapter describes business and operation models that have been examined in order to assess if they are suitable for the ELG legal entity (Section 3). Not only shall the ELG platform and initiative continue to exist, we also want to expand its functionalities further in order to serve and adapt to evolving user needs even better and to fulfil ELG's mission for the European LT community. We explore a number of different dimensions with regard to the shaping of the ELG legal entity and place special emphasis on the description of a set of products we specified that can be offered by the legal entity. At the same time, it is important to point out that the AI landscape – including LT – must still be characterised as highly dynamic (Rehm et al. 2020b). Precise predictions of where the field is headed in Europe in the next years are difficult to be made right now. It remains to be seen what the post-COVID market will look like, which breakthroughs will come next in AI and LT, what the impact of the various ongoing large-scale initiatives will be and how the LT/AI-related situation in the different European countries will develop in the future. This dynamic situation creates additional challenges when it comes to specifying the final shape of the ELG legal entity, which must consequently correspond to this agile and dynamic environment.

2 Long-term Vision and Mission of ELG

Our vision and long-term goal is to establish ELG as the primary platform and marketplace for all commercial and non-commercial Language Technologies developed and offered by the European LT community. In order to achieve this goal, multiple prerequisites need to be in place, e. g., the ELG cloud platform must have very high availability and it must exhibit near real-time performance for individual services, legally safe service level agreements need to be prepared so that services can be applied in production environments, simple mechanisms for billing need to be available and technical support needs to be offered. Trust in the platform and its reliability need to be established in a transparent manner. Operating these and other components of the platform and initiative incurs various system-relevant costs (Teece 2017).

2.1 Mission of the European Language Grid

To achieve the goal of becoming the primary platform for European LTs, ELG follows its mission of creating impact beyond the platform itself:

- Grow a vibrant community and help coordinate all European LT activities: ELG is an initiative *from* the European LT community *for* the European LT community, including industry, innovation and research. ELG can only be successful if the whole community makes active use of the platform and contributes as well as uses datasets and services. ELG collaborates with many related projects, companies, research organisations and further initiatives (see Chapters 10 and 11), most notably its sister project European Language Equality (ELE), which is currently developing a strategic agenda and roadmap that specify how to achieve digital language equality in Europe by 2030. In the agenda developed by ELE, ELG functions as the main technology platform of the ELE Programme so that the support of Europe's languages through technologies can be measured and monitored over time (Gaspari et al. 2022; Grützner-Zahn and Rehm 2022).
- Create and maintain a powerful, scalable and useful Language Technology platform: ELG's novel technological approach enables innovations and synergies between commercial and non-commercial LT demanders, suppliers and users (see Chapter 12). The unique ELG platform is based on the principle of encapsulating services in containers. This approach tackles and solves some of the issues of technical interoperability, which is a crucial obstacle on the way of cross-provider and cross-platform interoperability. ELG enables providers to deposit and deploy their services.
- Support the Multilingual Digital Single Market: ELG strengthens the commercial European LT landscape through the pan-European platform and marketplace. Offering powerful multilingual, cross-lingual and monolingual technologies, ELG aims to contribute to the emergence of a truly connected, language-crossing Multilingual Digital Single Market. European companies can showcase and offer their LTs and consulting services to customers on the ELG marketplace (see Chapter 12).

2.2 Added Value for Stakeholders

The implementation of this mission in the form of the ELG platform provides added value for all stakeholders, e. g., 1. ability to attract participants (i. e., customers, buyers, users, providers etc.), 2. ability to create demand economies of scale, 3. benefit of reduced time-to-market (especially from lab to market), 4. standardised quality, 5. ease of doing business and a 6. coherent ELG technology exploitation ecosystem.

Traditional, linear value chains are focused on a one-way process of value creation, e. g., raw materials are used and manufactured into products, which are then distributed and used by the consumer, until they are disposed of. For ELG, we foresee a two- or multi-way value creation. As a digital platform, ELG will maintain an ecosystem of reciprocity. LT providers, LT consumers, ELG stakeholders and the whole ELG community help to generate two-way and reciprocal value as a result of the combination of resources of its participants, cost benefits (demand economies of scale) and network effects. As such, marketplace participants will create value by tapping into resources and capacities that they do not have to own themselves. In addition, marketplace participants will enjoy cost benefits and positive compound effects, arising from demand aggregation, from efficiencies in networks and from technological improvements on the demand side. Third, there is value within the network itself: growth via network effects will lead to market expansion for each of the members of the ecosystem. New participants (buyers and suppliers) enter the marketplace, because they are attracted to ELG by the growing number of participants who are also part of the network. That way, value is created in a reciprocal, multi-sided (almost infinite) way. For more details, see Chapter 12.

3 Main Pillars of the Business and Operational Model

Given the large number of possible routes to evaluate as well as decisions to be made eventually, we stretched the consortium-internal discussion of the main pillars of the ELG legal entity's business and operational model over the whole project duration, initiating the consortium-wide discussion in late 2019, i. e., we started immediately after the implementation of the proof of concept of the ELG platform. The goal was to specify, in a step by step fashion, the main ingredients of the sustainability plan. Relevant intermediate results were presented at META-FORUM 2020 and 2021 as well as in a number of talks.

At the very start of the overall process we looked at the setup and models of various other organisations that might serve as potential blueprints for ELG or, the other way around, as examples of organisations that would *not* work for ELG. We paid special attention to the domain of Language Technology and related fields, to the aspect of community-driven organisations, to combining industry and research and to the relevance of Europe as an overarching umbrella. All organisations we examined in more detail operate in the sphere of IT, LT or AI. Some of them have been created as spin-offs of research projects. With regard to their size and setup, though, these organisations are very diverse; the similarities with ELG in terms of their respective starting points and target groups also vary considerably. The organisations are: DBpedia Association[1], World Wide Web Consortium (W3C)[2], Industrial Data Spaces (IDS)[3], LT Innovate[4], OpenAIRE[5], CLARIN ERIC[6], Big Data Value Association (BDVA)[7], Translation Automation User Society (TAUS)[8], ELRA/ELDA[9] and GATE Cloud[10]. While discussing and learning more about these organisations – especially with regard to the type of legal entity they use, their membership as well as governance and fee structure, revenue streams etc. – we realised that despite some superficial similarities, none of them could serve as a direct model for the ELG legal entity, i. e., we are not aware of any organisation that could serve as an actual blueprint. However, we have been able to derive some important questions from this comparison that have informed the subsequent steps of the process.

The following sections present the main pillars of the legal entity approx. in the order in which we discussed and designed them.

3.1 Expectations by the ELG Consortium's SME Partners

Next up in the overall process of designing the ELG legal entity, we initiated a discussion with the ELG consortium's SME partners, primarily to collect their expectations and demands towards a legal entity that operates and maintains the "primary platform for Language Technology in Europe". The most important aspects of their considerations can be summarised as follows.

Sales channel: ELG is, first and foremost, understood as a channel to promote and to sell the products and services offered by the SMEs. ELG should stir interest and convince potential customers to invest in European LT. This is also true for public administrations and governmental bodies, the European Institutions and NGOs with the general idea being that interested parties and stakeholders look at ELG first in their procurement processes for LT. It was suggested that, in the medium to long run, ELG should consider fulfilling or even establishing certain quality and security standards as well as some kind of quality seal.

Strategy and collaboration: Europe has strengths in certain areas and language combinations but new business opportunities can only be reached by joining

---

[1] https://www.dbpedia.org

[2] https://www.w3.org

[3] http://www.industrialdataspace.org

[4] https://lt-innovate.org

[5] https://www.openaire.eu

[6] https://www.clarin.eu

[7] https://www.bdva.eu

[8] https://www.taus.net

[9] http://www.elra.info

[10] https://cloud.gate.ac.uk

forces and combining the offers with those of other European players. Missing or needed tools and services from others will help expand one's own set of tools and services. The SMEs expect ELG to help in this regard, i. e., identifying and closing strategic partnerships (also see *Interoperability* below).

Buy-in from the whole community: According to the SME partners, ELG must be positioned in the right way with regard to other platforms and infrastructures, e. g., a controlled transition from META-SHARE to ELG should be achieved by also integrating those organisations who have participated in META-SHARE. Furthermore, ELG should be backed, i. e., supported and *actively* used, by national centres and institutions. In terms of the governance model, all stakeholders should be able to have their say, yet dominance must be avoided. ELG can also provide a channel so that the results of national and international funding programmes can be disseminated efficiently on an international level.

Information channel: The goal is for ELG to become the primary European platform for participants from academia, research institutions and commercial entities. Especially with regard to industry, the relevance, understanding and benefits of LT for companies of all sizes needs to be increased. ELG could function as a means to keep interested stakeholders informed by serving as an information source and matchmaker for buyers and suppliers alike (marketplace approach, see Chapter 12).

Interoperability: 1. Throughout Europe, there is a sizable number of other relevant platform and infrastructure initiatives including, among others, Gaia-X[11], the European AI-on-demand platform[12], EOSC[13] and NFDI[14]. The SMEs mentioned their expectation that ELG becomes part of this larger ecosystem of platforms around Artificial Intelligence, data economy, research data management and Open Science, i. e., that ELG should ideally be fully interoperable with these other infrastructures, eventually opening up additional markets (Rehm et al. 2020a). 2. Furthermore, providers of LT need to understand what the requirements are to participate in ELG and why it is beneficial for them. ELG needs to be compatible with existing businesses and should not duplicate existing systems. Since various companies already operate their own or managed cloud platforms, platform interoperability should be ensured so that ELG complements existing or emerging clouds rather than appearing like competition. ELG should avoid creating the impression of being yet another collection of data and tools but rather emphasise the ability to combine services and resources from different companies. 3. For this, however, full interoperability on the level of the actual tools and services, i. e., on the level of APIs, annotations, semantic descriptions, closed vocabularies etc. needs to be achieved (also see *Strategy and collaboration* above).

---

[11] https://gaia-x.eu

[12] https://www.ai4europe.eu

[13] https://eosc.eu

[14] https://www.nfdi.de

3.2 Key Aspects of the ELG Legal Entity

Informed by the SME partners' expectations and other desk research we performed (see above), we started defining key aspects of the ELG legal entity, as follows:

Not-for-profit or for-profit organisation?   There was a broad consensus in the consortium-internal discussions that the legal entity should be a not-for-profit organisation. This decision is rooted in the overall approach of ELG as an initiative *from* the European LT community *for* the European LT community. Moving into the for-profit direction would constitute a significant change of plan, effectively compromising the initiative's independence and ability to be perceived as neutral and non-competitive; this could also jeopardise the initiative's political standing with national and international administrations and funding agencies. In addition, the not-for-profit direction comes with additional benefits (e. g., in terms of taxation, more favourable funding conditions when participating in EU projects etc.).

Distributed team or central location?   Due to the fact that the ELG consortium is already a distributed team and that the development of the platform and its technical infrastructure is spread across different European countries, the decision was made to keep this distributed setup and to build the team virtually rather than in one physical location. Current technical setups for remote work enable efficient virtual meetings and distributed teams are very common in business by now anyway, which is why we made this decision. The suggestion was made to position the legal entity's "headquarter" in the country where the majority of the costs are likely to be incurred, which, for the time being, will be the rented cloud infrastructure plus part of the personnel costs.

Start small or big?   Given that developments in the AI/LT field and in Europe as a whole are very dynamic, the preparation of a detailed ten-year plan does not seem to be the right approach. A large organisation with a rigid hierarchical structure was perceived to be an obstacle in our consortium-internal discussions. Instead, we favour a flexible and agile setup that can react quickly and efficiently to changes and new framework conditions. However, the organisation must be large enough to ensure that the existing infrastructure and platform can be maintained and extended in a meaningful way and so that growth is possible. We currently assume a headcount of 10-15 employees for Phase 3 (see Table 1).

Abrupt transition or soft launch?   While the ELG EU project will end on 30 June 2022, various partners of the ELG consortium are involved in a number of new projects, in which the European Language Grid plays a certain role. Through these new projects, some of the costs of operating the cloud platform can be covered. This situation is ideal because it gives the consortium a bit more time and flexibility for completing the overall setup of the legal entity. Our goal is to establish the legal entity in the second half of 2022, performing a rather soft launch.

Membership organisation?   There are good reasons for having a setup that includes a membership structure, especially for actively including the many members of the European LT community and also because membership fees can be considered a constant, reliable source income if the ELG legal entity is able to continuously provide added value. On the other hand, the membership fee needs to be reasonable to make sure that interested parties are not deterred from the very outset. The specifics are still under discussion.

3.3 Assessment of Operational Costs

Operating the ELG legal entity will create costs, that need to be covered, even if the organisation itself will be a not-for-profit one. While the key tangible outcome of the EU project, the implemented and populated cloud platform, is an important prerequisite for the legal entity, several additional components need to be put in place. Crucially, the legal entity needs a team and director to take care of operations, maintenance and further development of the platform, associated tools and the ELG community. The main cost items are as follows.

Staff   Labour costs represent the largest share of the organisation's expenses. Even a minimal team includes employees for operations, development, marketing, support and management. It might not be necessary to hire full-time employees for each of these areas right away but in order to run a successful organisation, a stable team is essential.

Cloud hosting   To enable the legal entity to operate the ELG platform, a cloud infrastructure (including CPU, GPU, RAM, SSD and bandwidth) needs to be rented from a cloud service provider.

Overhead   This refers to costs like rent of office space, hardware like workstations and printers, furniture, electricity, heating, etc. Even if remote and part-time work might reduce these costs because there is no need to rent larger office spaces, overhead still accounts for part of the fixed costs of the organisation.

Legal   Especially in the ramp-up phase of an organisation, comprehensive and sound legal advice is crucial. The ELG legal entity will have to draw up and maintain model contracts and service level agreements for its products. Moreover, advice on GDPR, tax legislation and human resources issues is needed. The legal entity will not have the capacity for an inhouse legal expert, instead, legal services will be outsourced.

To facilitate future planning, a preliminary cost-structure has been developed (Table 1). It illustrates the foreseen soft start of the legal entity, which is separated into three phases. The gradual soft launch is meant to go from a small team that is working part-time (Phase 1) to a team of 10-15 full-time employees (Phase 3).

Cost Item	Phase 1 (start)	Phase 2 (ramp-up)	Phase 3 (stable)
Staff	2,500€	25,000€	100,000€
Cloud hosting	2,500€	10,000€	20,000€
Overhead	500€	2,500€	7,500€
Legal	–	2,500€	5,000€
Total	5,500€	40,000€	132,500€

Table 1 Estimated monthly costs in three phases (numbers are preliminary and indicative)

3.4 Business Model Canvas

The Business Model Canvas (BMC)[15] is a template used in strategic management for the development or documentation of existing or new business models. It is widely known and often serves as the first instrument applied when it comes to the visualisation and structuring of business models. The BMC helps to bring all essential elements of a business model into a scalable system. It consists of a visual chart with all necessary elements of an organisation or company. The idea is that the company or startup recognises its potential and weaknesses and understands where to align their activities by illustrating potential trade-offs (Osterwalder and Pigneur 2010). The nine "building blocks" of the business model design template that came to be called the Business Model Canvas were initially proposed by Osterwalder (2004) based on his work on a business model ontology. It outlines nine segments for the business model in a simple one-page canvas that can be inspected alongside each other. The nine BMC segments are: 1. Key Partners, 2. Key Activities, 3. Key Resources, 4. Value Proposition, 5. Customer Relationships, 6. Channels, 7. Customer Segments, 8. Cost Structure and 9. Revenue Streams. Below we explain how the ELG legal entity relates to each of the nine segments of the BMC. This ELG-specific BMC was prepared by all nine ELG consortium partners. First, we asked all partners to prepare a partner-specific BMC, i. e., to prepare their own vision and approach of the ELG legal entity. Afterwards we processed the nine individual, partner-specific BMCs into one consolidated BMC, which is the basis of the following description.

Segment: Key Partners   "Who are the key partners/suppliers? What are the motivations for the partnerships?"
One key partner in the ELG BMC are commercial and non-commercial LT service providers, either with or without their own cloud platform. Equally important are Language Resource and data providers that own existing data sets and repositories. These two key partners contribute to the thriving of the ELG platform. Their motivation is not (or not only) to use available services and resources, but they offer their own services and resources and create value or profit for their own organisations. Another key partner is the wider ELG community, including the ELG consortium, the 32 National Competence Centres, the national language communities, and all running EU projects and initiatives in the field of LT (includ-

---

[15] https://en.wikipedia.org/wiki/Business_Model_Canvas

ing ELE). This community consists of academic and research partners as well as a number of companies that need multilingual datasets and services for their research. Equally important for raising awareness are the European Commission and the European Parliament as well as national institutions such as ministries and funding agencies and other established networks and associations.

Segment: Key Activities   "What key activities does the value proposition require? What activities are the most important in distribution channels, customer relationships, revenue stream, etc.?"

The most crucial key activity is the maintenance, further development and operation of the ELG platform. It needs to provide an interesting and relevant offering in order to grow a critical mass of members and users and gain popularity in the whole European LT community and beyond. Regular posting of content and other outreach activities (such as events, tutorials, talks, publications, meetups etc.) are essential to generate visibility and create a strong reputation (see Chapter 10). All communication and dissemination activities have to be treated with the highest priority to retain existing users and keep attracting new ones. Leveraging existing communication networks and sales channels can support this process and will be further explored. Quick and reliable service and support helpdesks are needed to strengthen customer relationships. Licensing and billing models need to be maintained and promoted. Maintenance and management of cloud storage and computing for running services has to be ensured.

Segment: Key Resources   "What key resources does the value proposition require? What resources are the most important ones in distribution channels, customer relationships, revenue stream etc.?"

The most important resource is the ELG platform itself with all its functionalities and included services, corpora and additional information. ELG can be regarded as a set of seed technologies, tools and components that are extended over time. Customer feedback can be seen as a useful resource as well. It can come in many different forms such as evaluation from market data or helpdesk and user support feedback. Equally important is a dedicated ELG team, committed to not only maintaining existing technology, but growing it and promoting the importance of ELG on an international level. To achieve this, a wide international network is a key resource. The consortium combines vast experience and expertise, good knowledge of ongoing trends and access to numerous European networks in academia and industry.

Segment: Value Proposition   "Which customer needs are being satisfied? What core value is delivered to the customer?"

ELG is envisioned to become the primary LT platform for Europe and to function as a one-stop-shop, offering a rich portfolio of LT services, tools and datasets. One of its core values is the availability of state of the art services which are fast, effective, robust and high-quality. Another special attribute is the fact that ELG is "made *in* Europe, *for* Europe". This strong branding inspires trust and confidence and ensures that the system is compliant with European regulations, security constraints and ethics. For customer satisfaction, ELG needs to be customisable, cover niches, address verticals and offer direct access to providers. Furthermore, all solutions come with high usability and are easy to integrate. Stakeholders familiar with the European LT landscape are aware of the fragmentation of the community which impairs an effective exchange of resources. ELG is committed to tackle this existing fragmentation. Competitive pricing is another value that makes ELG attractive for customers. Unique about ELG is that it offers a new or additional channel for service providers and consumers. Suppliers can gain more visibility, easy portability between providers is guaranteed through joint standards. Workflow functionalities will eventually be integrated to combine services from different providers and even their own clouds. ELG also offers added value to academia. It allows the use of services and data and offers easy comparison between systems on the same data or different data with the same system. ELG is meant to act as a broker for European LT and as a catalyst to boost innovation that also makes both the European industry LT sector and academic institutions an attractive employer for young high-potentials.

Segment: Customer Relationships   "What relationship that the target customer expects are you going to establish? How can you integrate that into your business in terms of cost and format?"

The ELG brand is intended to be a quality seal for customers that guarantees state of the art services, a high level of security and compliance with all relevant EU regulations. Customers can use ELG through the web UI including code samples and libraries or through the APIs or SDKs. High quality guidelines and a user-friendly design make processes intuitive. Support through a service helpdesk is also possible. Technical onboarding and support packages will be offered and a fine-grained customer relationship model is being developed. Essential for targeting customers is strong brand building. Related marketing activities are tailored to different audiences and distributed regularly. While retaining customers is essential, new potential customers can be attracted through outreach and training events, tutorials, webinars and conferences. A brand that has earned people's trust can also create a need for other customer services such as consulting services around ELG and language-centric AI.

Segment: Channels   "Through which channels do customers want to be reached? Which channels work best? How much do they cost? How can they be integrated into customers' routines?"

Customers will be reached through a variety of channels. Events, both established and new ones, will play an important role, for example, events targeted at stakeholders in a specific industry domain. Dedicated networking sessions, conferences and presentations are also foreseen. Online advertising campaigns will accompany all events. Since ELG builds on an existing network of stakeholders, email marketing and social media campaigns have proven to be successful means of reaching out. Presence on social media channels such as Twitter or LinkedIn helps to promote events and maintain customer relationships. ELG itself is a channel through which customers can retrieve information, not only about services and datasets, but also about the community and events. Cloud platforms that are either currently being developed in other EU or national projects as well as existing commercial platforms can also act as channels to point potential customers to ELG. SEO can also help promoting ELG since users trust search engines.

Segment: Customer Segments "For which segment is value being created? Who is the most important customer?"

The ELG platform offers value to different customer segments. LT providers, both commercial and academic ones, can use ELG to offer their services and datasets. Research organisations can benefit immensely from the wide offer. Customers from industry that demand LT (including large enterprises, SMEs, startups etc.) represent an essential customer segment that contributes to turning ELG into a flourishing marketplace. The European Union, public administrations and NGOs can also integrate ELG services into their current solutions. The same holds true for funding agencies and policy makers, advertising companies etc. Other EU project consortia as well as project consortia on the national level can benefit from the value created by ELG.

Segment: Cost Structure "What are the highest costs? Which key resources or activities are most expensive?"

As mentioned earlier, the highest costs are created by the human resources and the digital infrastructure. Personnel costs are created by the team maintaining and further developing ELG including daily operations as well as customer support, but also community management work that requires marketing and communication activities. Further resources need to be assigned to management and administration work that includes budgeting, accounting and legal counselling. Moreover, overhead costs are to be covered.

Segment: Revenue Streams "For what value are customers willing to pay?"

Part of the overall revenue will be generated through different products including usage or subscription fees, brokerage fees (marketplace approach), commission fees and products such as LT as a Service (LTaaS; hosting of services, models, datasets), LT Platform as a Service (PaaS; combining ELG services into workflows) and Repository as a Service (RaaS; hosting service for whole repositories). Advertisements can, for instance, showcase companies, services, conferences etc. Sponsored content, services, data sets, companies etc. present another revenue stream as well as commission fees. Paid training events, tutorials, webinars etc. can be offered to commercial stakeholders. Conferences (event registration fees; sponsorship packages for companies) are also an opportunity to generate income as well as general consulting services around ELG and language-centric AI.

This brief summary of the nine segments is an extract of the ELG BMC, produced by consolidating the BMCs prepared by the ELG consortium partners. For many segments, there was broad agreement within the individual BMCs, especially with regard to *key partners*, *key activities* and *key resources*. Also, in *value proposition*, *customer relationships* and *channels* the answers were largely similar. The *customer segments* are quite heterogeneous, though, which may make a targeted approach more difficult. As far as the *cost structure* is concerned, there are few deviations. A crucial open question concerns the appropriate size and ambition of the ELG, in particular with regard to team size. The answers were rather diverse in the case of *revenue streams*; here, positions could be aligned more closely through the subsequent step of specifying and discussing the different ELG products. As a follow-up step, the exact revenue streams will be evaluated with regard to cost-effectiveness and sustainability.

3.5 Product Portfolio and Revenue Streams

Together with all partners of the ELG consortium we defined, in a process that included several iterations, a portfolio of products that the ELG legal entity can potentially offer. These products are targeted at members of the European LT community and also at stakeholders interested in using, implementing, integrating or purchasing European LT. The products are primarily foreseen as revenue streams for the ELG legal entity so that it is able to cover the fixed costs associated with operating the ELG legal entity and platform (Section 3.3).

Such a structured portfolio of products, including associated fees, is necessary for eventually preparing the budget plan of the legal entity. In the following, we briefly describe the main categories of the ELG product portfolio; due to space restrictions we are unable to include all the details (especially aspects such as competitors, pricing, technical preconditions and general prerequisites are left out), i. e., the description in this chapter is not meant to be exhaustive but rather indicative of the overall plan and vision of the legal entity. It is also important to note that not all products will be offered right from the start but that the set of products will be expanded gradually over time.

3.5.1 Product Category: Marketplace

Marketplace Commission   ELG features a directory of all European LT developers and can enable a match-making process, i. e., ELG facilitates, for potential buyers or integrators of LT, the discovery of the right LT provider. In this product, ELG receives a commission from every contract generated through the marketplace (approx. 5-10%). This product can be used by commercial LT developers to broaden their reach and to penetrate new markets, especially if the current is limited or if the developer is operating in a niche. On the demand side, we foresee this product to be used by larger organisations that want to buy LT or integrators that need a specific LT for a customer project. In order to participate in this marketplace, LT developer companies have to agree and to sign a marketplace participation framework agreement.

Public Request for Bids Model   This product is a potential extension of the *marketplace commission* product: Customers can publicly and maybe anonymously post the need for a certain technology or resource or perhaps for an integration task and ask supplier companies for bids. Multiple LT developers and integrators can post their bids (not publicly) so that the organisation that posted the original request for bids can identify a cost-effective way to move forward. Posting the original request for bids would require a small fee to be paid. If a contract is established, the usual ELG marketplace fee applies on top of this.

3.5.2 Product Category: Consulting

Technical ELG Platform Consulting   The ELG legal entity has enough expertise so that it can offer various types of technical consulting services, for example, regarding ELG, providing or using ELG services, combining services, training new models and making them available, i. e., services with a clear focus on the ELG platform, ecosystem and technical basis. This product is likely to be purchased by organisations that have a certain need for LT and that want to test and explore certain functionalities, models or tasks, but these organisations realise that they need some kind of help, e. g., implementation of prototypes, selection of technologies, evaluations etc. Using this product, organisations are able to make full use of the ELG platform and all its services. This product can be offered for a one-time fee or, for larger companies, also as part of a framework contract.

Conceptual ELG Community Consulting   This product is similar to the one described above; it primarily makes use of the ELG team's in-depth knowledge of the ELG community, i. e., of the European LT developer or provider landscape. In that regard, the ELG team can support organisations with a certain need for a general or specific type of LT in finding the right technology provider. Customers interested in this type of product know that they have a certain need for LT but they are unsure about the concrete next steps, i. e., where and how to find the provider company.

LT Market Intelligence Report   The ELG legal entity could exploit its in-depth knowledge of the European LT landscape and community and publish an annual or semi-annual market intelligence report about the European and maybe also global LT landscape including topics such as, among others, emerging trends, new players and rising stars, new projects and success stories. Such market analyses are highly relevant for a larger group of stakeholders including larger companies and enterprises (LT developers, LT users), non-governmental organisations, venture capital companies and others. These reports could be offered for a one-time fee or as packages that cover multiple reports with a slightly reduced fee.

3.5.3 Product Category: ELG APIs

ELG Power User Flatrate (for commercial users)   Through this product, commercial customers get unlimited and unrestricted access to the ELG APIs of all integrated services and tools. This product targets companies of any type (SMEs, integrators, enterprises) that have to pay a small monthly or annual fee to be able to use it. This subscription product provides direct to all ELG APIs for experimentation and evaluation purposes, enabling fast comparisons and immediate results.

It can also be used to develop smaller LT-driven applications by integrating ELG APIs into existing systems. Like with many other products, any surplus generated through this product will be transferred to those LT developing companies that have provided the ELG-integrated services that were used in the relevant month, based on the proportionate number of API calls.

ELG Power User Flatrate (for academic users)　Technically, this product is exactly like the first one but it targets academic users exclusively. The monthly or annual fee will be significantly lower than the fee of the power user flatrate for commercial users.

ELG Professional Flatrate　Conceptually, this product is similar to the first one but the professional flatrate includes additional features and support services, e. g., faster tools, more compute resources, faster helpdesk support, workflow or pipeline functionality etc. The price of this product will be significantly higher than the pricer for the first product.

3.5.4　Product Category: LT-as-a-Service

LT-as-a-Service (for commercial users)　This product targets commercial LT developers. Paying a certain fee, it enables them to host a limited number of LT tools or services within the ELG platform with guaranteed performance and availability. In order to be able to host more services or API endpoints in ELG, a different type of product needs to be purchased (see Section 3.5.6). This product is especially interesting for those companies that do not operate their own cloud infrastructures or that are eager to participate in the ELG initiative, i. e., ELG's LT-as-a-Service product can be seen as an alternative to renting cloud infrastructure. Another benefit of this product is that companies are able to extend their reach and to open up new markets, i. e., once again ELG can be used as an additional sales, promotion and distribution channel. This product can also be set up in multiple tiers, representing different maximum numbers of services and corresponding prices. While companies have to pay a certain fee for this product, the different ELG APIs products (see Section 3.5.3) will generate revenue, from which the companies will benefit. In that regard, it is important to identify the right balance over time.

LT-as-a-Service (for academic users)　Technically, this product is exactly like the previous one but it targets academic users exclusively. The monthly or annual fee will be significantly lower than the fee of the LT-as-a-Service product for commercial users. This product also targets research projects, for which ELG can function as a secondary or maybe even primary dissemination and exploitation channel for their research results. Like the ELG power user flatrate for academic users, we consider making this product available for free for academic users if and when the ELG legal entity has established stable revenue streams.

3.5.5 Product Category: Data-as-a-Service

Data-as-a-Service (for commercial users)   This product is very similar to LT-as-a-Service but instead of focusing upon running services or tools, it only allows making datasets or other (static) resources available on ELG, again, with guaranteed availability. Like LT-as-a-Service, this is an entry level product and, thus, only allows hosting a limited number of datasets (or up to a certain amount of data) on ELG. In case of more demand on the side of the customer, a different type of product needs to be purchased (see Section 3.5.6). This product needs to be priced lower than the LT-as-a-Service product.

Data-as-a-Service (for academic users)   Technically, this product is like the previous one but it targets academic users. The monthly or annual fee will be significantly lower than the fee of the Data-as-a-Service product for commercial users.

3.5.6 Product Category: Repository-as-a-Service, Platform-as-a-Service

Repository-as-a-Service, Platform-as-a-Service   Using this product, customers can host whole LT platforms or repositories on ELG while the ELG team takes care of all technical aspects including branding, availability, backups etc. This product targets a variety of stakeholders including goverments and ministries (e. g., for hosting national LT platforms on ELG), smaller or larger companies, smaller research groups and also whole research centres. The idea behind the product is that setting up and operating a cloud with an LT repository requires a lot of effort and expertise, which can be fully avoided by purchasing the corresponding ELG product. While the branding of the respective hosted platform or repository can be adapted to the brand and logo of the respective customer on the user interface level, at the same time, all hosted services, tools and other resources are automatically also part of the 'wider' ELG cloud platform, which will automatically broaden their reach significantly. We currently foresee three different tiers of this product: one entry level tier for research groups, one for SMEs and research centres and one for national LT repositories.

3.5.7 Product Category: Events

Training Events and Tutorials   In addition to the more technical products described above, training events and tutorials can be offered as products, especially for commercial customers. These can be, among others, general ELG-related training events (from half a day to multiple days) where the training relates to the ELG platform, using, providing and combining services etc. This type of event can be offered to organisations that have a need for certain LT and that want to be able to make the most of the ELG platform. This product is a pre-packaged and generic course, while those training events that involve customisation of content, tailoring the course to the respective customer and its specific needs, would be rather considered technical ELG platform consulting (see Section 3.5.2).

Annual Conference   The annual ELG conference assembles the whole ELG community, including commercial and academic participants, related projects and initiatives etc., and also the ELG team. While the annual ELG conference organised by the ELG EU project has been free of charge, this model could change (e. g., registration fees, sponsorship packages, paid presentation slots, booths for a fee in the industry exhibition etc.).

3.5.8 Product Category: Marketing and Advertisements

Conference Sponsorship   This product relates to typical conference sponsorship packages, which can be purchased by, typically, companies to position themselves as gold or platinum sponsors of the annual ELG conference. This product model is well established and accepted in industry and research but to be successful it requires the respective conference to be of very high relevance for its community.

Online Advertisements   The ELG platform could offer a small part of its screen real estate for online advertisements that can be purchased, among others, by members of European LT community to position their products or services in a more targeted way on the ELG website, for example, when certain keywords or search terms are used. In terms of revenue generated, this product only makes sense if the website has a very high number of users. Furthermore, it remains to be discussed and seen if online ads are a welcome addition on the ELG website or if they are perceived as not appropriate.

Sponsored Content   Similar to online advertisements, the idea behind this product is that customers can pay a small fee to get one or more of their products, services or resources or perhaps even their own organisation's or project's page in the ELG catalogue featured on the ELG website, clearly marked as "sponsored content" (for example, the first search result).

Merchandise   The final product relates to ELG-branded merchandise, which could be sold online, for example, tshirts, hats or pens with the ELG logo.

3.5.9 Miscellaneous

In addition to the actual products offered by the ELG legal entity, there are at least three other potential revenue streams or activities related to marketing the ELG products. These additional revenue streams cannot be considered products per se.

Foundations   The ELG legal entity could approach one or more foundations with the request to grant financial support. In return, the foundations could position themselves as supporters of the ELG initiative.

Project Grants   EU or national project grants are an obvious mechanism to support part of the ELG team and platform as well as its operation.

ELG Use Cases as Show Cases   Together with larger enterprises and some of the
commercial LT developer companies represented in ELG, interesting and relevant
show cases as well as success stories can be published on the ELG website, which
can function as marketing instruments and testimonials that demonstrate that ELG
is an important and valuable activity.

3.5.10 Summary and Assessment

The ELG product portfolio is diverse and broad, it offers multiple different options
of moving forward under the umbrella of the legal entity. As mentioned, we will
not start with all products right away but only with a selection. Before we make the
final selection, we will validate the products and their chance of being accepted by
the European LT community with a number of experts from the field. As the most
promising products we currently perceive the ELG APIs (Section 3.5.3) due to the
enormous market for this product, the LT-as-a-Service products (Section 3.5.4) due
to high demand, the marketplace (Section 3.5.1) as well as the consulting product
(Section 3.5.2).

Additionally, we see a lot of potential in offering countries the technical infrastructure for the purpose of supporting national LT platforms (Section 3.5.6). Especially
for smaller countries or regions, it is challenging to develop, operate and maintain
an elaborate technical platform all by themselves. For these, having their *National
LR/LT Repository* hosted as a service within ELG can be an attractive offer. For
ELG, in return, it appears to be an interesting financial pillar to operate such platforms, charging an annual hosting fee.

Making use of the ELG platform as the primary dissemination and exploitation
channel for research projects is another product idea that has a lot of potential (Section 3.5.4). It enables research projects to fully concentrate on the actual research
work without a need for developing complicated exploitation plans on their own because they can fully rely on ELG for this purpose. This approach can increase the
general visibility of European research results significantly.

3.6 Legal Entity Type

For the creation of a dedicated legal entity with European scope, we considered a
number of different entity types. The decision to move forward with a not-for-profit
organisation was made rather early in the process. The main options that we explored
were a professional association or a foundation. In that regard, each EU country has
its own set of different types of business entities as part of their legal system, which,
generally, all have their own specific sets of rules. These include, among others,
cooperatives, partnerships and limited liability companies. Looking at Germany, for
a not-for-profit organisation, a *gGmbH* (a not-for-profit private limited company), or
an *e. V.* (eingetragener Verein, registered association) would be two obvious options.

An alternative that enjoys some popularity with EU-funded projects is the Belgian Association without lucrative purpose (*AISBL*). As the ELG consortium does not have any partners in Belgium or Luxembourg, the AISBL option was ruled out for reasons of efficiency. In addition to national entities, there are several types of legal entities on the level of the European Union.

The *EEIG* (European Economic Interest Grouping) is part of European Corporate Law, created in 1985. An EEIG makes it easier for companies in different countries to do business together. Its activities must be ancillary to those of its members. Any profit or loss is attributed to its members. It is liable for VAT and social insurance of its employees but it is not liable to corporation tax and it has unlimited liability. Several thousand EEIGs exist and are active in various fields. This legal entity only applies to companies, it does not include research institutions.

The *SE* (Societas Europea) is a European company, established in 2001 by an EU Regulation. The SE has been growing in popularity ever since. It is a type of public limited-liability company and allows an organisation to operate its business in different European countries under the same rules. An SE offers many advantages such as easily setting up Europe-wide subsidiaries as well as an international holding company. The company headquarters can be relocated easily and the SE legal form conveys a strong European image. However, the SE comes with strict foundation criteria, such as the requirement of high initial capital.

The *SCE* (Societas cooperativa Europaea, European Cooperative Company) was established in 2006, it is related to the SE. An SCE can be established in the European Economy Area. This entity type was created to remove the need for cooperatives to establish subsidiaries in each EU Member State in which they operate, and to allow them to move their registered office and headquarters from one EU Member State to another. SCEs are governed by a single EEA-wide set of rules and principles which are supplemented by the laws on cooperatives in each Member State.

The *SPE* (Societas privata Europaea) is a European private limited company, it corresponds to an Ltd. in Anglo-Saxon countries or a GmbH in Germany, Austria and Switzerland. This legal entity type has been a European Commission proposal for more than ten years. As of now, it still does not exist.

For ELG, a crucial requirement is that the selected solution provides flexibility, agility and the ability to ramp up the operation of the legal entity in a careful way. The final decision must also be made on the basis of financial considerations, i. e., it must be specified which products or services can be offered to generate which profit.

At the time of writing, we will establish a registered association headquartered in Germany (e. V., *eingetragener Verein*). This option does not require any initial capital and frees ELG from the pressure of having to generate income immediately. Since some of the staff members who will be active in the ELG e. V. in the first phase are based in Berlin, it appears practical to set up the entity in Germany and under German law. It must be noted, however, that the legal entity will work in virtual teams primarily. The only legal entity type on the European level that could be appropriate for ELG, the SPE, does not exist yet.

4 Summary and Next Steps

This chapter presents the current state of planning of the ELG legal entity, which is foreseen to be established as an *eingetragener Verein, e. V.*, as a registered, not-for-profit association, in the second half of 2022. The legal entity will start small, with a soft launch, and is meant to be flexible and agile. The main pillars of this concept have been under development since late 2019 and cover most of the crucial aspects of the legal entity. In terms of financing, a mixed model is envisaged, driven by the product portfolio (Section 3.5), that includes shared revenue streams through LT provider companies that use ELG as a sales channel and their customers who use ELG to find the right providers and suppliers as well as services.

One aspect that still needs to be specified in more detail is the inclusion and active involvement of the European LT community and the governance structure of the legal entity. As an initiative *from* the European LT community *for* the community, its involvement is crucial to create trust and transparency as well as to provide representation to academic and industrial European LT developers. The proper inclusion of the community in a representative manner will require a number of discussions and deliberations. Fortunately, with regard to an *e. V.*, these matters do not need to be fully resolved before establishing the organisation but can also be taken on board and revised through updates of its statutes.

Originally we had envisioned to establish the legal entity within the project runtime and to start with a 'bigger' approach than is currently foreseen. The aforementioned delay of a few months in establishing the entity does not pose a problem because the overall framework conditions have changed in the last 12 to 18 months. Through recently started and publicly funded projects including ELE, ELE2, OpenGPT-X, NFDI4DataScience and AI as well as the upcoming EU projects DataBri-X and SciLake, which are about to start in October 2022 and early 2023 respectively, we are able to operate the ELG cloud platform and we can also perform some maintenance and other ELG-related work, including the extension of the ELG platform itself so that it is compatible with the emerging Gaia-X ecosystem. In addition, SciLake will establish the first bridges to the EOSC ecosystem.

Since the start of the project, we have been collaborating with the European AI on demand platform, especially with the AI4EU project, to ensure compatibility of our approaches in terms of semantically describing resources. Furthering these collaborative efforts will facilitate cross-platform search and discovery enabling ELG resources and other assets to be visible and usable by the wider AI community. Considering the EU's plan to deploy the European AI on demand platform, ELG is ready to act as the central language-related AI hub and marketplace providing access to and direct use of several thousands of LT services and related data.

While the future is always difficult to predict, it is clear already now that over the past three years the interest in ELG has risen constantly and that the legal entity that will take over the initiative after the EU project has ended has very good starting conditions. The ELG brand has been established in the community and a considerable buy-in can be observed already now. However, to take advantage of this momentum, the marketplace, broker, dissemination, exploitation and participation model needs to be extremely simple and easy to grasp to make sure users understand and accept it and the platform needs to be as user-friendly and all-encompassing as possible in every regard, including the various levels of technical interoperability. Quality and security aspects play a crucial role and can become the unique selling proposition as opposed to providers of LT services from the US or Asia.

References

Gaspari, Federico, Owen Gallagher, Georg Rehm, Maria Giagkou, Stelios Piperidis, Jane Dunne, and Andy Way (2022). "Introducing the Digital Language Equality Metric: Technological Factors". In: *Proceedings of the Workshop Towards Digital Language Equality (TDLE 2022; co-located with LREC 2022)*. Ed. by Itziar Aldabe, Begoña Altuna, Aritz Farwell, and German Rigau. Marseille, France, pp. 1–12. URL: http://www.lrec-conf.org/proceedings/lrec2022/workshops/TDLE/pdf/2022.tdle-1.1.pdf.

Grützner-Zahn, Annika and Georg Rehm (2022). "Introducing the Digital Language Equality Metric: Contextual Factors". In: *Proceedings of the Workshop Towards Digital Language Equality (TDLE 2022; co-located with LREC 2022)*. Ed. by Itziar Aldabe, Begoña Altuna, Aritz Farwell, and German Rigau. Marseille, France, pp. 13–26. URL: http://www.lrec-conf.org/proceedings/lrec2022/workshops/TDLE/pdf/2022.tdle-1.2.pdf.

Osterwalder, Alexander (2004). "The Business Model Ontology: A Proposition in a Design Science Approach". PhD thesis. France: University of Lausanne.

Osterwalder, Alexander and Yves Pigneur (2010). *Business Model Generation – A Handbook For Visionaries, Game Changers, And Challengers*. Wiley.

Rehm, Georg, Dimitrios Galanis, Penny Labropoulou, Stelios Piperidis, Martin Welß, Ricardo Usbeck, Joachim Köhler, Miltos Deligiannis, Katerina Gkirtzou, Johannes Fischer, Christian Chiarcos, Nils Feldhus, Julián Moreno-Schneider, Florian Kintzel, Elena Montiel, Víctor Rodríguez Doncel, John P. McCrae, David Laqua, Irina Patricia Theile, Christian Dittmar, Kalina Bontcheva, Ian Roberts, Andrejs Vasiļjevs, and Andis Lagzdiņš (2020a). "Towards an Interoperable Ecosystem of AI and LT Platforms: A Roadmap for the Implementation of Different Levels of Interoperability". In: *Proc. of the 1st Int. Workshop on Language Technology Platforms (IWLTP 2020, co-located with LREC 2020)*. Ed. by Georg Rehm, Kalina Bontcheva, Khalid Choukri, Jan Hajic, Stelios Piperidis, and Andrejs Vasiljevs. Marseille, France, pp. 96–107. URL: https://www.aclweb.org/anthology/2020.iwltp-1.15.pdf.

Rehm, Georg, Katrin Marheinecke, Stefanie Hegele, Stelios Piperidis, Kalina Bontcheva, Jan Hajic, Khalid Choukri, Andrejs Vasiļjevs, Gerhard Backfried, Christoph Prinz, José Manuel Gómez Pérez, Luc Meertens, Paul Lukowicz, Josef van Genabith, Andrea Lösch, Philipp Slusallek, Morten Irgens, Patrick Gatellier, Joachim Köhler, Laure Le Bars, Dimitra Anastasiou, Albina Auksoriūtė, Núria Bel, António Branco, Gerhard Budin, Walter Daelemans, Koenraad De Smedt, Radovan Garabík, Maria Gavriilidou, Dagmar Gromann, Svetla Koeva, Simon Krek, Cvetana Krstev, Krister Lindén, Bernardo Magnini, Jan Odijk, Maciej Ogrodniczuk, Eiríkur Rögnvaldsson, Mike Rosner, Bolette Pedersen, Inguna Skadina, Marko Tadić, Dan Tufiș, Tamás Váradi, Kadri Vider, Andy Way, and François Yvon (2020b). "The European Language Technology Landscape in 2020: Language-Centric and Human-Centric AI for Cross-Cultural Communication in Multilingual Europe". In: *Proceedings of the 12th Language Resources and Evaluation Conference (LREC 2020)*. Ed. by Nicoletta Calzolari, Frédéric Béchet, Philippe Blache, Christopher Cieri, Khalid Choukri, Thierry Declerck, Hitoshi Isahara, Bente Maegaard, Joseph Mariani, Asuncion Moreno, Jan Odijk, and Stelios Piperidis. Marseille, France: ELRA, pp. 3315–3325. URL: https://www.aclweb.org/anthology/2020.lrec-1.407/.

Rehm, Georg, Stelios Piperidis, Kalina Bontcheva, Jan Hajic, Victoria Arranz, Andrejs Vasiļjevs, Gerhard Backfried, José Manuel Gómez Pérez, Ulrich Germann, Rémi Calizzano, Nils Feldhus,

Stefanie Hegele, Florian Kintzel, Katrin Marheinecke, Julian Moreno-Schneider, Dimitris Galanis, Penny Labropoulou, Miltos Deligiannis, Katerina Gkirtzou, Athanasia Kolovou, Dimitris Gkoumas, Leon Voukoutis, Ian Roberts, Jana Hamrlová, Dusan Varis, Lukáš Kačena, Khalid Choukri, Valérie Mapelli, Mickaël Rigault, Jūlija Meļņika, Miro Janosik, Katja Prinz, Andres Garcia-Silva, Cristian Berrio, Ondrej Klejch, and Steve Renals (2021). "European Language Grid: A Joint Platform for the European Language Technology Community". In: *Proceedings of the 16th Conference of the European Chapter of the Association for Computational Linguistics: System Demonstrations (EACL 2021)*. Kyiv, Ukraine: ACL, pp. 221–230. URL: https://www.aclweb.org/anthology/2021.eacl-demos.26.pdf.

Teece, David J. (2017). "Dynamic Capabilities and (Digital) Platform Lifecycles". In: *Entrepreneurship, Innovation, and Platforms* 37 (Advances in Strategic Management), pp. 211–225. DOI: 10.1108/S0742-332220170000037008.

Vasiljevs, Andrejs, Khalid Choukri, Luc Meertens, and Stefania Aguzzi (2019). *Final study report on CEF Automated Translation value proposition in the context of the European LT market/ecosystem*. DOI: 10.2759/142151. URL: https://op.europa.eu/de/publication-detail/-/publication/8494e56d-ef0b-11e9-a32c-01aa75ed71a1/language-en.

Part IV
ELG Open Calls and Pilot Projects

Chapter 14
Open Calls and Pilot Projects

Lukáš Kačena, Jana Hamrlová, and Jan Hajič

Abstract We describe the two ELG open calls for pilot projects, the objective of which was to demonstrate the use and the advantages of ELG in providing basic LT for applications and as a basis for more advanced LT-based modules or components useful to industry. Our main goal was to attract SMEs and research organisations to either contribute additional tools or resources to the ELG platform (type A pilot projects) or develop applications using Language Technologies available in the ELG platform (type B pilot projects). We start with the detailed description of the submission and evaluation processes, followed by a presentation of the open call results. Afterwards we describe the supervision and evaluation of the execution phase of the projects, as well as lessons learned. Overall, we were very satisfied with the setup and with the results of the pilot projects, which demonstrate an enormous interest in ELG and the Language Technology topic in general.

1 Introduction

To demonstrate the advantages of ELG (Rehm et al. 2021) in providing LT for applications and as a basis for more advanced LT-based modules or components useful to industry, the ELG project set up a mechanism for using close to 30% of its budget for small scale demonstrator projects ("pilots") through two open calls. The calls were prepared using the ICT-29a call specification, making use of the Financial Support to Third Parties (FSTP) scheme according to the ICT Work Programme 2018-2020 (European Commission 2017). In total, we provided 1,950,000€ to the selected projects as FSTP with an awarded amount of up to 200,000€ per project. We established a lightweight submission procedure and a transparent evaluation process, in which external evaluators participated as reviewers.

The main objective of the open calls was to attract SMEs and research organisations to either contribute tools and services to ELG (type A projects) or develop

Lukáš Kačena · Jana Hamrlová · Jan Hajič
Charles University, Czech Republic, kacena@ufal.mff.cuni.cz, hamrlova@ufal.mff.cuni.cz, hajic@ufal.mff.cuni.cz

© The Author(s) 2023
G. Rehm (ed.), *European Language Grid*, Cognitive Technologies,
https://doi.org/10.1007/978-3-031-17258-8_14

applications using Language Technologies available in the ELG platform (type B projects). The results of the pilot projects are included in the ELG platform for dissemination, testing and external evaluation by other entities or the public.

2 Organisation of the Open Calls

2.1 Management Structure and Organisation

While agile, simple and lightweight from the proposers' point of view, the organisation of the two open calls was an internally complex procedure requiring close collaboration of three different teams (management team, technical team, Pilot Board) with support from a broad panel of external evaluators.

2.1.1 Pilot Board

The Pilot Board (PB) was set up for the supervision of the pilot projects. While the management team took care of the organisation and handling of the open calls and the execution of the pilots, the PB provided a forum so that the ELG project could discuss the progress of the pilots, their feedback and results. The PB was meant to be the main technical and strategic interface between the pilot projects and the ELG project proper, so that ELG could maximise its benefits from supporting the pilots and to make sure that the pilot projects benefit from ELG.

The PB operational procedures were drafted by the management team and approved by the ELG Steering Committee. Afterwards, seven PB members were nominated and approved. The operational procedures defined the main responsibilities of the PB as follows: approval of the open calls and related documentation; pilot project selection process; supervision of pilot project execution, including progress monitoring, evaluation of results and approval of the phased payments.

2.1.2 External Evaluators

An independent panel of experienced external evaluators ensured an open, transparent and expert-evaluation based selection process. The pool of evaluators was created using a separate open call. The evaluators were responsible for evaluating the project proposals and worked remotely using the web interface of the ELG Open Calls Platform. They were selected from the pool, avoiding any conflicts of interest. All evaluators were asked to sign a non-conflict of interest declaration and a confidentiality agreement before being accepted to perform the task.

2.1.3 Management Team

The management team organised the whole Open Calls process, including managing and directing the technical team. In line with Annex K of the Work Programme (European Commission 2017) and other relevant sections of the Rules for Participation, the management team prepared all prerequisites and procedures: the Open Calls Platform, web content, informational materials, forms, contract templates, presentation and reporting forms and templates, submission procedure, hiring and selection of external evaluators, call management structure, internal auditing and project results evaluation procedures. In the initial setup phase, the management team tapped the legal and financial expertise of the Technology Centre of the Czech Academy of Sciences, which is charged by the Czech government to host the National Contact Point (NCP) and other experts related to the preparation, execution and evaluation of EU framework programmes and projects.

2.1.4 Technical Team

An essential task was to set up the ELG Open Calls Platform for the proposal submission, evaluation and reporting process. We decided to develop the platform in-house to ensure that it fit our needs.[1] The technical team was responsible for developing the platform and for support during each phase of the process.

2.2 Timeline

Figure 1 shows the open calls execution timeline. After the announcement, each call was open for submissions for two months, followed by an evaluation procedure of approx. two months. After signing the contracts with the selected projects, the execution phase started. The expected project duration was 9-12 months. Four projects asked for a short extension of one or two months (which was accepted), mainly due to COVID-19 related delays of dissemination activities.

2.3 Communication with Stakeholders

Prospective applicants were targeted through various channels, e. g., the open calls website, a survey for stakeholders and other communication and dissemination activities carried out by all ELG consortium members.

From early 2019 onwards, the open calls were presented on the ELG website.[2] The content was regularly updated, starting from basic information including the

---

[1] https://opencalls.european-language-grid.eu

[2] https://www.european-language-grid.eu/open-calls

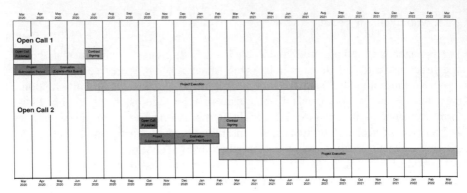

Fig. 1 Open Calls overall timeline

timeline and key parameters at the beginning of the project, followed by the call for evaluators[3] and complete information regarding the open calls[4].

We first monitored the interest in the open calls using a survey, which ran from May 2019 until June 2019. A total of 108 respondents participated. The result showed significant interest in the open calls and also a high demand for more information. Five months before the first call announcement, a second survey was prepared. We disseminated this survey during the first annual ELG conference META-FORUM 2019 in October 2019 in Brussels and collected answers from 47 respondents, 84% of which expressed an interest in taking part in the open calls.

The open calls were promoted through social media (Twitter, LinkedIn), various e-mail distribution lists, internal networks and collaborators, through the META-FORUM conference and through other means whenever an opportunity arose.

2.4 Submission Process

As explained in the previous section, in the preparatory period the overall open call procedure was set up, including all related documents and the development of the online platform for the management and evaluation of submissions. After the official announcement of one of our two open calls, applicants could then prepare and submit their project proposals. There was a continuous need for support, mainly answering questions we received by the participants via email.

With regard to the call announcement, we paid special attention to a well-prepared call documentation, which provided all necessary information for applicants, and a user-friendly submission platform. The documentation was prepared as an easy-to-understand document. It contained several annexes: Guide for Applicants, Third Party Agreement, Project Proposal Template and Evaluation Criteria.

---

[3] https://www.european-language-grid.eu/open-calls/call-for-evaluators

[4] https://www.european-language-grid.eu/open-calls

In the "Guide for Applicants" the management team showed, using screenshots, how to submit a project proposal through the platform, i. e., how to create an applicant account, how to log in and manage the account, how to create a new project proposal, fill in the forms and finally submit the proposal. We also maintained a list of (expected) frequently asked questions, for example "Who can apply for a pilot project?", "How much money is allocated for the pilot projects?", and "Does Brexit have any implications on eligibility?".

The Open Calls Platform was developed using the open source Content Management System Drupal with the guiding principle to keep the submission and evaluation process easy and straightforward for the participants and manageable for the call organisers. The platform runs under the ELG domain[5], while physically residing with the technical team to ensure quick reactions to any technical problems.

2.5 Evaluation Process

2.5.1 Preparation of the Evaluation Process

The most important part of the preparation of the evaluation process was the selection and specification of evaluation criteria that match the objectives to be achieved by the calls. At the same time, the criteria ought to be clear for the external experts evaluating each proposal.

The criteria were defined and described in detail in the call documentation. First, the submitted proposal should fulfill formal requirements (language, submission date, declaration of honor, legal status, eligible country, number of submitted proposals per applicant and no conflict of interest) which were checked by the management team before any further evaluation. Then, three independent evaluators checked the binary eligibility criteria: uniqueness, relevance for ELG, and whether the proposal contains all the required phases (experiment, integration, dissemination). These were followed by the graded and ranked evaluation criteria: objective fit, technical approach, business, integration and dissemination plan, budget adequacy, and team.

In order to identify evaluators with experience in language technologies and evaluation, a call for evaluators was published in February 2020. All relevant information (description of tasks, eligibility of candidates, selection criteria, contact email for questions, and a link to the registration form on the Open Call platform) was published on the ELG website as well as on the European Commission Funding and Tender portal. In addition, ELG consortium members disseminated the call through various channels. Potential evaluators were asked to fill in a registration form, through which contact information, CV, and professional experience related to evaluation and LT were collected. From about 156 applications, the management team selected 64 evaluators (a total for both project open calls) with relevant expertise in both the subject field(s) and in evaluating projects of at least similar size.

---

[5] https://opencalls.european-language-grid.eu

Before assigning projects to evaluators, we sent instructions via email and we organised webinars in which the evaluation process and criteria were explained.

All evaluators signed a contract with the ELG project. The contract included a clause to keep in strict confidence any technical or business information about the evaluated projects, as well as a no-conflict-of-interest declaration.

2.5.2 Execution of the Proposal Evaluation Process

Each proposal was evaluated by three independent external experts to ensure an transparent selection process. The evaluators were carefully assigned to the proposals by the management team. We also paid attention to gender (at least one female evaluator per proposal) and country of residence of the evaluator, avoiding at the same time possible personal or nationality-based conflicts of interest. The whole process was monitored by the Pilot Board. Each proposal was assigned to one of the PB members. These project coaches checked and confirmed or rejected the selection of evaluators with special regard to conflict of interest.

After the evaluation, the project coaches prepared summary reports for each proposal assigned to them. In these summaries, the coaches first reviewed the three reports by the external evaluators. They also suggested potential budget adjustments and changes of the total number of points (the maximum was 300 points, i. e., 100 points from each evaluator) in range of at most 30 points (open call 1) or 45 points (open call 2) up or down, where applicable. According to the evaluation criteria, project proposals by SMEs developing applications using LT available in ELG (B type projects) received 30 bonus points. Finally, the project coaches reviewed the eligibility criteria (uniqueness, relevance for ELG and project phases) as checked by the evaluators and suggested their decision on their fulfilment if the evaluators differed in opinion. The coaches also assessed the performance of the evaluators and quality of the reports. After all summary reports had been submitted by the coaches, a Pilot Board meeting was convened, in which the final ranking and selection was decided. All proposals were ranked by the total sum of points assigned. The ranked list was cut at the maximum available financial support (1,365,000€ for open call 1 and 585,000€ for open call 2).

3 Results

3.1 Open Call 1

3.1.1 Overview

The first call was opened on 1 March 2020 and closed on 30 April 2020 in accordance with the timeline (Figure 1). We accepted a total of 110 project proposals for evaluation from 103 applicants.

Submitted by	Type A	Type B	Total
Research organisation	43	5	48
SME	36	26	62
Total	79	31	110

Table 1 Proposals submitted to the first open call and accepted for evaluation

Seven applicants (five SMEs and two research organisations) submitted two proposals (one type A and one type B). Regarding the type of project, 79 submitted proposals were of type A (contribute resources, services, tools, or datasets to ELG) and 31 proposals were of type B (develop applications using language resources and technologies available in ELG), see Table 1. We received proposals from 29 different countries, including eligible countries outside the EU (Iceland, Israel, Norway, Serbia, South Africa, Switzerland, Turkey, United Kingdom). The total amount of financing requested by the submitted projects was 16,900,000€. One project requested 283,000€, which was over the limit of 200,000€ per project, and the lowest requested amount was 50,000€. The average amount requested per project was 153,000€.

At the end of June 2020, the results of the first open call were announced on the ELG website, including the list of projects selected for funding.[6] The two projects from the reserve list were informed that they might be selected for financial support if any of the selected projects rejected the financial support. The remaining projects were informed that they were not selected. In July 2020, contracts with all selected projects were signed, and the first payments were made (half of the awarded financial support), in line with the approved call documentation and procedures. All projects had started their execution phase by August 6. Furthermore, at the end of July 2020, abridged versions of the summary evaluation reports were provided to all applicants through the Open Calls Platform.

3.1.2 Selected Projects

The projects selected in open call 1 are listed in Table 2. All supported organisations are from the EU – three from Finland, two from Austria, Germany and Italy, and one from Spain. The awarded budget varies from 87,445€ to 167,375€.

Although we obtained more proposals from SMEs than from research organisations, there are three SMEs and seven research organisations among the selected projects. Similarly, although B type projects from SMEs were preferred, only two B type projects were accepted for financing which probably reflected the fact that the ELG platform was still being developed at the time of the first open call. Thus, it appeared to make more sense to create missing resources or tools rather than build applications using resources and tools available in ELG.

---

[6] https://www.european-language-grid.eu/open-calls/open-call-1

Organisation	Pilot Project	Type	Country	Funding
Fondazione Bruno Kessler	European Clinical Case Corpus	A	IT	139,370€
Lingsoft, Inc.	Lingsoft Solutions as Distributable Containers	A	FI	140,625€
Coreon GmbH	MKS as Linguistic Linked Open Data	A	DE	167,375€
Elhuyar Fundazioa	Basque-speaking smart speaker based on Mycroft AI	B	ES	117,117€
Universita' Degli Studi di Torino	Italian EVALITA Benchmark Linguistic Resources	A	IT	126,125€
University of Helsinki	Open Translation Models, Tools and Services	A	FI	154,636€
University of Vienna	Extracting Terminological Concept Systems from Text	A	AT	132,977€
University of Turku	Textual paraphrase dataset for deep language modelling	A	FI	166,085€
Weber Consulting KG	Virtual Personal Assistant Prototype	B	AT	87,445€
FZI Research Centre for Information Technology	Streaming Language Processing in Manufacturing	A	DE	132,160€

Table 2 List of pilot projects selected for financial support in the first open call

Four of the eight A type projects aimed to enrich the ELG platform with language resources and six of them planned to provide various language tools (i.e., two of the projects provide both resources and tools). The two B type projects promised speech applications – a smart speaker and a digital twin based on real-time language translation and analysis. The projects in general often dealt with underrepresented languages such as Basque, the Nordic languages, and European minority languages.

Technologically, the projects targeted a diverse set of goals and areas. There are projects targeting important interdisciplinary areas (medical informatics, manufacturing), modern technologies relating to language and semantic as well as world knowledge (Linked Open Data, paraphrasing) and core scalable technologies (distributable containers). Evaluation platforms as well as advanced and scalable machine translation still are and will be relevant issues for Language Technologies. Finally, the two speech-oriented applied projects broaden the portfolio of the usual Language Technologies in the desired direction, too.

3.1.3 Feedback provided and Survey for Proposers

With the goal of evaluating and improving our open call procedure, we conducted several surveys with everyone involved in the first open call. We started with the project proposers. After the evaluation process we also conducted a survey among all evaluators. The last survey was conducted among the Pilot Board members.

Two short surveys were designed for those who submitted a proposal (proposers) and those who uploaded an initial draft but did not submit a final version (non-proposers). The survey consisted of 15 questions, some open and some multiple choice. The survey topics were clustered into three sections: "motivation", "project proposals", and "your organisation". The information was collected anonymously.

The surveys were conducted in May 2020. Of the proposers, 73 out of 110 (66%) responded, and of the non-proposers, 6 out of 17 (35%) responded. The main conclusions from the proposers' survey that were relevant for the setup of the second open call: Almost 70% of respondents were interested in ELG because of both (functional) services and datasets. Slightly more than two thirds of the respondents preferred smaller, agile calls over large, consortium-based calls.

There was a demand for more detailed documentation (e. g., in the form of a webinar) that allows proposers to better interpret the strategic goals of ELG and get better information on already existing services in ELG. More details about the ELG API integration and about the infrastructure for working with data, applications and possibly also workflows were requested. Some improvements of the Open Calls Platform and its user-friendliness were made (e. g., limited space).

3.2 Open Call 2

The second open call was launched in October 2020 and experience from the first open call was reflected in its organisation.

3.2.1 Changes made between Open Call 1 and Open Call 2

The basic parameters, specified in the ELG Grant Agreement, remained the same for the second open call. Based on the lessons learned from open call 1, we implemented the following changes in the call documentation and the open call procedure:

- We improved the explanation of the strategic goals of ELG and the goals of the open calls. Links to an overview of ELG, its history and context and to an overview of the ELG platform were provided in the call documentation.
- We also improved the technical documentation of the ELG infrastructure and provided an easy-to-find list of currently available services – this was done with the launch of ELG Release 1 (June 2020).
- We organised a webinar, which took place during the submission period, on 12 November 2020. We explained the goals of the open call and presented the call documentation. The second part of the webinar was dedicated to questions and a discussion. A recording was made available to all applicants.
- The documentation, annexes, templates, and forms along with the Open Calls Platform were further improved.

- In the proposal template, budget breakdowns were requested in a fixed structure as well as a more detailed budget justification.
- New evaluators were recruited and added to the current group, with the aim to attract more experienced evaluators.
- It was decided that the second open call, like the first open call, should have no specific thematic focus.

3.2.2 Overview

The second call was opened on 1 October 2020 and closed on 30 November 2020 in accordance with the open calls timeline (Figure 1). We accepted 103 project proposals in total for evaluation.

Submitted by	Type A	Type B	Total
Research Organisation	38	5	43
SME	28	32	60
Total	66	37	103

Table 3 Proposals submitted to the second open call and accepted for evaluation

Five applicants (four SMEs and one research organisation) submitted two proposals (one type A and one type B). Regarding the project type, 66 proposals were of type A, and 37 project proposals were of type B. A total of 43 applicants who submitted a proposal in the second open call indicated that they had submitted the same or a similar proposal in the first open call. We received applications from 28 different countries, including eligible countries outside the EU (Iran, Israel, Norway, Serbia, Switzerland, Turkey, United Kingdom). The total amount of financing requested by the submitted projects was 13,257,919€. The average amount requested per project was 129,000€, which is less than in the first open call (153,000€).

In February 2021, the results of the second open call were announced on the ELG website.[7] All applicants were informed about the results. In February and March 2021, contracts with all selected projects were signed, and the first payments were made (half of the awarded financial support), in line with the call documentation and procedures. All projects had started their execution phase by 1 April 2021. Furthermore, in March 2021, abridged versions of the summary evaluation reports were made available to all applicants through the Open Calls Platform.

---

[7] https://www.european-language-grid.eu/open-calls/open-call-2

3.2.3 Selected Projects

The projects selected for financial support in open call 2 are listed in Table 4. The supported organisations are from five EU countries and the awarded budget varies between 85,421€ and 137,227€.

Organisation	Pilot Project Name	Type	Country	Funding
Institute for Bulgarian Language	Multilingual Image Corpus 2021	A	BG	110,960€
EDIA BV	CEFR Labelling and Assessment Services	B	NL	137,560€
University of West Bohemia	Motion-Capture 3D Sign Language Resources	A	CZ	85,421€
Sapienza University of Rome	Universal Semantic Annotator: A Unified API for Multilingual WSD, SRL and AMR	A	IT	113,228€
Sign Time GmbH	Sign language explanations for terms in a text	B	AT	137,227€

Table 4 List of pilot projects selected for financial support in the second open call

Although we obtained more project proposals from SMEs than from research organisations, there are two SMEs and three research organisations among the selected projects. Similarly, only two B type projects were accepted for financing.

Three A type projects aimed at providing tools to enrich the ELG platform. One project contributed multilingual annotated data, tools and services for image processing whilst the second one aimed at improving the ELG offer of linguistic tools by proposing a unified service powered by state-of-the-art neural models for carrying out annotations on three Natural Language Understanding tasks, i. e., Word Sense Disambiguation, Semantic Role Labelling and Semantic Parsing, in around 100 languages. The third A type project expanded the portfolio of language resources available in ELG by adding a dataset and search tool for Czech sign language. Regarding the B type projects, one of the projects also dealt with sign language. Its goal was to simplify text comprehension for deaf people by linking words and phrases to a sign language encyclopedia. The other project aimed to develop a set of tools, datasets, and services to enable automatic classification of the reading difficulty of texts on the Common European Framework of Reference.

3.2.4 Survey for Proposers to the Open Call 2

Just like for the first open call, a survey with 15 questions was designed for those who submitted a proposal. The survey had three sections: "motivation", "project proposals", "your organisation". In total, 39 out of 103 proposers (38%) responded. Regarding the motivation to submit a proposal, contributing services or resources to ELG to make them available to the ELG community and further development of an existing software or data project were the most frequent reasons reported by the respondents. The main expectations toward ELG were that the platform increases the visibility of the applicant's organisation on the European level and to get access to a large repository of tools and datasets. Also, almost all respondents think that more EU-funded activities dedicated to Language Technology and Language-centric AI are needed, preferably in the form of agile calls (with short proposals and quick evaluations, 9-12 months project run-time). Regarding the specialisation of respondents, most frequently they specialised in text analytics, machine translation or speech recognition. Respondents reported more than twenty domains that they specialise in (most frequently health sector), one fourth of all respondents have no particular specialisation.

4 Pilot Project Execution

Once the pilot projects were selected and the contracts signed, the continuous support from the ELG consortium started so that the projects could start their execution. The first opportunity where the newly selected pilot projects could become more familiar with ELG were the online meetings with the Pilot Board and other members of the ELG consortium. During these meetings, basic information about ELG and its technology as well as guidelines for project execution were presented.

Project execution (Figure 2) consisted of three phases: Phase 1 – Experiment; Phase 2 – Integration; Phase 3 – Dissemination. After finishing Phase 1, reporting from the applicants was required, and then the Pilot Board decided whether the project was allowed to continue execution (and consequently, whether the next payment, 35% of the awarded support, is made). After finishing Phase 3, a final report was required, and the Pilot Board evaluated the whole project and decided whether the project receives the final payment (15% of the awarded financial support).

As mentioned, each project was supervised by a project coach who was responsible for training the project team, collecting and answering questions during project execution, collecting reports, and guiding the team through the project phases.

To advertise them to a wider public, the pilot projects were presented at two annual ELG conferences, i. e., META-FORUM 2020 and META-FORUM 2021, in dedicated pilot project sessions in which all projects could present their main approaches and goals. In addition, workshops and training events organised by the ELG National Competence Centres (NCCs) were also used as opportunities to present certain pilot projects in the respective countries and regions.

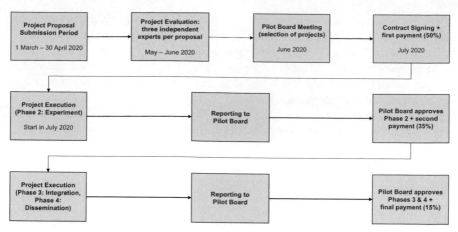

Fig. 2 Project execution scheme for pilot projects from the first open call

5 Conclusions

The results of the two open calls demonstrate an enormous interest in the European Language Grid and the Language Technology topic in general. The interest also indicates that the setup, including documentation, proposal template, platform etc., was easy to follow. In total, we received 213 project proposals from 156 different institutions (86 SMEs, 70 research organisations) in 32 different countries (including nine eligible countries outside the European Union); 15 projects were selected for funding, ten in the first open call and five in the second. The total amount requested was approx. 30 mil. €, while the available funding amounted to only 1.95 mil. € (an oversubscription of more than 15 times).

In the following we briefly summarise the main lessons learned, as gathered through the different surveys (see Sections 3.1.3 and 3.2.4):

- We aimed at a simple and light-weight procedure which led to a high number of submitted proposals. At the same time, the simplicity of the proposal template may have led to a higher number of low-quality proposals that were not adequately described or thought through. In both calls this rather high number of proposals required more person days and increased the costs related to the external evaluators.
- The quality of evaluation reports submitted by external evaluators was not entirely stable and, in some cases, could have been more profound. This was usually balanced by the project coach or Pilot Board.
- It was a good decision to develop the Open Calls Platform internally. Among others, it provided us with more flexibility, control over deadlines and quick and reliable support from the technical team.
- In the ELG project budget, the costs for the Open Calls Platform and for the proposal evaluation should have been planned more carefully.

Overall, we were very satisfied with the open calls setup and with the results of the pilot projects. While the results improved the ELG offering in terms of data, tools and services, and the applications developed using the ELG provided mutual benefit to the developers and ELG, we consider the overwhelming interest in the open calls an extremely important, albeit non-technical result: it demonstrates that Language Technologies are of tremendous interest to both researchers and commercial companies. It also shows that the open calls setup, as designed and implemented, was very attractive and can be considered as a model in similar undertakings in the future.

References

European Commission (2017). *Horizon 2020 – Work Programme 2018-2020. Annex K: Actions involving financial support to third parties*. Extract from Part 19 – Commission Decision C(2017)7124. Brussels, Belgium. URL: https://ec.europa.eu/research/participants/data/ref /h2020/other/wp/2018-2020/annexes/h2020-wp1820-annex-k-fs3p_en.pdf.

Rehm, Georg, Stelios Piperidis, Kalina Bontcheva, Jan Hajic, Victoria Arranz, Andrejs Vasiļjevs, Gerhard Backfried, José Manuel Gómez Pérez, Ulrich Germann, Rémi Calizzano, Nils Feldhus, Stefanie Hegele, Florian Kintzel, Katrin Marheinecke, Julian Moreno-Schneider, Dimitris Galanis, Penny Labropoulou, Miltos Deligiannis, Katerina Gkirtzou, Athanasia Kolovou, Dimitris Gkoumas, Leon Voukoutis, Ian Roberts, Jana Hamrlová, Dusan Varis, Lukáš Kačena, Khalid Choukri, Valérie Mapelli, Mickaël Rigault, Jūlija Meļņika, Miro Janosik, Katja Prinz, Andres Garcia-Silva, Cristian Berrio, Ondrej Klejch, and Steve Renals (2021). "European Language Grid: A Joint Platform for the European Language Technology Community". In: *Proceedings of the 16th Conference of the European Chapter of the Association for Computational Linguistics: System Demonstrations (EACL 2021)*. Kyiv, Ukraine: ACL, pp. 221–230. URL: https://w ww.aclweb.org/anthology/2021.eacl-demos.26.pdf.

Chapter 15
Basque-speaking Smart Speaker based on Mycroft AI

Igor Leturia, Ander Corral, Xabier Sarasola, Beñat Jimenez, Silvia Portela, Arkaitz Anza, and Jaione Martinez

Abstract Speech-driven virtual assistants, known as smart speakers, such as Amazon Echo and Google Home, are increasingly used. However, commercial smart speakers only support a handful of languages. Even languages for which ASR and TTS technology is available, such as many official EU member state languages, are not supported due to a commercial disinterest derived from their – relatively speaking – rather small number of speakers. This problem is even more crucial for minority languages, for which smart speakers are not expected anytime soon, or ever. In this ELG pilot project we developed a Basque-speaking smart speaker, making use of the open source smart speaker project Mycroft AI and Elhuyar Foundation's speech technologies for Basque. Apart from getting it to speak Basque, one of our goals was to make the smart speaker privacy friendly, non-gendered and use local services, because these are usual issues of concern. The project has also served to improve the state of the art of Basque ASR and TTS technology.

1 Overview and Objectives of the Pilot Project

Commercial smart speakers are increasingly popular despite the fact that their language coverage leaves much to be desired. Many large official national languages and practically all minority languages are unsupported by these devices. In many cases, the lack of support for a language in a smart speaker is not due to the lack of the necessary speech technologies, i. e., Automatic Speech Recognition (ASR) and Text To Speech (TTS). ASR and TTS technologies do exist for the Basque language

Igor Leturia · Ander Corral · Xabier Sarasola
Elhuyar Fundazioa, Spain, i.leturia@elhuyar.eus, a.corral@elhuyar.eus, x.sarasola@elhuyar.eus

Beñat Jimenez
Talaios Koop., Spain, jimakker@talaios.coop

Silvia Portela · Arkaitz Anza · Jaione Martinez
Skura Mobile, Spain, silvia@skuramobile.com, arkaitz@skuramobile.com, jaione@skuramobile.com

G. Rehm (ed.), *European Language Grid*, Cognitive Technologies,
https://doi.org/10.1007/978-3-031-17258-8_15

but it is unlikely that they will be implemented in smart speakers developed by the big technology enterprises because of its relatively small number of speakers.

On the other hand, there is a rather mature, open source smart speaker project called Mycroft AI.[1] Our ELG pilot project develops an open source smart speaker for the Basque language, based on Mycroft AI, that makes use of Elhuyar Foundation's ASR and TTS technologies. Apart from being open source and in Basque, other points of interest were the handling of privacy, gender and service locality issues.

One objective of the project was to improve the state of the art of Basque ASR and TTS technologies, since it would be necessary to adapt them to the context of a smart speaker. Specifically, we wanted to 1. improve the performance of Basque ASR technology for noisy environments; 2. create a grammar-based ASR system instead of a general vocabulary one to only recognise the commands of the speaker and, thus, improve precision; 3. create a neural network-based TTS system for Basque and replace the old HMM one; and 4. try to develop a gender-neutral voice.

2 Mycroft Localisation

A crucial and necessary part of the project was the localisation of Mycroft to Basque in its broadest sense. This involved not only a string translation process, but also making it understand speech commands and respond via speech in Basque. Thus, we had to develop plugins to connect Mycroft to Elhuyar's ASR and TTS services.

The localisation also involved the adaptation to Basque of Mycroft's linguistic module called *lingua-franca*, responsible for parsing numbers, days, times, durations, etc. in speech commands and to pronounce them correctly when responding.

Finally, the routine job of string translation of any software localisation process turned out not to be as straightforward for the commands' part. The parsing of many skills' intents from the commands is done by simply detecting some required or optional keywords and parameters, which is why their translation required more than just a simple sentence translation. We translated the Mycroft core module and 40+ of its skills (volume control, date, time, lists, alarms, audio record, radio, news, Wikipedia, weather, jokes, Wikiquote, e-mail etc.).

3 Privacy, Gender and Proximity

As mentioned in Section 1, we wanted to address the privacy and gender concerns often associated with smart speakers and also promote the use of local services. Regarding privacy, users and potential buyers have concerns with having a device in their homes with a microphone that is always on (Lau et al. 2018). However, respect for privacy is precisely one of Mycroft AI's unique selling propositions. They claim

---

[1] https://mycroft.ai

that they are "private by default" and that they "promise to never sell your data or give you advertisements" using their technology. This materialises in the fact that the wake word ("Hey, Mycroft") is detected locally, i. e., no audio is sent to remote servers except when saying a command after the detection of the wake word. On the other hand, if some big enterprise's cloud-based ASR or TTS services are used for the recognition of commands and the utterance of responses, there are logically some doubts as to what these companies will do with that data. Using Elhuyar's Basque ASR and TTS remote APIs from Mycroft, no data would be kept or collected.

Regarding gender treatment, smart speakers are known for their improper gender treatment, as stated in the Unesco report "I'd blush if I could: closing gender divides in digital skills through education" (West et al. 2019). According to this report, practically all commercial smart speakers exhibit a female voice and female personalities, and respond obligingly even to hostile requests, verbal abuse and sexual harassment, which may lead to reinforce and spread gender biases. The report ends with some recommendations that range from not making digital assistants female by default to developing neutral voices and personalities, which our project has tried to follow. The Basque voice installed at the moment is a male voice by default. Also, the speaker's name, Mycroft, – although fictional – is male, its "personality" is neutral, and it has no skill to respond in a docile manner to sexual comments or verbal abuse. However, we have also carried out some experiments in order to develop a gender-neutral synthetic voice (see Section 4.4).

We felt that our smart speaker should prioritise the local region and, for instance, allow listening to local radio stations, read the news from local media or buy goods or order food from local stores. We developed half a dozen local skills of our own, including local news, local radio stations, dictionary querying or Basque music.

4 Developments in Basque Speech Technology

4.1 ASR Robustness in Noisy Environments

One of the main challenges regarding the use of ASR technology in a smart speaker is making it robust enough to be reliable under non-optimal conditions: low volume, background noise, music, speech, room reverberation, low quality microphone, etc.

Elhuyar's ASR system for the Basque language is a general purpose system based on the Kaldi[2] toolkit. The speech data used to train the acoustic model comprises high quality clean parliamentary speeches. To make our acoustic model more robust, we used several synthetic data augmentation techniques during the training phase (Alumäe et al. 2018). This means that training data was 1. synthetically augmented by adding background noises from the MUSAN dataset (Snyder et al. 2015), which comprises several recordings of music, speech and a wide variety of noises;

---

[2] https://kaldi-asr.org

2. artificially reverberated with various real and simulated room impulse responses (Ko et al. 2017); and 3. augmented with threefold speed and volume perturbations.

4.2 ASR Closed Grammar-based Recognition

For general purpose ASR systems, typically a large language model is trained with a vast amount of diverse texts. For a smart speaker, however, where the user is expected to use a closed set of commands, limiting the ASR's vocabulary to just the necessary commands can increase the precision of the speech recognition.

Since Kaldi internally uses weighted finite state transducers (WFST) to model the language, simply by converting all the commands defined in Mycroft skills to the format used by Pynini (a Python library for WFST grammar compilation), we would obtain a language model limited to Mycroft's commands. But although Mycroft's skills were originally defined using its old-style intent parser Padatious (where the whole command is defined), nowadays most skills use the new intent parser Adapt, which defines commands using a few keywords and parameters. This makes it unfeasible to automatically generate all possible commands containing the keywords and parameters. Rewriting all skills to the Padatious format would have made the code much more difficult to maintain as well as losing Adapt's recall gain. This is why the creation of a custom grammar was eventually discarded.

4.3 Neural Network-based Basque TTS

Elhuyar's previous Basque TTS service was based on Hidden Markov Models (HMMs). In the ELG pilot project we developed a new neural network-based TTS service. Since the first neural system was published in 2013 (Zen et al. 2013), these have taken a clear advantage over HMM-based approaches and systems like Tacotron 2 (Shen et al. 2018) have achieved naturalness comparable to natural voice.

The key challenge with neural TTS systems is the size of the training dataset. The original Tacotron 2 monospeaker system was trained with 24.6 hours of speech, and subsequent research concluded that 10 hours is the minimum time required to obtain maximum quality (Chung et al. 2019). The only publicly available database of Basque speech of that size is a multispeaker database created by Google (Kjartansson et al. 2020), which contains recordings from 53 speakers with a maximum of 15 minutes per speaker. Modified configurations of Tacotron 2 using speaker embeddings have proved successful providing good quality multispeaker TTS systems (Jia et al. 2018), i.e., systems trained using combined recordings of multiple speakers, capable to synthesise the voice of each of them. We recorded a small multispeaker database, combined it with the Google database, and trained a multispeaker TTS using speaker embeddings, obtaining our own neural quality TTS voices.

4.4 Gender-neutral Voice

Apart from the interventions to address gender issues (Section 3), we conducted experiments towards obtaining a gender-neutral voice. Tolmeijer et al. (2021) observed that we do not regard voices of intermediate pitch (which is what could be understood as gender-neutral) as genderless, that we assign them one gender or the other, and that those that could be best considered as ambiguous in terms of gender or genderless were those with the greatest division of opinion.

Most of the literature on the field of generating gender-ambiguous voices seek gender neutrality through pitch modification, such as Tolmeijer et al. (2021), or the first genderless voice Q (Carpenter 2019). We employed a different and innovative approach. We first calculate the average speaker embedding for each gender with the embeddings obtained in the training and then we compute the embedding that is midway between the average male and female embeddings. Using this embedding in the trained Tacotron 2, we can synthesise sentences with a voice which has produced divided opinions as to its gender and which can thus be considered genderless.

5 Conclusions and Results of the Pilot Project

This ELG pilot project developed an open source Basque-speaking smart speaker based on Mycroft AI, which respects privacy and which uses a more appropriate approach regarding the voice's gender than commercial smart speakers. We connected Mycroft to Elhuyar's Basque ASR and TTS services, and we improved the state of the art of Basque speech technologies. Our ASR for Basque performs better in noisy environments and we developed a new deep neural network-based TTS for Basque and made experiments towards a gender-ambiguous synthetic voice. We translated more than 40 Mycroft skills and developed half a dozen new ones addressing local services. We tested the Basque Mycroft in PCs and Google AIY Kits.

Anyone can now download, install on a device and try Mycroft in Basque. While the ELG pilot project is finished, we continue to work on the project with the aim of, if possible, bringing a Basque smart speaker device to the market. We believe that the work carried out, the experience gained and the code developed in the ELG pilot project can be very useful for other minority language communities that would like to have access to a smart speaker that speaks their own language.

Acknowledgements The work described in this article has received funding from the EU project European Language Grid as one of its pilot projects. The project has also been helped by the Basque Government through its Hazitek programme (project DomEus) and the Gipuzkoa Provincial Council through its Etorkizuna eraikiz programme (project Mycroft.eus).

References

Alumäe, Tanel, Ottokar Tilk, and Asad Ullah (2018). "Advanced rich transcription system for Estonian speech". In: *Human Language Technologies – the Baltic Perspective: Proc. of the Eighth Int. Conference (Baltic HLT 2018)*. Ed. by Kadri Muischnek and Kaili Müürisep. Amsterdam, the Netherlands: IOS Press, pp. 1–8. DOI: 10.3233/978-1-61499-912-6-1.

Carpenter, Julie (2019). "Why Project Q is More than the World's First Nonbinary Voice for Technology". In: *Interactions* 26.6, pp. 56–59. DOI: 10.1145/3358912.

Chung, Yu-An, Yuxuan Wang, Wei-Ning Hsu, Yu Zhang, and RJ Skerry-Ryan (2019). "Semi-supervised training for improving data efficiency in end-to-end speech synthesis". In: *ICASSP 2019*. IEEE, pp. 6940–6944.

Jia, Ye, Yu Zhang, Ron J Weiss, Quan Wang, Jonathan Shen, Fei Ren, Zhifeng Chen, Patrick Nguyen, Ruoming Pang, Ignacio Lopez Moreno, et al. (2018). "Transfer learning from speaker verification to multispeaker text-to-speech synthesis". In: *Proceedings of the 32nd International Conference on Neural Information Processing Systems*. Red Hook, NY, USA: Curran Associates, pp. 4485–4495.

Kjartansson, Oddur, Alexander Gutkin, Alena Butryna, Isin Demirsahin, and Clara E. Rivera (2020). "Open-Source High Quality Speech Datasets for Basque, Catalan and Galician". In: *SLTU-CCURL 2020*. 11–12 May, Marseille, France, pp. 21–27.

Ko, Tom, Vijayaditya Peddinti, Daniel Povey, Michael L. Seltzer, and Sanjeev Khudanpur (2017). "A study on data augmentation of reverberant speech for robust speech recognition". In: *ICASSP 2017*, pp. 5220–5224. DOI: 10.1109/ICASSP.2017.7953152.

Lau, Josephine, Benjamin Zimmerman, and Florian Schaub (2018). "Alexa, Are You Listening? Privacy Perceptions, Concerns and Privacy-Seeking Behaviors with Smart Speakers". In: *Proc. of Human-Computer Interaction* 2.CSCW, pp. 1–31. DOI: 10.1145/3274371.

Shen, Jonathan, Ruoming Pang, Ron Weiss, Mike Schuster, Navdeep Jaitly, Zongheng Yang, Zhifeng Chen, Yu Zhang, Yuxuan Wang, Rj Skerrv-Ryan, et al. (2018). "Natural TTS Synthesis by Conditioning Wavenet on Mel Spectrogram Predictions". In: *ICASSP 2018*. IEEE, pp. 4779–4783.

Snyder, David, Guoguo Chen, and Daniel Povey (2015). "Musan: A music, speech, and noise corpus". In: *arXiv preprint arXiv:1510.08484*.

Tolmeijer, Suzanne, Naim Zierau, Andreas Janson, Jalil Sebastian Wahdatehagh, Jan Marco Marco Leimeister, and Abraham Bernstein (2021). "Female by Default? – Exploring the Effect of Voice Assistant Gender and Pitch on Trait and Trust Attribution". In: *Conference on Human Factors in Computing Systems (CHI)*. New York, NY, USA: ACM, pp. 1–7.

West, Mark, Rebecca Kraut, and Han Ei Chew (2019). *I'd blush if I could: closing gender divides in digital skills through education*. Unesco EQUALS.

Zen, Heiga, Andrew Senior, and Mike Schuster (2013). "Statistical parametric speech synthesis using deep neural networks". In: *2013 IEEE International Conference on Acoustics, Speech and Signal Processing*. IEEE, pp. 7962–7966.

Chapter 16
CEFR Labelling and Assessment Services

Mark Breuker

Abstract Our pilot project aims to develop a set of text collections and annotation tools to facilitate the creation of datasets (corpora) for the development of AI classification models. These classification models can automatically assess a text's reading difficulty on the levels described by the Common European Framework of Reference (CEFR). The ability to accurately and consistently assess the readability level of texts is crucial to authors and (language) teachers. It allows them to more easily create and discover content that meets the needs of students with different backgrounds and skill levels. Also, in the public sector using plain language in written communication is becoming increasingly important to ensure citizens can easily access and comprehend government information. EDIA already provides automated readability assessment services (available as APIs and an online authoring tool) for the CEFR in English. Support for Dutch, German and Spanish are added as part of this project. Using the infrastructure developed in this project the effort for creating high quality datasets for additional languages is lowered significantly. The tools and datasets are deployed through the European Language Grid. The project is scheduled to be completed in the second quarter of 2022.

1 Overview and Objectives of the Pilot Project

The CEFR (Common European Framework of Reference for Languages: Learning, Teaching, Assessment, Council of Europe 2020) aims to provide a comprehensive learning, teaching and assessment method that can be used for all European languages. Indicating the level of learners of foreign languages, the CEFR facilitates the assessment of a person's language proficiency. By now, most are familiar with the six reference levels (A1 – C2) used for this purpose (Figure 1).

CEFR levels are the foundation for a communicative approach to (foreign) language acquisition, teaching and certification. Although the CEFR levels represent a widely supported approach, the availability and quality of (educational) content la-

Mark Breuker
EDIA b. v., The Netherlands, mark@edia.nl

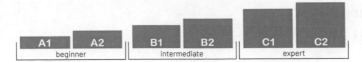

Fig. 1 CEFR proficiency levels

belled with CEFR levels are limited. This is because the highly laborious, error-prone labelling process is performed manually (save for some exceptions). This results in several practical obstacles regarding publishing, teaching, and learning:

- Content creators (publishers, authors, teachers, government officials) struggle to use consistent criteria for checking a text's difficulty level.
- Teachers have trouble finding or creating appropriate texts for their students.
- Content managers struggle to monitor the readability level of their content collections over time.

To tackle this problem, we have developed an automated text classification technology using Natural Language Processing. Our technology can perform CEFR text levelling in a scalable and consistent manner for multiple languages at a very granular level. By removing blockers through automation, we expect to impact the practical application of CEFR, enabling the labelling of more content in less time in a highly consistent manner. This way, we will lay the foundation for making written content with properly labelled text levels more widely available, adhering to the CEFR standard. After all, practical obstacles will have been eliminated.

The European Language Grid (Rehm et al. 2021) provides EDIA with a marketplace to promote, sell and distribute its CEFR services to a broad audience. Through the standardised ELG catalogue and API specification, developers can more easily adopt the services provided by EDIA in their applications.

2 Methodology

The infrastructure for the CEFR readability services developed during the pilot project consists of various components (Figure 2). The infrastructure facilitates the creation of the CEFR readability assessment services, using the following process:

1. Data collection – collect (unlabelled) texts for each language
2. Data labelling – label the texts on CEFR reading level using human experts
3. Model training – train classification models on the datasets
4. Integration – expose the models as REST services on ELG using API proxies
5. Authoring – integrate the services in a CEFR levelling and authoring application

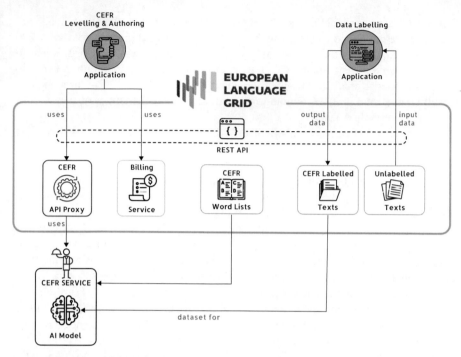

Fig. 2 CEFR infrastructure diagram

3 Implementation

To create the corpus, we collected approx. 1,200 texts per language from various public sources such as newspapers, magazines, educational sources and government websites. To speed up the text collection process we developed several text-scraping algorithms. Each text was stored as plain-text in a database together with information about its source and copyright licence. To ensure that the unlabelled dataset was well balanced and covered both easy and more difficult reading levels, we used texts from sources known to be targeted at basic, intermediate and advanced language users. In addition we used heuristics-based methods of readability assessment. This provided us with an initial indication of the reading difficulty of each text.

Our first attempt at a data labelling application was based on a pairwise comparison algorithm (Crompvoets et al. 2020). We applied this approach on a collection of 1,200 Dutch texts. The rationale for this approach was that comparing two texts on reading difficulty is a relatively easy task for teachers and would suffer less from inconsistent and subjective criteria used when evaluating a text directly on its CEFR-level. This approach resulted in a rank-ordered list of texts on reading difficulty. Next we set the boundaries for the CEFR-reading levels within this rank-ordered list. Unfortunately we found that we were not able to train a classification model on the dataset. Upon closer inspection (based on a random sample of 100 texts) we found that many texts were labelled incorrectly (i. e., 25 percent more than two levels off). Although we compared each text with six other texts (resulting in a total of 7,200 annotations), possibly the number of comparisons per text was still insufficient to create a reliable measurement. This means the pairwise comparison approach also offers no benefits compared to labelling each text on CEFR level by three experts (resulting in a total of 3,600 annotations) with regard to the number of annotations needed to a reliable dataset.

In our second attempt we labelled texts directly regarding their CEFR reading level. This new labelling application provides functionality for organising the unlabelled texts into various projects which supports working with multiple languages and creating subsets from the total corpus to label the texts in smaller batches. This allows us to annotate the texts iteratively which means we can better monitor the quality of the annotations during the labelling process. Within each project, annotation tasks are created and are assigned to language experts. Each text is evaluated by three different experts to ensure high quality CEFR assessments. For each text annotators complete an assessment form with criteria described in the CEFR reading level descriptors (such as vocabulary and grammatical complexity, Alderson et al. 2006). We have based this approach in part on the CEFR Estim Grid project (Tardieu et al. 2010). Prior to completing the content labelling tasks, annotators participate in an (online) workshop to collaboratively assess the CEFR level of a small subset of texts to align on the CEFR level descriptors.

Once we labelled all texts and completed the datasets we were able to develop the CEFR readability classification models. The models we created return the predicted difficulty on a linear scale, which means that we can predict the reading difficulty more granularly than the 6-level CEFR scale. In other words, we can say, for example, that a text is on the more difficult end of the B2 level. Based on the models, we created web services for assessing the overall readability of a text, difficult words in the text and alternative words (suggestions) for these difficult words.

We then integrated our CEFR services into the ELG platform using proxy services. A proxy service maps incoming ELG requests onto our classification API running on our web servers. The proxy service was packaged as a Docker container, stored in our company's Docker registry and then deployed on ELG. To improve performance and avoid blocking requests, we used the Asyncio library to support asynchronous processing of service requests. To speed up the development of the proxy services, we switched to using ELG's Python SDK for later versions of our service implementations.

For the authoring application we chose to integrate our CEFR services with the Fonto editor[1] as an add-on. This allowed us to focus on developing the text analysis rather than basic text editing features. In addition we used the Fonto Content Quality component to highlight relevant sections in the text and provide feedback to authors which allows them to improve the readability and quality of their texts. The Fonto editor is a popular tool by major (educational) publishers, which enables easy integration and adoption of our technology by new clients.

---

[1] https://www.fontoxml.com

4 Evaluation

For collecting the texts for our dataset we had planned to use the C4 Corpus (public domain part)[2] which is a huge collection of plain texts, released under a Creative Commons licence, which appeared to be very useful for our project. However, upon closer inspection we found that the licence detection algorithm that was used is not very accurate and that the structure of the texts was not very suitable for our purposes. Also, the sheer size of this corpus added to the complexity of its processing. We therefore decided not to use the C4 Corpus, but create a new corpus instead. We tried various methods for data labelling. Unfortunately the pairwise comparison did not yield a useful dataset from which we could create a classification model. Possible explanations may be that the number of comparisons per text was too low, that we did not select the right pairs of texts for the language teachers to compare, or that the teachers did not consistently select the most difficult text from each set. This would need to be investigated further.

Integrating our services into the ELG was straightforward and easy. Using the ELG Python SDK we were able to make our services available through ELG. We also appreciated the thorough review process of our submitted services and datasets by the ELG team. We received good feedback and support to improve the required metadata, code performance and overall compatibility with the ELG API specification. The standards-based ELG integration (e. g., using the ELG Python SDK) makes it significantly easier for third-party developers to consume and integrate our services in their language learning applications. We have not yet been able to evaluate the billing services of the ELG in a production setting. We can see that the services we deployed on ELG have been used multiple times, but we have little information about the use over time and the types of users (e. g., commercial vs. academic).

5 Conclusions and Results of the Pilot Project

Our goals with this project were to extend our CEFR service to additional languages beyond English and to use the European Language Grid as a marketplace for commercialising our services. Although the project has not yet been completed we can already see that the project has helped us to improve our data collection and labelling process, which helps to create high quality datasets for training additional language models. We created CEFR readability classification models using these datasets which we have made available on ELG as services.[3] The services are integrated into a text authoring application which helps authors assess and improve the readability of their (educational) texts in multiple languages. Deploying services on the ELG is currently easy and useful for demonstration and trial purposes. We

---

[2] https://live.european-language-grid.eu/catalogue/#/resource/service/corpus/1186
[3] https://live.european-language-grid.eu/catalogue/project/5258

believe the ELG SDKs enable third party developers to more easily discover and consume our APIs.

Acknowledgements The work described in this article has received funding from the EU project European Language Grid as one of its pilot projects. We thank Cito Labs for their valuable expertise and support in the pairwise labelling experiment; all language teachers involved in labelling hundreds of texts on the CEFR; FontoXML for their support with integrating our NLP services with their product; the ELG team for funding our pilot project and the help we received for deploying our CEFR services and datasets on the ELG platform.

References

Alderson, J. Charles, Neus Figueras, Henk Kuijper, Guenter Nold, Sauli Takala, and Claire Tardieu (2006). "Analysing Tests of Reading and Listening in Relation to the Common European Framework of Reference: The Experience of The Dutch CEFR Construct Project". In: *Language Assessment Quarterly* 3.1, pp. 3–30. URL: https://doi.org/10.1207/s15434311laq0301_2.

Council of Europe (2020). *Common European Framework of Reference for Languages: Learning, teaching, assessment – Companion volume*. Strasbourg: Council of Europe Publishing, pp. 53–59. URL: https://www.coe.int/lang-cefr.

Crompvoets, Elise A. V., Anton A. Béguin, and Klaas Sijtsma (2020). "Adaptive Pairwise Comparison for Educational Measurement". In: *Journal of Educational and Behavioral Statistics* 45.3, pp. 316–338. DOI: 10.3102/1076998619890589. URL: https://doi.org/10.3102/107699861989 0589.

Rehm, Georg, Stelios Piperidis, Kalina Bontcheva, Jan Hajic, Victoria Arranz, Andrejs Vasiļjevs, Gerhard Backfried, José Manuel Gómez Pérez, Ulrich Germann, Rémi Calizzano, Nils Feldhus, Stefanie Hegele, Florian Kintzel, Katrin Marheinecke, Julian Moreno-Schneider, Dimitris Galanis, Penny Labropoulou, Miltos Deligiannis, Katerina Gkirtzou, Athanasia Kolovou, Dimitris Gkoumas, Leon Voukoutis, Ian Roberts, Jana Hamrlová, Dusan Varis, Lukáš Kačena, Khalid Choukri, Valérie Mapelli, Mickaël Rigault, Jūlija Meļņika, Miro Janosik, Katja Prinz, Andres Garcia-Silva, Cristian Berrio, Ondrej Klejch, and Steve Renals (2021). "European Language Grid: A Joint Platform for the European Language Technology Community". In: *Proceedings of the 16th Conference of the European Chapter of the Association for Computational Linguistics: System Demonstrations (EACL 2021)*. Kyiv, Ukraine: ACL, pp. 221–230. URL: https://www.aclweb.org/anthology/2021.eacl-demos.26.pdf.

Tardieu, Claire, Raili Hildén, Magda Lehmann, and Monique Reichert (2010). *The CEF-ESTIM Grid*. URL: http://cefestim.ecml.at.

Chapter 17
European Clinical Case Corpus

Bernardo Magnini, Begoña Altuna, Alberto Lavelli, Anne-Lyse Minard, Manuela Speranza, and Roberto Zanoli

Abstract Interpreting information in medical documents has become one of the most relevant application areas for language technologies. However, despite the fact that huge amounts of medical documents (e. g., medical examination reports, hospital discharge letters, digital medical records) are produced, their availability for research purposes is still limited, due to strict data protection regulations. Aiming at fostering advanced information extraction technologies for medical applications, we present E3C, a corpus of clinical case narratives fully based on freely licensed documents. E3C (European Clinical Case Corpus) contains a vast selection of clinical cases (i. e., narratives presenting a patient's history) that cover different medical areas, are based on different styles and produced in different languages. A portion of the corpus has been manually annotated to be used for training and testing purposes, while a larger set of documents has been automatically tagged to serve as a baseline for future research in information extraction.

1 Overview and Objectives of the Pilot Project

The interest in information extraction from clinical narratives has increased in recent decades, including clinical entity extraction and classification (Schulz et al. 2020; Grabar et al. 2019; Dreisbach et al. 2019; Luo et al. 2017), clinical prediction systems, e. g., MIMIC III (Johnson et al. 2016), and the organisation of challenges at CLEF (Kelly et al. 2019), and Semeval. However, only a few shared datasets have been created, limiting the potential of developing applications in this area.

Bernardo Magnini · Alberto Lavelli · Manuela Speranza · Roberto Zanoli
Fondazione Bruno Kessler, Italy, magnini@fbk.eu, lavelli@fbk.eu, manspera@fbk.eu, zanoli@fbk.eu

Begoña Altuna
Fondazione Bruno Kessler, Italy, HiTZ Centre, University of the Basque Country, Spain, begona.altuna@ehu.eus

Anne-Lyse Minard
Université d'Orléans, France, anne-lyse.minard@univ-orleans.fr

© The Author(s) 2023
G. Rehm (ed.), *European Language Grid*, Cognitive Technologies,
https://doi.org/10.1007/978-3-031-17258-8_17

We report upon the E3C (European Clinical Case Corpus) ELG pilot project, which resulted in a large collection of clinical cases in five European languages: English, Spanish, French, Italian and Basque. A clinical case is a statement of a clinical practice, presenting the reason for a clinical visit, the description of physical exams, and the assessment of the patient's situation. Clinical cases are typically reported and discussed in research papers, and are often used for education purposes in medicine. In addition, published clinical cases are de-identified, overcoming privacy issues, and are rich in clinical entities as well as temporal information.

> A 25-year-old man with a history of Klippel-Trenaunay syndrome presented to the hospital with mucopurulent bloody stool and epigastric persistent colic pain for 2 wk. Continuous superficial ulcers and spontaneous bleeding were observed under colonoscopy. Subsequent gastroscopy revealed mucosa with diffuse edema, ulcers, errhysis, and granular and friable changes in the stomach and duodenal bulb, which were similar to the appearance of the rectum. After ruling out other possibilities according to a series of examinations, a diagnosis of GDUC was considered. The patient hesitated about intravenous corticosteroids, so he received a standardized treatment with pentasa of 3.2 g/d. After 0.5 mo of treatment, the patient's symptoms achieved complete remission. Follow-up endoscopy and imaging findings showed no evidence of recurrence for 26 mo.

The sample clinical case reported in the box above is about a patient presenting gastric symptoms, who is finally diagnosed with gastroduodenitis associated with ulcerative colitis (GDUC). To reach the diagnosis, two medical tests (colonoscopy and gastroscopy) were performed. Treatment, outcome (complete remission) and follow-up (no evidence of recurrence) are also present in the text.

2 Corpus Collection and Annotation

The document collection was determined by the available resources for each language (e. g., PubMed, scientific journals, medicine leaflets). First, we identified possible document sources as well as their licenses and re-distribution policies. We selected sources that were either already available under Creative Commons licenses (i. e., CC-BY or CC-BY-SA), possibly asking for re-distribution permission to the right holders. In the case of the SPACCC[1] and NUBes[2] corpora, the texts were ready to be used by us in terms of licensing and formatting. We automated the text collection as much as possible, for example, in some cases we were able to identify and extract the section with the clinical case. All English and some French documents were automatically extracted from PubMed[3], through its API, while medicine leaflets were automatically crawled and stored in a single file for each language. Journal articles with clinical cases that could not be extracted automatically were filtered through the search query "clinical case" in the different languages. In addition to the

---

[1] https://github.com/PlanTL-GOB-ES/SPACCC

[2] https://github.com/Vicomtech/NUBes-negation-uncertainty-biomedical-corpus

[3] https://pubmed.ncbi.nlm.nih.gov

extraction of the relevant documents, corresponding metadata was stored to allow accurate documentation.

The annotation of temporal information was performed following an adaptation of the THYME annotation guidelines (Styler et al. 2014).[4] Temporal information refers to the events in a text as well as to chronological references and relations. To encode temporal information, we defined the following tags and relation types. Events, time expressions, temporal relations and aspectual relations are widely used in temporal information tasks, while actor, body part and RML annotations were added as they convey relevant information of the clinical domain.

- *Events* are the events or states relevant to the patient's clinical timeline.
- *Time expressions* refer to points and intervals in time.
- *Temporal relations* (TLINK) implement relations that chronologically order events and time expressions.
- *Aspectual relations* (ALINK) are created between an aspectual event and its subordinated non-aspectual event.
- *Actors* are the people (or animals) mentioned in the text.
- *Body parts* are the parts of the body that are bigger than cells.
- *Results, measurements and lab and test results (RML)* are lab test and analytics' results, formulaic measurements and measurement values.

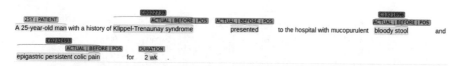

Fig. 1 A sentence in a clinical case annotated with both temporal information and clinical entities (i. e., disorders) with their UMLS codes (marked in red)

The annotation of clinical entities is mainly based on the guidelines of SEM-EVAL 2015 Task 14 "Analysis of Clinical Text"[5] and on the ASSESS CT guidelines (Miñarro-Giménez et al. 2018). The annotation of Layer 1 was done fully manually, while for Layer 2 the automatic annotation was produced with a distant supervision method that matches clinical entities with disorder concepts in UMLS.

3 Implementation

The E3C corpus is organised in three different layers:

Layer 1: about 25k tokens per language of clinical narratives with full manual or manually checked annotation of clinical entities, temporal information and factuality, for benchmarking and linguistic analysis.

---

[4] http://clear.colorado.edu/compsem/documents/THYME_guidelines.pdf

[5] http://alt.qcri.org/semeval2015/task14/data/uploads/share_annotation_guidelines.pdf

Layer 2: 50-100k tokens per language of clinical narratives with automatic annotation of clinical entities. Distant supervision was used to annotate 8,972 clinical entities with their corresponding concepts in UMLS.

Layer 3: about 1m tokens per language of non-annotated medical documents (not necessarily clinical narratives) to be exploited by semi-supervised approaches.

Table 1 shows the sizes of the layers (document and token numbers). Table 2 shows the numbers of Layer 1 tags to indicate information density in clinical cases.

	English	French	Italian	Spanish	Basque
Layer 1	84 / 25142	81 /25196	86 / 24319	81 / 24681	90 / 22505
Layer 2	171 / 50371	168 / 50490	174 / 49900	162 / 49351	111 / 12541
Layer 3	9779 / 1075709	25740 / 66281501	10213 / 13601915	1876 / 1030907	1232 / 518244

Table 1 Documents/tokens in each language and layer in the E3C corpus.

Entity	English	French	Italian	Spanish	Basque
CLINENTITY	1024	1327	869	1345	1910
EVENT	4885	4312	3385	4767	7910
ACTOR	682	427	338	319	505
BODYPART	968	659	328	814	1410
TIMEX3	380	333	298	383	638
RML	480	508	383	391	1101
ALINK	114	71	109	92	113
TLINK	4852	4084	1150	4700	7981

Table 2 Annotations in each language in Layer 1 in the E3C corpus.

4 Evaluation

For temporal information and clinical entity annotation tasks, we performed inter-annotator agreement (IAA) tests. We measured whether the guidelines had been defined and were understood correctly, and we ensured that the quality of annotations in the corpus was similar. The IAA phase had been done on the English part of the corpus. IAA for temporal entities (EVENT, TIMEX3, ACTOR, BODYPART) was measured using three annotators and six documents. To compute the agreement, we used the F1-measure metric, which produced the same results as using the Dice coefficient. The agreement is high for EVENT and ACTOR entities (with an average of 0.81 and 0.87), but a bit lower for TIMEX3 and BODYPART (with an average of 0.50 and 0.57). The IAA for temporal relations (TLINK) was split in two phases: three documents were annotated, the results discussed by the annotators and then three new documents were annotated. To measure the agreement, we used the Tempeval-3 scorer (UzZaman and Allen 2011), implemented for the evaluation of systems based on the comparison of temporal graphs built from annotations. The average F1-measure for the first phase was 0.43 and 0.53 for the second.

The annotation of the clinical entities in Layer 1 was performed by four annotators. Again, the agreement is calculated using F1, whereas for the CUI attribute we computed the accuracy taking into consideration only the entities identified by two annotators. The agreement for clinical entity recognition is 0.70 on average (from 0.64 to 0.78). In the entity linking task, the accuracy on entities identified by both annotators starts at 0.86 (on average 0.89).

The clinical entities in Layer 2 were annotated automatically using distant supervision and UMLS as a controlled vocabulary. A manual assessment of the quality of these annotated entities would be too demanding in terms of human resources. For this reason, the quality of Layer 2 has been estimated through an indirect evaluation that uses the results obtained by distant supervision on Layer 1 (Table 3) as an estimation of the quality of the Layer 2 annotations. This approximation is possible because the documents in Layer 1 and Layer 2 are clinical cases and because they were extracted from the same kind of publications or from the same existing corpora.

	English	French	Italian	Spanish	Basque
Accuracy	48.33	54.92	58.09	63.64	55.35

Table 3 Estimated accuracy (F_1-measure) of the clinical entities in Layer 2.

5 Conclusions and Results of the Pilot Project

The E3C pilot project aims at fostering advanced information extraction technologies for medical applications. Results include a large corpus of annotated clinical cases in five languages. The corpus is available on the ELG platform.

Acknowledgements The work described in this article has received funding from the EU project European Language Grid as one of its pilot projects and from the Basque Government post-doctoral grant POS_2020_2_0026.

References

Dreisbach, Caitlin, Theresa A. Koleck, Philip E. Bourne, and Suzanne Bakken (2019). "A systematic review of natural language processing and text mining of symptoms from electronic patient-authored text data". In: *Int. Jour. of Medical Informatics* 125, pp. 37–46. DOI: 10.1016/j.ijmedinf.2019.02.008.

Grabar, Natalia, Cyril Grouin, Thierry Hamon, and Vincent Claveau (2019). "Recherche et extraction d'information dans des cas cliniques. Présentation de la campagne d'évaluation DEFT 2019". In: *Actes du Défi Fouille de Textes 2019*. Toulouse, France: Actes DEFT 2019, pp. 7–16. URL: https://www.irit.fr/pfia2019/wp-content/uploads/2019/07/actes_DEFT_CH_PFIA2019.pdf.

Johnson, Alistair E.W., Tom J. Pollard, Lu Shen, Li-wei H. Lehman, Mengling Feng, Mohammad Ghassemi, Benjamin Moody, Peter Szolovits, Leo Anthony Celi, and Roger G. Mark (2016). "MIMIC-III, a freely accessible critical care database". In: *Scientific Data* 3. DOI: 10.1038/sdata.2016.35.

Kelly, Liadh, Hanna Suominen, Lorraine Goeuriot, Mariana Neves, Evangelos Kanoulas, Dan Li, Leif Azzopardi, Rene Spijker, Guido Zuccon, Harrisen Scells, and João Palotti (2019). "Overview of the CLEF eHealth Evaluation Lab 2019". In: *Experimental IR Meets Multilinguality, Multimodality, and Interaction*. Ed. by Fabio Crestani, Martin Braschler, Jacques Savoy, Andreas Rauber, Henning Müller, David E. Losada, Gundula Heinatz Bürki, Linda Cappellato, and Nicola Ferro. Cham: Springer, pp. 322–339.

Luo, Yuan, William K. Thompson, Timothy M. Herr, Zexian Zeng, Mark A. Berendsen, Siddhartha R. Jonnalagadda, Matthew B. Carson, and Justin Starren (2017). "Natural Language Processing for EHR-Based Pharmacovigilance: A Structured Review". In: *Drug Safety* 40 (11), pp. 1075–1089. DOI: 10.1007/s40264-017-0558-6.

Miñarro-Giménez, José Antonio, Catalina Martínez-Costa, Daniel Karlsson, Stefan Schulz, and Kirstine Rosenbeck Gøeg (2018). "Qualitative analysis of manual annotations of clinical text with SNOMED CT". In: *PLoS ONE* 13.12. URL: https://www.ncbi.nlm.nih.gov/pmc/articles/PMC6307753/pdf/pone.0209547.pdf.

Schulz, Sarah, Jurica Ševa, Samuel Rodríguez, Malte Ostendorff, and Georg Rehm (2020). "Named Entities in Medical Case Reports: Corpus and Experiments". In: *Proceedings of the 12th Language Resources and Evaluation Conference*. Marseille, France: ELRA, pp. 4495–4500. URL: https://www.aclweb.org/anthology/2020.lrec-1.553.

Styler, William F., Steven Bethard, Sean Finan, Martha Palmer, Sameer Pradhan, Piet C. de Groen, Brad Erickson, Timothy Miller, Chen Lin, Guergana Savova, et al. (2014). "Temporal Annotation in the Clinical Domain". In: *Transactions of the Association for Computational Linguistics* 2. Ed. by Ellen Riloff, pp. 143–154. URL: http://aclweb.org/anthology/Q14-1012.

UzZaman, Naushad and James Allen (2011). "Temporal Evaluation". In: *Proceedings of the 49th Annual Meeting of the Association for Computational Linguistics: Human Language Technologies*. Portland, Oregon, USA: ACL, pp. 351–356. URL: https://aclanthology.org/P11-2061.

Chapter 18
Extracting Terminological Concept Systems from Natural Language Text

Dagmar Gromann, Lennart Wachowiak, Christian Lang, and Barbara Heinisch

Abstract Terminology denotes a language resource that structures domain-specific knowledge by means of conceptual grouping of terms and their interrelations. Such structured domain knowledge is vital to various specialised communication settings, from corporate language to crisis communication. However, manually curating a terminology is both labour- and time-intensive. Approaches to automatically extract terminology have focused on detecting domain-specific single- and multi-word terms without taking terminological relations into consideration, while knowledge extraction has specialised on named entities and their relations. We present the Text2TCS method to extract single- and multi-word terms, group them by synonymy, and interrelate these groupings by means of a pre-specified relation typology to generate a Terminological Concept System (TCS) from domain-specific text in multiple languages. To this end, the method relies on pre-trained neural language models.

1 Overview and Objectives

Domain knowledge is paramount to any specialised communication setting. A structured representation of domain-specific terminology fosters the acquisition of new domain knowledge, the expansion of existing knowledge, and optimises specialised discourse by supporting terminological consistency (Budin 1996). Extracting Terminological Concept Systems from Natural Language Text (Text2TCS) is a pilot project supported by the European Language Grid (ELG) to develop a language technology that automatically extracts a Terminological Concept System (TCS) from domain-specific texts in multiple languages. A TCS is a terminological resource that conceptually structures domain-specific terms and provides hierarchical and non-hierarchical relations between them. Within the context of terminology science, a *term* signifies a domain-specific designation that linguistically represents a domain-specific concept (ISO1087 2019). A *concept* groups terms by meaning, which is

Dagmar Gromann · Lennart Wachowiak · Christian Lang · Barbara Heinisch
University of Vienna, Austria, dagmar.gromann@univie.ac.at, lennart.wachowiak@univie.ac.at, christian.lang@univie.ac.at, barbara.heinisch@univie.ac.at

G. Rehm (ed.), *European Language Grid*, Cognitive Technologies,
https://doi.org/10.1007/978-3-031-17258-8_18

generally represented as unique characteristics shared by a set of real-world entities. Once terms have been grouped into concepts based on their synonymous meaning within languages and equivalent meaning across languages, terminology science foresees interrelations of concepts by terminological relations. Such relations are categorised into hierarchical, i. e., generic and partitive, and non-hierarchical, e. g., causal and spatial, relations. For instance, the sentence *COVID causes coughing* can be depicted as a causal relation from the concept that represents the cause *COVID* to the effect concept designated by *coughing*. However, in practice, publicly available terminologies rarely contain any relations, since manually creating them is time- and labour-intensive. While Automated Term Extraction (ATE) methods have proliferated (e. g., Astrakhantsev 2018; Lang et al. 2021), additionally structuring extracted terms by concepts and relations has been neglected. To address this issue, Text2TCS provides a method and tool to extract terms and interrelations between domain-specific synonym sets across languages and domains. The Text2TCS implementation has been integrated and is available on the ELG plattform.[1]

2 Methodology

The Text2TCS methodology depicted in Figure 1 builds on a pipeline approach with the following steps: preprocessing, term extraction, relation extraction and postprocessing. The pipeline takes domain-specific natural language sentences or text as input and outputs a TCS in the TermBase eXchange (TBX) format and as a concept map. We experimented with several joint term and relation extraction methods, especially relying on pre-trained Neural Machine Translation and Sequence to Sequence models such as mT5 (Xue et al. 2021). However, a pipeline approach relying on fine-tuning XLM-R (Conneau et al. 2020) was finally preferable due to a smaller model size as well as a substantially higher inference speed and performance reliability. In order to fine-tune pre-trained models, training data needs to be available. To this end, two terminologists annotated 51 texts spanning distinct domains from computer science to ecology in English and German with a total of 6,327 terms and 9,460 relations.

2.1 Preprocessing

In a first step, the input text's language is detected and it is split into individual sentences. The former relies on the Python library PYCLD2[2] that supports 83 languages. Language detection is required in order to issue a warning in case the input language is unsupported and to indicate the language in the final TBX output file. Furthermore,

---

[1] https://live.european-language-grid.eu/catalogue/tool-service/8122

[2] https://github.com/aboSamoor/pycld2

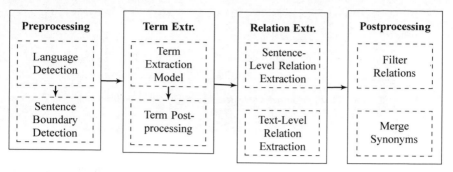

Fig. 1 Text2TCS extraction pipeline

the detected language is passed on to the sentence boundary detection module that relies on language-specific rules.

Sentence boundary detection is achieved using the rule-based Python module pySBD (Sadvilkar and Neumann 2020), which officially supports 22 languages. This step is required due to limited input length of current neural language models and to allow for a sentence-based relation extraction step. Thus, the pipeline can be sure to support 22 languages (two-digit ISO language codes): am, ar bg, da, de, en, es, el, fa, fr, hi, hy, it, ja, kk, mr, my, nl, ru, pl, ur, zh. However, the term and relation extraction models potentially support up to 100 languages.

2.2 Term Extraction

From several distinct experiments with term extraction, which we detail in Lang et al. (2021), the best performing classifies each token of an input sentence separately, utilising the same fully connected layer for all tokens after they have been processed by XLM-R. In term extraction, an established method is (e. g., Hazem et al. 2020) to first generate all possible term candidates from a sequence/sentence and input the candidate together with its context for the model to predict whether it is a term or not. This requires first generating all possible n-grams of a pre-specified length from a text. Instead, the token classification we propose assigns one of three labels to each token in a sequence: B-T for beginning of term, T for continuation of term, and n for not a term (component). For instance, the input sequence "motor vehicle means any power-driven vehicle." would be labeled as B-T, T, n, n, B-T, T, n, extracting the terms "motor vehicle" and "power-driven vehicle". This approach leads to a substantial reduction in training and inference time compared to previous methods. In XLM-R's own tokeniser, which we utilise, we noticed an issue with trailing punctuation, e. g. a comma after a term. Thus, we apply an additional cleaning step in which we remove trailing punctuation from a standard punctuation list, unless the punctuation appears multiple times in the term, e. g. "U.S.A.".

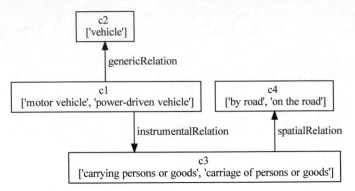

Fig. 2 Example TCS from sequence "motor vehicle means any power-driven vehicle, which is normally used for carrying persons or goods by road or for drawing, on the road, vehicles used for the carriage of persons or goods"

2.3 Relation Extraction

Related domain-specific mentions in text can either occur within the same sentence or across sentence boundaries. Thus, two separate models in the pipeline predict relations: a sentence-level and a text-level model. For sentence-level relation extraction, we input a mention pair followed by a contextualising sentence containing both mentions to a fine-tuned pre-trained XLM-R model that predicts a relation taking the relation direction into account (see Wachowiak et al. 2021, for details). We apply our own relation typology of hierarchical relations, i. e., generic and partitive, and non-hierarchical relations, i. e., activity, causal, instrumental, origination, spatial, property, and associative. Generic relations and synonyms frequently occur across sentence boundaries, which is why we additionally train a text-level relation extraction model to detect these two, building on our previous model (Wachowiak et al. 2020) fine-tuning XLM-R. This model takes a mention pair as input and classifies it as a generic relation, synonymy or random, which means no or any other relation. Since predicting relations for individual term pairs drastically impacts inference time, we optimize the pipeline to process multiple term pairs and their context sentence simultaneously.

2.4 Postprocessing

In the last step, synonyms predicted on sentence- and text-level are merged into concepts. Furthermore, the relations predicted by the two models are filtered to only include those with high confidence scores and to remove duplicates to provide the final TCS exemplified in Figure 2.

3 Evaluation

We evaluated individual steps in the pipeline as well as the overall system on manually TCS-annotated texts in English, German, Spanish, Portuguese, French, Italian,
Romanian and Russian as well as on standard datasets, where available, for a better comparison. The term extraction model outperforms previous neural approaches
(Hazem et al. 2020) from the TermEval challenge by up to 11.6 F1 score and obtained
74% (Precision: 70%, Recall: 78%) on our dataset. The sentence-level relation extraction model obtained a weighted F1 score of up to 53% (Precision: 56%, Recall:
53%) and the text-level relation extraction model of up to 78% (Precision: 78%, Recall: 77%) on our manually annotated datasets. The sentence-level extraction is also
compared to a mixed dataset of the SemEval 2007 Task 4 and SemEval 2010 Task 8
relations, on which the model obtains a weighted F1 score of 87% (see Wachowiak
et al. 2021, for details).

4 Conclusions and Results of the Pilot Project

Automatically extracting and structuring domain-specific knowledge from text is
a challenging task. Text2TCS innovatively fine-tunes pre-trained neural language
models in a pipeline approach to first extract terms, second relations on sentence-
and text-level, and finally group synonyms. To this end, this pilot project proposed a
novel typology of terminological relations. A consistent use of relation types across
languages aims to ease the alignment of resulting monolingual TCS across languages.
Integrating such an alignment method is future work. At the moment, the method
takes terms and relations into consideration, however, text frequently contains (parts
of) natural language definitions and their extraction would represent a valuable future addition to the method.

Acknowledgements The work described in this article[3] has received funding from the EU project
European Language Grid as one of its pilot projects. The computational results presented have been
achieved in part using the Vienna Scientific Cluster (VSC).

References

Astrakhantsev, Nikita (2018). "ATR4S: toolkit with state-of-the-art automatic terms recognition
    methods in Scala". In: *Language Resources and Evaluation* 52.3, pp. 853–872.
Budin, Gerhard (1996). *Wissensorganisation und Terminologie: Die Komplexität und Dynamik wis-
    senschaftlicher Informations- und Kommunikationsprozesse*. Vol. 28. Forum für Fachsprachen-
    Forschung. Gunter Narr Verlag.

---

[3] https://text2tcs.univie.ac.at

Conneau, Alexis, Kartikay Khandelwal, Naman Goyal, Vishrav Chaudhary, Guillaume Wenzek, Francisco Guzmán, Edouard Grave, Myle Ott, Luke Zettlemoyer, and Veselin Stoyanov (2020). "Unsupervised Cross-lingual Representation Learning at Scale". In: *Proceedings of the 58th Annual Meeting of the Association for Computational Linguistics*. Ed. by Dan Jurafsky, Joyce Chai, Natalie Schluter, and Joel Tetreault. ACL, pp. 8440–8451. DOI: 10.18653/v1/2020.acl-main.747. URL: https://www.aclweb.org/anthology/2020.acl-main.747.

Hazem, Amir, Mérieme Bouhandi, Florian Boudin, and Beatrice Daille (2020). "TermEval 2020: TALN-LS2N System for Automatic Term Extraction". In: *Proceedings of the 6th International Workshop on Computational Terminology*. Ed. by Béatrice Daille, Kyo Kageura, and Ayla Rigouts Terryn. Marseille, France: ELRA, pp. 95–100.

ISO1087 (2019). *ISO 1087:2019: Terminology work and terminology science – Vocabulary*. Standard. Geneva, CH: International Organization for Standardization.

Lang, Christian, Lennart Wachowiak, Barbara Heinisch, and Dagmar Gromann (2021). "Transforming Term Extraction: Transformer-Based Approaches to Multilingual Term Extraction Across Domains". In: *Findings of the Association for Computational Linguistics: ACL-IJCNLP 2021*. ACL, pp. 3607–3620. DOI: 10.18653/v1/2021.findings-acl.316.

Sadvilkar, Nipun and Mark Neumann (2020). "PySBD: Pragmatic Sentence Boundary Disambiguation". In: *Proceedings of Second Workshop for NLP Open Source Software (NLP-OSS)*. ACL, pp. 110–114.

Wachowiak, Lennart, Christian Lang, Barbara Heinisch, and Dagmar Gromann (2020). "CogALex-VI Shared Task: Transrelation - A Robust Multilingual Language Model for Multilingual Relation Identification". In: *Proceedings of the Workshop on the Cognitive Aspects of the Lexicon*. Ed. by Rong Xiang, Emmanuele Chersoni, Luca Iacoponi, and Enrico Santus. ACL, pp. 59–64.

Wachowiak, Lennart, Christian Lang, Barbara Heinisch, and Dagmar Gromann (2021). "Towards Learning Terminological Concept Systems from Multilingual Natural Language Text". In: *3rd Conference on Language, Data and Knowledge (LDK 2021)*. Ed. by Dagmar Gromann, Gilles Sérasset, Thierry Declerck, John P. McCrae, Jorge Gracia, Julia Bosque-Gil, Fernando Bobillo, and Barbara Heinisch. Vol. 93. Open Access Series in Informatics (OASIcs). Dagstuhl, Germany: Schloss Dagstuhl – Leibniz-Zentrum für Informatik, 22:1–22:18. DOI: 10.4230/OASIcs.LDK.2021.22.

Xue, Linting, Noah Constant, Adam Roberts, Mihir Kale, Rami Al-Rfou, Aditya Siddhant, Aditya Barua, and Colin Raffel (2021). "mT5: A Massively Multilingual Pre-trained Text-to-Text Transformer". In: *Proceedings of the 2021 Conference of the North American Chapter of the Association for Computational Linguistics: Human Language Technologies*. ACL, pp. 483–498. DOI: 10.18653/v1/2021.naacl-main.41.

Chapter 19
Italian EVALITA Benchmark Linguistic Resources, NLP Services and Tools

Viviana Patti, Valerio Basile, Andrea Bolioli, Alessio Bosca, Cristina Bosco, Michael Fell, and Rossella Varvara

Abstract Starting from the first edition held in 2007, EVALITA is the initiative for the evaluation of Natural Language Processing tools for Italian. We describe the EVALITA4ELG project, whose main aim is to systematically collect the resources released as benchmarks for this evaluation campaign, and make them easily accessible through the European Language Grid platform. The collection is moreover integrated with systems and baselines as a pool of web services with a common interface, deployed on a dedicated hardware infrastructure.

1 Overview and Objectives of the Pilot Project

In Natural Language Processing (NLP), periodic campaigns are a popular means to set benchmarks for specific tasks, stimulate the development of comparable systems and ultimately promote research advancement (Nissim et al. 2017). The validation of NLP models on different datasets strongly depends on the possibility of generalising their results on data and languages other than those on which they have been trained and tested (Magnini et al. 2008). Recent trends are pushing towards proposing benchmarks for multiple tasks (Wang et al. 2018), or for testing the adaptability of systems to different textual domains, genres, and languages, including under-researched and under-resourced ones. The recent specific emphasis on multilingual assessment is also driven by a growing awareness that language technologies can help promote multilingualism and linguistic diversity (Joshi et al. 2020). In this context, the EVALITA4ELG project integrates linguistic resources and language technologies developed under the umbrella of the EVALITA evaluation campaign into the European Language Grid.

Viviana Patti · Valerio Basile · Cristina Bosco · Michael Fell · Rossella Varvara
University of Turin, Italy, viviana.patti@unito.it, valerio.basile@unito.it, cristina.bosco@unito.it, michael.fell@unito.it, rossella.varvara@unito.it

Andrea Bolioli · Alessio Bosca
CELI, Italy, andrea.bolioli@h-farm.com, alessio.bosca@h-farm.com

G. Rehm (ed.), *European Language Grid*, Cognitive Technologies,
https://doi.org/10.1007/978-3-031-17258-8_19

EVALITA[1] is an initiative of the Italian Association for Computational Linguistics (Associazione Italiana di Linguistica Computazionale, AILC[2]). Since 2007, it has been providing a shared framework where different systems and approaches can be evaluated and compared with each other with respect to a large variety of tasks, organised by the Italian research community. The focus of EVALITA is to support the advancement of methodologies and techniques for natural language and speech processing in an historical perspective, beyond the performance improvement, favouring reproducibility and cross-community engagement.

The main goal of the EVALITA4ELG project is to leverage more than a decade of findings of the Italian NLP community, in order to provide easier access to resources and tools for Italian through ELG. We worked towards the achievement of multiples goals, namely: (i) a survey of the tasks organised in the seven editions of EVALITA, released as a knowledge graph; (ii) an anonymisation procedure for improving compliance with current data standard policies; (iii) the integration of resources and systems developed during EVALITA into the ELG platform; (iv) the creation of a unified benchmark for evaluating Italian Natural Language Understanding (NLU); (v) the dissemination of a shared protocol and a set of best practices to describe new resources and tasks in a format that allows a quick integration of metadata into the European Language Grid.

2 Methodology

We started by surveying the tasks organised in EVALITA, collecting the resources and their metadata for upload, and organising this set of information in an ontology. We anonymised the resources according to the current policies for the protection of people's privacy. Finally, we integrated systems and baselines as a pool of web services with a common interface.

2.1 Surveying the EVALITA Tasks

Starting in 2007, EVALITA has been devoted to the evaluation of NLP tools for Italian, providing a shared framework in which participating systems are evaluated on a growing set of different tasks. Rather than being focused on a single task, EVALITA has always been characterised by a wider variety of tasks: each edition of the EVALITA campaign, held in 2007 (Magnini et al. 2008), 2009, 2011 (Magnini et al. 2013), 2014 (Attardi et al. 2015), 2016 (P. Basile et al. 2017), 2018 (Caselli et al. 2018) and 2020 (V. Basile et al. 2020), has been organised around a set of shared tasks dealing with both written and spoken language, varying with respect to the

---

[1] http://www.evalita.it

[2] https://www.ai-lc.it

challenges tackled and datasets used. The number of tasks has considerably grown, from five tasks, in the first edition in 2007, to 14 tasks in the latest edition held in 2020. Following the trends of other national and international evaluation campaigns, like, e. g., SemEval[3], the typology of tasks also evolved, progressively including a larger variety of exercises oriented to semantics and pragmatics. In particular, the 2016 edition brought a focus on social media data and on the use of shared data across tasks. Open access to resources and research artifacts is deemed crucial for the advancement of the state of the art (Caselli et al. 2018) and the availability of shared evaluation benchmarks is crucial for fostering reproducibility and comparability of results. Organisers were encouraged to collaborate, stimulated to the creation of a shared test set across tasks, and to eventually share all resources with a wider audience. This has resulted in the creation of GitHub public repositories.[4]

2.2 The EVALITA Knowledge Graph

Starting from the semi-structured repositories mentioned in the previous section and from the information collected by surveying seven editions of EVALITA, we built a knowledge graph (KG) that provides the essential information about the editions of the EVALITA evaluation campaign. The KG describes EVALITA in terms of organised tasks, but also of people and institutions that constitute the EVALITA community throughout the years. The KG is structured around an ontology implemented in OWL and it is available both on the website of the EVALITA4ELG project[5] and as a service on the ELG platform. The current version of the ontology comprises 148 classes, 37 object properties and nine data properties. The ontology and the KG are thoroughly described in Patti et al. (2020). As an example, Figure 1 depicts the structure of the KG around the HaSpeeDe2018 task.

The knowledge graph can be queried through a SPARQL endpoint, which allows to inspect the ontology by selecting some variables that occur among the set of triples (subject, predicate, object) composing the knowledge graph. It is thus possible to answer relevant questions related to the EVALITA campaign, extracting information from the KG such as, e. g., "What is the total number of institutions involved as organisers of tasks in all seven EVALITA campaigns?":

```
SELECT  (COUNT(distinct ?institution) AS ?totalInstitutions)
where {
   ?task e4e:hasInstitution ?institution.
}
>>>> result: 55 <<<<
```

---

[3] https://semeval.github.io
[4] https://github.com/evalita2016/data
[5] http://evalita4elg.di.unito.it

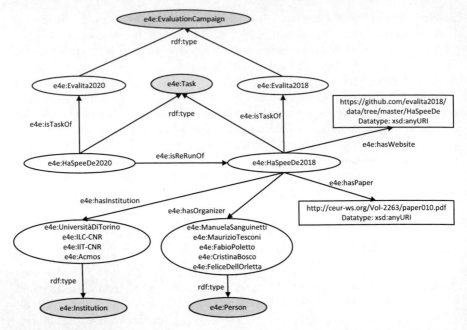

Fig. 1 EVALITA knowledge graph; primary classes are colored and their relations illustrated around the HaSpeeDe2018 task

2.3 Anonymisation of Resources

The EVALITA resources to be made accessible in the ELG platform had to be carefully checked and made compliant with the current policies about data releasing and sharing (e. g., GDPR, Rangel and Rosso 2018), therefore particular attention has been paid to data anonymisation. The datasets collected for EVALITA4ELG were anonymised relying on an automatic anonymisation tool developed in the context of the AnonymAI research project, and then manually reviewed in order to assess their quality. AnonymAI is a nine months research project co-financed by the H2020 project NGI Trust focusing on providing legally compliant anonymisation profiles customised to the needs of end users.

The anonymisation profile applied to the EVALITA4ELG dataset detects and masks person names, phone numbers, email addresses, mentions/replies/retweets, and URLs. The most frequent entities that were masked in the anonymisation process consist of person names and mentions (e. g., in the SardiStance dataset about 50 person names and 150 mentions).

2.4 Release of Data and Models through ELG

At the time of this writing, 51 Language Resources and Technologies are linked to the EVALITA4ELG project in ELG.[6] Eight services were fully integrated into ELG: four of them from the EVALITA 2018 edition, and four of them from the most recent EVALITA 2020 edition. Of the 2018 systems, three are hate speech detection systems (HaSpeeDe 2018 task) and one is Gender Detection (GxG). Of the 2020 systems, two are hate speech detectors (HaSpeeDe 2020 task), one is a POS tagger for spoken language (KIPoS task), and one is a misogyny detection system (AMI task). All datasets and services are accessible interactively from the ELG website or programmatically by means of REST API calls or the ELG-provided Python SDK.

3 Conclusions and Results of the Pilot Project

EVALITA4ELG has been a successful effort towards the inclusion of resources for the Italian language in the European Language Grid. We created a catalogue of resources and models developed during the various editions of the EVALITA campaign, designed in the form of a knowledge graph that can be inspected through SPARQL queries. We collected the original distribution of the resources used for EVALITA tasks and we created 44 entries. For 13 resources, together with CELI, we developed and applied an anonymisation procedure to mask personal and sensitive data. We integrated eight available systems from different tasks into ELG. Finally, we organised an event on September 2021 with hybrid participation[7], including an overview of the project and the results obtained, a tutorial about integrating systems and resources on ELG, and a round table with 14 invited speakers chosen among the most active organisers of tasks of EVALITA.

Acknowledgements The work described in this article has received funding from the EU project European Language Grid as one of its pilot projects. The work has also received funding from the EU's Horizon 2020 research and innovation programme under grant agreement no. 825618 (AnonymAI, NGI Trust).

References

Attardi, Giuseppe, Valerio Basile, Cristina Bosco, Tommaso Caselli, Felice Dell'Orletta, Simonetta Montemagni, Viviana Patti, Maria Simi, and Rachele Sprugnoli (2015). "State of the Art Language Technologies for Italian: The EVALITA 2014 Perspective". In: *Intelligenza Artificiale* 9, pp. 43–61.

---

[6] https://live.european-language-grid.eu/catalogue/project/1397

[7] http://evalita4elg.di.unito.it/conference

Basile, Pierpaolo, Malvina Nissim, Rachele Sprugnoli, Viviana Patti, and Francesco Cutugno (2017). "EVALITA Goes Social: Tasks, Data, and Community at the 2016 Edition". In: *Italian Journal of Computational Linguistics* 3.1, pp. 93–127.

Basile, Valerio, Danilo Croce, Maria Di Maro, and Lucia C. Passaro (2020). "EVALITA 2020: Overview of the 7th Evaluation Campaign of Natural Language Processing and Speech Tools for Italian". In: *Proc. of the 7th Evaluation Campaign of Natural Language Processing and Speech Tools for Italian. Final Workshop (EVALITA 2020), 17 Dec. 2020*. Vol. 2765. CEUR Workshop Proceedings.

Caselli, Tommaso, Nicole Novielli, Viviana Patti, and Paolo Rosso (2018). "Evalita 2018: Overview on the 6th Evaluation Campaign of Natural Language Processing and Speech Tools for Italian". In: *Proceedings of the Sixth Evaluation Campaign of Natural Language Processing and Speech Tools for Italian. Final Workshop (EVALITA 2018)*. Ed. by Tommaso Caselli, Nicole Novielli, Viviana Patti, and Paolo Rosso. Torino: CEUR Workshop Proceedings, pp. 3–8.

Joshi, Pratik, Sebastin Santy, Amar Budhiraja, Kalika Bali, and Monojit Choudhury (2020). "The State and Fate of Linguistic Diversity and Inclusion in the NLP World". In: *Proc. of the 58th Annual Meeting of the Association for Computational Linguistics*. ACL, pp. 6282–6293.

Magnini, Bernardo, Amedeo Cappelli, Fabio Tamburini, Cristina Bosco, Alessandro Mazzei, Vincenzo Lombardo, Francesca Bertagna, Nicoletta Calzolari, Antonio Toral, Valentina Bartalesi Lenzi, Rachele Sprugnoli, and Manuela Speranza (2008). "Evaluation of Natural Language Tools for Italian: EVALITA 2007". In: *Proc. of the 6th Int. Conference on Language Resources and Evaluation (LREC 2008)*. Marrakech: ELRA, pp. 2536–2543.

Magnini, Bernardo, Francesco Cutugno, Mauro Falcone, and Emanuele Pianta, eds. (2013). *Evaluation of Natural Language and Speech Tools for Italian, International Workshop, EVALITA 2011, Rome, Italy, January 24-25, 2012, Revised Selected Papers*. Vol. 7689. Lecture Notes in Computer Science. Springer. URL: https://doi.org/10.1007/978-3-642-35828-9.

Nissim, Malvina, Lasha Abzianidze, Kilian Evang, Rob van der Goot, Hessel Haagsma, Barbara Plank, and Martijn Wieling (2017). "Last Words: Sharing Is Caring: The Future of Shared Tasks". In: *Computational Linguistics* 43.4, pp. 897–904.

Patti, Viviana, Valerio Basile, Cristina Bosco, Rossella Varvara, Michael Fell, Andrea Bolioli, and Alessio Bosca (2020). "EVALITA4ELG: Italian Benchmark Linguistic Resources, NLP Services and Tools for the ELG Platform". In: *Italian Journal of Computational Linguistics* 6.6-2, pp. 105–129. DOI: https://doi.org/10.4000/ijcol.754.

Rangel, Francisco and Paolo Rosso (2018). "On the Implications of the General Data Protection Regulation on the Organisation of Evaluation Tasks". In: *Language and Law* 5.2, pp. 95–117.

Wang, Alex, Amanpreet Singh, Julian Michael, Felix Hill, Omer Levy, and Samuel Bowman (2018). "GLUE: A Multi-Task Benchmark and Analysis Platform for Natural Language Understanding". In: *Proceedings of the 2018 EMNLP Workshop BlackboxNLP: Analyzing and Interpreting Neural Networks for NLP*. Brussels: ACL, pp. 353–355.

Chapter 20
Lingsoft Solutions as Distributable Containers

Sebastian Andersson and Michael Stormbom

Abstract Lingsoft is one of the leading language technology and language service providers in the Nordic countries. In the Lingsoft Solutions as Distributable Containers (LSDISCO) project, we packaged our language technology tools for distribution as containerised services via the European Language Grid (ELG). As a result, Lingsoft's speech recognition, machine translation, proofing, and morphological analysis was made available to users of the European Language Grid. The services primarily cover Finnish (general and healthcare domain), Swedish (also Finland Swedish), Danish, Norwegian bokmål and nynorsk, and English. The distribution as containerised services is a straightforward way of making our tools available and updated on ELG and we intend to continue to update our service offerings on ELG with new tools and languages as we develop them.

1 Overview and Objectives of the Pilot Project

Lingsoft is one of the leading providers of language technology solutions in the Nordic countries and one of the 100 largest language service providers in the world. The tools and models that Lingsoft contributed to ELG via the Lingsoft Solutions as Distributable Containers (LSDISCO) project already existed and in most cases they were already actively used in production by Lingsoft or our customers. The goal of the LSDISCO project was to make those tools and models available as ELG-compatible services for ELG users (Rehm et al. 2021). This included four types of services:

- *Speech recognition*, with the supported languages being Finnish (general and healthcare domain), Swedish and Norwegian bokmål
- *Machine translation*, for language pairs involving Finnish, Swedish, and English in any combination, as well as both directions of Finnish – German

Sebastian Andersson · Michael Stormbom
Lingsoft, Finland, sebastian.andersson@lingsoft.fi, michael.stormbom@lingsoft.fi

- *Proofing, entailing spelling and grammar error detection* for Finnish, Swedish, Danish, Norwegian bokmål, and spelling for Norwegian Nynorsk and English
- *Text analysis*, entailing morphological analysis (lemmatization and morphology) and named entity recognition (NER) for Finnish, Swedish, Danish, Norwegian Bokmål, Nynorsk, and English

The end result of the project was a set of high quality NLP tools for the Nordic languages available through ELG, for both commercial and non-commercial use, allowing companies and public organisations throughout Europe to efficiently incorporate Nordic language support in their solutions and services.

2 Methodology

The four types of tools and services in scope for the LSDISCO project – speech recognition, machine translation, proofing and text analysis – have been originally developed at Lingsoft in different periods in the company and software development history and for different primary use cases. The least common denominator was a need for refactoring the tools and service architecture to comply with the ELG requirements. Especially the machine translation tools needed conversion from an internally used tool to enable also external distribution as a service via ELG.

The LSDISCO project was divided into three phases per requirements in the ELG call outline: 1. Experiment; 2. Integration; 3. Dissemination. The Experiment phase consisted of refactoring Lingsoft's tools and architecture to comply with ELG's integration requirements. This phase also included enabling a licensing mechanism for the services and creation or upgrade of the terms of service documentation. For the Integration phase, we selected the option to integrate our services to ELG via a proxy container, as this was the most practical option for us requiring the least amount of additional maintenance. This means that all calls to the ELG service are forwarded to and processed by Lingsoft's back end. Upgrades to the services in Lingsoft's back end per our normal release update cycle, e. g., model improvements, are then immediately available also in ELG. The dissemination phase consisted of advertising Lingsoft's services and the ELG platform on Lingsoft's website and in suitable forums such as conferences and trade fairs.

3 Implementation

Lingsoft's proofing, text analysis and speech recognition services were already to a large extent ready for ELG integration. The improvements made for those largely followed the existing development roadmap. The biggest implementation and refactoring effort in the LSDISCO project was for enabling serving Lingsoft's neural machine translation (NMT) to external users, in this case ELG. The NMT engine and models were migrated from a solution serving "only" Lingsoft's own translation production to the same Software as a Service infrastructure as our speech recognition. This gave us a scalable back end and the possibility to provide user credentials for NMT usage, thus making important improvements to commercialising Lingsoft's machine translation and serving also external organisations.

To integrate our services with ELG, we implemented the Lingsoft ELG adapter. The Lingsoft ELG adapter is an API proxy container, illustrated in Figure 1. It exposes the ELG platform's internal LT Service API specification compatible endpoints and acts as a proxy to the Lingsoft APIs:

ASR API   Lingsoft Speech Recognition API
NMT API   Lingsoft Machine Translation API
LMC API   Lingsoft Language Management Central API (text analysis)

In the proxy container, we implemented the conversion between the ELG and the Lingsoft API specifications. The proxy container also includes the mechanism for forwarding authentication via ELG for Lingsoft's back end service.

The Lingsoft ELG Adapter was packaged into a Docker image and submitted to DockerHub. Lingsoft then filled in the ELG XML metadata specifications for Lingsoft's services on the ELG platform, and the ELG technical team could proceed with the actual integration. The DockerHub image of the Lingsoft ELG Adapter was created for ELG, but it can be deployed by other organisations in a Docker environment and integrated with the organisation's own solutions. All that another

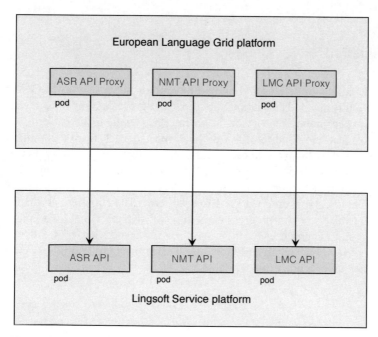

Fig. 1 API proxy containers relay Lingsoft's services to ELG

organisation would need to deploy the same Docker image into their environment are credentials from Lingsoft that allows calling the Lingsoft back end services.

As the ELG technical team preferred one service per functionality and language. This meant that Lingsoft provided a total of 35 services for ELG integration. The full set of services is presented in Table 1.

Service	Supported Languages/Domains
Speech recognition	Finnish, Finnish Healthcare, Swedish, Norwegian bokmål
Machine translation	Finnish ↔ English, English ↔ Swedish, Finnish ↔ Swedish, German ↔ Finnish
Proofing	Finnish, Finnish Healthcare, Swedish, Finland Swedish, Danish, Norwegian bokmål and nynorsk, English
Morphological analysis (incl. Lemmatization)	Finnish, Swedish, Danish, Norwegian bokmål and nynorsk, English
Named Entity Recognition (NER)	Finnish, Finnish Wikidata, Finnish YSO, Swedish, Danish, Norwegian bokmål and nynorsk, English

Table 1 Lingsoft services and languages

4 Evaluation

Generally, online guidelines and human integration support from ELG were clear and sufficiently detailed throughout the course of the project. The integrated services work per expectation in the "try out" user interface on the ELG platform.

Lingsoft also provided the ELG project with feedback from a commercial perspective regarding the integration process and platform functionality. For example, the demonstration services available in the "try out" box are quite slow. Lingsoft's speech recognition supports near real-time "live" subtitling/dictation, but this is not yet possible to demonstrate via the ELG platform. The commercial aspects of the platform are also work-in-progress at the time of writing, with no working solution for billing an ELG end user for the use of, e. g., Lingsoft's services. At present, we provide our solutions through ELG mainly for demonstration purposes, as a marketing channel, and for non-commercial use.

5 Conclusions and Results of the Pilot Project

The ELG project allowed us to upgrade our service infrastructure for easier distribution via ELG as well as through other channels. We believe that we will continue to utilise other providers' ELG resources and services for our benefit, especially open source tools and resources. From our experience with trying to utilise open source tools from the academic community, the ELG approach of researchers (and other developers) providing their open source tools as shareable docker containers with an exposed API is a great improvement over the current situation.

For Lingsoft, ELG can be seen as an additional distribution channel for tools and services we already provide. As an SME from Finland, it is expected that an official EU platform will increase the findability of our services and raise the credibility of our solutions outside of Finland, where we are well known. ELG is therefore expected to facilitate reaching customers outside of Finland and the Nordics.

We provide our tools both for commercial usage (on a Software as a Service subscription model) by companies and organisations, and for research purposes (free of charge for non-commercial use). In our internal work processes, e. g., subtitling and translation, the dockerised tools and API access is ideal, as this facilitates keeping our technology pipeline modular, and the core language technology tools easily replaceable and/or upgradable.

A centralised catalogue of European language technology, if widely adopted, will be beneficial to private providers of language technology, such as Lingsoft, for reaching new customers with our tools and services offerings. Conversely, we hope our contribution to the platform with our services benefit ELG in becoming widely adopted by providing more quality items for the ELG catalogue. Our solutions are robust and widely used with a proven track record. Our spelling and grammar tools have been distributed with the Microsoft Office suite and are used by the Finnish Digital and Population Data Agency, as well as several of the largest newspapers in Sweden; we have collaborated with the Swedish Post and Telecom Authority and the public service broadcaster SVT in creating speech-to-text for Swedish and our Finnish speech-to-text is in use for transcription in a number of Finnish organisations, including the Finnish parliament.

As ELG grows, we believe we will get good exposure for our services by having them on display at ELG. The service adapter ELG integration allows us to continuously improve the content of our ELG services with a minimum of additional maintenance effort. We also intend to continue to release new tools and covered languages in line with our general development roadmap.

Lingsoft is proud to have been one of the selected organisations for the ELG integration projects. We look forward to being part of the continued development of the ELG platform and hope that a substantial part of the ELG visions are fulfilled in the near future.

Lingsoft's services can be found in the European Language Grid.[1]

---

[1] https://live.european-language-grid.eu/catalogue/search/Lingsoft

Acknowledgements The work described in this article has received funding from the EU project European Language Grid as one of its pilot projects.

References

Rehm, Georg, Stelios Piperidis, Kalina Bontcheva, Jan Hajic, Victoria Arranz, Andrejs Vasiļjevs, Gerhard Backfried, José Manuel Gómez Pérez, Ulrich Germann, Rémi Calizzano, Nils Feldhus, Stefanie Hegele, Florian Kintzel, Katrin Marheinecke, Julian Moreno-Schneider, Dimitris Galanis, Penny Labropoulou, Miltos Deligiannis, Katerina Gkirtzou, Athanasia Kolovou, Dimitris Gkoumas, Leon Voukoutis, Ian Roberts, Jana Hamrlová, Dusan Varis, Lukáš Kačena, Khalid Choukri, Valérie Mapelli, Mickaël Rigault, Jūlija Meļņika, Miro Janosik, Katja Prinz, Andres Garcia-Silva, Cristian Berrio, Ondrej Klejch, and Steve Renals (2021). "European Language Grid: A Joint Platform for the European Language Technology Community". In: *Proceedings of the 16th Conference of the European Chapter of the Association for Computational Linguistics: System Demonstrations (EACL 2021)*. Kyiv, Ukraine: ACL, pp. 221–230. URL: https://www.aclweb.org/anthology/2021.eacl-demos.26.pdf.

Chapter 21
Motion Capture 3D Sign Language Resources

Zdeněk Krňoul, Pavel Jedlička, Miloš Železný, and Luděk Müller

Abstract The new 3D motion capture data corpus expands the portfolio of existing language resources by a corpus of 18 hours of Czech sign language. This helps alleviate the current problem, which is a critical lack of quality data necessary for research and subsequent deployment of machine learning techniques in this area. We currently provide the largest collection of annotated sign language recordings acquired by state-of-the-art 3D human body recording technology for the successful future deployment of communication technologies, especially machine translation and sign language synthesis.

1 Overview and Objectives of the Pilot Project

Sign language (SL) is a natural means of communication for deaf people. About 70 million people use SL as their first language and there are more than 100 different dialects used around the world. Although significant progress has been made in recent years in the field of language machine learning techniques, the field of SL processing struggles with a critical lack of quality data needed for the successful application of these techniques. SL resources are scarce – they consist of small SL corpora usually designed for a specific domain such as linguistics or computer science. There are some motion capture datasets for American Sign Language (ASL) and French Sign Language (Lu and Huenerfauth 2010; Naert et al. 2017) with a total recorded time of motion of up to 60 minutes. The situation is even worse for "small" languages.

The 3D reconstruction of human body motion using images and depth cameras is a common approach for capturing the movement of the human body (MMPose Contributors 2020). Current large SL datasets are mostly based on 2D RGB videos (Vaezi Joze and Koller 2019; Zelinka and Kanis 2020). The main goal of our project is to deliver a large 3D motion dataset collected using high precision optical marker-based motion capture and to extend the existing ELG portfolio of language resources

Zdeněk Krňoul · Pavel Jedlička · Miloš Železný · Luděk Müller
University of West Bohemia, Czech Republic, zdkrnoul@ntis.zcu.cz, jedlicka@ntis.zcu.cz, zelezny@ntis.zcu.cz, muller@kky.zcu.cz

© The Author(s) 2023
G. Rehm (ed.), *European Language Grid*, Cognitive Technologies,
https://doi.org/10.1007/978-3-031-17258-8_21

by Czech sign language (CSE) data. For comparison SIGNUM, one of the largest video-based SL datasets, contains approximately 55 hours of SL recordings (Koller et al. 2015) and one of the largest 3D motion capture datasets contains only 60 minutes of SL recordings (Naert et al. 2017).

Motion capture technology guarantees precise recording of the signer's movements in 3D space at the cost of a more complex preparation phase compared to standard video recording. Optical marker-based motion capture has become the industry standard for capturing movement of the human body. In Jedlička et al. (2020), we collected the first 3D motion capture dataset for CSE, covering the weather forecast domain. It has a rather limited size and contains recordings of one signer only.

Our contribution can be summarised as follows:

- Proof of concept of large-scale motion capture recording of multiple SL speakers;
- Provide 3D motion capture data to cover wider domains, grammatical context and more signers. We perform proper data post-processing, annotate glosses, and develop tools for data extraction from the collected dataset;
- The largest SL motion capture dataset consisting of recordings of continuous SL phrases and a vocabulary of six native SL speakers from carefully selected domains, in total more than 18 hours;
- Tools that allow searching for individual glosses, phrases, or small movement sub-units (e. g., given hand shape/action) in the dataset.

2 Methodology and Experiment

A new recording procedure for a large amount of 3D motion capturing of SL was investigated to ensure sufficient diversity of SL speakers, grammar, and sign contexts. This makes the new language resource more versatile and useful in many different research fields such as further linguistic and SL motion analyses. The integral part of the experiment is data processing.

In Jedlička et al. (2020), the experimental recording setup with VICON 18 cameras was used as proof of the intended concept. The negative aspect of this setup was its high complexity; the setup was very time demanding and not suitable for large-scale data and multiple speakers.

The new procedure simplifies the process by dividing the setup into two separate parts: large-scale body movement and small-scale, highly detailed finger movement are recorded with two separate motion capture camera setups, each of which uses a reduced number of capture cameras and is adjusted slightly for different speakers.

2.1 Recording Setup

We used our laboratory equipment, i.e., the VICON motion capture system with eight cameras. We extended it with a standard color video camera for a reference video. The frame rate was 100 frames per second (fps) for the motion capture and 25 fps for the reference video. The VICON system records movement using passive retro-reflexive markers attached to the human body. Movement is modeled as a set of movements of the rigid parts connected by the skeleton; the marks are placed on the poles of the rotation axis of the main skeleton joints. Each body part is defined by at least four markers, except fingertips, see Figure 1.

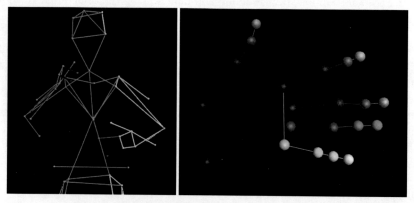

Fig. 1 Visualisation of SL body marker setup (left) and SL hand-shape marker setup (right)

The SL body marker setup is based on marker positions defined by the VICON three-finger standard. It uses a total of 43 markers for tracking upper body, head, arms, and palms movement. A simple hand pose is provided at the same time and incorporates tracking of thumb, index, and little fingertips. Moreover, this setup includes face tracking providing a non-manual component of SL, that is reduced to seven facial markers. The SL hand-shape marker setup is designed for detailed hand-shapes recording. Each hand-shape is recorded separately. Data is recorded for the right hand only. The movement starts from the relaxed hand-shape, then changes to the given hand-shape and back to the relaxed hand-shape. For both setups, data capturing was supervised by CSE linguists.

2.2 Data Annotation

An essential step is the annotation of captured SL utterances. We use time-synchron-ised reference video, the ELAN tool (Figure 2) and SL experts. The annotation of a sign is done by giving the information of the sign's meaning (gloss), and the right and the left hand-shape. If the sign consists of more than one defined hand-shape, the hand-shapes are annotated as a set of hand-shapes. Both the activities are very laborious and time-consuming. To successfully complete this task, we involved several trained annotators who worked in parallel.

2.3 Data Post-processing

Post-processing consists of data-cleaning, whole-body motion reconstruction, and data-solving. Data-cleaning removes noise and fills gaps in the raw 3D data caused by frequent mutual occlusions of markers during signing, and other noise caused by the environment. Motion reconstruction and data-solving recalculate marker positions into the movement of the skeletal model.

The data of both setups was post-processed. We reconstructed small gaps by the interpolation standard technique as long as the trajectory was simple enough. Note, that the recording speed is 100 fps, which is fast enough to contain minimal changes in trajectory between frames. We used semi-automatic 3D reconstruction of marker trajectories and labeling, and manual cleaning of swaps and gaps. For the body parts defined by at least four markers, filling in the trajectories of the marker is well automatised because at least three points are enough to define the missing position.

The body marker setup uses only one marker per fingertip and some larger gaps caused by more complex self-occlusions of body parts can obscure three or more markers in one rigid segment. Post-processing in those cases is more complicated and gaps must be filled in manually.

The full SL body movement is achieved as a composition of the body movement and corresponding data of the hand-shapes setup. For this purpose, the annotation of hand-shapes provides us temporal segmentation of the recordings. Thus the fingertip motion segments can provide information about dynamic changes during the performance of a particular SL hand-shape in a particular data frame.

The middle part of a given segment is always completed according to the hand-shape(s) assigned by the annotation. We captured full fingers motion only for the transition of the given hand-shape from and to the neutral hand-shape. Thus, for the other frames of the segment, the nearest hand pose with the smallest reconstruction

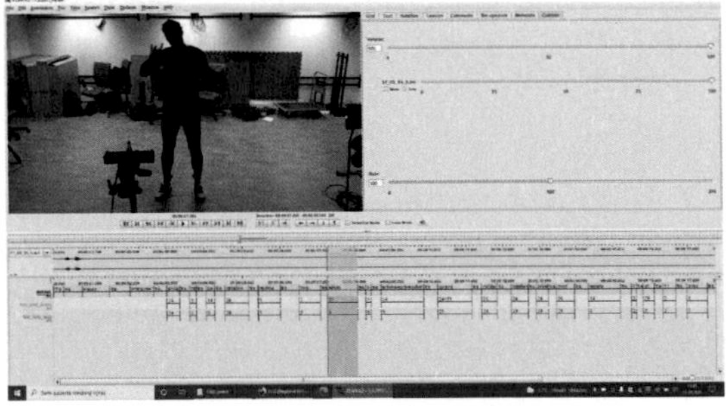

Fig. 2 Example of annotation work in ELAN, specifically designed software for the analysis of sign languages, and gestures

error can be used. We consider only those frames that have an alignment error below a given threshold. The remaining frames will have gaps in the final trajectories.

We solved the above problem as point-set alignment via Procrustes analysis that arises especially in tasks like 3D point cloud data registration. The rigid transformation of two sets of points on top of each other minimises the total distance in 3D between the corresponding markers (Arun et al. 1987). Since the data is noisy, it minimises the least-squares error:

$$err = \sum_{i=1}^{N} ||RM_f^i + t - M_{rf}^i||, \tag{1}$$

where M_f and M_{rf} are current and reference frame(s) respectively as a set of 3D points with known correspondences, R is the rotation matrix and t the translation vector. We define $N = 7$ as three fingertips (thumb, index, little finger), two wrist markers, and two knuckles of the index and little fingers. We aligned just the rotation and translation because the 3D transformation preserves the shape and size (same hand-shape and SL speaker). For the left hand, we mirrored the reference frame(s).

The last step is data-solving. It is a process of reconstruction of the 3D motion of the skeleton from the marker trajectories. For this purpose, we use the VICON software. The skeleton is well defined to directly control the SL avatar animation or handle animation retargeting.

2.4 Dataset Parameters

We limited the linguistic domain to two specific fields to reduce the number of unique signs. Weather forecasts and animal descriptions from the zoological garden domain were selected by CSE linguists. We were also given a list of all hand-shapes which occur in these domains. The dataset is collected from six SL speakers, who differ in their body size, age, and gender.

3 Conclusions and Results of the Pilot Project

SLs are not sufficiently supported through technologies and have only fragmented, weak, or no support at all. Our ELG pilot project offers a new SL resource designed for the development of language technologies (LTs) and multilingual services for Czech. The results contribute to the establishment of the Digital Single Market as one of ELG's objectives. In contrast to the all-in-one recording setup, the body movement is recorded separately from the highly detailed recording of hand poses. This separation reduces the camera setup complexity and the complexity of data during post-processing, which makes SL recording more flexible and adjustments for new SL speakers or data easier.

The project delivered a professionally created SL dataset via state-of-the-art 3D motion capture technology. The project provides data for the wider research community through ELG. We have recorded 18 hours of sign language and recorded six different speakers for two different domains.

We assume our results will be beneficial for other applications such as next generation SL synthesis that uses a 3D animated avatar for natural human movement reproduction or SL analysis or gesture recognition and classification in general.

Acknowledgements The work described in this article has received funding from the EU project European Language Grid as one of its pilot projects.

References

Arun, K. S., T. S. Huang, and S. D. Blostein (1987). "Least-Squares Fitting of Two 3-D Point Sets". In: *IEEE Transactions on Pattern Analysis and Machine Intelligence* PAMI-9.5, pp. 698–700. DOI: 10.1109/TPAMI.1987.4767965.

Jedlička, Pavel, Zdeněk Krňoul, Jakub Kanis, and Miloš Železný (2020). "Sign Language Motion Capture Dataset for Data-driven Synthesis". In: *Proceedings of the LREC2020*. Marseille, France: ELRA, pp. 101–106.

Koller, Oscar, Jens Forster, and Hermann Ney (2015). "Continuous sign language recognition: Towards large vocabulary statistical recognition systems handling multiple signers". In: *Computer Vision and Image Understanding* 141. Pose & Gesture, pp. 108–125.

Lu, Pengfei and Matt Huenerfauth (2010). "Collecting a motion-capture corpus of American Sign Language for data-driven generation research". In: *Proceedings of the NAACL HLT 2010 Workshop on Speech and Language Processing for Assistive Technologies*. ACL, pp. 89–97.

MMPose Contributors (2020). *OpenMMLab Pose Estimation Toolbox and Benchmark*. URL: https://github.com/open-mmlab/mmpose.

Naert, Lucie, Caroline Larboulette, and Sylvie Gibet (2017). "Coarticulation Analysis for Sign Language Synthesis". In: *Universal Access in Human – Computer Interaction. Designing Novel Interactions*. Cham: Springer, pp. 55–75.

Vaezi Joze, Hamid and Oscar Koller (2019). "MS-ASL: A Large-Scale Data Set and Benchmark for Understanding American Sign Language". In: *BMVC*.

Zelinka, Jan and Jakub Kanis (2020). "Neural Sign Language Synthesis: Words Are Our Glosses". In: *2020 IEEE Winter Conference on Applications of Computer Vision (WACV)*, pp. 3384–3392. DOI: 10.1109/WACV45572.2020.9093516.

Chapter 22
Multilingual Image Corpus

Svetla Koeva

Abstract The ELG pilot project Multilingual Image Corpus (MIC 21) provides a large image dataset with annotated objects and multilingual descriptions in 25 languages. Our main contributions are: the provision of a large collection of high-quality, copyright-free images; the formulation of an ontology of visual objects based on WordNet noun hierarchies; precise manual correction of automatic image segmentation and annotation of object classes; and association of objects and images with extended multilingual descriptions. The dataset is designed for image classification, object detection and semantic segmentation. It can be also used for multilingual image caption generation, image-to-text alignment and automatic question answering for images and videos.

1 Overview and Objectives of the Pilot Project

Significant progress has been achieved in many multimodal tasks, such as image caption generation, aligning sentences with images in various types of multimodal documents and visual question answering. The shift of traditional vision methods challenged by multimodal big data motivates the creation of a new image dataset, the Multilingual Image Corpus (MIC21).

The MIC21 dataset is characterised by carefully selected images from thematically related domains and precise manual annotation for segmentation and classification of objects in over 20,000 images. The annotation is performed by drawing of or correcting automatically generated polygons, from which bounding boxes are automatically constructed. This allows for wide application of the dataset in various computer vision tasks: image classification, recognition and classification of single objects in an image or of all object instances in an image (semantic segmentation).

The annotation classes which are used belong to a specially designed ontology of visual objects which provides options for extracting relationships between objects in images; the construction of diverse datasets with different levels of granularity of

Svetla Koeva

Institute for Bulgarian Language, Bulgarian Academy of Sciences, Bulgaria, svetla@dcl.bas.bg

© The Author(s) 2023

G. Rehm (ed.), *European Language Grid*, Cognitive Technologies,
https://doi.org/10.1007/978-3-031-17258-8_22

object classes; and the compilation of appropriate sets of images illustrating different thematic domains. The ontology classes and their definitions, accompanied by illustrative examples, have been translated into 25 languages, which can be used for automatic interpretation of an image, caption generation and alignment of images with short texts such as questions and answers about the image content.

2 Methodology

We have divided the annotation process into four main stages: 1. definition of an ontology of visual objects; 2. collection of appropriate images; 3. automatic object segmentation and classification; and manual correction of object segmentation and manual classification of objects. The dataset contains four thematic domains (sport, transport, arts, security), which group highly related dominant classes such as *Tennis player*, *Soccer player*, *Limousine*, *Taxi*, *Singer*, *Violinist*, *Fire engine*, and *Police boat* in 130 subsets of images. We have used the COCO Annotator (Brooks 2019), which allows for collaborative work within a project, and offers tracking object instances and labelling objects with disconnected visible parts.

2.1 Ontology of Visual Objects

In current practice, WordNet is typically used in generating text queries for the creation of search-based image collections. For example, ImageNet uses 21841 synsets for image collection and their labeling (Russakovsky et al. 2015). A Visual Concept Ontology is proposed which organises concepts (Botorek et al. 2014), containing 14 top-level ontology classes divided into 90 more specific classes. Other datasets use a hierarchical organisation of object classes and mutually exclusive classes (Caesar et al. 2018), however, the number of concepts is usually relatively small.

The ontology of visual objects created for MIC21 embraces concepts that are thematically related and can be depicted in images. The four thematic domains (sport, transport, arts, security) are represented by 137 dominant classes, which show the main "players" within these domains. The ontology also embraces the hypernyms of the dominant classes up to the highest hypernym, which denotes a concrete object, and non-hierarchically related classes (called attributes) (Koeva 2021). The type of dominant class and the type of attribute class determine the type of the relation between them: *has instrument*, *wears*, *uses*, *has part*, etc. For example, the attribute classes for *Billiard player* are *Pool table*, *Billiard ball*, and *Cue*, while for *Bowler* – *Bowling alley*, *Bowl*, *Bowling pin*, *Bowling shoe* etc.; the hypernym classes for *Billiard player* and *Bowler* are *Player*, *Contestant* and *Person*.

Some of the classes and relations are inherited from WordNet (Miller et al. 1990). Additional classes and relations are included in the ontology in case they are not present in WordNet, for example *Bowler wears Bowling shoes*. Using the ontology of visual objects ensures the selection of mutually exclusive classes; the interconnectivity of classes by means of formal relations and an easy extension of the ontology with more concepts corresponding to visual objects.

2.2 Collection of Images and Metadata

The images in the dataset are collected from a range of repositories offering APIs: Wikimedia (images with Public Domain License or Non-copyright restrictions license)[1]; Pexels (images with a free Pexels license allowing free use and modifications)[2]; Flickr (images with Creative Commons Attribution License, Creative Commons Attribution ShareAlike License, no known copyright restrictions, Public Domain Dedication, Public Domain Mark)[3]; Pixabay (images with a free Pixabay license allowing free use, modifications and redistribution)[4]. The Creative Commons Search API is also used for searches on content available under Creative Commons licenses[5]. Over 750,000 images were collected in total and automatically filtered further by image dimensions, license types and for duplication. Each image is equipped with metadata description in JSON format: *filepath*; *source* (name of the repository or service used to obtain the image); *sourceURL* (URL of this repository or service); *license*; *author* (if available); *authorURL* (if available); *domain* (the domain the image belongs to); *width and height* (in pixels) etc.

3 Criteria for the Selection of Images

After the collection of images, we performed additional manual selection to ensure the quality of the dataset, applying the following criteria: i) The image has to contain a clearly presented object described by a given dominant class; ii) The object should (preferably) have no occluded parts; iii) The target object should be in its usual environment and in a position or use that is normal for its activity or purpose; iv) The instances of the target object in different images should not represent one and the same person, animal or artefact; v) Images with small objects, unfocused objects in the background or images with low quality are not selected; vi) Images which represent collages of photos or are post-processed are not selected.

The final selection of images is triple-checked independently by different experts: after the automatic collection, after the automatic generation of segmentation masks and during manual annotation.

---

[1] https://commons.wikimedia.org/wiki/Commons:Licensing

[2] https://www.pexels.com/license/

[3] https://www.flickr.com/services/developer/api/

[4] https://pixabay.com/service/license/

[5] https://api.creativecommons.org/docs/

3.1 Generation and Evaluation of Suggestions

To accelerate the manual annotation, an image processing pipeline for object detection and segmentation was developed. Two software packages – YOLACT (Bolya et al. 2019) and DETECTRON2 (Wu et al. 2019), and Fast R-CNN (Girshick 2015) models trained on the COCO dataset (Lin et al. 2014) were used for the generation of annotation suggestions. We also performed automatic relabelling for some of the predicted classes (usually for the dominant class and for some of its attribute classes), e. g., the COCO category *Person* within the subset *Golf* from the thematic domain *Sport* is replaced with the class *Golf player*. The performance of the models was evaluated over all domain-specific datasets within the domain *Sport* (see Figure 1).

Fig. 1 Annotation results: human (left), YOLACT (middle) DETECTRON2 (right)

The results demonstrate similar behaviour with a slight predominance of one of the models, which was further used to predict the object classes in the datasets from the other three thematic domains. Altogether 253,980 segmentation masks were automatically generated, 194,212 of which were manually adjusted.

3.2 Annotation Protocol

The task for annotators was to outline polygons for individual objects in the image (either by approving or correcting the automatic segmentation or by creating new polygons) and to classify the objects against the classes from the predefined ontology. The annotation follows several conventions:

- An object within an image is annotated if it represents an instance of a concept included in the ontology.
- All objects from the selected dominant class and its attribute classes are annotated (for example, *Gondola* and the related objects *Gondolier* and *Oar*).
- If the object can be associated with different classes, this is recorded within the metadata (for example, for a female soldier – *Soldier* and *Woman*).

Quality control is provided by a second annotator who validates the implementation of the conventions and discusses the quality with the annotation group on a regular basis. If necessary, some of the images are re-annotated.

4 Multilingual Classes

For the purpose of the multilingual description of the images, all ontology classes have been translated into 25 languages: English (Princeton WordNet), Albanian, Bulgarian, Basque, Catalan, Croatian, Danish, Dutch, Galician, German, Greek, Finnish, French, Icelandic, Italian, Lithuanian, Polish, Portuguese, Romanian, Russian, Serbian, Slovak, Slovene, Spanish, and Swedish.

Openly available wordnets have been used from the Extended Open Multilingual WordNet.[6] For the ontology classes which are not inherited from WordNet the appropriate WordNet hypernyms are used. Where WordNet translations are not available, additional sources of translations as BabelNet[7] are employed. The multilingual translations of classes are presented in a separate JSON file which contains information about the language and the translation source. The translations of the ontology classes are accompanied by their synonyms, the concept definition and usage examples (if available in the sources).

5 Conclusions and Results of the Pilot Project

The Multilingual Image Corpus provides fully annotated objects within images with segmentation masks, classified according to an ontology of visual objects, thus offering data to train models specialised in object detection, segmentation and classification (Table 1). The ontology of visual objects allows easy integration of annotated images in different datasets as well as learning the associations between objects in images. The ontology classes are translated into 25 languages and supplied with definitions and usage examples. The explicit association of objects and images with appropriate text fragments is relevant for multilingual image caption generation, image-to-text alignment and automatic question answering for images and video.

Domain	Subsets	Number of Images	Number of Annotations
Sport	40	6,915	65,482
Transport	50	7,710	78,172
Arts	25	3,854	24,217
Security	15	2,837	35,916
MIC21	130	21,316	203,797

Table 1 Multilingual Image Corpus: basic statistics

---

[6] http://compling.hss.ntu.edu.sg/omw/summx.html

[7] https://babelnet.org/guide

All annotations and image metadata are available for commercial and non-commercial purposes in accordance with the Creative Commons Attribution-ShareAlike 4.0 International (CC BY-SA 4.0).

Acknowledgements The work described in this article has received funding from the EU project European Language Grid as one of its pilot projects.

References

Bolya, Daniel, Chong Zhou, Fanyi Xiao, and Yong Jae Lee (2019). "YOLACT: Real-time Instance Segmentation". In: pp. 9156–9165. DOI: 10.1109/ICCV.2019.00925.

Botorek, Jan, Petra Budíková, and Pavel Zezula (2014). "Visual Concept Ontology for Image Annotations". In: *CoRR*. URL: http://arxiv.org/abs/1412.6082.

Brooks, Justin (2019). *COCO Annotator*. URL: https://github.com/jsbroks/coco-annotator/.

Caesar, Holger, Jasper Uijlings, and Vittorio Ferrari (2018). "COCO-Stuff: Thing and Stuff Classes in Context". In: *Conference on Computer Vision and Pattern Recognition*, pp. 1209–1218.

Girshick, Ross (2015). "Fast R-CNN". In: pp. 1440–1448. DOI: 10.1109/ICCV.2015.169.

Koeva, Svetla (2021). "Multilingual Image Corpus: Annotation Protocol". In: *Proceedings of the International Conference on Recent Advances in Natural Language Processing (RANLP 2021)*. INCOMA, pp. 701–707.

Lin, Tsung-Yi, Michael Maire, Serge Belongie, Lubomir Bourdev, Ross Girshick, James Hays, Pietro Perona, Deva Ramanan, C. Lawrence Zitnick, and Piotr Dollár (2014). "Microsoft COCO: Common Objects in Context". In: *European Conference on Computer Vision (ECCV)*. Zürich, pp. 740–755.

Miller, George, R. Beckwith, Christiane Fellbaum, Derek Gross, and Katherine J. Miller (1990). "Introduction to WordNet: An on-line lexical database". In: *International Journal of Lexicography* 3, pp. 235–244.

Russakovsky, Olga, Jia Deng, Hao Su, Jonathan Krause, Sanjeev Satheesh, Sean Ma, Zhiheng Huang, Andrej Karpathy, Aditya Khosla, Michael Bernstein, Alexander C. Berg, and Li Fei-Fei (2015). "ImageNet Large Scale Visual Recognition Challenge". In: *International Journal of Computer Vision* 116, pp. 157–173.

Wu, Yuxin, Alexander Kirillov, Francisco Massa, Wan-Yen Lo, and Ross Girshick (2019). *Detectron2*. URL: https://github.com/facebookresearch/detectron2.

Chapter 23
Multilingual Knowledge Systems as Linguistic Linked Open Data

Alena Vasilevich and Michael Wetzel

Abstract Creation and re-usability of language resources in accordance with Linked Data principles is a valuable asset in the modern data world. We describe the contributions made to extend the Linguistic Linked Open Data (LLOD) stack with a new resource, Coreon MKS, bringing together concept-oriented, language-agnostic terminology management and graph-based knowledge organisation. We dwell on our approach to mirroring of Coreon's original data structure to RDF and supplying it with a SPARQL endpoint. We integrate MKS into the existing ELG infrastructure, using it as a platform for making the published MKS discoverable and retrievable via a industry-standard interface. While we apply this approach to LLOD-ify Coreon MKS, it can also provide relevant input for standardisation bodies and interoperability communities, acting as a blueprint for similar integration activities.

1 Overview and Objectives of the Pilot Project

In a world depending on knowledge sharing, data-driven businesses and research communities are concerned with the creation, sharing, and use of language resources in accordance with Linked Data principles, which ensure better data discoverability, standardised structure, and cost savings for all parties involved in the creation of structured data. Robust, coherent, and multilingual information standards are needed to enable information exchange among public organisations, similar to standards that have been fostering technical interoperability for decades (Guijarro 2009).

We extend the Linguistic Linked Open Data (LLOD) stack with a new resource, Multilingual Knowledge System (MKS). MKS caters for the discovery, access, retrieval, and re-usability of terminologies and other interoperability assets organised in knowledge graphs (KG) in a taxonomic fashion. As a semantic knowledge repository, its main forte is the ability to exchange information among acting systems, ensuring that its precise *meaning* is understood and preserved among all parties, in any language. Injecting structure into the language data and expanding the result-

Alena Vasilevich · Michael Wetzel
Coreon GmbH, Germany, alena@coreon.com, michael@coreon.com

G. Rehm (ed.), *European Language Grid*, Cognitive Technologies,
https://doi.org/10.1007/978-3-031-17258-8_23

ing KG with multilingual terminologies, Coreon uses the European Language Grid (ELG) as a platform for making the published resources discoverable and retrievable through SPARQL, a protocol widely used for the retrieval of information from Semantic Web resources. While existing SPARQL tools enable users to query knowledge graphs, they are rarely used for termbases and other terminology resources, i. e., core data sources for translation and localisation (Stanković et al. 2014). This step makes Coreon integration into other systems tool-independent: instead of using the proprietary API, it relies on LLOD standards.

The goal of our contribution is to deliver MKS resources to the Semantic Web community, enabling it to query concept-oriented multilingual structured data with a well-established industry-standard syntax, and to promote the development of data multilingualism within the Semantic Web. In the long run, MKS as a LLOD resource can provide relevant input for standardisation bodies and interoperability communities: acting as a blueprint for similar integration activities, it can be viewed as a starting point for an international standard. We share our experience with ISO/TC37 SC3[1] working groups as a draft for a technical recommendation on how to represent TermBase eXchange (TBX) dialects as RDF.

2 Making Coreon Data Structure LLOD-compatible

Resource Description Framework (RDF) and Web Ontology Language (OWL) are standardised formats for representing Semantic Web data. They support data integration and offer a plethora of tools and methods for data access. SPARQL operates on RDF/OWL resources allowing users to retrieve structured responses to submitted queries. To express queries, it utilises triple patterns that are to be matched by RDF/OWL triples and filter conditions, imposing ranges for literals (Almendros-Jiménez and Becerra-Terón 2021). Despite the emerging interest in publishing terminological resources as linked data, the LLOD stack has not been heavily utilised for this purpose so far (Buono et al. 2020).

We implemented a solution for Coreon MKS, making termbases discoverable and accessible for LLOD systems (Chiarcos et al. 2013). Normally data owners deploy a technology like a RDF triple store for their terminology tool, often developing or setting up a tedious data-mirroring process. We go beyond the limits of RDF/knowledge graph editors, which tend to be good at relation modeling but have weaknesses when it comes to capturing linguistic information.

At the core of the MKS lies a language-independent KG. Unlike other popular solutions within terminology management, linking is performed *not* at the *term* but at the *concept* level; therefore, abstracting from terms, we can model structured knowledge for phenomena that reflect the non-deterministic nature of human language, such as word sense ambiguity, synonymy, and multilingualism. Linking *per concept* also ensures smooth maintenance of relations without additional data clutter:

---

[1] https://www.iso.org/committee/48136.html

relation edges are independent from labels, terms and their variants, and other metadata. Besides the mirroring process between the Coreon data model and an RDF graph, the RDF vocabulary was established, covering classes, relations, additional term-descriptive information, and administrative metadata. It binds elements into RDF triples. At this stage it was critical to identify information objects and mapping of predicates and literals.

```
 1  {"created_at": "2021-04-20T13:04:59.816Z",
 2      "terms": [
 3              {"lang": "en",
 4              "value": "screen" ,
 5              "id": "607ed17b318e0c181786b549" ,
 6              "concept_id": "607ed17b318e0c181786b545",
 7              "properties": []},
 8              {"lang": "de",
 9              "value": "Bildschirm" ,
10              "id": "607ed195318e0c181786b55e" ,
11              "concept_id": "607ed17b318e0c181786b545",
12              "properties": []}
13      ],
14      "id": "607ed17b318e0c181786b545" }
```

Listing 1 Excerpt of the Coreon data structure.

Listing 1 shows relevant lines within the original JSON data structure that represents the sample concept "screen", with *concept* ID and individual *term* IDs and their values highlighted. To transform this data structure into an RDF graph, the concept and its two terms are bound together in statements, i. e., RDF triples. Each triple comprises a subject, a predicate and an object; in our case, the concept will act as the subject, the terms become objects and the required predicate is named hasTerm. The complete sample set of triples serialised in RDF/Turtle is provided in Listing 2, with highlighted lines 9-10 indicating that the resource with ID 606336dab4dbcf018ed99308 belongs to the OWL class *coreon:Concept* and contains a term with ID 606336dab4dbcf018ed99307.

In RDF and LOD, data is stored in an atomic manner, with predicates and uniform resource identifiers (URIs) linking elements together. In our case, all instances represented as classes receive unique identifiers. Together with unique IDs, the namespace coreon: unambiguously identifies any given element, regardless of whether it is a concept, term, property or a concept relation. Table 1 lists our RDF vocabulary, derived from the original MKS data structure. During the Coreon-to-RDF conversion, there were obvious candidates for classes, like Concept and Term; yet mirroring descriptive information like Definition or TermStatus and mapping taxonomic and associative concept relations turned out to be challenging. For the predicates we had to specify what information can be used, defining owl:range and owl:domain;

```
 1  coreon:607ed17b318e0c181786b547 a coreon:Edge;
 2    coreon:edgeSource coreon:606336dab4dbcf018ed99308;
 3    coreon:edgeTarget coreon:607ed17b318e0c181786b545;
 4    coreon:type "SUPERCONCEPT_OF" .
 5
 6  coreon:606336dab4dbcf018ed99307 a coreon:Term;
 7    coreon:value "peripheral device"@en .
 8
 9  coreon:606336dab4dbcf018ed99308 a coreon:Concept;
10    coreon:hasTerm coreon:606336dab4dbcf018ed99307 .
11
12  coreon:607ed17b318e0c181786b545 a coreon:Concept;
13    coreon:hasTerm coreon:607ed195318e0c181786b55e ,
14      coreon:607ed17b318e0c181786b549 .
15
16  coreon:607ed17b318e0c181786b549 a coreon:Term;
17    coreon:value "screen"@en .
18
19  coreon:607ed195318e0c181786b55e a coreon:Term;
20    coreon:value "Bildschirm"@de .
```

Listing 2 Triples serialised in RDF / Turtle

```
 1  coreon:hasTerm
 2    rdf:type owl:ObjectProperty ;
 3    rdfs:comment "makes a term member of a concept" ;
 4    rdfs:domain coreon:Concept ;
 5    rdfs:label "has term" ;
 6    rdfs:range coreon:Term .
```

Listing 3 Specification of a predicate

e. g., the predicate hasTerm can only accept resources of type coreon:Concept as a subject (owl:domain). Listing 3 provides a full specification of this predicate.

	OWL Type	Coreon RDF Vocabulary
Classes	owl:Class	coreon:Admin, coreon:Edge, coreon:Concept, coreon:Flagset, coreon:Property, coreon:Term
Predicates	owl:ObjectProperty	coreon:hasAdmin, coreon:hasFlagset, coreon:hasProperty, coreon:hasTerm
Values	owl:AnnotationProperty	coreon:edgeSource, coreon:edgeTarget, coreon:id, coreon:name, coreon:type, coreon:value

Table 1 Derived Coreon RDF vocabulary

3 Real-Time Data Access via a SPARQL Endpoint

With the vocabulary defined, we equipped Coreon's export engine with a RDF publication mechanism, including the export in relevant syntax flavours (Turtle, N3,
JSON-LD). The Coreon cloud service was supplied with a real-time accessible
SPARQL endpoint via Apache Jena Fuseki.[2] It conforms to all published standards
and tracks revisions and updates in the under-developed areas of the standard. Running as a secondary index in parallel with the repository's data store, Fuseki catches
any changes made by data maintainers, updating the state of the repository in real
time. Listing 4 demonstrates a sample SPARQL query over a MKS that deals with
wine varieties: here, we want to return all terms, including the values of the *Usage*
flag in case the terms have them.

```
SELECT ?t ?termvalue ?usagevalue
    WHERE { ?t rdf:type coreon:Term .
            ?t coreon:value ?termvalue .
            OPTIONAL {  ?t coreon:hasProperty ?p .
                        ?p coreon:key "Usage" .
                        ?p coreon:value ?usagevalue .
            }
    }
```

Listing 4 Sample SPARQL query over MKS

Table 2 shows a subset of the linked data structures returned by this query, i. e., a
term's URI, its value, and usage recommendation if available.

[t]	termvalue	usagevalue
http://www.coreon.com/coreon-rdf#[...]8b8aa	Riesling	
http://www.coreon.com/coreon-rdf#[...]8b8bb	Cabernet Sauvignon	Preferred
http://www.coreon.com/coreon-rdf#[...]8b8be	CS	Not allowed
http://www.coreon.com/coreon-rdf#[...]8b8c2	Merlot	

Table 2 Results of the sample SPARQL query (Listing 4): returned grape varieties

4 Conclusions and Results of the Pilot Project

We developed a pipeline to make MKS resources LLOD-compatible, mapping
Coreon data structure to RDF, conceiving the Coreon-RDF vocabulary and publishing MKS resources via ELG. Besides making the SPARQL endpoint available

---

[2] https://jena.apache.org

through ELG, we implemented a productised piece of software, providing TermBase eXchange-like terminology resources in the RDF and Semantic Web context; a set of demo repositories is accessible via the endpoint through ELG. Beyond establishing structural interoperability, the implemented interface bridges Coreon with other Semantic Web systems, enabling querying of elaborate multilingual terminologies. Our mirroring approach can act as a blueprint for similar conversion and integration activities, viewed as a starting point for an international standard. Deployed through ELG, Coreon's SPARQL interface enables the Semantic Web community to query rich heterogeneous MKS data with a familiar, industry-standard syntax, promoting data accessibility and contributing to the development of multilingual resources within the Semantic Web.

Acknowledgements The work described in this article has received funding from the EU project European Language Grid as one of its pilot projects.

References

Almendros-Jiménez, Jesús Manuel and Antonio Becerra-Terón (2021). "Discovery and diagnosis of wrong SPARQL queries with ontology and constraint reasoning". In: *Expert Systems with Applications* 165, p. 113772. DOI: 10.1016/j.eswa.2020.113772.

Buono, Maria Pia Di, Philipp Cimiano, Mohammad Fazleh Elahi, and Frank Grimm (2020). "Terme-à-LLOD: Simplifying the Conversion and Hosting of Terminological Resources as Linked Data". In: *Proc. of the 7th Workshop on Linked Data in Linguistics, LDL@LREC 2020, Marseille, France, May 2020*. Ed. by Maxim Ionov, John P. McCrae, Christian Chiarcos, Thierry Declerck, Julia Bosque-Gil, and Jorge Gracia. ELRA, pp. 28–35.

Chiarcos, Christian, Philipp Cimiano, Thierry Declerck, and John P. McCrae (2013). "Linguistic Linked Open Data. Introduction and Overview". In: *Proceedings of the 2nd Workshop on Linked Data in Linguistics (LDL-2013): Representing and linking lexicons, terminologies and other language data*. Pisa, Italy: ACL, pp. i–xi.

Guijarro, Luis (2009). "Semantic interoperability in eGovernment initiatives". In: *Computer Standards & Interfaces* 31.1, pp. 174–180. DOI: 10.1016/j.csi.2007.11.011.

Stanković, Ranka, Ivan Obradović, and Miloš Utvić (2014). "Developing Termbases for Expert Terminology under the TBX Standard". In: *Natural Language Processing for Serbian-Resources and Applications*, pp. 12–26.

Chapter 24
Open Translation Models, Tools and Services

Jörg Tiedemann, Mikko Aulamo, Sam Hardwick, and Tommi Nieminen

Abstract The ambition of the Open Translation Models, Tools and Services (OPUS-MT) project is to develop state-of-the art neural machine translation (NMT) models that can freely be distributed and applied in research as well as professional applications. The goal is to pre-train translation models on a large scale on openly available parallel data and to create a catalogue of such resources for streamlined integration and deployment. For the latter we also implement and improve web services and computer-assisted translation (CAT) tools that can be used in on-line interfaces and professional workflows. Furthermore, we want to enable the re-use of models to avoid repeating costly training procedures from scratch and with this contribute to a reduction of the carbon footprint in MT research and development. The ELG pilot project focused on European minority languages and improved translation quality in low resource settings and the integration of MT services in the ELG infrastructure.

1 Overview and Objectives of the Pilot Project

OPUS-MT (Tiedemann and Thottingal 2020) provides ready-made server solutions that can be deployed on regular desktop machines to run translations using any NMT model that has been released through the project.[1] The service is powered by Marian-NMT[2] (Junczys-Dowmunt et al. 2018), an efficient open-source framework written in pure C++ with implementations of state-of-the-art neural machine translation architectures. OPUS-MT provides two implementations that can be deployed on regular Ubuntu servers or through containerised solutions using docker images. Both solutions can easily be configured using JSON and can be deployed with a wide range of OPUS-MT models. Multiple translation services and nodes can be combined in one access point through a lightweight API. The coverage is constantly growing and

Jörg Tiedemann · Mikko Aulamo · Sam Hardwick · Tommi Nieminen
University of Helsinki, Finland, jorg.tiedemann@helsinki.fi, mikko.aulamo@helsinki.fi, sam.hardwick@helsinki.fi, tommi.nieminen@helsinki.fi

[1] https://github.com/Helsinki-NLP/Opus-MT

[2] https://marian-nmt.github.io

© The Author(s) 2023
G. Rehm (ed.), *European Language Grid*, Cognitive Technologies,
https://doi.org/10.1007/978-3-031-17258-8_24

improved models are continuously released through our repository as a result of our on-going model training efforts.

A dockerised web app is implemented using the Tornado Python framework, which we adapted for the integration into the European Language Grid environment providing an interface that can seamlessly be deployed in the ELG infrastructure. The essential metadata records for the ELG service catalogue are generated from pre-defined templates using information available from released translation models. The routines support bilingual as well as multilingual models and can also be used to set up access points that serve several translation services. Appropriate docker images are compiled using installation recipes and scripts. We host them on Docker Hub from where they can be pulled by ELG requests to serve translation requests directly through the online APIs. Detailed deployment documentation is available from the repository.[3]

At the time of writing, OPUS-MT provides 89 registered MT services within ELG including a wide variety of bilingual and multilingual models. Registered services can be tested online and can also be accessed through the web API and ELG Python SDK. The translation runs on regular CPUs with minimal resource requirements thanks to the efficient decoder implementation in Marian-NMT. Multilingual models are handled in a special way: multiple source languages can be handled by a single access point whereas multiple target languages require separate access points. Metadata records include the relevant information to describe the service provided.

We also developed plugins for professional translation workflows under the label of OPUS-CAT[4] (Nieminen 2021). Our tools include a local MT engine that can run on regular desktop machines making MT available without the security and confidentiality risks associated with online services. OPUS-CAT integrates with popular translation software such as Trados Studio, memoQ, OmegaT and Memsource. It also provides an integrated fine-tuning procedure for domain adaptation. All OPUS-MT models can be downloaded and used locally with the MT engine, some of the plugins can also fetch translations directly from the OPUS-MT services in ELG.

2 Increasing Language Coverage

The general goal of OPUS-MT is to increase language coverage of freely available machine translation solutions. The project already provides over a thousand pre-trained translation models covering hundreds of languages in various translation directions. The ongoing effort is documented by public repositories and regular updates and we omit further details here as this is a quickly moving target.

Within our ELG pilot project, we further developed our pipelines and recipes to systematically train additional NMT models. The effort resulted in the model de-

---

[3] https://github.com/Helsinki-NLP/Opus-MT/tree/master/elg
[4] https://helsinki-nlp.github.io/OPUS-CAT/

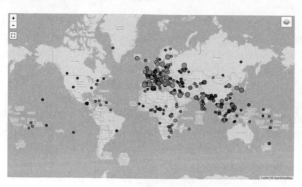

Fig. 1 OPUS-MT map: A visualisation of language coverage and model quality according to automatic evaluation metrics and the Tatoeba MT challenge benchmarks; here: models that translate from a source language mapped on their glottolog location to English; larger circles indicate bigger benchmark test sets and the color scale goes from green (high quality) to red (poor quality)

velopment framework OPUS-MT-train[5] with support for bilingual and multilingual models that can be trained on data provided by OPUS[6] and the Tatoeba translation challenge[7] (Tiedemann 2020).

In order to keep track of the development, we heavily rely on the Tatoeba benchmarks and we implemented an interactive tool to visualize the current state of our released models. Figure 1 shows an example screenshot.

The geographic distribution of released models is an appealing way to uncover blind spots in the NLP landscape. The lack of appropriate data resources is one of the major bottlenecks that block the development of proper MT solutions for most language pairs of the world. Another issue is the narrow focus of research that typically overemphasises well established tasks for reasons of comparability and measurable success. OPUS-MT does not have a strict state-of-the-art development focus based on major benchmarks but rather emphasises language coverage and the focus on under-researched translation directions. The OPUS-MT map and the Tatoeba MT challenge try to make this work visible and more attractive.

The main strategy to tackle issues with *limited data resources* is to apply transfer learning and some type of data augmentation. In OPUS-MT we are constantly facing the problem of limited training data and noise and the ELG pilot project specifically focused on low-resource scenarios and European minority languages.

The idea of transfer learning is based on the ability of models to pick up valuable knowledge from other tasks or languages. In MT, the main type of transfer learning is based on cross-lingual transfer where multilingual translation models can be used to push the performance in low-resource settings (Fan et al. 2021). The effect is typically pronounced with closely related languages where strong linguistic similarities can lead to big improvements across language boundaries (Tiedemann 2021).

---

[5] https://github.com/Helsinki-NLP/OPUS-MT-train

[6] https://opus.nlpl.eu

[7] https://github.com/Helsinki-NLP/Tatoeba-Challenge/

In OPUS-MT, we therefore focused on multilingual models of typologically related languages. In our setup, we rely on language groups and families established within the ISO 639-5 standard. A dedicated tool for mapping languages to language groups and connecting them with the hierarchical language tree has been developed to allow a systematic development of multilingual NMT models based on typological relationships.[8] The procedures have been integrated in the OPUS-MT training recipes and can be applied to arbitrary datasets from the Tataobea MT Challenge.

Table 1 illustrates the effect of cross-lingual transfer with multilingual models on the example of the Belarusian-English translation benchmark from the Tatoeba MT Challenge. All models apply the same generic transformer-based architecture (Vaswani et al. 2017) with identical hyper-parameters and training recipes.

NMT model	Belarusian $\longrightarrow$ English	English $\longrightarrow$ Belarusian
Belarusian – English	10.0	8.2
East Slavic – English	38.7	20.8
Slavic – English	**42.7**	**22.9**
Indo-European – English	41.7	18.1

Table 1 Machine translation between Belarusian and English with different NMT models; scores refer to BLEU scores measured on the Tatoeba MT Challenge benchmark

The bilingual baseline model is very poor due to the limited training data that is available from the Tatoeba dataset (157,524 sentence pairs). Augmenting the training data with closely related languages such as other (East) Slavic languages leads to significant improvements, which is not very surprising. The effect can be seen in both directions. Note that the multi-target models need to be augmented by language tokens to indicate the output language to be generated. The importance of systematic benchmarks is also shown in the table where we can see that Indo-European language model struggles and the effect of positive transfer diminishes due to the capacity issues of such a complex model setup.

Finally, we also tested a novel type of data augmentation using a rule-based system (RBMT) for back-translation (Sennrich et al. 2016) to produce additional data for the translation from Finnish to Northern Sámi (Aulamo et al. 2021). Our results revealed that knowledge from the RBMT system can effectively be injected into a neural MT model significantly boosting the performance as shown in Table 2.

We use two benchmarks in our evaluations: the UiT set[9], and the YLE set of 150 sentence pairs from news stories about Sámi culture.[10] Preliminary manual evaluation revealed that the NMT-based model was often unable to correctly translate proper names. Adding copies of monolingual data as suggested by Currey et al. (2017) helps to alleviate that issue. Furthermore, we also added experiments with subword regularisation (Kudo 2018) and data tagging (Caswell et al. 2019) to bet-

---

[8] https://github.com/Helsinki-NLP/LanguageCodes

[9] 2,000 sentence pairs sampled from the Giellatekno Free corpus https://giellatekno.uit.no

[10] Collected from https://yle.fi

	Training Data	UiT	YLE
Baseline	25,106	18.9	4.3
+ NMT-bt	422,596	34.0	9.8
+ RBMT-bt	378,567	36.3	15.5
+ NMT-bt + RBMT-bt	885,301	**40.1**	10.8
+ NMT-bt + copy	845,192	35.7	12.5
+ RBMT-bt + copy	757,134	35.7	**18.6**
+ NMT-bt + RBMT-bt + SR + TB	885,301	40.0	17.2

Table 2 Training data sizes (sentence pairs) and results (BLEU) for the Finnish-Northern Sámi translation models using original parallel data (Baseline), augmented data with back-translations from NMT and RBMT systems (NMT-bt, RBMT-bt), added monolingual data (copy), subword regularisation (SR) and tagged back-translations (TB) evaluated on the UiT and YLE test sets

ter exploit the distributions in the training data and to distinguish between sources with different noise levels. Preliminary results are encouraging and deserve further investigations. In future work, we plan to add pivot-based translation and multilingual models to further improve the performance of the system, to support additional input languages and to include other Sámi language varieties, too.

3 Conclusions and Results of the Pilot Project

OPUS-MT is an on-going effort to make MT widely available for open research and development with an extensive language coverage and well established deployment and integration procedures. Our ELG pilot project made it possible to strengthen the focus on minority languages and to further exploit transfer and data augmentation strategies to improve the quality of MT for under-resourced language pairs.

Acknowledgements The work described in this article has received funding from the EU project European Language Grid as one of its pilot projects. We would also like to acknowledge the support by the FoTran project funded by the European Research Council (no. 771113) and CSC, the Finnish IT Center for Science, for computational resources.

References

Aulamo, Mikko, Sami Virpioja, Yves Scherrer, and Jörg Tiedemann (2021). "Boosting Neural Machine Translation from Finnish to Northern Sámi with Rule-Based Backtranslation". In: *Proceedings of the 23rd Nordic Conference on Computational Linguistics (NoDaLiDa)*. Reykjavik, Iceland: Linköping University Electronic Press, pp. 351–356. URL: https://aclanthology.org/2021.nodalida-main.37.
Caswell, Isaac, Ciprian Chelba, and David Grangier (2019). "Tagged Back-Translation". In: *Proc. of the Fourth Conf. on Machine Translation*, pp. 53–63.

Currey, Anna, Antonio Valerio Miceli Barone, and Kenneth Heafield (2017). "Copied Monolingual Data Improves Low-Resource Neural Machine Translation". In: *Proceedings of the Second Conference on Machine Translation*. Copenhagen, Denmark: ACL, pp. 148–156. DOI: 10.18653/v1/W17-4715. URL: https://aclanthology.org/W17-4715.

Fan, Angela, Shruti Bhosale, Holger Schwenk, Zhiyi Ma, Ahmed El-Kishky, Siddharth Goyal, Mandeep Baines, Onur Celebi, Guillaume Wenzek, Vishrav Chaudhary, Naman Goyal, Tom Birch, Vitaliy Liptchinsky, Sergey Edunov, Michael Auli, and Armand Joulin (2021). "Beyond English-Centric Multilingual Machine Translation". In: *Journal of Machine Learning Research* 22.107, pp. 1–48. URL: http://jmlr.org/papers/v22/20-1307.html.

Junczys-Dowmunt, Marcin, Roman Grundkiewicz, Tomasz Dwojak, Hieu Hoang, Kenneth Heafield, Tom Neckermann, Frank Seide, Ulrich Germann, Alham Fikri Aji, Nikolay Bogoychev, André F. T. Martins, and Alexandra Birch (2018). "Marian: Fast Neural Machine Translation in C++". In: *Proceedings of ACL 2018, System Demonstrations*. Melbourne, Australia: ACL, pp. 116–121. URL: http://www.aclweb.org/anthology/P18-4020.

Kudo, Taku (2018). "Subword Regularization: Improving Neural Network Translation Models with Multiple Subword Candidates". In: *Proc. of the 56th Annual Meeting of the Association for Computational Linguistics*, pp. 66–75.

Nieminen, Tommi (2021). "OPUS-CAT: Desktop NMT with CAT integration and local fine-tuning". In: *Proceedings of the 16th Conference of the European Chapter of the Association for Computational Linguistics: System Demonstrations*. ACL, pp. 288–294. DOI: 10.18653/v1/2021.eacl-demos.34. URL: https://aclanthology.org/2021.eacl-demos.34.

Sennrich, Rico, Barry Haddow, and Alexandra Birch (2016). "Improving Neural Machine Translation Models with Monolingual Data". In: *Proceedings of the 54th Annual Meeting of the Association for Computational Linguistics (Volume 1: Long Papers)*, pp. 86–96.

Tiedemann, Jörg (2020). "The Tatoeba Translation Challenge – Realistic Data Sets for Low Resource and Multilingual MT". In: *Proceedings of the Fifth Conference on Machine Translation (WMT)*. ACL, pp. 1174–1182. URL: https://aclanthology.org/2020.wmt-1.139.

Tiedemann, Jörg (2021). "The Development of a Comprehensive Data Set for Systematic Studies of Machine Translation". In: *Multilingual Facilitation*. Ed. by Mika Hämäläinen, Niko Partanen, and Khalid Alnajjar. Finland: University of Helsinki, pp. 248–262. DOI: 10.31885/9789515150257.

Tiedemann, Jörg and Santhosh Thottingal (2020). "OPUS-MT – Building open translation services for the World". In: *Proceedings of the 22nd Annual Conference of the European Association for Machine Translation (EAMT)*. Lisboa, Portugal: European Association for Machine Translation, pp. 479–480. URL: https://helda.helsinki.fi/bitstream/handle/10138/327852/2020.eamt_1_499.pdf.

Vaswani, Ashish, Noam Shazeer, Niki Parmar, Jakob Uszkoreit, Llion Jones, Aidan N Gomez, Łukasz Kaiser, and Illia Polosukhin (2017). "Attention is all you need". In: *Proceedings of the 31st International Conference on Neural Information Processing Systems*, pp. 6000–6010.

Chapter 25
Sign Language Explanations for Terms in a Text

Helmut Ludwar and Julia Schuster

Abstract The ELG pilot project SignLookUp serves the goal of developing a function that makes text documents easier to comprehend for deaf people. This is important as many of them are functional illiterates.

1 Overview and Objectives of the Pilot Project

The ELG (Rehm et al. 2021) pilot project SignLookUp aims to make texts easier to comprehend for deaf people. Deaf people have a difficult access to texts (Luckner et al. 2005). Learning a written language is a challenge with a hearing impairment (Harris et al. 2017). Therefore, about 75 percent of deaf people are functional illiterates.

Fig. 1 LookApp visualisation

The ideal form of accessibility for the deaf would be the complete translation of texts into sign language. However, this is usually not possible due to limited resources and budgets. The LookApp technology is an intermediate solution and serves the goal of making texts easier to understand for the deaf.

SignLookUp is a technology that links texts to a sign language encyclopedia. Deaf people thus have the possibility to click on difficult or unknown terms in a text and

Helmut Ludwar · Julia Schuster
Sign Time GmbH, Austria, helmut.ludwar@signtime.media, julia.schuster@signtime.media

© The Author(s) 2023
G. Rehm (ed.), *European Language Grid*, Cognitive Technologies,
https://doi.org/10.1007/978-3-031-17258-8_25

immediately receive the explanation or description of the word in their sign language which is displayed adjacent to the text. Using mouseover or clicking on the term, a window pops up and a sign language video is played. Often the explanation of a word or term in sign language is sufficient to make a whole sentence understandable.

SignLookUp starts with two sign languages, but is developed in such a way that it can be easily expanded. The product will be licensed for companies and is free for the end-user (deaf people). This technology thus supports the deaf in accessing and making sense of text information on the internet and at the same time promotes the integration of this marginalised group in our society.

2 Methodology

Selecting the terms that are most important for deaf people to better understand the whole text is a special challenge. On the one hand, it must of course be those that are of central importance, but on the other hand, consideration must also be given to how deaf people experience and understand facts. Last but not least, linguistic peculiarities such as idiomatic expressions, onomatopoeic terms and language images must also be taken into account when finding terms.

Therefore, for the creation of the sign language explanations of an item within a text on a website the following method is used:

1. *Determine the target audience or readers for the website*, e. g., language competence, relevant prior knowledge, thematic interest, age, gender, education.
2. *Perform word analysis* (Egle 2020):

   a. Does the author paraphrase or avoid certain terms in a noticeable manner (euphemisms, taboos)?
   b. Does the text contain words and expressions that must be understood in a figurative sense (linguistic images, metaphors, similes)?
   c. What language-layers or language-uses can be identified?
   d. Does the text contain a foreign word or technical expressions?
   e. Are there words and phrases in the text that can be associated or connoted with other ideas (e. g., "She's feeling blue" → "She's feeling sad")?
   f. Do buzzwords, empty phrases, or other stereotypes occur (e. g., "low-hanging fruit")?
   g. Do certain words acquire a special meaning when the context is taken into account (broadening or narrowing of meaning, emotional coloring)?
   h. From what time do the words used originate? Are they already obsolete (archaism) or newly formed (neologism)? What is their purpose?
   i. Can certain words be assigned to a specific area (e. g., technology, art, sports)? What is the effect?
   j. Are there exaggerations/understatements?
   k. Is only a part of a whole addressed: synecdoche (e. g., pars pro toto)?
   l. Are synonyms (different terms but describing the same in context) used?

3. *Analysis of the text and selection of items:* An automatic analysis of the text to show the comprehensibility and complexity of the text and individual words are used as a starting point, e. g., creation of the readability index (LIX, W. Lenhard and A. Lenhard 2011).[1]

Thereafter a specialist who is fluent in the languages, e. g., a deaf person or an interpreter, checks whether the passages and terms are understandable for deaf people and selects the candidates for explanation based on the following criteria:

   a. Which terms are of central importance to the content?
   b. Special meaning, e. g., opposite of what is written (irony)
   c. Special words from item 2

4. *Providing the following (meta) information:* Concept (named entity), lemma, context, web link, text language, sign language, version.
5. *Term explanation (for each term):*

   a. Explanation of the term in simple language using the guidelines (Netzwerk Leichte Sprache 2013).
   b. It must not exceed 30 words and must be as brief as possible.
   c. Must be universal and general so that it is suitable for all uses in a text with the same context.
   d. Begins with a relationship to a higher-level or more general term.
   e. Includes the typical features of the term, using semes (the smallest unit of meaning) for this purpose.
   f. Add examples

As a reference for the creation of explanations available sources may be used, e. .g., medicine DGS[2], medicine ÖGS[3].
6. *Translation into sign language:*

   a. If there is a common sign for the item, it must be used at the beginning, followed by the signed explanation.
   b. Translation into sign language glosses
   c. Transfer into sign language animations
   d. Producing a sign language explanation video

7. *Quality assurance according to the four-eyes-principle:* The draft version of an entry including sign language videos must be checked by a hearing sign language interpreter for completeness and correctness of content. In this way, native speaker competencies of both languages, written and sign language, are included.

---

[1] https://wortliga.de/textanalyse/

[2] https://www.sign-lang.uni-hamburg.de/glex/intro/inhalt.html

[3] https://www.equalizent.com

3 Implementation

The beta-version of LookApp (preliminary product name) is implemented in Java-Script on the server where the respective website to be analysed is located. The workflow described below is also shown in Figure 2:

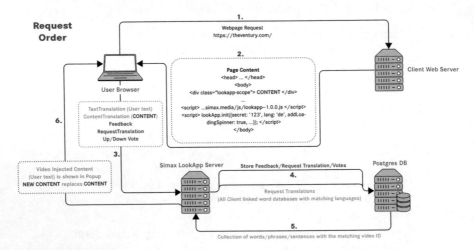

Fig. 2 LookApp concept

1. End user goes to a website that offers LookApp.
2. The web server returns the content of the page which includes:

    a. Parts of the content with the LookApp-scope class
    b. The LookApp JavaScript is fetched from the LookApp server or served in a static way.
    c. The script is initialised with certain parameters.

3. The request 3 actually represents multiple calls between browser and client

    a. At first the "custom options" are loaded
    b. The client-specific CSS file is loaded
    c. Any LookApp action

4. Depending on the action

    a. Store feedback, requested translations, votes in the database → workflow ends here
    b. Query a list of translations belonging to the client side and corresponding to the passed parameter lang

5. Collection of words and explanations

    a. The server then replaces found words with an icon
    b. JavaScript will interpret as hover or clickable video translations

6. The page content is sent back and replaced by JavaScript.

4 Evaluation

In order to verify the usefulness of the application, a preliminary study was conducted. This involved providing a website with LookApp to a small group of deaf people and then performing a qualitative survey through sign language interpreters.

The results show consistently positive feedback regarding assistance for understanding as well as the avatar used. In order to be able to make reliable statements, however, a survey with a larger test group that represents the deaf community must be carried out.

5 Conclusions and Results of the Pilot Project

As part of the pilot project, a beta version of LookApp was created, which is already being used on early adopter websites, which is why it is evident that the concept and implementation can be used with a positive benefit. Further development of the functions (e. g., use of NLP methods) and the creation of high quality explanations of as many terms as possible are planned next.

It has already been shown in this phase of development that there are multiple advantages. Deaf people have better access to information that cannot be fully translated into sign language due to time or resource constraints. Although our reading aid does not provide the convenience of a full sign language translation, it supports text comprehension in a significant way. Customers who provide large amounts of information or whose content is updated frequently cannot translate all of their content into sign language due to time and economic constraints. With LookApp, even such content can be made much more accessible. Existing and future customers can thus be offered hybrid solutions. In addition to summaries of a website's content in sign language videos according to "Accessibility of websites and mobile applications" (European Parliament, Council of the European Union 2016), LookApp can be implemented for the entire content of the website. Implementing LookApp in a specific website requires only a small financial and organisational effort on the side of the customer but can produce great effects on the side of deaf users.

Acknowledgements The work described in this article has received funding from the EU project European Language Grid as one of its pilot projects.

References

Egle, Gert (2020). *Leitfragen zur sprachlichen Analyse.* URL: http://teachsam.de/deutsch/d_schre ibf/schr_schule/txtanal/txtanal_6_1a.htm.

European Parliament, Council of the European Union (2016). *Directive 2016/2102 of 26 Oct. 2016 on the Accessibility of the Websites and Mobile Applications of Public Sector Bodies.* URL: http://data.europa.eu/eli/dir/2016/2102/oj/eng.

Harris, Margaret, Emmanouela Terlektsi, and Fiona E. Kyle (2017). "Literacy Outcomes for Primary School Children Who Are Deaf and Hard of Hearing: A Cohort Comparison Study". In: vol. 60. American Speech-Language-Hearing Association. URL: https://pubs.asha.org/doi/pdf /10.1044/2016_JSLHR-H-15-0403.

Lenhard, Wolfgang and Alexandra Lenhard (2011). *Berechnung des Lesbarkeitsindex LIX nach Björnson.* URL: http://rgdoi.net/10.13140/RG.2.1.1512.3447.

Luckner, John, Ann Sebald, John Cooney, John Young, and Sheryl Muir (2005). "An Examination of the Evidence-Based Literacy Research in Deaf Education". In: *American Annals of the Deaf* 150, p. 443.

Netzwerk Leichte Sprache (2013). *Regeln für Leichte Sprache.* URL: https://www.leichte-sprache .org/wp-content/uploads/2017/11/Regeln_Leichte_Sprache.pdf.

Rehm, Georg, Stelios Piperidis, Kalina Bontcheva, Jan Hajic, Victoria Arranz, Andrejs Vasiļjevs, Gerhard Backfried, José Manuel Gómez Pérez, Ulrich Germann, Rémi Calizzano, Nils Feldhus, Stefanie Hegele, Florian Kintzel, Katrin Marheinecke, Julian Moreno-Schneider, Dimitris Galanis, Penny Labropoulou, Miltos Deligiannis, Katerina Gkirtzou, Athanasia Kolovou, Dimitris Gkoumas, Leon Voukoutis, Ian Roberts, Jana Hamrlová, Dusan Varis, Lukáš Kačena, Khalid Choukri, Valérie Mapelli, Mickaël Rigault, Jūlija Meļņika, Miro Janosik, Katja Prinz, Andres Garcia-Silva, Cristian Berrio, Ondrej Klejch, and Steve Renals (2021). "European Language Grid: A Joint Platform for the European Language Technology Community". In: *Proceedings of the 16th Conference of the European Chapter of the Association for Computational Linguistics: System Demonstrations (EACL 2021).* Kyiv, Ukraine: ACL, pp. 221–230. URL: https://w ww.aclweb.org/anthology/2021.eacl-demos.26.pdf.

Chapter 26
Streaming Language Processing in Manufacturing

Patrick Wiener and Steffen Thoma

Abstract Often underestimated, (semi-)structured textual data sources are an important cornerstone in the manufacturing sector for product and process quality tracking. The ELG pilot project SLAPMAN develops novel methods for industrial text analytics in the form of scalable, reusable, and potentially stateful microservices, which can be easily orchestrated by domain experts in order to define quality anomaly patterns, e. g., by analysing machine states and error logs. The results are fully available as open source and integrated into the IIoT toolbox Apache StreamPipes.

1 Overview and Objectives of the Pilot Project

Continuous process and product quality monitoring is a critical task in the manufacturing sector for early detection of anomalies, e. g., gathering insights on potential machine failures, breakouts or performance degradation. Often underestimated, a large part of data sources that are able to provide insights to quality deviations are textual data sources. This includes machine status data and error data, but also production plans. Such information is very important for tracking anomalies and an important source to shop floor workers and other domain experts for identifying potentially critical situations and root causes. While the analysis of real-time measurements is well explored, the automated analysis of textual data is underexplored and hindered by language barriers and often confusing text codes specific to companies or domains. The goal of the SLAPMAN project is the development and integration of streaming language technology (LT) modules from the European Language Grid (ELG, Rehm et al. 2021) to process, analyse and exploit non-structured or semi-structured manufacturing process data. These modules have been integrated into the open-source IIoT toolbox Apache StreamPipes. StreamPipes provides services for self-service data analytics by pursuing a graphical flow-based modeling approach. This allows the description of stream processing applications in the form of processing pipelines composed of multiple, interconnected pipeline elements. This sig-

---

Patrick Wiener · Steffen Thoma
FZI Research Center for Information Technology, Germany, wiener@fzi.de, thoma@fzi.de

G. Rehm (ed.), *European Language Grid*, Cognitive Technologies,
https://doi.org/10.1007/978-3-031-17258-8_26

nificantly lowers rather high technological entry barriers towards making streaming language processing in particular, and LT in general, accessible for non-technical domain experts. SLAPMAN developed novel extensions to Apache StreamPipes that can be easily added to StreamPipes in the form of modular standalone services, e. g., streaming adapters to quickly connect textual data sources (e. g., production plans from MES systems), or pipeline elements for NLP including named entity recognition (NER), tokenising, word embeddings or translation.

2 Graphical, Flow-based Modeling with Apache StreamPipes

Apache StreamPipes[1] is an incubator project of the Apache Software Foundation, that provides a reusable toolbox to easily connect, analyse and exploit a variety of IIoT-related data streams without any programming skills. It leverages different technologies especially from the fields of stream processing, distributed computing, and the semantic web. Riemer et al. (2014) proposed a methodology for semantics-based management of event streams based on the dataflow programming paradigm which is the foundations of StreamPipes. In this regard, StreamPipes allows modelling stream processing applications in the form of processing pipelines. Pipelines comprise a sequence of pipeline elements provided by arbitrary event-driven microservices from an extensible toolbox. Such event-driven microservices are operated in a distributed environment consisting of multiple, potentially heterogeneous runtime implementations. In doing so, this facilitates the distributed execution of pipeline elements to account for business or application-specific requirements. Figure 1 gives a rudimentary overview of a basic named entity recognition pipeline in StreamPipes. The pipeline consists of three pipeline elements, a textual quality report data source for a group of flow rate sensors, a named entity recognition processor based on an ELG service, and a dashboard sink to visualise results.

The decomposition of complex analytical challenges into smaller function blocks allows StreamPipes to mitigate the problem of committing to a single stream processing technology. On top, it uses semantics to guide non-technical domain experts throughout the pipeline creation process. In recent years, several profound extensions to the knowledge base of StreamPipes were implemented to improve and extend existing capabilities. This includes StreamPipes Connect (Zehnder et al. 2020), a semantics-based adapter model and edge transformation functions, and StreamPipes Edge Extensions (Wiener et al. 2020), a methodology for geo-distributed pipeline deployment and operation. Besides StreamPipes, other solutions for low-code dataflow programming exist, e. g., Apache Nifi[2], or Node-RED[3].

---

[1] https://streampipes.apache.org

[2] https://nifi.apache.org

[3] https://nodered.org

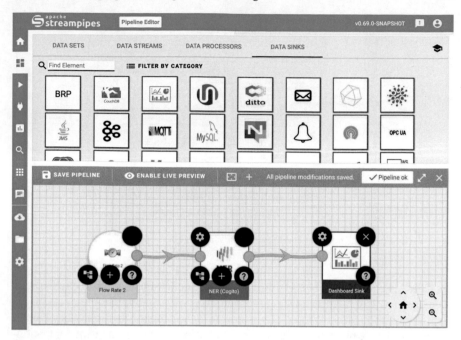

Fig. 1 Example pipeline in StreamPipes

3 Architecture

From an architectural point of view, SLAPMAN follows the microservice architecture of StreamPipes and provides a seamless integration with LT services offered by the ELG platform as shown in Figure 2. In general, the ELG platform provides various LT services that allow to perform language processing and LT-related operation. From a technical perspective, LT services are remotely accessible via REST over HTTP. As such, requests comprising textual data are issued against corresponding LT services that process the incoming call and in return provide the analysis results. For instance, using a machine translation service allows to translate quality defect reports from various plants in different source languages into a common target language, e. g., English, in order to globally investigate certain defect patterns.

In this context, StreamPipes allows to design and develop arbitrary pipeline elements using an SDK. Therefore, arbitrary LT services available on the ELG platform can be wrapped as specific pipeline elements providing language processing capabilities to domain experts to be leveraged in a reusable and self-service manner. Once a user models and deploys a pipeline using one of the LT pipeline elements, textual data is continuously transferred between participating pipeline elements in an event-driven manner by means of a topic-based publish/subscribe pattern. As such, output events from preceding pipeline elements are published to a message broker proto-

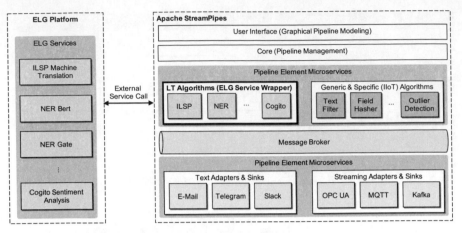

Fig. 2 Architecture: ELG platform and StreamPipes integration

col, e. g., Apache Kafka[4]. Succeeding pipeline elements subscribe to relevant topics in order to retrieve the previously published events. The complete life cycle of the event-driven application is internally managed by the core of StreamPipes which is responsible for the pipeline management. This includes pipeline element compatibility based on semantic verification to provide user support and guidance throughout the pipeline modeling process. In addition, this incorporates message broker protocol negotiation including system-side topic management of the publish/subscribe pattern. At run-time, streaming textual events subscribed by LT pipeline elements of deployed pipelines issue REST calls to remote LT services on the ELG platform to perform the essential processing tasks. Results are sent back and published again to the corresponding message broker protocol for further usage. The architectural design of standalone pipeline element microservices facilitates to extend StreamPipes with additional LT components.

4 Implementation

The main activities in SLAPMAN were focused on the development of new extensions for Apache StreamPipes related to language technology. As such, the extensions were focused on i) wrapping and integrating existing services from the ELG platform (e. g., NER, rumour veracity, sentiment analysis, machine translation), ii) developing new data processors and data sinks for Apache StreamPipes related to LT (e. g., chunker, language detection, part-of-speech-tagger, sentence detection, tokeniser), iii) developing additional adapters to connect text-focused data sources (e. g., Telegram, Slack, Manual Input) and iv) developing technical extensions to the

---

[4] https://kafka.apache.org

toolbox itself to ease the integration of new NLP models along with general usability improvements (e. g., file management, word cloud visualization).

In addition, a new Client API was developed which allows to adapt existing pipelines and to configure pipeline elements from external applications. This enables users to easily update trained language models using a convenient Java client. Moreover, from a deployment and orchestration perspective, StreamPipes relies on Docker as its default installation option. To further alleviate the integration into the ELG platform based on Kubernetes, a helm chart[5] for StreamPipes was developed which is available for public use. This helm chart paired with the general extensibility of StreamPipes to install new pipeline elements providing LT capabilities at run-time allows to integrate additional LT algorithms as demands change.

5 Conclusions and Results of the Pilot Project

In the future, we plan on pursuing the following key activities resulting from lessons learned along the way. In order to better facilitate the integration in existing enterprise architectures, StreamPipes is planned to support standard identity and access management systems such as Keycloak to complement the existing user management. This will also be beneficial for a smoother interaction with the ELG platform itself. In addition, the work on the StreamPipes Python wrapper to simplify the development of new pipeline elements and especially the integration of ELG services is continued. Similarly, the work on the Client API for external pipeline control from code is planned to be pursued.

Acknowledgements The work described in this article has received funding from the EU project European Language Grid as one of its pilot projects.

---

[5] https://helm.sh

References

Rehm, Georg, Stelios Piperidis, Kalina Bontcheva, Jan Hajic, Victoria Arranz, Andrejs Vasiļjevs, Gerhard Backfried, José Manuel Gómez Pérez, Ulrich Germann, Rémi Calizzano, Nils Feldhus, Stefanie Hegele, Florian Kintzel, Katrin Marheinecke, Julian Moreno-Schneider, Dimitris Galanis, Penny Labropoulou, Miltos Deligiannis, Katerina Gkirtzou, Athanasia Kolovou, Dimitris Gkoumas, Leon Voukoutis, Ian Roberts, Jana Hamrlová, Dusan Varis, Lukáš Kačena, Khalid Choukri, Valérie Mapelli, Mickaël Rigault, Jūlija Meļņika, Miro Janosik, Katja Prinz, Andres Garcia-Silva, Cristian Berrio, Ondrej Klejch, and Steve Renals (2021). "European Language Grid: A Joint Platform for the European Language Technology Community". In: *Proceedings of the 16th Conference of the European Chapter of the Association for Computational Linguistics: System Demonstrations (EACL 2021)*. Kyiv, Ukraine: ACL, pp. 221–230. URL: https://www.aclweb.org/anthology/2021.eacl-demos.26.pdf.

Riemer, Dominik, Ljiljana Stojanovic, and Nenad Stojanovic (2014). "SEPP: Semantics-Based Management of Fast Data Streams". In: *Proceedings of IEEE 7th International Conference on Service-Oriented Computing and Applications, SOCA 2014*. IEEE, pp. 113–118. DOI: 10.1109/SOCA.2014.52. URL: http://ieeexplore.ieee.org/document/6978598/.

Wiener, Patrick, Philipp Zehnder, and Dominik Riemer (2020). "Managing Geo-Distributed Stream Processing Pipelines for the IIoT with StreamPipes Edge Extensions". In: *Proceedings of the 14th ACM International Conference on Distributed and Event-Based Systems*. DEBS '20. Montreal, Quebec, Canada: ACM, pp. 165–176. DOI: 10.1145/3401025.3401764. URL: https://doi.org/10.1145/3401025.3401764.

Zehnder, Philipp, Patrick Wiener, Tim Straub, and Dominik Riemer (2020). "StreamPipes Connect: Semantics-Based Edge Adapters for the IIoT". In: *The Semantic Web*. Ed. by Andreas Harth, Sabrina Kirrane, Axel-Cyrille Ngonga Ngomo, Heiko Paulheim, Anisa Rula, Anna Lisa Gentile, Peter Haase, and Michael Cochez. Cham: Springer, pp. 665–680.

Chapter 27
Textual Paraphrase Dataset for Deep Language Modelling

Jenna Kanerva, Filip Ginter, Li-Hsin Chang, Valtteri Skantsi, Jemina Kilpeläinen, Hanna-Mari Kupari, Aurora Piirto, Jenna Saarni, Maija Sevón, and Otto Tarkka

Abstract The Turku Paraphrase Corpus is a dataset of over 100,000 Finnish paraphrase pairs. During the corpus creation, we strived to gather challenging paraphrase pairs, more suitable to test the capabilities of natural language understanding models. The paraphrases are both selected and classified manually, so as to minimise lexical overlap, and provide examples that are structurally and lexically different to the maximum extent. An important distinguishing feature of the corpus is that most of the paraphrase pairs are extracted and distributed in their native document context, rather than in isolation. The primary application for the dataset is the development and evaluation of deep language models, and representation learning in general.

1 Overview and Objectives of the Pilot Project

Natural language processing research focuses increasingly more at a deeper understanding of language meaning, which is the enabling factor for the next generation of language technology applications. Of especially recent interest are neural meaning representations that are robust to non-trivial re-phrasing of statements with equivalent or near-equivalent meaning. While deep learning methods have effectively solved many supervised learning tasks where large amounts of task-specific training data are available, their performance in representation learning tasks is much weaker (Glockner et al. 2018; Tsuchiya 2018; McCoy et al. 2019). In practical terms, we do not yet have well-proven general methods that, given arbitrary statements with the same contextual meaning but very different wording, would reliably produce highly similar representations for the statements. The fundamental limitation has been the lack of appropriate training data and learning procedures that are able to infer the projection from observable surface forms to faithful semantic representations.

In this ELG pilot project, we set out to address this limitation by building a fully manually annotated paraphrase corpus for Finnish, the Turku Paraphrase Corpus. In

Jenna Kanerva · Filip Ginter · Li-Hsin Chang · Valtteri Skantsi · Jemina Kilpeläinen · Hanna-Mari Kupari · Aurora Piirto · Jenna Saarni · Maija Sevón · Otto Tarkka
University of Turku, Finland, jmnybl@utu.fi, lhchan@utu.fi, figint@utu.fi

G. Rehm (ed.), *European Language Grid*, Cognitive Technologies,
https://doi.org/10.1007/978-3-031-17258-8_27

343

addition to building this resource, we also gathered experience and data regarding how such a resource can be built efficiently and what human resources are needed, built initial models based on the new resource, and produced baseline results.

2 Methodology

The primary distinguishing feature of our corpus compared to other related efforts is its fully manual annotation (as opposed to automatic candidate generation), resulting in paraphrase pairs that are non-trivial and challenging in not being highly lexically related. In other words, an important objective was to avoid bias due to automatic candidate selection so as to obtain a more realistic estimate of the performance of machine learning models on natural language understanding tasks. To this end, we gather source documents that are potentially rich in paraphrases for fully manual paraphrase candidate extraction. These documents include alternative translations of movie subtitles, news headings and articles reporting the same event, discussion forum messages with identical titles and topics, alternative student translations from translation course assignments, and student essays answering the same prompts.

Along with the manual extraction, all paraphrase candidates are manually classified into categories of paraphrases and non-paraphrases according to the developed annotation scheme. The design of the annotation scheme strives to capture varying levels of paraphrasability of candidate paraphrase pairs. We use a scale of four base labels, 1–4, similar to those used in some other paraphrase corpora (Creutz 2018). We define the four base labels as label *1* unrelated sentences, label *2* related but not paraphrases, label *3* paraphrases in the given context but not universally so, and label *4* universal paraphrases. In addition, label *4* paraphrases can be marked with optional flags $>$ or $<$ for subsumption, *s* for style, and *i* for minor deviations. These flags mark properties of the paraphrases that do not fulfill the strict universality criteria of the label *4* due to one of several defined reasons. The subsumption flag means that the paraphrasability is directional; one sentence can be universally substituted by the other, but not the other way around. The style flag means that the paraphrases convey the same meaning, but may have differing tones or registers, which make them not interchangeable in certain circumstances. The minor deviation flag marks minimal differences in meaning (for example, "this" vs. "that"), or grammatical number, person, tense, etc. that can be trivially identified automatically. These flags are independent of each other and thus one label *4* paraphrase pair can have multiple flags, disregarding the directional subsumption flags. More detailed description of the labels together with example annotations is given in the annotation guidelines (Kanerva et al. 2021a).

3 Implementation

The annotation work was carried out by six main annotators, each being a native Finnish speaker with a strong background in language studies by having completed or ongoing studies in a field related to languages or linguistics. Each annotator worked 5–9 months either full or part time in a strong collaboration with a broader project team including supportive roles in the annotation work.

An annotator starts the process by going through the automatically aligned source document pair presented side-by-side in a custom annotation tool[1] developed for the paraphrase extraction, and extracts all interesting paraphrase candidates by selecting the corresponding text passages from both documents. While saving the candidate, together with the text passage pair the tool also saves the actual position of the text passage in the original document, therefore supporting studying the paraphrase pairs in their original document context. To our knowledge, this is the first paraphrase corpus that includes the document context for the released paraphrase pairs. After extracting all interesting paraphrase candidates from the source document pair, the annotator marks the document finished and moves on to the next one.

The extracted paraphrase candidates are automatically transferred to a separate annotation tool[2] developed specifically for paraphrase labeling. In this tool, each pair of paraphrase candidates is shown separately, and the annotator can see the original contexts if necessary. The annotator labels the original paraphrase pair, and has the option to copy the original text and rewrite the texts into full paraphrases (label *4* without flags). In cases where the annotator decided to provide a rewritten pair, two or more pairs of paraphrases are obtained for the corpus: the original pair, and the rewritten pair(s). The annotators are instructed to rewrite the paraphrase candidates in cases where a simple edit, such as word deletion, insertion or synonym replacement, can be naturally constructed and does not require too much effort.

4 Evaluation

The paraphrase label annotation was guided using a shared annotation manual, daily meetings, and regularly assigned double annotation batches in order to ensure annotation consistency between the six annotators. The manual paraphrase extraction did not involve a similarly careful annotator training or consistency monitoring throughout the project. Instead of ensuring each annotator extracting the same segments if given the same text, the objective is to collect a diverse set of different paraphrase candidates, where minor deviations in the personal extraction habits only creates more diversity to the data. In order to study the extraction behaviour of the annotators, we measure the average number of paraphrase pairs extracted from one docu-

---

[1] https://github.com/TurkuNLP/pick-para-anno
[2] https://github.com/TurkuNLP/rew-para-anno

ment pair, indicating how eager the annotator was to include or exclude borderline uninteresting, extremely difficult or otherwise debatable pairs from the corpus.

While the data sources used in the paraphrase extraction step have distinct characteristics in terms of extraction ratios, we use the subset originating from the alternative subtitles (approx. 80% of the full corpus) for this study in order to account for differing source text proportions between the annotators. We measure the average number of paraphrases extracted from one subtitle document pair (about 15 minutes worth of the subtitled program's runtime), while taking into account all document pairs where the extraction and labeling was carried out by the same annotator, and the document pair resulted at least one extracted paraphrase. The statistics are shown in Table 1, the individual extraction rates falling between 13 and 50 pairs indicating some amount of diversity between the annotators. When measuring the mean lexical similarity of the extracted paraphrase pairs (together with standard deviation) as well as annotated paraphrase label distribution for each annotator, we do not notice any significant difference between annotators oriented towards higher or lower extraction rates. The label distributions are visualised in Figure 1. Finally, in Table 1 we measure the proportion of extracted paraphrase pairs each annotator chose to rewrite during the label annotation (row *Rewritten*), showing large differences among the annotators, between 1.4% and 29.5% of rewritten paraphrase pairs.

	Ann1	Ann2	Ann3	Ann4	Ann5	Ann6
Extracted pairs	28,685	18,908	9,553	7,713	6,359	1,897
Total extracted (%)	39.1	25.8	13.0	10.5	8.7	2.6
Extracted/doc	23.4	13.2	13.4	22.0	48.9	23.4
Rewritten (%)	6.8	23.4	1.3	29.5	14.9	1.4

Table 1 Comparison of the six annotators in terms of the average number of paraphrase pairs extracted from one 15-min subtitle pair (Extracted/doc), as well as the percentage of paraphrase pairs, where the annotator provided a rewrite (Rewritten); in addition to these two metrics, we also illustrate the total amount of the paraphrase pairs extracted by the annotator (both raw count and percentage); note that the number of extracted paraphrases does not sum up to the total corpus size as the comparison is done on the subtitle subset only (approx. 80% of the full corpus)

In order to ensure the consistency of the label annotation, approx. 2% of the paraphrase pairs are double annotated, where two different annotators annotate the labels independently from one another for the same paraphrase candidates. The two individual annotations are merged and conflicting labels resolved together with the annotation team, resulting in a consolidated subset of consensus annotation. The overall accuracy of the individual annotations against the consensus labels is around 70%, on the full set of labels permitted in the annotation scheme. The level of agreement is on par with similar numbers reported in other paraphrase studies (Dolan and Brockett 2005; Creutz 2018). The agreement measures when calculated separately for each annotator vary between 64% and 76%, the most common disagreements being between the semantically nearest labels (i. e., labels *3* and *4</>*, or labels *4</>* and *4*), or whether to include or not include the rare additional flags *s* or *i*.

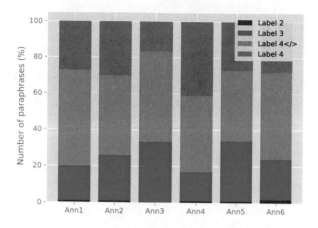

Fig. 1 Label frequencies illustrated separately for the six annotators using the same subtitle subset of the corpus as in Table 1

5 Conclusions and Results of the Pilot Project

The project resulted in a high quality corpus of Finnish paraphrases including a total of 104,645 manually classified pairs, 91,604 being naturally occurring pairs directly extracted from the source documents, while 13,041 are produced through manual rewriting. The manual extraction method presented in the article both skews the label distribution towards true paraphrases ensuring efficient use of human resources (98% being labeled positive) as well as preserves the original document context, making this the first released corpus of paraphrasing in context. The contextual information is used in Kanerva et al. (2021b), where we present a novel approach to paraphrase detection by framing the task as detecting the target paraphrase span from the given document, a similar setting as used in question answering. In addition to the actual corpus, the project also provided models trained for paraphrase classification and fine-tuned sentence representations.

All resources presented in this article are available through the European Language Grid[3] and also on the TurkuNLP website[4] under the CC-BY-SA license.

Acknowledgements The work described in this article has received funding from the EU project European Language Grid as one of its pilot projects. In addition, this work was supported by the Academy of Finland and the Digicampus project. Computational resources were provided by CSC – IT Center for Science.

---

[3] https://live.european-language-grid.eu/catalogue/corpus/7754
[4] https://turkunlp.org/paraphrase.html

References

Creutz, Mathias (2018). "Open Subtitles Paraphrase Corpus for Six Languages". In: *Proceedings of the 11th International Conference on Language Resources and Evaluation (LREC 2018)*. Ed. by Nicoletta Calzolari, Khalid Choukri, Christopher Cieri, Thierry Declerck, Sara Goggi, Koiti Hasida, Hitoshi Isahara, Bente Maegaard, Joseph Mariani, Hélène Mazo, Asuncion Moreno, Jan Odijk, Stelios Piperidis, and Takenobu Tokunaga. Miyazaki, Japan: ELRA, pp. 1364–1369.

Dolan, William B. and Chris Brockett (2005). "Automatically Constructing a Corpus of Sentential Paraphrases". In: *Proceedings of the Third International Workshop on Paraphrasing (IWP 2005)*, pp. 9–16.

Glockner, Max, Vered Shwartz, and Yoav Goldberg (2018). "Breaking NLI Systems with Sentences that Require Simple Lexical Inferences". In: *Proceedings of the 56th Annual Meeting of the Association for Computational Linguistics (Volume 2: Short Papers)*. ACL, pp. 650–655. DOI: 10.18653/v1/P18-2103. URL: https://aclanthology.org/P18-2103.

Kanerva, Jenna, Filip Ginter, Li-Hsin Chang, Iiro Rastas, Valtteri Skantsi, Jemina Kilpeläinen, Hanna-Mari Kupari, Aurora Piirto, Jenna Saarni, Maija Sevón, et al. (2021a). "Annotation Guidelines for the Turku Paraphrase Corpus". In: *arXiv preprint arXiv:2108.07499*.

Kanerva, Jenna, Hanna Kitti, Li-Hsin Chang, Teemu Vahtola, Mathias Creutz, and Filip Ginter (2021b). "Semantic Search as Extractive Paraphrase Span Detection". In: *arXiv preprint arXiv:2112.04886*.

McCoy, Tom, Ellie Pavlick, and Tal Linzen (2019). "Right for the Wrong Reasons: Diagnosing Syntactic Heuristics in Natural Language Inference". In: *Proceedings of the 57th Annual Meeting of the Association for Computational Linguistics*. ACL, pp. 3428–3448. DOI: 10.18653/v1/P19-1334. URL: https://aclanthology.org/P19-1334.

Tsuchiya, Masatoshi (2018). "Performance Impact Caused by Hidden Bias of Training Data for Recognizing Textual Entailment". In: *Proceedings of the 11th International Conference on Language Resources and Evaluation (LREC 2018)*. Miyazaki, Japan: ELRA, pp. 1506–1511. URL: https://aclanthology.org/L18-1239.

Chapter 28
Universal Semantic Annotator

Roberto Navigli, Riccardo Orlando, Cesare Campagnano, and Simone Conia

Abstract Explicit semantic knowledge has often been considered a necessary ingredient to enable the development of intelligent systems. However, current state-of-the-art tools for the automatic extraction of such knowledge often require expert understanding of the complex techniques used in lexical and sentence-level semantics and their linguistic theories. To overcome this limitation and lower the barrier to entry, we present the Universal Semantic Annotator (USeA) ELG pilot project, which offers a transparent way to automatically provide high-quality semantic annotations in 100 languages through state-of-the-art models, making it easy to exploit semantic knowledge in real-world applications.

1 Overview and Objectives of the Pilot Project

Natural Language Processing (NLP) is the field of Artificial Intelligence (AI) which aims at enabling computers to process, understand and generate text in the same way as we humans do. Although AI systems are nowadays able to process massive amounts of text, they are still far from achieving true Natural Language Understanding (NLU). Indeed, current systems still struggle in explicitly identifying and extracting the meaning or semantics conveyed by a text of interest. Nonetheless, the integration of explicit semantics has already been successfully exploited in a wide array of downstream tasks that span multiple areas of AI from NLP with information retrieval, question answering, text summarisation, and machine translation, to computer vision with visual semantic role labeling and situation recognition. Unfortunately, expert knowledge of lexical semantics, sentence-level semantics and complex deep learning techniques often becomes a roadblock in the integration of explicit semantic information into downstream tasks and real-world applications, especially in multilingual scenarios. To lower the entry point for semantic knowledge integration into multilingual applications, we present the Universal Semantic Anno-

Roberto Navigli · Riccardo Orlando · Cesare Campagnano · Simone Conia
Sapienza University of Rome, Italy, navigli@diag.uniroma1.it, orlando@diag.uniroma1.it, campagnano@di.uniroma1.it, conia@di.uniroma1.it

G. Rehm (ed.), *European Language Grid*, Cognitive Technologies,
https://doi.org/10.1007/978-3-031-17258-8_28

tator (USeA) project, the first unified API for three core tasks in NLU: Word Sense Disambiguation (WSD), Semantic Role Labeling (SRL), and Abstract Meaning Representation (AMR) parsing. With USeA, we offer a simple yet efficient way to use state-of-the-art multilingual models within a single framework accessible via REST API, browsers, and programmatically. This will ease the integration of NLU models in NLP pipelines (also for low-resource languages), allowing them to exploit explicit semantic information to improve their performance.

2 Methodology

USeA is the first unified set of APIs for high-performance multilingual NLU, supporting 100 languages. USeA employs state-of-the-art multilingual neural networks to provide automatic semantic annotations for WSD, SRL and AMR Parsing.

Word Sense Disambiguation (WSD) is the task of associating a word in context with its most appropriate sense from a sense inventory (Bevilacqua et al. 2021b). USeA provides word sense labels using an improved version of the state-of-the-art WSD model proposed by Conia and Navigli (2021), which, differently from other ready-to-use tools for WSD based on graph-based heuristics (Moro et al. 2014; Scozzafava et al. 2020) or non-neural models (Papandrea et al. 2017), is built on top of a Transformer encoder. Crucially, thanks to BabelNet 5 (Navigli et al. 2021), a multilingual encyclopedic dictionary, USeA is able to disambiguate text in 100 languages.

Semantic Role Labeling (SRL) is the task of answering the question "Who did What, to Whom, Where, When, and How?" (Màrquez et al. 2008), providing a structured and explicit representation of the underlying semantics of a sentence. Differently from other available SRL systems, USeA encapsulates an improved version of the neural model introduced by Conia et al. (2021a), which performs state-of-the-art cross-lingual SRL with heterogeneous linguistic inventories.

Abstract Meaning Representation (AMR) parsing is the task of capturing the semantics of a sentence through a rooted directed acyclic graph, with nodes representing concepts and edges representing their relations (Banarescu et al. 2013). USeA offers a multilingual version of SPRING (Bevilacqua et al. 2021a), a recent state-of-the-art, end-to-end system for Text-to-AMR generation.

3 Implementation

The USeA pipeline is organised in five self-contained modules that are transparent to the end user, as shown in Figure 1.

Orchestrator Module. The Orchestrator Module is the core of USeA and serves as an entry point for the semantic API. Being an end-to-end system, the end user

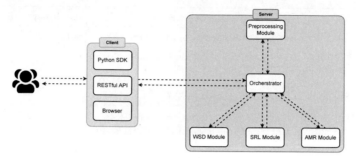

Fig. 1 USeA architecture: a user sends text to the USeA server and receives semantic information; in the server, the orchestrator processes the input using task-specific modules

is only required to send raw text to our service. The input text is then processed by the Preprocessing Module and the result sent to the WSD, SRL and AMR Parsing modules. In particular, since the SRL and AMR Parsing tasks are more demanding, we offload the WSD module to CPU and run SRL and AMR Parsing requests on GPU to optimise hardware usage. The responses from the three semantic modules are then combined and sent back to the end user.

Preprocessing Module. The preprocessing module takes care of producing the pre-processing information that is usually needed by NLP systems, i. e., language iden-tification, document splitting, tokenisation, lemmatisation, and part-of-speech tag-ging. In order to support as many languages as possible while keeping low hardware requirements, the preprocessing module is built around Trankit (Nguyen et al. 2021) and supports 100 languages with a single model.

WSD Module. We developed AMuSE-WSD (Orlando et al. 2021) as our WSD module. Its neural architecture is based on XLM-RoBERTa (Conneau et al. 2020), a multilingual Transformer model. More specifically, given a word in context, the WSD module i) builds a contextualised representation of the word using the hidden states of XLM-RoBERTa, ii) applies a non-linear transformation to obtain a sense-specific representation, and iii) computes the output score distribution over all the possible senses of the input word.

SRL Module. InVeRo-XL (Conia et al. 2021b) is the SRL system we developed for USeA. Similarly to the WSD module, the SRL module is also based on XLM-RoBERTa. In particular, given an input sentence, the SRL module i) builds a se-quence of contextualised word representations using the hidden states of XLM-RoBERTa, ii) identifies and disambiguates each predicate in the sentence, and iii) for each predicate, produces its arguments and their semantic roles.

AMR Parsing Module. The AMR Parsing Module is heavily based on SPRING (Blloshmi et al. 2021), which we extended to support multiple languages. SPRING is a sequence-to-sequence Transformer model that operates as a parser by "translating" an input sentence into a linearised AMR graph. We extend SPRING to support 100 languages by replacing BART with the multilingual version of T5.

	English datasets						Multilingual datasets		
	Se2	Se3	Se07	Se13	Se15	All	Se13	Se15	Xl-Wsd
Moro et al. (2014)	67.0	63.5	51.6	66.4	70.3	65.5	65.6	–	52.9
Papandrea et al. (2017)	73.8	70.8	64.2	67.2	71.5	–	–	–	–
Scozzafava et al. (2020)	71.6	72.0	59.3	72.2	75.8	71.7	73.2	66.2	57.7
USeA (WSD)	**77.8**	**76.0**	**72.1**	**77.7**	**81.5**	**77.5**	**76.8**	**73.0**	**66.2**

Table 1 English WSD results in F1 scores on Senseval-2 (SE2), Senseval-3 (SE3), SemEval-2007 (SE07), SemEval-2013 (SE13), SemEval-2015 (SE15), and the concatenation of the datasets (ALL); we also include results on multilingual WSD in SemEval-2013 (DE, ES, FR, IT), SemEval-2015 (IT, ES), and XL-WSD (average over 17 languages, English excluded)

	Catalan	Czech	German	English	Spanish	Chinese
AllenNLP's SRL demo	–	–	–	86.5	–	–
InVeRo	–	–	–	86.2	–	–
USeA (SRL)	**83.3**	**85.9**	**87.0**	**86.8**	**81.8**	**84.9**

Table 2 Comparison between USeA and other recent automatic tools for SRL; F1 scores on argument labeling with pre-identified predicates on the CoNLL-2012 English test set and the CoNLL-2009 test sets converted from dependency-based to span-based

4 Evaluation

USeA offers state-of-the-art models for multilingual WSD, SRL and AMR Parsing. Here, we report its results on standard gold benchmarks for each task.

Results in WSD. We evaluate our WSD Module against other disambiguation tools on gold standard benchmarks for English and multilingual WSD, covering 17 languages. The results (Table 1) show that USeA outperforms its competitors by a wide margin, especially in multilingual WSD (+8.5% in F1 Score on XL-WSD).

Results in SRL. We report the performance of our SRL Module on two gold standard benchmarks for SRL, CoNLL-2009[1] and CoNLL-2012, covering six languages. USeA is the first package to provide annotations in languages other than English while also outperforming its competitors in English (Table 2).

Results in AMR Parsing. Finally, we examine the performance of our AMR Parsing Module on AMR 3.0[2], which is currently the largest AMR-annotated corpus. Even though USeA supports 100 languages, it is still competitive with other recently proposed English-only AMR parsing systems (Table 3).

---

[1] The CoNLL-2009 dataset was originally intended for dependency-based SRL. We convert dependency-based annotations to span-based annotations using the gold syntactic trees.

[2] https://catalog.ldc.upenn.edu/LDC2020T02

	SMATCH
Lyu et al. (2021)	75.8
Zhou et al. (2021)	81.2
SPRING (Bevilacqua et al. 2021a)	83.0
USeA (AMR-Parsing)	80.9

Table 3 SMATCH score obtained by USeA compared with recent literature on AMR 3.0 (English)

5 Conclusions and Results of the Pilot Project

We presented the USeA project, providing an overview on its objectives and on how we worked towards achieving them. We hope that USeA will represent a useful tool for the integration of explicit semantic knowledge – word meanings, semantic role labels, and graph-like semantic representations – into real-world applications.

Acknowledgements The work described in this article has received funding from the EU project European Language Grid as one of its pilot projects.

References

Banarescu, Laura, Claire Bonial, Shu Cai, Madalina Georgescu, Kira Griffitt, Ulf Hermjakob, Kevin Knight, Philipp Koehn, Martha Palmer, and Nathan Schneider (2013). "Abstract Meaning Representation for Sembanking". In: *Proceedings of the 7th Linguistic Annotation Workshop and Interoperability with Discourse*, pp. 178–186. URL: https://aclanthology.org/W13-2322.

Bevilacqua, Michele, Rexhina Blloshmi, and Roberto Navigli (2021a). "One SPRING to Rule Them Both: Symmetric AMR Semantic Parsing and Generation without a Complex Pipeline". In: *Proc. of AAAI* 35.14, pp. 12564–12573. URL: https://ojs.aaai.org/index.php/AAAI/article/view/17489.

Bevilacqua, Michele, Tommaso Pasini, Alessandro Raganato, and Roberto Navigli (2021b). "Recent Trends in Word Sense Disambiguation: A Survey". In: *Proc. of IJCAI-21*, pp. 4330–4338. DOI: 10.24963/ijcai.2021/593.

Blloshmi, Rexhina, Michele Bevilacqua, Edoardo Fabiano, Valentina Caruso, and Roberto Navigli (2021). "SPRING Goes Online: End-to-End AMR Parsing and Generation". In: *Proceedings of EMNLP*, pp. 134–142. URL: https://aclanthology.org/2021.emnlp-demo.16.

Conia, Simone, Andrea Bacciu, and Roberto Navigli (2021a). "Unifying Cross-Lingual Semantic Role Labeling with Heterogeneous Linguistic Resources". In: *Proceedings of NAACL*, pp. 338–351. URL: https://www.aclweb.org/anthology/2021.naacl-main.31.

Conia, Simone and Roberto Navigli (2021). "Framing Word Sense Disambiguation as a Multi-Label Problem for Model-Agnostic Knowledge Integration". In: *Proceedings of EACL*, pp. 3269–3275. URL: https://www.aclweb.org/anthology/2021.eacl-main.286.

Conia, Simone, Riccardo Orlando, Fabrizio Brignone, Francesco Cecconi, and Roberto Navigli (2021b). "InVeRo-XL: Making Cross-Lingual Semantic Role Labeling Accessible with Intelligible Verbs and Roles". In: *Proceedings of EMNLP*, pp. 319–328. URL: https://aclanthology.org/2021.emnlp-demo.36/.

Conneau, Alexis, Kartikay Khandelwal, Naman Goyal, Vishrav Chaudhary, Guillaume Wenzek, Francisco Guzmán, Edouard Grave, Myle Ott, Luke Zettlemoyer, and Veselin Stoyanov (2020). "Unsupervised Cross-lingual Representation Learning at Scale". In: *Proceedings of the 58th*

Annual Meeting of the Association for Computational Linguistics. Ed. by Dan Jurafsky, Joyce Chai, Natalie Schluter, and Joel Tetreault. ACL, pp. 8440–8451. DOI: 10.18653/v1/2020.acl-main.747. URL: https://www.aclweb.org/anthology/2020.acl-main.747.

Lyu, Chunchuan, Shay B. Cohen, and Ivan Titov (2021). "A Differentiable Relaxation of Graph Segmentation and Alignment for AMR Parsing". In: *Proc. of EMNLP*, pp. 9075–9091. URL: https://aclanthology.org/2021.emnlp-main.714.

Màrquez, Lluís, Xavier Carreras, Kenneth C. Litkowski, and Suzanne Stevenson (2008). "Semantic Role Labeling: An Introduction to the Special Issue". In: *Comp. Linguistics* 34.2, pp. 145–159. URL: https://aclanthology.org/J08-2001.

Moro, Andrea, Alessandro Raganato, and Roberto Navigli (2014). "Entity Linking meets Word Sense Disambiguation: A Unified Approach". In: *TACL* 2, pp. 231–244. URL: https://aclanthology.org/Q14-1019.

Navigli, Roberto, Michele Bevilacqua, Simone Conia, Dario Montagnini, and Francesco Cecconi (2021). "Ten Years of BabelNet: A Survey". In: *Proc. of IJCAI-21*, pp. 4559–4567. DOI: 10.24963/ijcai.2021/620.

Nguyen, Minh Van, Viet Dac Lai, Amir Pouran Ben Veyseh, and Thien Huu Nguyen (2021). "Trankit: A Light-Weight Transformer-based Toolkit for Multilingual Natural Language Processing". In: *Proceedings of the 16th Conference of the European Chapter of the Association for Computational Linguistics: System Demonstrations*. ACL, pp. 80–90. DOI: 10.18653/v1/2021.eacl-demos.10. URL: https://aclanthology.org/2021.eacl-demos.10.

Orlando, Riccardo, Simone Conia, Fabrizio Brignone, Francesco Cecconi, and Roberto Navigli (2021). "AMuSE-WSD: An All-in-one Multilingual System for Easy Word Sense Disambiguation". In: *Proceedings of the 2021 Conference on Empirical Methods in Natural Language Processing: System Demonstrations*. ACL, pp. 298–307. DOI: 10.18653/v1/2021.emnlp-demo.34. URL: https://aclanthology.org/2021.emnlp-demo.34.

Papandrea, Simone, Alessandro Raganato, and Claudio Delli Bovi (2017). "SupWSD: A Flexible Toolkit for Supervised Word Sense Disambiguation". In: *Proceedings of the 2017 Conference on Empirical Methods in Natural Language Processing: System Demonstrations*. Copenhagen, Denmark: ACL, pp. 103–108. DOI: 10.18653/v1/D17-2018. URL: https://www.aclweb.org/anthology/D17-2018.

Scozzafava, Federico, Marco Maru, Fabrizio Brignone, Giovanni Torrisi, and Roberto Navigli (2020). "Personalized PageRank with Syntagmatic Information for Multilingual Word Sense Disambiguation". In: *Proceedings of the 58th Annual Meeting of the Association for Computational Linguistics: System Demonstrations*. ACL, pp. 37–46. DOI: 10.18653/v1/2020.acl-demos.6.

Zhou, Jiawei, Tahira Naseem, Ramón Fernandez Astudillo, and Radu Florian (2021). "AMR Parsing with Action-Pointer Transformer". In: *Proceedings of the 2021 Conference of the North American Chapter of the Association for Computational Linguistics: Human Language Technologies*. ACL, pp. 5585–5598. DOI: 10.18653/v1/2021.naacl-main.443. URL: https://aclanthology.org/2021.naacl-main.443.

Chapter 29
Virtual Personal Assistant Prototype YouTwinDi

Franz Weber and Gregor Jarisch

Abstract YouTwinDi is the next step in a digitised world in which the digital twin evolves and interacts with other digital twins and makes autonomous decisions in the interest of its human twin. In this scenario, security and digital ethics assure ethical decisions and IT specialists concur on improving the digital landscape with ethical models. This vision also includes overcoming language barriers. A continuous match of supply and demand as well as tailored searches help human twins to improve their lives in all respects. YouTwinDi uses the most advanced translation and language analysis technologies, allowing the user and its digital twin to interact with all European citizens without being blocked by language barriers.

1 Overview and Objectives of the Pilot Project

The goal of this ELG (Rehm et al. 2021) pilot project was to build the prototype of a personal virtual assistant, which can be installed on a small device or integrated in an ELG-compatible container. We wanted to demonstrate that this can be accomplished using ELG language resources and technologies while keeping highest security standards. We use the open source software EDDI which is running in a docker container for the natural language interface. This prototype is the basis for the development of a minimum viable product ready for market launch.

We believe that conversational AI applications are well suited to support interactions between people that speak different languages due to their real-time nature and the ability to create personalised customer experiences at scale.

In line with the broader ELG principle that "with 24 official EU and many more additional languages, multilingualism in Europe and an inclusive Digital Single Market can only be enabled through Language Technologies", the YouTwinDi[1] solution was developed on top of our existing technology and integrated into the European Language Grid. We use APIs to translate text input (or speech input, via speech-

Franz Weber · Gregor Jarisch
Labs.ai, Austria, franz@labs.ai, gregor@labs.ai

[1] https://www.youtwindi.com

to-text technologies) and to recognise intents to query specific data sources and to provide feedback in the language spoken by the user either in written or spoken form (via text-to-speech technologies). YouTwinDi uses these features to add translations of web audio and video streams and to convert the channels into text streams – two appropriate examples are the automatic translation of the European Commission's LinkedIn broadcast events or the automatic translation of local radio stations. Through the integration of ELG APIs we can also integrate technologies such as sentiment analysis into YouTwinDi. Such features are fundamental especially for public institutions to better support citizens.

2 Methodology

The basis for the Digital Twin prototype is our open source chatbot framework EDDI (Enhanced Dialogue Driven Intelligence).[2] This solution has several features that simplify the integration of and with the available ELG resources.

Our software development process is based on the agile software development approach, in particular on Scrum. All product features are listed and prioritised in a product backlog, which consists of what needs to be done to successfully deliver a working software system, including bug fixes and non-functional requirements.

Cross-functional teams estimate and sign up to deliver potentially shipable increments of software during successive sprints, typically lasting 30 days. Once a sprint's backlog is committed, no further functionality can be added to the sprint except by the team. Once a sprint has been delivered, the product backlog is analysed and re-prioritised, if necessary, and the next set of deliverables is selected for the next sprint. From the lean product development best practices we have adopted the concept of minimum viable product (MVP) as a strategy to avoid building products that customers do not need or want, realising often the product with the agreed number of features and the minimum level of quality that can be easily verified by senior users. We develop our solution keeping in mind the ability to interface with external services and resources via APIs and building software development kits. This allows us to integrate fast and to test the integration with available ELG building blocks.

Each feature under development was monitored in terms of costs (human resources and hardware as well as software resources) and in terms of delivery. Acceptance tests were linked to use cases and test criteria. Integration has always been important for us as an open source solution provider, which is why all our software features are available at the API level. Modern concepts as Graph API and authentication and authorisation security are at the core of our software development methodology, allowing for easy testing and integration with existing systems.

Our development strictly follows the Service Oriented Architecture (SOA) concept, removing the bottleneck of dependencies and permitting the usage of independent layers to achieve the development goals. We also subscribe to the concept of

---

[2] https://www.eddi.labs.ai

microservices (already adopted by ELG), which allows us to easily embed our solution in the ELG ecosystem. Our goal was to develop a portable solution that can
run on a small hardware solution (e. g., Raspberry Pi) and that can also be interfaced
with the ELG platform or directly embedded in ELG as a container.

We value change management and have documented all steps to integrate our
solution using "how to" documents and guidelines.

2.1 Use Case 1: Automated Translation of local News

The Newbly[3] use case relates to the delivery of local news in foreign languages (see
Figure 1). In this use case, the user interacts via text or voice with YouTwinDi.

- The automated translation translates the topic expressed in the search query into
  the local language (set in the configuration).
- YouTwinDi initiates a look up for the topic in local news and social media in the
  local language.
- YouTwinDi checks if the news is categorised as fake, in which case the user is
  alerted and asked if they want to proceed anyway.

If the news is not categorised as fake, the user is presented with the news and the
news is stored in order to be periodically checked against the fake news database,
which case YouTwinDi will notify the user accordingly.

2.2 Use Case 2: Secure Communication between Virtual Assistants

The second use case revolves around communication between *multiple* virtual assistants. Imagine a friend has a wish list on an ecommerce platform – you could ask
your friend for access to this list, but that would make your friend anticipate the
present. One solution for this challenge can be personal assistants negotiating for
a piece of information. Your bot could ask your friend's bot what to gift the friend
based on the online wish list, which, in the case of Amazon, is provided by Alexa. As
your and your friend's virtual assistants are "friends" themselves (trusted domain),
they are allowed to communicate such information without your friend receiving a
notification.

3 Implementation

The pilot project consisted of five work packages. Work Package 1 was dedicated
to the research of potential suitable hardware to be used for the prototype. In addi-

---

[3] https://newb.ly

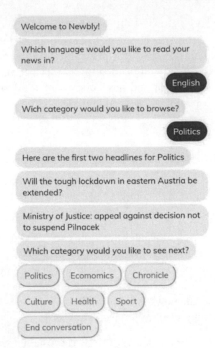

Fig. 1 YouTwinDi use case 1: automated translation of local news

tion we verified if running a containerised version of EDDI would be possible on the shortlisted hardware. For the prototype we decided to use a standard Android smartphone. We also specified the use cases (see Sections 2.1 and 2.2).

Work Package 2 focused upon the integration of EDDI into the ELG platform and setting up the needed containers. We implemented the two use cases, as defined in WP1, on the Android phone. The first use case is defined as translating news from the German language into other languages, such as Romanian or Croatian using machine translation tools available in ELG. The second use case concentrates on the communication between two virtual assistants where one wants to obtain a birthday wish list from the other assistant's owner.

Work Package 3 concentrated on preparing the hardware and installing the software including the use cases on the selected Android smartphone running in a container. In order to accomplish this some modifications had to be applied to the operating system. Afterwards we could easily install EDDI running in a container, however, we came to realise that the ELG language technology tools would be too large to run on the smartphone in a container. From a security point of view our goal was to have all technologies on the device in order to provide maximum security and privacy to users. As this was not possible, we decided for the prototype to be able to call remote services.

Work Package 4 was dedicated to finalising and testing the prototype. In addition, we created a presentation and documented which compromises we had to engage in compared to the initial specification in WP 1 and WP 2.

Work Package 5 took care of all dissemination activities. This was an ongoing process from the beginning to the end of the pilot project. We set up a project website[4] which was updated on a regular basis with updates and news about the pilot project. We also posted updates on social media, such as LinkedIn and Twitter. The audience reached with the project website was, on average, 145 unique users per month. In total, users were reached from Austria, USA, Czech Republic, China, Netherlands, Canada, Germany, United Arab Emirates, Switzerland and Croatia.

4 Conclusions and Results of the Pilot Project

The main technology achievements of our pilot project can be summarised as follows. We could successfully demonstrate that Docker containers can run on small devices such as Android smartphones and that applications such as EDDI and databases such as MongoDB can run within these containers. We could also show that peer-to-peer networks for communication between virtual assistants are possible with both a public and a private section of the accessible data and a handshake and identity check mechanisms to verify both users of the virtual assistants with key exchange and end-to-end encryption in order to achieve highest security standards. Based on the research work during the pilot project and the implemented prototype, we plan to develop the software further to a minimum viable product.

YouTwinDi is the next step in a digitised world in which the digital twin evolves and interacts with other digital twins and makes autonomous decisions in the interest of its human twin. In this scenario, security and digital ethics assure ethical decisions and IT specialists concur on improving the digital landscape with ethical models. This vision also includes overcoming language barriers. A continuous match of supply and demand as well as tailored searches help human twins to improve their lives in all respects. YouTwinDi uses the most advanced translation and language analysis technologies, allowing the user and its digital twin to interact with all European citizens without being blocked by language barriers.

We use our existing open source software EDDI which is running in a docker container for the natural language interface. This prototype is the basis for the development of a minimum viable product ready for market launch.

The ELG pilot project YouTwinDi had two major innovation aspects:

Technical innovation   For the first time an AI application runs within a Docker container on a small hardware device without any technical limitations.

Creative-economical innovation   The creative-economical innovation relates to the idea that the digital twin interacts with other digital twins and makes autonomous decisions in the interest of its human twin.

---

[4] https://youtwindi.com

Acknowledgements The work described in this article has received funding from the EU project European Language Grid as one of its pilot projects.

References

Rehm, Georg, Stelios Piperidis, Kalina Bontcheva, Jan Hajic, Victoria Arranz, Andrejs Vasiļjevs, Gerhard Backfried, José Manuel Gómez Pérez, Ulrich Germann, Rémi Calizzano, Nils Feldhus, Stefanie Hegele, Florian Kintzel, Katrin Marheinecke, Julian Moreno-Schneider, Dimitris Galanis, Penny Labropoulou, Miltos Deligiannis, Katerina Gkirtzou, Athanasia Kolovou, Dimitris Gkoumas, Leon Voukoutis, Ian Roberts, Jana Hamrlová, Dusan Varis, Lukáš Kačena, Khalid Choukri, Valérie Mapelli, Mickaël Rigault, Jūlija Meļņika, Miro Janosik, Katja Prinz, Andres Garcia-Silva, Cristian Berrio, Ondrej Klejch, and Steve Renals (2021). "European Language Grid: A Joint Platform for the European Language Technology Community". In: *Proceedings of the 16th Conference of the European Chapter of the Association for Computational Linguistics: System Demonstrations (EACL 2021)*. Kyiv, Ukraine: ACL, pp. 221–230. URL: https://www.aclweb.org/anthology/2021.eacl-demos.26.pdf.

Printed in the United States
by Baker & Taylor Publisher Services